Shiptown

CONTEMPORARY ETHNOGRAPHY

Kirin Narayan and Alma Gottlieb, Series Editors

A complete list of books in the series is available from the publisher.

Shiptown

Between Rural and Urban North India

Ann Grodzins Gold

PENN

UNIVERSITY OF PENNSYLVANIA PRESS

PHILADELPHIA

Published by
University of Pennsylvania Press
Philadelphia, Pennsylvania 19104-4112
www.upenn.edu/pennpress

Printed in the United States of America on acid-free paper
1 3 5 7 9 10 8 6 4 2

Library of Congress Cataloging-in-Publication Data
Names: Gold, Ann Grodzins, author.
Title: Shiptown : between rural and urban North India / Ann Grodzins Gold.
Other titles: Contemporary ethnography.
Description: 1st edition. | Philadelphia : University of Pennsylvania Press, [2017] |
Series: Contemporary ethnography
Identifiers: LCCN 2016055422 | ISBN 9780812249255 (hardcover : alk. paper)
Subjects: LCSH: Market towns—India—Rajasthan—Social life and customs—
21st century. | City and town life—India—Rajasthan—History—
21st century. | Ethnology—India—Rajasthan. | Rajasthan (India)—Social life and
customs—21st century.
Classification: LCC HT147.I5 G65 2017 | DDC 307.760954/4—dc23 LC record
available at https://lccn.loc.gov/2016055422

All photographs by Ann Grodzins Gold unless otherwise acknowledged.
Photographs are from the 2010–11 fieldwork period unless otherwise specified.

For Mariam, Colorado, and Cheyenne: I love you

This book was coproduced (researched and developed) in close association with Bhoju Ram Gujar, Madhu (Hemalata) Gujar, and Chinu (Lalita) Gujar.

Contents

Preface

Between August 2010 and June 2011 I lived in the town of Jahazpur in Rajasthan, North India, and practiced anthropology as best I could. Bhoju Ram Gujar and his daughters were companions, helpers, and genuine partners in producing whatever ethnographic knowledge I am able to offer here. The writing is mine, for better or worse. I relied on so much assistance from my Rajasthani family that I intended their names to appear on the title page as coproducers, although not as coauthors, of the study. Paperwork obstacles prevented this or rendered it a struggle for which I had not sufficient gumption. I have highlighted their contributions on the dedication page to acknowledge up front my respect, gratitude, and dependence on their help.

I liked living in Jahazpur. The people I met were kind and cordial. I perceived a straightforwardness to relationships and attitudes, even when sporadically contentious. If my husband wrangled with our somewhat difficult landlord over money, members of the landlord's family still regularly brought us plates with samples of the special delicious treats they prepared for innumerable festivals. Our sitting room was, after all, right above their cooking area, and many enticing fragrances came through the open grating. When a friend's son was injured in a brief street squabble among young men, the person who injured him appeared at the door the next day, utterly contrite, and bringing *prasad* (blessed leftovers) from the goddess temple as a peace offering. While proximity can sometimes lead to unredeemable fissures, as recent global history depressingly shows, part of my larger point in this book is that proximity untroubled by political manipulations normally leads to benign forms of familiarity: to greet, to share food, to chat about banalities. These simple interchanges are worth something.[1]

After about a third of my time in Jahazpur was up, I wrote the following:

I have become acquainted with a lot of extraordinary characters; no one could ever convince me that small-town people are boring, or "all the same."[2] There are, to sample just a few: our Brahmin neighbor-woman who keeps an extraordinary variety of vows and fasts every month—twenty days out of thirty without exaggeration —and whose house is lavishly adorned with her own decorative handiwork in every medium from needlework to woven plastic; the goldsmith who shut down his jewelry shop to work for the Tulip insurance network and describes this lucrative sales enterprise as divine; the college lecturer who lives in one of Jahazpur municipality's tiny hamlets with his nonliterate wife and who has meticulously researched, written, and self-published in collaboration with the temple committee a detailed history of his lineage deity, the herogod Malaji; the crippled tailor (born into a caste specializing in dairy production) married to his elder brother's widow, a woman who looks old enough to be his mother, who sits at the bus stand sewing pennants for deities as well as simple clothing items; the passionate Muslim devotee of a local *pir*, a businessman with a flourishing side trade in protective amulets in spite of some in his community disapproving strongly of such magical props; the young single mother who is studying for a teaching certificate and who insisted on showing me her glamorous, costly wedding album with apparently unmitigated pride in spite of having been unceremoniously abandoned and divorced by her handsome groom; the middle-aged man of the wine-selling caste who went on a hunger strike to try to get the local government behind a plan to clean up Jahazpur's oncesacred Nagdi River; an enterprising member of the once-stigmatized formerly "butcher" community whose fleet of buyers on motorbikes assist him in purchasing every kind of unwanted materials from beer bottles to women's hair to candy boxes, which he sorts and resells in diverse areas at a tidy profit; the old entrepreneur-cum-patriarch from a farming caste who as a young man cornered the market on manufacturing lime used in construction and whose burgeoning prosperity allows him to import a Brahmin from a remote sacred center to do multiday rituals to ward off astrological impediments to his business.

These and other unique individuals—many of whom make cameo appearances in the pages that follow—are slivers of the whole that is

Jahazpur. It is not always easy to see how their highly diverse, exquisitely particular stories and viewpoints converge. This is why the place Jahazpur—its name, its history, its gates and walls and markets and temples and mosques, its river, its trash, its cows and pigs and grasshoppers—this is why Jahazpur as place is the subject of my ethnographic story.

Although the town name Jahazpur would literally translate as *Shiptown*, you may rightly assume that in titling this book, I had metaphors in mind. However counterintuitive it might be, I ask you to imagine a town in motion, a town as transport, a town providing a specific form of transport linking rural with urban. I suggest that Shiptown is a place providing passages, sometimes regular shuttles back and forth, between an agropastoral economy and a market economy. All travel is risky. Ships cross the high seas. These twenty-first-century passages we understand to be subject to dangerous swells, currents, storms. Still, my title intends to imply Shiptown's potential to provide less sudden transitions, less high-speed transport than, let's say, a rocket. I might liken transitions from village to megacities such as Mumbai or Delhi to shockingly disorienting dislocations involving blastoffs. By contrast, ships travel in stately fashion. On board a ship it is sometimes possible to imagine oneself not going anywhere at all, that is, to experience a sense of stasis while actually in motion.

Around the time when I began to write *Shiptown* in earnest, I encountered in translation Rahi Masoom Reza's novel, *A Village Divided* (*Adha Gaon*, first published in 1966).[3] I felt simultaneously elated and downhearted. Reza portrays aspects of human interaction in a pluralistic *qasba* in ways that unfold much I had longed to understand in Jahazpur. *Shiptown* cannot bring to the page the intimacies and intricacies of small-town life as does a novel or memoir. Accepting that ethnography is a lesser art, my hope is to align myself with Reza's insistent grounding in humanity; or maybe more accurately, in the human comedy.

In this work I frequently acknowledge deficiencies of ambition and capacity and own up to inadequacy of research scope and skill. These statements are less apologies than reflections arising from an acute awareness of limitations.[4] Such acknowledged deficiencies of aims or abilities might be counterbalanced by another posture, which is pride in what I have been able to convey through intimacy and resonance. If shyness is my greatest deficit (and I have no doubt *Shiptown* would be far richer were I less withdrawn a personality), another asset I possess as a researcher is willing pliability; I allow myself to be led, pushed, diverted, instructed, and in these passive modes I find I often garner glimpses of an otherwise elusive cultural reality.

Because I remain a professor, an academic, a scholar, I have not been able to free myself of ingrained habits: tracking relevant sources and writing notes. These should provide helpful cross-references for a study so idiosyncratically qualitative.

From my fieldwork journal the first week, August 2010:

> the aging ann
> anthropologist I meant to type
> why am I here?
> no longer ambitious
> and no longer physically strong

I want Jahazpur to be a good place, a place of which I can say look: by calling themselves pitiless they somehow keep in their consciousness the need for compassion, as the mynah birds on Huxley's island calling "Karuna Karuna"

So what will I find out about *insan ka jivan* [human life] in Jahazpur? probably that it is no better and no worse than anywhere on earth.

A Brief Note on Names, Transliteration, and Related Matters

For evident reasons, I could not give the town of Jahazpur a pseudonym. As in all my earlier ethnographic writings (excepting Gold 2014b), when I name persons, I supply real names. It is both my conviction and my experience that people who give their valuable time to express views or share knowledge want to be credited. In rare cases where I am at all concerned that a particular individual would not wish to be named in a particular context, I have simply not used any name and withheld or blurred identifying details.

In accord with current fashion and a post-Orientalist rationale, I eschew the use of diacritics in the text of this book for words or names transliterated from Hindi, Urdu, or Rajasthani. The only exception is when I directly cite a publication that does employ them. When I use for the first time in my own writing a Hindi word, I italicize it; after that it appears in roman. For terms from Hindi and Rajasthani that occur very frequently in the text, a selective glossary provides limited diacritics. When a translated interview text includes English words within Hindi or Rajasthani speech, I flag them with an asterisk before the word or phrase, unless they are fully incorporated loanwords such as "colony." Those South Asian words that have come into English are neither italicized nor starred; for them I use the *OED* spelling (e.g., purdah, qawwali). A single important exception is to write *qasba*, not casbah; the latter would mislead because, although etymologies merge, North Indian usage is particular and qasba as place is the subject of *Shiptown*.

Caste names in this part of Rajasthan are often used as surnames. I capitalize them when they serve as proper names and also when I use the local caste name categorically, for example, Khatik, Regar. However, when I translate to a professional identity often still associated with a named group even if abandoned by the majority of its members, I do not capitalize: for example, butcher, leather worker.

In Jahazpur it is quite common in polite conversation to employ the government designation SC (Scheduled Caste) to refer to persons belonging to birth groups (*jati*) that elsewhere are known collectively as Dalit (oppressed). The SC designation originated in colonial times but has gained increased significance with post-Independence India's affirmative action efforts. Speaking generally, SC encompasses all those communities once discriminated against as "untouchable." In Jahazpur the most visible SC groups would be Harijan, Khatik, and Regar. Members of communities identified as indigenous peoples may be called ST, which stands for Scheduled Tribe. Around Jahazpur the largest ST population is Mina. Minas have a fair measure of local clout and dignity; no euphemism is required when naming them so ST is heard less often. The ST designation is nonetheless of high salience for Minas, as it too is linked with advantageous government programs (Moodie 2014).

Introduction

This book is about a small town in Rajasthan called Jahazpur (literally, "shiptown") and the people I met there in the second decade of the twenty-first century. What kind of a place is Jahazpur? First, it is a *qasba*, a market town that not so long ago was walled and gated. As a qasba Jahazpur united mercantile and bureaucratic functions—a common pattern in this region of North India.[1] Jahazpur is a bounded place, an expanding place, an environmentally endangered place, a communally "sensitive" place, a peaceful and beautiful place with a motley but attractive built landscape rendering fragments of its complex history visible. To me it is, most importantly, a peopled place.

I sustained two simultaneous aims while composing *Shiptown*. My primary aim is to offer descriptions of, and insights into, small-town life in provincial North India. I especially seek to convey the ways a town is both distinct from its rural surroundings and a dynamic hub where businessmen and farmers are in near constant interaction, where two-way passages between two symbiotic but quite different modes of life are normal and persistent processes. *Shiptown* does not claim to offer a comprehensive portrait of qasba life, but it does attempt to portray some pervasive textures of society, materiality, and popular imagination in such a place at a particular time.

This work's secondary aim is to contribute to an ever-growing body of literature on ethnographic practice. While not a fieldwork memoir, the text provides more self-disclosure than is usually the case: struggles, trials, errors, inner turmoil, and dependence on the kindness of others. While I do not propose methodological models, I do try to display the ways in which my Jahazpur research was fruitfully collaborative.

Just as Jahazpur qasba is multifaceted, *Shiptown* the book is a hybrid product. Composed of diverse viewpoints, snapshots, routes, events, and explorations, this text offers a patchwork of descriptive prose, images, journal entries, narratives, conversations, and even a poem (I began several

Figure 1. View of Jahazpur from hilltop, showing mosque with tall minaret
and many small temple domes.

during fieldwork but finished exactly one). Different chapters reflect different approaches to understanding and different interpretive modes and
moods; they are voiced in subtly varying tones and composed in varying
styles.

This introductory chapter sets the scene for what follows, drawing on
my earliest interviews (August–September 2010) to sketch the nature of
Jahazpur qasba as articulated by its residents. Readers should be able to
gather gradually, as I did, some of the ways people in Jahazpur talk about
where they live. How shall we think about a qasba? Is it no more than a
glorified village or merely a plotted point on the less citified end of an
urban continuum? I argue that it is more helpful to see the qasba as a
particular kind of North Indian place with characteristics all its own. If the
view from the big city deems Jahazpur only dubiously urban, the view from
the village understands it as a place with urban amenities (*suvidha*) both
domestic and public. Rural people know Jahazpur as a place where you
can "get your work done"—whether it has to do with shopping or with

relatively minor bureaucratic negotiations. With numerous government offices and a hospital, Jahazpur is a hub for services unavailable in villages. You cannot obtain a driver's license in Jahazpur, but you can get a ration card, open a bank account, file a police case, register a land transfer, and conduct similar business.

Qasba comes into English (as *casbah*) from Arabic via French colonial usage in Algeria. It arrived in Indian languages from the same origin but along a different route. The Arabic term is often translated "citadel," while the South Asian gloss becomes simply "town." In Hindi usage I found *qasba* roughly defined—both by dictionaries and by people I interviewed—as a settlement "larger than a village but smaller than a city." With its population around 19,000 in 2001 and 20,586 in the 2011 census, Jahazpur fit that bill.[2] The semantics of qasba in North India evidently engages more than demography. Not every small town of comparable size is appropriately referred to as a qasba—a designation comprising some ineffable and some very concrete qualities. These have to do with a richly plural cultural heritage, administrative functions, trade, and indeed walls.[3] To my mind qasba is a genuine and distinctive third category—neither mini-city nor overgrown village.

Writing of the "globalized city" worldwide, Bayart observes that it "is not anathema to the countryside. The city remains attached to the countryside through rural migration, supply lines, leisure activities, family visits, election campaigns and the political mobilisation of notables" (2007:24). In a sweeping study of Indian cities, through the ages and across geographies, Heitzman states: "A large percentage of the small and middle cities in South Asia existed primarily as marketing nodes and, to a lesser extent, as administrative hubs for rural hinterlands" (2008:208).[4] Both observations are precisely true of Jahazpur qasba, and the village/town interface is absolutely crucial to Jahazpur's market economy. There are constant and multiple exchanges—physical, psychological, political, economic, and social—between town and country. Many qasba families still own village land even if they have lived for generations inside the walls. Marriage ties send city girls to villages and vice versa, sometimes with unhappy homesickness resulting. Every interviewee testified that people from surrounding villages constitute the majority of customers in the market which lies at the heart of the qasba's very existence.

Jahazpur's bus stand and streets are crammed with shopping opportunities. I was fascinated by what Jahazpur market sold and equally by what was not available. For example, toilet-bowl cleaner (much advertised on TV and copiously applied to porcelain "squat-latrines") was on display in every little shop; toilet paper was nowhere. A single brand of preservative-infused white sliced bread could be purchased at a few places in the central market; but in most grocery stores bread came only as hard, cold pieces of toast, sold by the slice and considered good for upset stomachs. As for jam—a legacy of colonialism that has become a drearily gelatinous red staple throughout urban India—it was nowhere to be found. Our simple toaster, purchased in Jaipur, was a curiosity even to wealthy neighbors.

Most of the literature on the North Indian qasba is historical.[5] One of the few contemporary sociological approaches to an urban center comparable in size, diversity, and several other features to Jahazpur is K. L. Sharma's extensive work on the qasba of Chanderi in Madhya Pradesh. Sharma vacillates on ways to describe the mentality of Chanderi. In his monograph published in 1999 he asserts that the town exhibits "true urban consciousness" (16–17). In a later article, Sharma states emphatically that Chanderi may be urban, but "village-like ethos and culture" are "hidden within it" (2003:412). Far from accusing Sharma of contradicting himself, I point out these alternative assessments as illuminating affirmations of the impossibility of characterizing a qasba as either rural or urban. It is definitively both and equally neither—a characterization around which pretty much all interviewees concurred.

Perhaps symbolic of Jahazpur's dual nature: goods arrive on huge transport trucks from manufacturing centers all over the country and world, but must be delivered to shops in the old city by handcarts. Motorcycles clog the qasba lanes; cars improbably manage to negotiate passage when the need is imperative; large transport trucks are altogether out of the question. Jahazpur is undeniably and self-consciously a "provincial" place: *mofussil*, or—as people there frequently told me, using English words, a "backward area."[6] Before passing through the gates, as we shall do in Chapter 2, let us listen to Jahazpur describe itself.

Kalu Singh, a Mina man in his eighties, grew up in Jahazpur but has seen a great deal of the world. He served in the army and was stationed first in South India and then in Kashmir. After the army, Kalu Singh worked for years in both Mumbai and Ahmedabad, returning in his old age to settle in his hometown with his wife—with whom, he confided, he had a "love marriage." (Still unusual today in Jahazpur, love marriage was practically unheard of for his generation.)

Eager to elicit his comparison between the cosmopolitan places he had sampled in his long life and Jahazpur, I posed this question: "Mumbai is the biggest and most modern [*sab se bara, sab se adhunik*] city in India, so what is Jahazpur?" Kalu, echoing my simplistic locution with gentle mockery, replied: "It is the most *backward! [*sab se backward*]."

During my first months of fieldwork I often began with simple questions either about Jahazpur as a place, or about the meaning of qasba. Something which puzzled me during this initial period was the way so many town residents were quick to express a negative assessment of their home, just as Kalu did. Based on my experience, albeit limited, of visiting or passing through other small towns in the region, Jahazpur struck me as endowed with many quality-of-life pluses. Its geophysical landscape and its architecture both possessed attractive features. I found the social ambiance equally pleasant—a comfortable union of urban "mind your own business" with provincial courteousness.

Yet it soon became clear that the town had a collectively professed inferiority complex. Many residents told me they were hoping to leave or planning to send their children elsewhere to study and maybe to work. Rarely if ever did anyone mention the lovely view from the fort, the vital charms of the markets, the religious diversity and abundance of temples, shrines, and saints' tombs. In short, all that made Jahazpur picturesque to my foreigner's eyes was unexceptional to them. Their big complaint: the town had made "no *progress."[7]

Equally perplexing to me were the frequent invidious comparisons I heard made with nearby Devli. Jahazpur, people said, was stagnant while Devli was advancing. In my view, Devli lacked everything that I liked about Jahazpur: gorgeous vistas, deep history, dramatic geography. Devli was a product of colonialism, grown up around a British army camp. It is still the site of a military base, to which many attribute its superior progress, both economic and social. I never properly explored Devli, though I put in plenty of restless time at the bus stand there. Initially a few strolls around the Devli bus stand did not yield an elevated view of greater amenities. However, when I had to wait there at night, I began to see distinguishing features. For example, around 8 P.M. at one of the tea stalls I observed a huge vat of milk at the boil; what would they be doing with so much milk at that time of night, I wondered out loud. To my surprise, I learned that the tea shop stays open all night. Come to think of it, why was I so often pacing at the Devli bus stand? Because, of course, Devli is a transportation hub and buses come and go from larger cities (Jaipur, Kota, Udaipur, Delhi, Gwalior) twenty-four hours a day. Jahazpur's bus stand, by stark contrast, would be dark and shut down well before midnight.

Chetan Prakash Mochi's family fled Pakistan in 1947, landing in Jahazpur not many years thereafter. They now have a pleasant home and lovingly tended garden in Santosh Nagar colony—the recently settled suburb of Jahazpur where I too lived. "Mochi" means "shoemaker," but Chetan and his wife Vimla, probably now in their fifties, have successfully changed professions. Both are tailors, sewing for gents and ladies, respectively. On my first of many visits to their home (for Vimla sewed all my salvar suits that were not ready-made), I was served assorted delicious delicacies and given a tour of the house. I noted in one back bedroom a framed portrait of Dr. B. R. Ambedkar, the revered twentieth-century leader of oppressed communities in their struggles for rights and dignity. Mochis, I realized with a start, of course would be SC or "Scheduled Caste"— formerly untouchable as are all groups dealing with leather. But it wasn't until I saw the picture of Ambedkar that it dawned on me that this family, hard-working but living a comfortable suburban life, might embrace the shared identity of downtrodden communities or Dalits. No Regars or Chamars (Rajasthan's two most populous leather worker castes) lived in Santosh Nagar, to my knowledge—certainly not at this end of the colony where Brahmins and Jats predominated with a sprinkling of Gujars, Vaishnavs, Rajputs, Baniyas.[8]

> *Ann*: Tell me about Jahazpur. What is it? It seems it is neither a
>   village nor a city.
> *Chetan*: It is a qasba!
> *Ann*: So, if you had to compare a qasba with a village or a city what
>   would you say?
> *Chetan*: In the city there is education, there are hospitals, and in the
>   village you don't have these things, and if you get sick you have
>   to go to the city. Well, in Jahazpur there *is* a hospital, but it
>   doesn't have facilities (*suvidha*). It isn't even a good place to go
>   for *delivery [of babies]—not even *normal delivery.
> *Ann*: Where do you go that is near?
> *Chetan*: Devli!

Suvidha might be the word that recurred most often when I asked for a simple town versus village contrast. Suvidha encompasses all kinds of comforts, amenities, conveniences. These include indoor latrine facilities, a reliable, plentiful *nal* (running water connection), electric power at least somewhat more regular than in rural areas and all that it brings, from basic lighting to fridges, ceiling fans, and the ability to watch your favorite TV serial uninterrupted. Often people used suvidha to cover diverse positive attributes of town versus village. Here, however, Chetan uses it *against* Jahazpur. Suvidha may stretch beyond domestic comfort to encompass transportation facilities, high-class shopping options, access to competent medical care, and educational choices beyond the basic government school. It is on that second level that Devli particularly outstripped Jahazpur in people's estimations.[9]

Madan Lohar moved from his village birthplace to Jahazpur in pursuit of a good living and a good market for his fine craftsmanship in metal. His well-made and attractive metal storage cupboards were objects of desire. He had been operating a highly successful business manufacturing and selling metal furnishings for about two decades in Jahazpur, and his large family lived in a spacious home they had built adjacent to his shop on the Santosh Nagar road. But Madan told us he had already laid plans to move to Devli.

Bhoju Ram, my research collaborator, asked Madan what change he had seen in Jahazpur in the twenty-some years he had lived here, and he answered, "There is no special change! Jahazpur is a village-like town (*gaom jaisa qasba*), but Devli!—their way of life (*rehen sahan*), their clothes, in all things they have made progress, in Devli!" A successful Brahmin shopkeeper we called "Lovely," whose English nickname derived from the name of his store, also posed an extreme contrast between Jahazpur and Devli with an emphasis on Devli's rapid development. He told us, "When I studied in Devli, there was zero there, but now Devli is ten times better than Jahazpur!"

Many theories were advanced on the reasons for Devli's rapid progress, which is rooted both in historical and economic circumstances. One is the proximity of military camps and industrial enterprises.

In my conversation with the tailor Chetan Prakash, I said, "I've heard that Devli is smaller than Jahazpur, so why is there greater development in Devli?" He explained:

When India wasn't free, there was an English army camp in Devli, and conveniences (suvidha) were created for the camp at that time; even now there is still a military base and training center there, so that development has continued into the present.

And today there are also other nearby enterprises like the Bisalpur Dam . . . factories, mines, and highways. Jahazpur, on the other hand, is completely isolated, and that is why it isn't developed.

At this juncture our conversation took a turn to reveal some advantages to Jahazpur after all. I admit to provoking this shift with a leading question:

Ann: But I've heard that Jahazpur is a more peaceful place.
Chetan: Yes there is peace here, but nothing more! Here there is no looting, no theft. In Devli, if you don't put a lock on your house when you go out, even in the day or just for a few hours, you could get robbed.

Suddenly Devli looks less appealing, and we glimpse at least a tinge of civic pride beneath the rhetoric of self-disparagement.

Neelam Pandita, a young Brahmin woman studying for her nursing degree, had recently moved to the "suburb" of Santosh Nagar with her parents and brother, leaving behind a crowded and unharmonious joint family household "inside the walls." By nature cheerful, positive, and friendly, Neelam had mostly good things to say about Jahazpur. However, she did critique the availability of educational supplies, telling us emphatically, "You can't get books in Jahazpur—not any of the books you need to study for the competitive exams, and you absolutely can't get any books on nursing; I order them from Bhilwara or Ajmer." Neelam considered space the key causal factor in Jahazpur's lack of progress, perhaps because a crowded house presented difficulties for her own family that were still fresh in her memory.

When I asked Neelam to speculate on the reasons for the sluggish development of Jahazpur, she explained, "Jahazpur is a small, congested area, and the population has increased. But they are all gathered into a small place. So that is why there is less development here. . . . Devli is spread out, and there are big suburbs where you can build big houses."

Another young woman we interviewed, called Tinku, came from a predominantly agricultural community. She stood out among my early interviewees as assessing Jahazpur in a more positive way. I describe her in my mid-August journal as "very voluble," noting, "Tinku had a lot to say about Jahazpur, she had a lot to say about everything."[10] In our recorded interview with Tinku she readily made comparisons between village and town:

> In the village the atmosphere (*vatavaran*) is good but the education isn't good. Here there are good schools nearby; business is good also in Jahazpur. Jobs are here. You can't do business in the village!
>
> The qasba is better than the village; you don't have to go too far for your work. [She unites here two senses of *kam*, or work, which can mean in this phrase both "to get things done" and "to get the things you need"]. You can do it all right here. But if you live in a village, you have to go outside the village to take care of your work [whether shopping or bureaucratic]. For that reason Jahazpur is better than a village.

This voice from a young woman with village experience presents what can be appreciated about Jahazpur if you have tried living in both kinds of places (and if you cease indulging in a grass-is-greener yearning for the dubious charms of Devli). The very things Tinku highlighted I also appreciated, for I too had shifted from village to town.[11]

Each of the five chapters in Part I—Origins, Gateways, Dwellings, Routes, and Histories—recounts in detail how people and communities use and transform places through imagining, residing in, and traversing them.

The first chapter relates the mythic origins of Jahazpur, well known to all its residents, and offers ethnographic elaborations embroidering these legends' meanings. Chapter 2 enters Shiptown, the place and the book, through multiple openings. The town is walled and gated, thus not only contained but permeable. While gazing both ways through its five and a half gates, I highlight thematic motifs that crisscross the whole.

Chapter 3 begins from my own fieldwork circumstances and practices as they emerge from the increasingly undisciplined discipline of anthropology. Fieldwork produces a particular kind of lived relationship to place and to neighbors; cohabiting is a method of sorts. From attending to those neighbors with whom I interacted regularly, it requires no shift in focus to talk about gender roles in a new kind of place: a small town's still smaller suburb or "colony" (an English word fully incorporated into Hindi). Fieldwork is ever permeable to emotions even while generating data.[12]

Chapter 4 focuses on how, in a fundamentally plural place, religion periodically overflows its primary interiority (whether temples, mosques, or hearts) to fill up town streets with visual and aural sensations generating sensory surfeit. Equally, this chapter about parades and other festive modes of claiming space may enhance understandings of identity, tension, and peacekeeping. Chapter 5 turns to the depths of the past in order to ponder how these do and do not appear on the surface in present times. It is in part about the layers of displacement that centuries precipitate, and how some groups organize themselves regularly to remember the places they once lived and ritually revisit them. It is also, in part, about how some people accidentally rediscover the past underground and respond to it. Here I seek to evoke the ways places speak of history and history speaks through places—processes that are meaningful to communities.

Part I thus begins with names and tales, then meanders in and out the qasba gates and up and down the road leading from the bus stand to the colony Santosh Nagar. It parades noisily all around the qasba streets and makes several quick excursions to the surrounding hamlets, attuned to oral histories tapping the depths of the past. Of course there remains a great deal left to learn about Jahazpur and its residents.

Each of the three chapters composing Part II of *Shiptown* grapples with a particular set of complicated, purposeful human activities which develop around areas glossed, for drama and convenience, as Ecology, Love, and Money. My selection of these three foci for human endeavors is based (as I believe most honest ethnographic explorations are) on a partially serendipitous, partially plotted blend of what fascinated me, what presented itself readily to me, and what I realized I had better not ignore if I wanted to stay true to my larger project. That ultimately was to write a good book about a qasba and its relationship to the rural that surrounds it.[13] Each of these clusters of activity—ecological, social, and commercial—offers a panoramic window onto rural and urban interchanges, fusions, transformations, oscillations.

Environmental protection, marriage, and trade as human projects exist throughout the globe, inflected by locality. Sometimes alone, more often in association with Bhoju and his daughters, I observed, experienced, and queried these projects in Jahazpur. Whether focused on unique instantiations or seeking connective threads among multiple cases, my attempt remains above all to be attentive to myriad locally embedded specificities. Part II thus fleshes out ethnographic explorations of Jahazpur as place in three different ways. These are how to protect and sustain valued environments; how ritually and materially to ensure the future happiness of couples and satisfy the pressures of society; and how to keep one's business afloat in the unstable world of the market ridden with uncertainties but also with promises. Part II's chapters represent learning experiences for me as an ethnographer—sometimes tentatively, delicately, blindly groping my way; sometimes racing into the purely unknown, as if on a dare; sometimes beckoned by others, sometimes barging in quite uninvited. Each project I consider also constitutes for participants a kind of activity involving the acquisition of knowledge, the development of strategies, the transformation of selves.

I drew the content of Part I from my whole year's study and organized the bits and pieces in order to layer content and build up understanding. By contrast, a fieldwork chronology loosely structures Part II. That is, I follow my own learning experiences: the trees predated and overlook this fieldwork, while the river occupied Bhoju and me between Diwali (mid-November) and winter. The wedding was a bright gash in the midst of my research and dominated the brief cold season. The market, my last big focus, we pursued in the relentlessly increasing heat from March into June. There's a neat circularity too, as the very latest effort to save the river, observed on social media and my most recent return visit in 2015, is above all a shopkeepers' movement, aligned with ideals of self-improvement within qasba culture. Underlying these ideals is the conviction that an improved environment would also improve business.

Chapter 6 also follows closely from the last chapter of Part I, because one of the wooded hilltops, the first one to which Bhoju called my attention, is protected by the Mautis Minas. Engaging with trees and river has in some ways framed my entire encounter with Jahazpur. The trees brought me there to begin with, drawing me from rural to urban, from village to town, via Malaji's sacred grove. The river and its travails flowed or trickled into my consciousness only when I heard in the fall of 2010 about a hunger striker's efforts to save it. Thus Chapter 6 bridges two contexts and eras of my Rajasthan anthropology, juxtaposing successful tree protection and an ongoing struggle for river restoration, asking why the former has been more easily executed than the latter.

In Chapter 7 I practice full participant observation during about a month of preparation for, as well as aftermath of, the wedding of my research collaborator Bhoju Ram Gujar's three daughters, two of whom are coproducers of this book. You could say I suspended my fieldwork, or you could say I was more intensely engaged than during any other time period. When the date was first set, the family was undecided as to whether the wedding would be held in the brides' home village of Ghatiyali (my former fieldwork site and Bhoju's birthplace), or in Jahazpur, where most of the family currently resided. I remained a neutral listener while different persons advocated for different venues. Grandma really wanted the village; the girls were rooting for Jahazpur with their collective if modestly muted might. They knew that in the end the choice of location, just like the choice of bridegrooms, would be Papa's, not theirs, and Papa would do what was best. When it finally was settled that it would be a town wedding, town elements, costly ones too, were incorporated into it. I intuited, but never heard expressed in words, that the decision was based in part on the young women's wishes, in part on the prudence of avoiding certain difficult relatives in Ghatiyali, and in part on the ways that town life had genuinely transformed this family's aspirations.

The market, of course, is the paradigmatic meeting place of town and country. Vegetables come in from villages, as do shoppers whose needs, from blue jeans to tractors, are served by town tradespeople. In Chapter 8, the last substantial chapter of *Shiptown*, I finally arrive at its (mercenary) heart. Arguably, I might have come to the market immediately following Chapter 2: every gate, after all, leads to or from its central space. As periphery, Santosh Nagar depends on the center; if there were no qasba, there would be no colony. However, my choice to retreat in Chapter 3 to Santosh Nagar (thus to gender, to domesticity) was reasoned and deliberate. Shopping lists begin at home.

When in Chapter 4 we look at the carefully negotiated routes of religious processions and the defining, peace-producing fear of *danga* (riots) as bad for *dhandha* (business), we of course traverse the market streets and listen attentively to shopkeepers' concerns. Pluralism is as much or more a by-product of commercial life as it is of peace committees. We begin to apprehend that the priorities of having a peaceful environment for buying and selling was a large component of the "good-feeling" (*sadbhavana*) process. Moreover, shopping stimulates integration across religious communities: even modest young Hindu women will venture into a Muslim shop (for example, Gaji Pir Gota Center) in search of sparkling trim, if the variety and quality of selection is, after all, the best in town.

The intricately intertwined histories of nonviolent Jain merchants and Minas as farmers/soldiers—presented in Chapter 5 as crucial to contemporary Jahazpur society and politics—also importantly underlies market transactions. In the market, most shopkeepers spoke fondly if somewhat patronizingly of Mina customers, who account for a huge percentage of their trade and were regularly characterized as ever eager to buy the latest fashion. Finery-loving Minas pit their wits against merchants determined to empty their pockets. How might this resonate with goat-sacrificing Minas possessing access to the dangerous power and potent blessings of the non-vegetarian goddess who requires respect from vegetarian Jains? These stereotypical roles seem set in an eternal dance in which each plays their part with vehemence and an underlying awareness, I am pretty sure, of the scripted nature of their interactions.

The refreshingly secular self-help "Save the Nagdi" cleanup team, invoked at the close of Chapter 6, emerged a few years after my fieldwork concluded and includes Hindu, Jain, and Muslim shopkeepers. The salient term here is shopkeepers; religious identities seem to lack relevance. I by no means intend to imply that religious identities are not important in the qasba; the accelerated proliferation of processions and construction projects among all Jahazpur's religious groups depends heavily on donations from businesspeople—donations that depend in turn on profit, that is, on surplus. However, alliances can and do form across religious difference on the basis of improving the atmosphere and reputation of the market; an improved market enhances resources available to fund separate religious projects.

As Chapter 7 will highlight, to point to the commercialization of items used in wedding rituals may epitomize apparently trivial but cumulatively consequential aspects of urbanization, especially for those traveling on the slow passage by "ship" from rural to urban. These ritual props are not terribly costly, but with apparently increasing sales volume they seem to add up to worthwhile business opportunities. I don't know what percentage of business in Jahazpur is generated by weddings or more broadly by life cycle ritual celebrations. Festivals such as Diwali and Id were mentioned by every purveyor of cloth and clothing as highlights of the business year. Still, it would not surprise me if the commerce stimulated by weddings were calculated to be equivalent to the staggering proportion of sales dependent on Christmas in the USA. Just that protracted cloth-giving ritual, the *mayro*, means many thousands of rupees to dealers in cloth, as merchants emphasized in our interviews. The sellers of silver and gold ornaments could hardly stay afloat without the trade generated by gifts at weddings and requisite dowry items. In addition, think of the sweet makers, the tent house at the bus stand that rents out all kinds of hospitality necessities, the light decoration people, even the tailors. Weddings in general are vital to a healthy market in many different areas.

If the trees brought me bodily to Jahazpur, at the time I saw the town only as a blob adjacent to the hilltop. What eventually drew my mind into investigating Jahazpur as place were the legends naming it a pitiless land. As they initially provoked the research on which this book is based, I begin with these tales.

PART I

Origins, Gateways, Dwellings,
Routes, Histories

Chapter 1

Legends

Of Names, Snakes, and Compassion

They say that on a dark night in the month of Asharh, at
the start of the monsoon, a chieftain of Tughlaq, Saiyid
Masood Ghazi, crossed the swollen Ganga and attacked
Gadipuri. Accordingly, the town changed its name from
Gadipuri to Ghazipur. The roads are the same, the lanes
too, and the houses—just the name changed. Perhaps
names are outer shells which can be changed. There is no
unbreakable bond between names and identity, because if
there were then Gadipuri too should have changed when it
became Ghazipur. (Reza 2003:4)[1]

Like Ghazipur which was once Gadipuri, as my epigraph taken from Reza's
novelistic memoir of another qasba explains, Jahazpur also experienced a
name change of which it is fully conscious. But while Jahazpur's name
change is associated with a period of history—"Mughal times"—it differs
from Ghazipur's in that no specific ruler or event precipitated the transformation. Moreover, at least until very recently, Jahazpur's name was locally
meaningful only in its provocation of curiosity. Jahazpur is a landlocked
place, and a town by definition is set on the ground; so why "Shiptown"?[2]

On a brief revisit to Jahazpur in 2013 I had one short encounter with a
young and visionary Jain nun, an outsider who had taken up residence
there in the wake of a miracle (see the Epilogue). She showed me a poster
with her design for a new temple to be built on the outskirts of town.[3] The
temple would have the form of a stylized ship so that, as she expressed it to
me, people from elsewhere would come to distinguish this special place,

Figure 2. Site of new Jain temple under construction, showing poster
with design in the form of a ship, 2015.

would learn, easily recognize, and recollect its name. This Jain nun's design
and her vision marked the singular instance of reference I ever heard in
Jahazpur to the literal meaning of the town's name, and of course it comes
from someone who arrived from some other place. The name does indeed
have a story, or stories, but the stories have nothing to do with a ship.

The story of Jahazpur's name, which I first heard casually on a brief
visit in 2006 when fieldwork there was not even a gleam in my eye, offers
no explanation for why the place is called Shiptown. Rather, Jahazpur origin legends project into the past a wholly different name replete with meaningful stories and witnessed by stone shrines—if you know where to look
for them (one is in the jungle; one is in the penumbra of larger, more
beautiful structures). These legends perplexed and intrigued me, becoming
ultimately the seeds of this book (or to sustain nautical imagery, my tug-
boats to fieldwork).

Jahaz means ship, but there is no large body of water anywhere in sight
in this semiarid region of central Rajasthan. It is only natural to ask how

the name arose; Jahazpur residents are therefore well accustomed to this very question. They have a pat and ready answer. They explain that their town was the site of the mythic snake sacrifice performed by King Janame-jaya in Mahabharata times, and they offer an etymology of the town's name having nothing to do with a ship. Common lore has it that, although today it is spelled and pronounced Jahazpur (*jahaz* "ship," from the Arabic, *-pur* "city"), it was originally Yagyapur (*yagya* "sacrifice," from the Sanskrit, *-pur*). Whatever its facticity, this etymology appears in the government-issued District Census Handbook (Census of India 1994:lxxii).

The shift from Sanskrit *y* to vernacular Hindi *j* does not necessarily involve the influence of Urdu or Perso-Arabic vocabularies. For example, *yatra* for pilgrimage becomes *jatra* in Rajasthani without losing its San-skritic origins. However, the word *jahaz* is an Urdu word, and it really doesn't sound all that much like *yagya*. In short, the linguistic transforma-tion operative here is not simply the common *y* to *j* shift from classical to spoken tongue. Rather the substitution is of an entire meaningful lexeme. There are no stories about a ship because it seems the name "ship" was an expedient accident.

It took me about four years post-fieldwork to realize that my initial question—"Why is your town called Jahazpur, Ship City, when the sea is nowhere in sight?"—had perpetually gone unanswered. In relating the story of Yagyapur as the town's origin tale, Jahazpur residents simply left it as self-evident that Yagyapur had morphed to Jahazpur. No one ever pin-pointed an episode or exact moment in history when an official renaming occurred. We might speculatively fill in the blanks and assume that *jahaz* was easier to pronounce and to write, perhaps for revenue collectors in the Mughal period who would have kept their records in the Arabic script used for both Persian and Urdu.

In any case, the question of how Jahazpur got its name always led directly to Yagyapur. Diverted by the strangely negative stories associated with "Sacrifice City" I simply forgot to keep wondering: why "Ship"? Yagya-pur is an immediate jumping-off place for two compelling and puzzling place legends—each linked to, but departing from, one of India's great epics, the Mahabharata and the Ramayana. As we arrive in Shiptown, I present these brief, perplexing tales of Yagyapur. Their foundational signifi-cances for the town, and for this book, should be self-evident. I relate them with scraps of performative context and in the translated words of diverse tellers rather than simply in synopsis. How and where stories are told matters. And conversational follow-ups sometimes add depth to simple narrative content.

In the indirect nature of this passage to meaning—from "Why a ship?" to "Let me tell you about the ancient sacrifice"—I also would suggest an analogy to some of my fieldwork methods, which rarely involve a single-minded or persistently linear pursuit of specific information. In the incomplete nature of my grasp of Jahazpur's name transformation, my ethnographic style is foreshadowed. Throughout this work, I try to acknowledge at least some of what I did not learn, or forgot to ask, or did not care to know, or could never find out. Moreover, and importantly, these stories obliquely provide a bridge between an agricultural economy and a market economy—a transition congruent with the subject of *Shiptown*, the book.

The two brief tales of Sacrifice City, taken together, I will call for convenience the "pitiless land" cycle. These begin with a king who appears in the prologue to the Mahabharata. Janamejaya, the son of King Parikshit, is descended from Arjuna—one of the five Pandava brothers who are the epic heroes. Although Janamejaya ruled four generations after the events of the epic, his tale is related in the prologue as part of a frame story. After his father is killed by a snakebite, Janamejaya determines to hold a great sacrifice during which, by the power of verbal spells (*mantras*), all kinds of snakes are drawn into the fire pit to perish. Although ultimately thwarted, Janamejaya's intention is to destroy the entire snake species.[4]

Many Jahazpur people relate this basic opening, embellished with greater or lesser detail and names from the epic. The locally salient tale, which to the extent of my knowledge appears in no published versions, begins with an inserted premise: because of Janamejaya's vengeful intentions—basically snake genocide—his sacrifice requires a "pitiless land" (*nirday desh*).

Bhoju and I had sought out Ram Swarup Chipa, a man in his sixties who belonged to the community of cloth makers—dyers and printers. We asked him, "How old is Jahazpur?" Here is his reply:

Once there was a King, Janamejaya, and his father was Parikshit. A snake king bit King Parikshit. So his son went to Sukhdev Muni and asked him to find some pitiless land, where he could hold a sacrifice.

He wanted all the sinful souls [that is, snakes] to come into this sacrificial fire.

So, King Janamejaya came wandering this way with his companions. Near Jahazpur is Nagola and a man there was irrigating with
leather buckets, and in his wife's arms was a six-month-old child.
So the water kept overflowing and she thought, "The water is overflowing and the child is crying," so she thrust her child in the place
where the water came flowing through.[5]

King Janamejaya thought there could not be any place on earth
with less compassion than this—if a mother could do such a thing.
So this is the place where they held the snake sacrifice.

And nine lineages of snakes were wiped out in the sacrificial fire
(*havan*). In that place is a stone image [of a snake].

We elicited and recorded another telling from a retired teacher who
reported his age as seventy-six. Asked what he did, the man replied with
much dignity: "I am old, I sit and sleep." His father had been a fourth-class
peon for the Jahazpur court before Independence; he himself had been
posted as a teacher four times inside the town of Jahazpur. I asked about
the transformation of the town's name, "I heard it was Yagyapur—how did
it become Jahazpur?" He did not answer the question even in a cursory way
but simply launched into the heart of the "pitiless land," skipping over even
the epic king and his father:

It is said that some people wanted to do a sacrifice (yagya) and they
thought, "where is this pitiless land where we can do a sacrifice?"

Thus wandering on their quest, they came to a place, [now
called] Nagola. At this place, the people who were looking for a
pitiless land, saw a man who was irrigating his field; his oxen were
pulling the water from the well in leather buckets and his wife was
building mud barricades to channel the water.

But the water kept breaking through her mud barrier and flowing into the beds [instead of through the irrigation channels as
desired]. It just wasn't stopping. When she saw that the water
wouldn't stop, she picked up her baby and thrust him into the gap,
to block the water.

The people decided this had to be the pitiless place. Everyone
thought, "How could a mother use her child to block the water?
There couldn't be any land more pitiless!"

Figure 3. Snake shrine in Nagola said to be site of King Janamejaya's sacrifice.

> In this sacrifice, they recited spells (mantras), and from the power of the mantras, all nine lineages of snakes arrived and dropped into the pit of their own accord, into the sacrificial pit. This place's name was Nag Havan [Snake Oblations], and from that came the place name Nagola, and also Nagdi, the name of the river today.

This version omits all epic references but provides more detail about the agricultural laborer's work and her extreme frustration. It charters not only the town's name but the name of Jahazpur's river, the Nagdi (Chapter 6).

The problematic attempt to exterminate snakes (normally revered if also healthily feared by rural Hindus) seems a fertile generator of additional stories set in the recent past. These stories might be categorized by folklorists as a Rajasthani version of "urban legends." I found compelling an insistence on redress for the ancient violence perpetrated against snakes. We gathered several tales about a regional taboo on preparing the soil with a cultivating blade called *kuli* (which I'm told is particularly dangerous to snakes). In the stories, snakes themselves enforce the taboo, with sanctions ranging from fear to death.

An elderly Mina man in Borani, one of the outlying hamlets that belong to Jahazpur municipality, related the main tale and concluded: "This is why they used to call Jahazpur Yagyapur." Bhoju Ram asked him if there existed any "proof" that the ancient sacrifice took place right here.

Here is how the old man answered that challenge: "Right now, even today, at Sarsia village, whenever the people were plowing their fields with a kuli, and not with a plow, snakes obstructed their kuli. The snakes do not bite, but they don't let farmers use the kuli. So the farmers got together and made a golden kuli and did a sacrifice (yagya), and after that they were able to use kuli in their field. *This* is proof." This puts a satisfying "nature bats last" coda to the snake sacrifice tale, allowing us to see it as ecological parable. It shows that humans ought to negotiate rather than exterminate, even to negotiate with a compensatory sacrifice. Note this is a sacrifice offered *to* snakes, a complete reversal of the prior sacrifice *of* snakes.

In the heart of Jahazpur qasba we interviewed a very old Vaishnavite priest, Mohandas Vairagi, and his grandson Ram Charan, who looked to be in his twenties. I began by asking about the origin legend of the Nagdi River, telling them I heard it was created "from the blood of snakes." Ram Charan agreed to the truth of this. He went on to speak of current problems with snakes in the fields. This urban priestly family still cultivates farmland just outside Jahazpur town. "We don't plow our fields with the kuli; if we do, then we have trouble and see lots of snakes. . . . One year I used the kuli, and I saw snakes every day. The next year, I stopped using it and we didn't see nearly so many snakes." I asked if this problem with the use of the kuli was true only in the area around the Nagdi Dam, but Ram Charan said it applied to the whole region.

> *Ann*: So, is the kuli "forbidden?" [I employ the word *pratibandh*, which I learned when researching the prohibitions kings put on peasants such as "don't wear gold" or "don't eat white sugar."]
>
> *Ram Charan*: No, this [taboo] is something we embrace as moral duty (*dharmik maneta*).
>
> *Bhoju*: Was there some event when someone tried to use the kuli?

Ram Charan: Yes, yes! There was someone who died! He was bit by
    a snake and died. And maybe five or seven years ago I tried
    myself to use the kuli and so many snakes appeared, beyond
    counting! I saw a black snake this thick [he demonstrates
    expansively with his fingers] after plowing with the kuli.
Bhoju: So after that you stopped using the kuli?
Ram Charan [an excitable fellow]: No, no, no! We don't even say
    the word *kuli*!"
Bhoju [always persistent]: So now you *never* see any snakes?
Ram Charan: Well, yes, sometimes we see one; but at that time
    [when he had dared to employ a kuli] we sighted a snake every
    single day, one at least. I've seen these things with my own eyes.

The second tale in the pitiless land cycle has nothing to do with snakes
or farming. It propels us directly into the urban realm of the market, by
definition a realm of monetary transactions. This story draws on one figure,
the well-known Shravan Kumar, who appears briefly in Hinduism's other
major epic, the Ramayana. Shravan Kumar's story was often told immediately after the snake sacrifice story.[6]

In the classic Ramayana epic, Shravan Kumar's story constitutes a fatal
intervention in the plot. His figure remains revered as a model for filial
service. He is known as the devoted son who carried his blind parents on
pilgrimage and who was accidentally killed—mistaken for an elephant—by
Lord Rama's father King Dasaratha while on a youthful hunting excursion.
Shravan's parents curse Dasaratha to die in sorrow separated from his own
beloved son—the same unhappy fate the young king's misplaced arrow has
forced upon them. In the Ramayana this curse, which Dasaratha relives in
a dreamlike state on his deathbed, serves to determine the karmic necessity
for Ram's exile and his father's mortal grief.[7]

The first individual to tell me about Shravan Kumar's Jahazpur moment
was an elder in the Khatik community. Durga Lal Khatik had been instrumental in founding the Khatiks' Satya Narayan temple—a watershed in
their history as well as in Jahazpur's (Gold 2016). He told us that Jahazpur
was known far and wide as a pitiless land because when Shravan placed his
foot within the town boundary, the young man halted in his tracks and
demanded *kiraya* or "fare" from his parents. They said, "Wait, son, the
ground beneath your feet must be what causes you to speak in such pitiless
fashion. Just keep walking until you have passed once again outside the

border of this place." Sure enough, as soon as Shravan Kumar stepped outside of Jahazpur territory, he once again became a model of filial devotion.[8]

If Jahazpur's mythic snake sacrifice charters both name and character of place, Shravan Kumar's story builds on and reinforces the notion that Jahazpur ground is somehow stamped with, or programmed for, primal violations of moral order: the ascendance of business over kinship. To me this story brings us to the heart of things. A market is a place, so unlike a family, where everyone must pay their way.

Individuals occasionally add a few narrative embellishments to their tellings, but there is little significant variation. A few examples suffice to show the ways a particular teller may inflect the basic story.

Kamala Dholin—a woman from the community of drummers, who serve as bards and whose verbal skills are renowned—located her telling of the Shravan Kumar story in Nagola, which, as we just heard, is reputed to be the actual site of Janamejaya's sacrifice and which is a bit of a way out of town. But she quickly merges the two places in her story:

In Nagola, Shravan Kumar was carrying his parents. Then he stopped and said to them, "I have taken you on a pilgrimage around the entire world. Now you pay me the fare (kiraya)!"

They said, "You didn't ask for the fare before. Why do you ask for it here in Jahazpur?"

Shravan's father told his son, "Pick up some of this soil (mitti) and take it with you." After they crossed the Banas River, his mother said, "All right, so you want your fare now?" But he had no idea what she was talking about.[9]

Then his mother put down the Jahazpur soil and as soon as he put his foot on it he began all over again, demanding from his parents their fare.

But the moment he moved his foot to the actual soil belonging to that far side of the Banas, he said he didn't want the fare.

Kamala concluded: "Such are the qualities (gun) in Jahazpur's soil." Hers was the most explicit and dramatic telling in that the son does not even remember his demand once his feet are no longer touching the soil of the pitiless land.

Chittar Gujar belonged to one of the few Gujar families rooted in Jahazpur. He was among the first elders we visited in 2010, due to Bhoju's feeling comfortable with Gujars.[10] Historically, of course, Chittar's community was associated with herding and dairy production, as are Gujars throughout Rajasthan. But he had successfully developed a truck transport business. As does Kamala's, Chittar's concise telling establishes a precise boundary for the pitiless land: "Shravan Kumar was carrying his parents on a pilgrimage. When he reached Jahazpur, he asked them—his mother and father—for the fare. They said, 'OK, we'll pay you the fare if you want it . . . but in this place there is no compassion. Between Jahazpur and the Banas River is the pitiless territory. So just go a little farther.'" And of course, no sooner do they cross the Banas River than Shravan Kumar becomes the perfect son once again.

Satyabala, a vivacious Brahmin woman who lived in the qasba, had rented rooms in her house to Bhoju Ram and two of his children for several years before Bhoju purchased his own property in Santosh Nagar. I had also stayed with her on one of my earlier visits. She was therefore one of the people we knew best in the qasba. Moreover, Jahazpur was both her natal home and her in-laws' home, making her a lifelong Jahazpurite and a nice resource in that regard, as many women I interviewed had only moved here after marriage. On one visit I asked her about Jahazpur being a pitiless land, and she launched into the Shravan Kumar story without even mentioning the snake sacrifice. She told it like this:

> Once Shravan Kumar was serving his mother and father, by taking them on pilgrimage. He took them throughout Mewar, but when he came to Jahazpur, he asked them for money: "Give me my fare (kiraya)."
>
> His mother and father were both blind and they had nothing to give him, so they said to go forward, and he did, and when they came out from Jahazpur he didn't ask anymore—and that is why people say this is sinful earth (papi dharti).

One Santosh Nagar neighbor, Ayodhya Vaishnav, was about forty years of age and had scant education. I met her in the company of Bhoju's two daughters. Ayodhya surprised me by stating early on in our conversation that people like me (that is foreigners, non-Indians) had "more love among yourselves than we do here."

She then without prompting launched straight into the story of Shravan Kumar or, as she called him, Shravan Beta (Son). "He took his mother and father everywhere," she told us, "but only near the Nagdi did he ask for money. He asked for it when he came to Pander Road." Thus embroidering the story in maplike local geography, she related the basic episode and concluded with a flourish: "It is a true story." I asked her then to go back to the topic of love and explain what she had said earlier. She answered firmly, as if the Shravan Kumar narrative had served to prove her point, "You see, there is more love in your country than there is in Jahazpur."

Ayodhya's reference to America serves my purposes as this opening chapter's final pitiless land telling (we return to Shravan Kumar in Chapter 8). I wish here to emphasize another effort and motif running throughout this book: the two-way gaze, and two-way passages of understanding—or at times misunderstanding. Looking back, I recollect during my first research three decades ago that people in the village of Ghatiyali (less than thirty kilometers from Jahazpur) were sometimes naive enough to believe that American streets were made of glass. At the same time they were severely critical of American culture that shunned its duties to the elderly as well as to children (and that I put my son in boarding school was perfect proof). Many people I met during my earlier village research claimed that my land so rich in possessions lacked love, a quality they insisted was more abundant in India.

So why would Ayodhya, in Jahazpur in 2010, idealize relationships in America? Possibly she wished to emphasize her own bitter assessment of the local: even in the materialistic USA she might have met with more kindness than in pitiless Jahazpur. I learned that Ayodhya had her private troubles, as was the case with most interviewees who agreed with the legends and attributed a genuine harshness to human relationships in Jahazpur. Such people were, I emphasize, in the minority.

By beginning with the pitiless land cycle, and by taking it not only as origin tale but as a kind of chartering mythology, I do not intend in any fashion to take it as valid judgment. Neither do most Jahazpur residents. Interviewees generally related the pitiless land cycle without a lot of reflection or reflexivity. It was simply part of a ready store of local lore, and a query as to whether it were true that Jahazpur had such a nature, or was any worse than other towns, would meet most often with dismissive replies.

However, there were a number, such as Ayodhya Vaishnav, for whom the pitiless land cycle served, as does the Mahabharata itself, to provoke pondering what Gurcharan Das has called "the difficulty of being good" (2010). That is, some people use the tales to rethink their own life experiences and even their own actions. Some people may conclude that snake slaughter is not the answer after all. As the young Vaishnav man was so determined to make us understand, snakes demand respect; if humans ignore this, retribution follows. Moreover, one's aged parents must not be charged the fare even though it taxes you—financially, emotionally, and physically—to care for them.

Most of the time the following chapters engage the everyday. Jahazpur's origin legends and the ways people interpret them reveal that the everyday may be stippled with troublesome snakes, heartless relatives, vengeance, and cupidity. Except for the snakes, we could say the same about anywhere on earth. My intention is to emphasize throughout this book that the everyday is equally wondrous in manifestations of concern, curiosity, hospitality, solidarity, integrity. This is my ethnographic version of the free newspaper I sometimes pick up in Ithaca called *Positive News*.

In Ghatiyali in 1980 village people often told me I was far too *bholi*—naive and gullible. Many anthropologists in these turbulent times provide accounts of violence, conflict, and suffering, and I read and teach their work with enormous-admiration and even awe.[11] In claiming my calling to report on easier matters I certainly acknowledge my lack of aptitude and appetite for painful stuff. But I also argue simply that it is good to know not only the worst of which human beings are capable, but to document some of the ways and modes humans' everyday actions resist or temper the influence of pitiless soil on which we all may find at times that we have (inadvertently or deliberately) placed a foot. One remedy, as the old blind parents advised, is to lift that foot up again. There is some comfort in knowing that the land without compassion is bounded.

Chapter 2

Entries

Five Gates and a Window

From the remote time when walled towns and royal
strongholds were first built it was instinctive for men to
attribute anagogical, allegorical and topological meanings
to gateways. (Smith 1978:10)

I first arrived for a long-term fieldwork spell in Jahazpur on 5 August 2010.
I was sixty-three and hardly a novice. Over a period of time extending back
more than thirty years I had pursued diverse anthropological projects in
this region of Rajasthan. Moreover, I had already spent several nights in
Jahazpur and met a number of people there during three consecutive summer visits in 2006, 2007, and 2008. My aim now was to study the nature of
small-town life in North India in what I planned would be a wide-ranging,
if far from comprehensive, fashion. I had proposed to ground my topic by
looking at three specific types of places: neighborhoods, shops, and shrines.
These were all around me, in delightful if daunting abundance. Even so,
methodological avenues eluded me. How to begin finding meaningful patterns in everyday routes and activities?

Once again, I was working collaboratively with Bhoju Ram Gujar, but
only when his schedule as a full-time middle-school headmaster and dedicated government servant permitted. He fitted my work as best he could
into the cracks and crevices of what seemed to me to be an inordinately
busy and complicated life.[1] Bhoju himself, while eager as ever to embark
upon ethnographic research, did not radiate his usual confidence as we
confronted this vast new space of investigation.

In the past when we had worked together in villages, Bhoju considered himself fully cognizant of, and comfortable in, the social milieu; his gifts as an interlocutor were unparalleled. Now, well-educated and well-traveled though he was, Bhoju remained a village-born person only lately come to town. Although it wasn't in his nature to declare it, I could tell that Jahazpur society was partially mysterious to him, almost as opaque in some respects as it was to me.[2] An economy ruled by trade, not farming, was certainly new territory for both of us. Some important groups here—for example, the former butchers and the former wine sellers—were not present at all in Ghatiyali, Bhoju's birthplace and my previous fieldwork base.

It says something of significance about the kind of place Jahazpur is that Bhoju and I were initially baffled by a very strong contrast between Jahazpur and Ghatiyali. Ghatiyali was the second-largest village in the twenty-seven-village dominion of Sawar. Most people living within that former kingdom, even in the late 1990s and early 2000s, possessed vivid memories or knowledge of the time preceding India's independence in 1947 when kings had ruled. They particularly recollected and could tell stories about the last king of Sawar, who had died without progeny the same year that India gained freedom from colonial rule. Even those far too young to have actual memories produced stories about Vansh Pradip Singh, a ruler so attentive to the goings-on in his estates that he was said to have personally and literally sniffed out poached game from his ramparts and sent his guards to arrest whoever was cooking it (Gold and Gujar 2002). Moreover, as recently as 2010 a member of the former ruling family who resides at least part of the time in Ghatiyali's fort won a local democratic election there.

Jahazpur by contrast was located well beyond the olfactory range of rulers whether they were based in Udaipur, Ajmer, or even relatively nearby Shahpura, and whether they were Hindu, Mughal, or British. The pervasive memories of a "time of kings" that we had relied upon for our research on environmental history in the kingdom of Sawar were perplexingly absent here. Jahazpur politics inside the walls is dominated by merchants, Brahmins, and Deshvali Muslims (the three groups that own the most qasba land as well). In greater Jahazpur—the Nagar Palika, or municipality, incorporating twelve hamlets surrounding the town—Minas have put their numbers to work in block voting and triumphed in a series of recent mayoral elections.[3]

Participation in Jahazpur politics by members of the former ruling class, the Rajputs, is negligible. Mansions belonging to families once connected

Figure 4. Maps of Rajasthan and Bhilwara District (produced by Joseph W. Stoll).

with royal power are empty, overgrown, and crumbling; no one in the general public seems to know or care where the owners went. Sawar's fort remains inhabited by the ruling lineage, but Jahazpur's is in ruins and long ago was stripped of anything valuable that could be removed (except for images of the gods that still abide there and continue to receive worship and service). Rumor had it that Jahazpur fort had been put up for sale by the government. I have not been able to document this assertion, but a few people jokingly proposed that I purchase the ruins and open a heritage hotel. In sum, in contemporary Jahazpur, the decline of Rajput fortunes seemed complete. Those few remaining members of families slightly related to royalty are poor, disempowered, and command scant interest from the public.[4]

Bhoju was initially stunned at how few people in Jahazpur could even name the last ruler, and certainly no one spoke of royalty with any kind of affection or reverence, not even with intense hatred. Much of what we did glean through persistent questioning about the former rulers in these parts had to do with dissolute behavior: unsavory alliances, substance abuse, crushing debt. For the most part, these figures from the past were not a live topic of conversation. This could not have presented a greater contrast with our previous experience.

For a month, during which there were predictable preoccupations connected with domestic and bureaucratic arrangements, I flailed around to match my research agenda to my whereabouts. To counter my hesitations, Bhoju initiated some excellent pragmatic steps. First, he rustled up persons willing to be interviewed on a general level about town and place. These interviews, mostly with busy, senior members of Jahazpur's merchant community, we conducted in the evening after business hours. Bhoju's two older daughters, meanwhile, were easily persuaded to help me meet and have conversations with neighbor women, a morning enterprise that proved not only productive but pleasant, even as it stimulated a whole new set of concerns around gender and neighborhood (see Chapter 3). My neighbors lived in Santosh Nagar, on the outskirts of town, where we had decided to settle for excellent reasons. But I worried about the need to keep my attention focused on Jahazpur proper, the qasba, "inside the walls" (*kot ke andar*) as the local phrase went.

We were into September, and there was plenty of daylight to spare. Bhoju's school was still on the hot season schedule, so he normally returned fairly early in the afternoon. Bhoju suggested that we survey the built landscape, especially those landmarks or places in which history was embedded. Of course, I had been several times up to the fort on the hill for the hike, the views, and to visit the tomb of Gaji Pir and adjacent Muslim shrines. But now we would tour the flats systematically and visit the old qasba gates. I had already passed in and out of the grandest gate, the one connecting the bus stand to the market, countless times; but I had taken only sporadic note of the others.

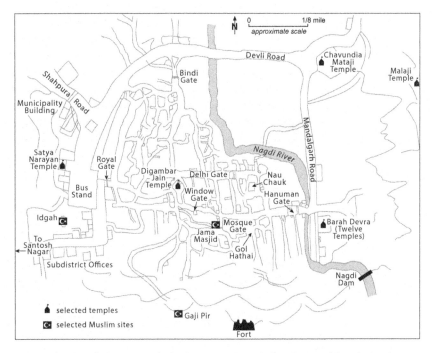

Figure 5. Hand-drawn map of Jahazpur, selected sites (original by Bhoju Ram Gujar, redesigned and produced by Joseph W. Stoll).

Although portions of the old ramparts are no longer standing, Jahazpur's market and residences were originally contained within a fully walled area. Five major doorways remain intact, three of which lead to the exterior; another opens on an important outdoor square, and another marks the significant Muslim presence within Jahazpur qasba and sets apart the entrance to the mosque as sacred space (Bianca 2000). Lastly, there is a small gate to the exterior, more a window than a doorway. This "Window Gate" was regularly included when our most thorough informants enumerated ways to enter and exit the qasba. That made a total, you might say, of five and a half gates—or as I have put it in my chapter title, five gates and a window.[5]

We had already conducted some interviews with elderly people whose memories reached back into the 1940s, and there would be many more. We heard repeatedly that right up to Independence, the gates were locked at night, some manned by watchmen. For industrious farmers who lived in the town but farmed in the surrounding countryside, the walls and locked gates could become major inconveniences. I don't know when the walls were constructed, exactly. But the process of walling market towns to protect from robbers appears to have been a nineteenth-century process elsewhere in the region.[6] At certain seasons, farmers must work long past dusk. They were forced to sleep in their fields. Even if a watchman might allow a human to climb through a small window set within the massive door, the big doorways through which livestock might pass were kept closed throughout the night.

These practices were explained to us repeatedly as intended to protect the town with its goods from thieves and wild animals. The wall portions that are still standing have signs of past military functions (slits through which rifles or arrows could be shot). However, although some notations in historical accounts mention battles involving Jahazpur's fort on the hill, I found neither written nor oral traces of battles around the town itself.

Bhoju and I toured all the gates by motorcycle, me in my usual sidesaddle position behind him. This gave us a happy sense of continuity with our previous successful research in the twenty-seven-village kingdom of Sawar, much of which relied on similar if more grueling motorcycle excursions (Gold and Gujar 2002). It also provided a feeling of current accomplishment. At each gate we disembarked, and I took photographs. When we looked at them later on the computer, I failed to identify all the images correctly. To my recalcitrant brain, with its unusually weak visual recognition skills, three of the six gates were somehow indistinguishable. So we took another round. Frustrated with my deficiencies in visual memory, I digitally pasted my photographs into a document with notes on each gate, cramming my geography lessons.

I knew that however irrelevant the now perpetually open gates seemed today, the life of the qasba had once been channeled through them. I knew I needed to get the layout of Jahazpur. People and their stories, true and mythic, have always been my most passionate ethnographic calling. As such they trump not just architecture but politics, economics, institutions, and theory. This is not to say that I deny the many ways material and invisible structures of power condition the human tales I gather; it is rather a question of what takes precedence in my writing, and in my fieldwork practice too. I was pleased to see a monkey striding along the top of Hanuman Gate, an entry named for a nearby temple dedicated to Hanuman, the monkey deity beloved as Lord Rama's loyal companion.

I lead readers into Shiptown (aka Sacrifice City) via five gates and a window. I present these entrances as specific, named, located, visible, solid structures. Equally I use them metonymically as contiguous with particular themes and topics running through this book. Each physical gate offers passages in two directions. Each metonymical gate stretches into key elements of my ethnography and may equally be taken as double-faced in that it intentionally links the world of Jahazpur, as far as I was able to participate in or learn about it, with the world of anthropology and South Asian studies, in which I dwell professionally and intellectually.[7]

Walls, gates, and windows are comforting frames, providing simultaneously apprehensions of containment/protection and access/visibility. The gates are inarguably emblematic of the place Jahazpur, and I deploy each gate to open up one or a set of related themes that readers will encounter in *Shiptown*. The matchup of gate to theme or subject, as sketched here, is inevitably loose. Nonetheless, I propose that the suggestive affinities are strong enough to sustain a set of topics central to this book and thus to suggest to readers particular kinds of passage.

None of the six built gates or the six conceptual pathways to and from Shiptown posed here is exactly congruent with the content of the six chapters to follow. However, the introductory sections, or entries, that comprise the remainder of Chapter 2 will resonate most strongly in specific additional chapters (as indicated parenthetically below, with the fullest convergence listed first):

1. Royal Gate (Bhanvarkala Gate): Commercial passages (Chapters 8, 4)
2. Delhi Gate: Historical passages (Chapters 5, 4)
3. Bindi Gate: Sociological passages (Chapters 4, 5)
4. Mosque Gate: Pluralistic passages (Chapters 4, 8)
5. Hanuman Gate: Ecological passages (Chapter 6)
5½. Window Gate: Ethnographic passages (Chapters 3, 7)

Those larger themes suggested by passages through the gates are woven throughout the whole text of this book as they are woven throughout life in Jahazpur. All of them characterize aspects of passages between rural and urban lives and livelihoods—this book's overarching and underlying subject.

Walls no longer contain the place called Jahazpur, if they ever did. Of the chapters to follow not a single one takes place only inside the walls, and three are set almost totally outside them. And yet, the walled qasba *is* Jahazpur. Nor was Bhoju mistaken in giving significance to the gates. As is frequently the case, I am following his lead or am propelled on my way by his polite push from behind.

Royal Gate: Commercial Passages

In many regions of the world and many eras of human history, gateways carry a set of meanings related to political, economic, and cosmological power. Paul Wheatley's magnum opus on Asian cities names Rajasthan's capital Jaipur, a city of very imposing gates, as one of the most recent examples of cosmos-replicating town planning (1971:440). Wheatley writes: "The city gates, where power generated at the axis mundi flowed out from the confines of the ceremonial complex towards the cardinal points of the compass, possessed a heightened symbolic significance which, in virtually all Asian urban traditions, was expressed in massive constructions whose size far exceeded that necessary for the performance of their mundane functions of granting access and affording defense" (1971:435). It is unlikely that Jahazpur was designed to replicate the cosmos. Still, it is reasonable to conclude that the inspiration for the size and shape of Jahazpur's Royal Gate was found in one or another of the region's grander urban spaces. And it is indisputably the case that processions both sacred and secular regularly pass through Royal Gate, making an impressive sight even in the twenty-first century. Surely these processions with their clamorous if temporary claims on public space draw upon that ancient symbolic resonance.

A literal translation for the name of the gate I am calling "Royal" cannot readily be extracted from the Rajasthani-Hindi dictionary. According to Bhoju, Bhavarkala in the local language might awkwardly be rendered into English, putting the pieces together, as the "King's Grandson's Big Gate." When I proposed "Royal" as a convenient gloss, he agreed with some relief, averring that it made perfect sense. Royal Gate's name is the same as the name of the nearby water reservoir (*talab*) which has town-wide uses both practical and ritual—the latter including the bathing of gods every Jal Jhulani Gyaras (Jahazpur's most ambitious and spectacular Hindu festival; see Chapter 4).

Royal Gate is the largest of the gates, so large that within its structure, set into each side of the passageway, are two venerable bangle shops. Commerce, which is the raison d'être of the qasba, thus insinuates its presence

Figure 6. Looking outward from market to bus stand through Royal Gate, 2015.

into the majesty of the gate itself. Jahazpur's Royal Gate sees a constant two-way flow of people, animals, handcarts, and motor vehicles. On one side of this massive structure is the bus stand with its constant bustle of noisy ordered chaos. On the other side is the main market. If after entering you veer to the right, you will immediately arrive in Chameli Market, where Muslim-run businesses including meat, fish, and cotton quilts are clustered near the smaller of Jahazpur's mosques, known as Takiya Mosque.[8] Or you can wend more or less directly through the main market, eventually to reach Delhi Gate and pass through to the fenced, open parklike square known as Nau Chauk (discussed below). If you did not stop to chat, browse, or shop—which honestly never happens—you could easily walk the distance between Royal and Delhi Gates, or between the bus stand and Nau Chauk, in about ten minutes.

Jahazpur's main market is utterly crammed with shops; the shops themselves are equally crammed with goods. Whether you are in the street or inside a shop there is a feeling of tightness, density, and abundance of merchandise. Perhaps most common are the grocery stores (*kirane ki dukan*), followed by unstitched cloth, and increasingly popular (although largely for men and children) ready-made clothing. But the market also holds, in random order: shoe stores, photo studios, cookware, toys, electronics, sweets, gold and silver ornaments, stationery and school supplies, a dairy, plastic utensils, "fancy" (cosmetics, bangles, costume jewelry, and other trinkets and finery), supplies for festivals and rituals, and a lot more. There are barbers and tailors, for example, trading in services rather than goods. With just a few exceptions, any and all of life's everyday necessities as well as its pleasures, comforts, and minor entertainments may be obtained inside the walls. There are no restaurants, but the largest sweet shop has a few tables. There is no cinema, but to my amazement, late in my stay, I was led down a few steps into a videogame parlor, a site I had passed countless times but simply never seen. I have noted just one pharmacy inside the market; the rest are conveniently lined up in a row near the hospital, which is down the road that leads to Santosh Nagar well beyond the bus stand and far outside the walls.

Between the two sides of Royal Gate, the bus stand, and the market, there is both continuity of merchandise and contrasts. Besides transport, the central and most vital feature of Jahazpur bus stand's central space is the produce market; this space houses the vast majority of stalls conducting a flourishing produce trade—a wide variety of fresh fruits and vegetables in season. Some of the same items are available from small, individual gardener-vendors at the other end of the market, outside Delhi Gate at Nau Chauk. None of the grocery stores inside the walls sells fresh produce, although they do deal in garlic, onions, chilies, and other spices.

Outside Royal Gate at the bus stand we encounter, appropriately for a transport hub, various ways that the town of Jahazpur is hooked into the world around it. Obvious are those actual moving vehicles—buses, trucks, jeeps, and cars for hire—absorbing and disgorging passengers. Ever increasing in number are parked motorcycles, still the vehicle of choice for men with jobs or businesses that have endowed them with middle-class status but whose means are still limited.[9] A car is not simply a one-time investment of capital; to drive one regularly requires outlays for petrol that far outstrip the cost of running a motorcycle. Nonetheless, private cars are also multiplying in numbers, and an automobile showroom was the latest business to arrive in the town some years after my fieldwork time.

The Hotel Prakash with its colorful facade stands out on one side of the bus stand. I understand decent, simple accommodations may be had there, but I never did enter its premises. There are places at the bus stand where you can eat a cooked meal, but they are not considered to be proper restaurants. Rather they are *dhabas* (roadside eateries), in that they have no menus and, like the Hotel Prakash, would rarely if ever be patronized by women or families.[10] Another flourishing business is the fully stuffed "tent house" which rents out all the requisite hospitality accoutrements for a wedding or funeral feast, including the tent itself, cookware, and bedding for guests. There is a jam-packed store I privately called the "everything" store, where soap, toothpaste, vitamins, padlocks, cookies, undershirts, socks, and countless other useful items may be acquired, although you must know what you need and ask for it.

Ranged around the bus stand's periphery are the high-speed Internet place, the bank, the cash machines (two of them), and several mobile phone recharge shops also offering fax services and other forms of telecommunication. (Some dispensers of similar services are also found in the interior market.) Also located at the bus stand, doing business with Jahazpur residents and villagers, are agents selling insurance, notable because their shops appear strangely vacant in contrast to the densely packed merchandise on display in most stores. Insurance, however invisible, sells.

One of the town's oldest sweet shops, where we often purchased our favorite "milk cakes," is located there. Next to the sweet shop is a paan stall; its owner reminisced about bygone days when lengthy lines of customers waited patiently to savor his special betel leaf concoctions. Now they may prefer to purchase inferior prepackaged substitutes at a far lower cost, lacking flavor, complexity, and art. Fried snacks including delicious *kachoris* are available at the bus stand. In the hot season there is a sugar-cane juice press in constant operation, producing lovely frothy green drinks; next to it, run by the same family, a year-round stall features cigarettes and such. The shops at the bus stand in the vicinity of Royal Gate continue to expand. The municipality profits from opening up space for the construction of new stalls to house additional businesses; two rows were under way in 2011.

If everything described thus far could easily apply to hundreds or even thousands of small-town bus stands in South Asia (and likely other parts of the developing world as well), Jahazpur's bus stand also has a distinctive landscape, tapping the town's particular histories of devotion and struggle. These permanent sites and moveable events reflect pan-Indian as well as local traditions. The Tejaji shrine, dedicated to an epic regional hero-god with the power to cure snakebites, is located right here.[11] The Ram Lila

Figure 7. Vegetable market at bus stand showing Satya Narayan
temple in background.

stage is set up here in advance of Dashera—the fall festival marking Lord
Rama's defeat of Ravana and his return with the rescued Sita to Ayodhya.
Here the epic tale is performed for ten nights running.[12] Devotional songs
(bhajans) to Ramdevji are performed on the bright second of every lunar
month (when the waxing moon is just a sliver).[13] Every major procession
taken out in Jahazpur, whether Hindu, Jain, Muslim, or secular (as well as
most minor ones, and there are plenty of them), will at some point take a
halt and congregate for a time at the bus stand—whether processing from
an interior site to the water reservoir or from an outlying shrine passing
into the market through Royal Gate (see Chapter 4).[14]

The Satya Narayan temple established by the Khatik community in the
mid-1980s is perhaps the most potently evocative structure at Jahazpur bus
stand, signaling as it does the shifts of changing times and presiding in
certain ways over economic developments in Jahazpur as much as religious
ones. The Khatiks traded in live animals destined to be butchered and
sometimes were butchers; they have SC status. As I understand it (although

the timing is approximate), the Khatiks acquired the land where the Satya Narayan temple stands, as well as adjacent property now housing lucrative shops, sometime in the 1970s, when they had used their block voting power to support a politician who, when successful, rewarded them with this land. At that time, of course, the land had less commercial value than it does today. It did not take long for the Khatik community to begin their transformative actions, sacred and secular, devotional and commercial—the establishment of the Satya Narayan temple and of the vegetable auction and associated market (Gold 2016).

Sometimes urban Jahazpur would surprise me by keeping a tradition I had imagined to be wholly rural. This could happen even at the bus stand, with its urban air uniting globalized commerce with village-bound transport. On the day of Makar Samkrant—the winter solstice according to the Hindu lunar calendar, which comes in early January—there are a number of regional traditions. The best known among these is kite flying, which happens all over North India and Pakistan. In rural Rajasthan, however, Samkrant is memorably a day on which individuals purchase bundles of fodder and spread it out for the cattle. This is said to provide merit to the donor. To me it had seemed a sweet and wholly rustic notion: giving cows a day off the hard work of grazing and letting them feast lazily. The beneficiaries of this tradition would be any settlement's collective herd, so the donor of fodder does not favor their own animals even though theirs might be among the herd, and many people who do not own livestock still donate fodder. In Ghatiyali village, this pampering of skinny livestock takes place on the banks of the water reservoir, rather far from all habitations, a purely pastoral landscape.

I was unprepared on Samkrant morning to encounter urban vendors at Jahazpur bus stand throwing down heaps of carrots for the ill-behaved cows that hang around here. This surprised me, especially as on ordinary days these indolent, pesky creatures, well aware of their sacred status, or so it seems, were often roundly cursed and smacked smartly on the rump or even on the head (though never actually beaten) for helping themselves, uninvited, to some choice, ill-guarded produce. Vendors keep sticks handy expressly for this purpose. But on Makar Samkrant at Jahazpur bus stand, cows feasted on carrots willingly donated. I note this here not only for its being a sign of rural-urban synthesis but because it offers a lesson about change.

The bus stand has not always been the bus stand. Before 1978, when that transformation took place, this site I know as Jahazpur bus stand was, it seems, the site where every morning the herd of cows and buffalo owned by town residents assembled to be taken to graze by a collectively employed herdsman. In villages such as Ghatiyali this gathering place is exactly the spot where people donate fodder on Makar Samkrant. In Jahazpur, we may thus assume that cows have a historically, spatially, and ritually chartered right to be fed just here. Carrots, abundant at this season, are more accessible than fodder to vegetable vendors in town—businesspeople who value the idea of acquiring religious merit.

For those living inside the walls, it would be Royal Gate from which they would most commonly emerge to set forth on many kinds of errands to places near and distant. Royal Gate was my gate, too, through which I both approached and departed the qasba. When I turned homeward I would walk through the bus stand, down Santosh Nagar Road, past the fresh squeezed juice stand (also a Khatik innovation), the subdistrict offices, the hospital, the post office, the *idgah*, the graveyard, all the way to Santosh Nagar's very last side street where I lived.

Delhi Gate and Nau Chauk: Historical Passages

Only one store among dozens of small grocery or provision shops carried large jars of Nescafé, which I personally consumed in shocking amounts. Dan and I discovered this store at the far end of the market, not far from Delhi Gate. At first it surprised me that such a well-stocked store would be at what I assumed was the lesser end of the bazaar. But it all depends on your position, perspective, and moment in history. A town's spatial orientations shift and change not only over time but according to where one stands. Picture the qasba opening up inwardly from Delhi Gate, not Royal Gate. For some who live at that end of town, most probably it still does. In Jahazpur's not-so-remote past, Delhi Gate was definitely not the tail of the market.

Suresh Sindhi gave a very general account of the shift in orientations of Jahazpur's commercial and transportation life. He told us, "The people didn't used even to come to the Royal Gate, because where the bus stand is now was jungle, and no one came there; besides that, in the evening the gate was closed. The bus stand used to be at Nau Chauk." Just outside of Delhi Gate is the rectangular fenced clearing known as Nau Chauk. *Nau chauk* means "nine squares" or "nine markets" or perhaps "nine corners."

Today the space called Nau Chauk is a small park surrounded by shops. It is worth looking further into the history of this space, which is Jahazpur's only town square. Once it was adjacent to almost all the local government offices. Once it was connected with the royal residences inside the walls. Once Nau Chauk, and not the current bus stand, was the site of the annual Ram Lila.

Delhi Gate offers passage to a complicated history of town rule, and its passage denotes shifting orientations of both power and place. Try to picture Jahazpur in an earlier era: imagine today's bus stand nonexistent. Also nonexistent were the fruit market, the Satya Narayan temple, and Santosh Nagar colony. The road south from the bus stand to Santosh Nagar, which today is flanked with government offices and the small businesses that grow up around them, at that time led only to the Muslim graveyard, the adjoining idgah, and the jungle with its common-property grazing ground. All the town's administrative functions were in and around Nau Chauk. Today only the Patwari (land revenue office), the Cooperative Bank, and a few other minor offices remain in the Nau Chauk vicinity.[15]

In 2010–11, the vegetable sellers who squatted on the periphery of Nau Chauk displayed notably less attractive produce than those who stood proudly behind proper (if movable) stalls at the bus stand. Nau Chauk itself was a far quieter place than the bus stand with far fewer vehicles. However, there are still some quality stores ranged around Nau Chauk, including an excellent "fancy" store favored by Bhoju's daughters.

Our passage through Bindi Gate will lead us to some social structural aspects of qasba life; here I set Jahazpur town in broader currents of Rajasthan histories. In the flat lands of Jahazpur are several Hindu temples that town citizens declare to be "very old." Inside the walls is Juna Char Bhuja ("ancient Four-Arms," that is, Vishnu); outside are Barah Devra ("Twelve Temples") beyond Hanuman Gate; and Narsinghdwara ("Door of the Man-Lion," again an avatar of Vishnu) on the banks of the Nagdi River. I have heard all of these attributed to the eleventh or twelfth centuries, but I have no documentation of their age. There is significant archaeological evidence of an ancient Jain presence in this region, dating to a period well before the Mughuls (Chattopadhyaya 1994:47; Sethia 2003:25; see also Chapter 5).

From recorded history, we know that in the second half of the fifteenth century, Kshetra Singh of Mewar (ruled 1364–82) conquered Jahazpur along with Mandalgarh and Ajmer, taking it from the Pathans and annexing it to Mewar (Purohit 1938:69). Jahazpur's hilltop fort was among many that were built during an immense fortification project for the expanding kingdom of Mewar undertaken by Maharana Kumbha (ruled 1433–68) in the mid-fifteenth century (Hooja 2006:341–47; Purohit 1938:66).[16] In the sixteenth century Jahazpur came under Mughal rule but not for long. Documented sources report that the emperor Akbar gave Jahazpur to Maharana Pratap's rebellious half-brother Jagmal after the death of their father Udai Singh (Hooja 2006:466). This would have been just following the time period when Yagyapur became Jahazpur and when some local groups converted to Islam.

Jahazpur's fort was captured by the small neighboring kingdom of Shahpura in the early eighteenth century and recaptured by Mewar about a hundred years later (Dāngī 2002). According to Purohit (1938), during the Maratta rebellion Jahazpur was for some time under the domination of Jhala Zalim Singh of Kota. Except for those relatively brief interludes between the Mughals and Independence, Jahazpur qasba and its surrounding farmlands remained under Mewar. Jahazpur's last deputized local ruler, Vijay Pratap Singh, died in 1931 (some say he was murdered).

From chasing such slight references to Jahazpur as may be gleaned from history books, old gazetteers, and district census handbooks, the impression I have is that among the capitals from which Jahazpur was governed, only Shahpura was nearby, and Shahpura was too small to hold on to it. The capital of Rajputana's preeminent kingdom, Mewar, within which Jahazpur was most often included, was at a considerable distance. Even in 2011, when I traveled by car from Jahazpur to Udaipur for a conference, I was struck by the distance, compounded by a very poor road for a significant stretch of the journey. I thought a lot on that trip about how far this distance might have seemed in the times of the Ranas.

Although it was certainly a pawn in royal doings for many centuries, my conjecture is that Jahazpur, intermittently but for lengthy periods of history, flew largely under the radar of rulers in any capital. There were for example wild fluctuations in revenue collection (Sehgal 1975:53). Because of the large Mina population in the region, this was never an easy place to rule. Minas were by reputation fiercely independent and powerful fighters. Sometimes they served whoever was ruling but just as often effectively defied impositions (taxes, conscriptions) from any outside power. Tellingly, when Colonel Tod visited in 1818 it was Minas who greeted him (see Chapter 5). It may well have been a matter of little regret for a ruler to hand off Jahazpur to someone else, as Akbar did to Jagmal. It is also advisable in considering Jahazpur history to take into account that dominant communities in Jahazpur qasba proper were never Rajput and were concerned with trade, not war. No matter who was ruling, opportunities to buy and sell would be ongoing.[17]

In 1997 I recorded, in Ghatiyali, Sukhdevji Gujar's memories. The most critical juncture of his young adult life took place in the early 1940s and involved Jahazpur's Nau Chauk. It was there that he went to enlist in the army. He walked thirty-three kilometers alone in the night, from Ghatiyali to Jahazpur. He told me:

> I wasn't afraid of anything, and nothing attacked me! I didn't meet anyone at all, I went on foot. [To walk alone in the night requires a lot of courage.] In Jahazpur, at the place called Nau Chauk, people were enlisting in the military; in the middle of the city.
>
> There were hundreds of people there, who had come in order to enlist. . . . carpenters, gardeners, ironworkers, Minas, Rajputs, lots of people, all the *jatis*. And a gentleman came, a fair-skinned gentleman, an Englishman. There was just one: "Duke Sahab" [presumably a British military officer]. He arrived, sitting on a horse, and wearing a hat on his head. . . . People were lined up there in rows, three by three, and the gentleman walked in-between the rows, looking, looking. And then he put a mark on me.
>
> And the ones who had marks, they took them over to one side, so they put me on one side with them. On that day, in one day, in the same fashion, 150 people were selected; out of many hundreds who wanted to enlist. (Gold and Gujar 2002:168–69, condensed and slightly reworded)

Sukhdevji's memory is evidence that in late colonial times, during World War II, Nau Chauk had its official functions and was put to use by the British, in spite of Jahazpur being part of Mewar and governed under paramountcy rather than direct rule. I imagine Duke Sahab would have taken permission from the Rana in Udaipur to use Nau Chauk in Jahazpur as a recruitment site, but that is pure speculation. I do know with certainty that Nau Chauk and much that lies in its vicinity is intimately connected with the checkered history of rule in Jahazpur.

Adjacent to Nau Chauk is a building that is now Jahazpur's overflowing upper secondary school. The school building is grafted onto a former royal residence in an architecturally odd fusion. On the grounds of the school or former palace is a large, gated shrine to the Hindu deity Ganesh, which everyone knows as a place where a powerful authority once sat, whether it was Jahangir, Shah Jahan, or the delegated royal agent for this area (*hakim*). Ram Swarup Chipa, for example, told us that Ganesh's place was once a meeting hall built by Jahangir. Another Hindu man from an artisan community speculated for us that Hindus had installed Ganesh there in order to claim it for themselves, as a preemptive move against Muslim ownership.

However, a Muslim interviewee told us explicitly that Ganeshji was put there deliberately by a Mughal ruler to ensure that no ordinary mortal being could ever sit on the same spot where the emperor had held court. A different Muslim interviewee had told us in 2008, "Shah Jahan was sitting where Ganesh is now. He thought, 'after me, no one can sit on my chair,' so he himself installed the Ganesh image." Shravan Patriya, a Brahmin journalist, told us that Ganesh was installed in this courtyard "to keep the place pure." In all its variations, the installation of Ganesh would seem to mark an amiable delegation of power from Muslims back to Hindus in Jahazpur's past.

A number of persons from different communities referred to Nau Chauk in interviews as a site of significance to the history of the town, or of their own families and trades. Some further tidbits about Nau Chauk are compelling.

Kailash, whose caste identity was wine seller (although this was not his current business) told us that the liquor storehouse maintained by his community had been located in Nau Chauk. To measure out the liquor, he said, "they used a little brass pot, and distributed it straight from a small storage tank." He told us that his great-aunt would "measure out liquor with the brass pot and sell it there."[18] Another man, from the leatherworking community, spoke of his grandfather who was a "tantric magician." Once, one of the great kings of Udaipur came to Jahazpur and summoned our interviewee's grandfather, demanding that he perform his magical arts. Where did this take place? In Nau Chauk. The man asserted that his grandfather did not disappoint the king; he took a broom and transformed each one of its straws into scorpions.

As they piled up, Nau Chauk stories began to remind me of Bob Dylan's *Highway 61*—an ironic venue for every kind of weird, game-changing performance in the history of humankind. Even today, many ritually significant events take place at Nau Chauk. The *taziya*, symbolic tomb of

Figure 8. Children drum at Nau Chauk on Muharram procession morning.

heroic martyrs whose deaths were a turning point in Islamic history, spends the entire night on the edge of Nau Chauk, before both annual Muharram processions (separated by forty days). Although Jahazpur had many Holi fires in many different neighborhoods, a major Holi effigy is staked and burned at Nau Chauk. This was the only Holi where I saw a Brahmin priest perform a worship ritual before igniting the demoness wreathed in firecrackers. On both Hindu and Muslim festivals, demonstrations of physical prowess, commonly called *akara* by both religious communities, took place at Nau Chauk.

Note well that these things do not happen inside the fenced square, although presumably Sukh Devji's recruitment into the British Army did. All the other events of public import described here take place around the edge of that park. The actual space within the square offers another complicated story from recent times of which I am certainly missing some key elements, but which nonetheless I shall attempt to sketch. The fenced center of Nau Chauk was somewhat unkempt during most of my fieldwork.

There were some trees and other greenery including flowering vines inside, but the ground was dry and brown and the space unattractive. Sometime in 2011 all that began to change. While I was still living there the town chairman (mayor), influenced doubtless by some patronage group, had the interior spruced up and planted with flowers. He had a decorative fountain and a stone lion's head on a pillar installed there. Later a cardboard image of Maharana Pratap (ruled Mewar 1572–97) appeared.

Over a year after I departed, a proper stone statue of Maharana Pratap was installed inside Nau Chauk with festive pomp including rains of rose petals. Although locals such as Bhoju Ram were drawn to participate, the event organizers and sponsors were part of a statewide organization of Rajput patriots; few hailed from Jahazpur where, as already noted, Rajput power has thoroughly dwindled. The entire transformative process was marred (I heard after the fact) by minor but prickly "communal" incidents expressive of rancor. These included small vandalisms to the new fence followed by disputes over who would pay the cost of repair for said vandalisms.

I confess that Maharana Pratap, as an icon of Rajasthan's glorious martial history, has never warmed my heart. I would prefer to refuse ethnographic responsibility for reporting on a development that happened, after all, more than a year beyond my fieldwork's conclusion. But there are two things I must add to update my account of Nau Chauk. First, on my most recent visit in 2015 the space inside the fence was very nicely maintained, with green grass and colorful flowers pleasing to the eye. Yet it is hardly a public park in the Euro-American sense, designated for democratized enjoyment of its pleasant features. Nau Chauk is fenced and the gate kept locked. Second, in spite of the local Muslim community's objection to the statue, and Hindu rebuttals, there has been a kind of reconciliation, at least on the surface. The taziya continues to spend the nights before Muharram in its usual place near the small park with its new statue. For the time being, Jahazpur's inner spirit of "live and let live" prevails.

Bindi Gate: Sociological Passages

In late August 2010, well before my systematic tour of the gates, Bhoju and I made our first foray into the leather workers' neighborhood inside the walls.

Then we drove through Bindi Gate and into the Regar *mohalla*, where firewood is stacked in huge piles, where fans don't run, where I sweated for the hour of the interview. There was *arati* [ritual of circling lights before an image] going on at the Ram Devji temple, and the children crowded round me in an amazingly non-Jahazpur way, more like village children. The arati was extensive and beautiful; I took pictures, the children wanted to be in the pictures and nearly wrenched the camera from my hand in their excitement to see themselves in the small screen.

Then we want to the home of a Regar teacher whose old father talked to us. I appreciated the respect the younger man gave to the older, letting his father's interview finish, before he began speaking to us with eloquence about the disadvantages faced by his community, even in recent years: the slights they suffered in schools, as workers, when bridegrooms go to villages, at tea stalls, and worst of all the story of the Ambedkar statue purchased 6 years ago but not yet installed due to high caste objections.[19] (field journal, 29 August 2010)

Bindi Gate may be the most dilapidated of the old doorways, and its part of town feels the most "villagey," as my journal exclaims. Children are more numerous and more of them are wearing torn T-shirts, while few dress in the ornate, costly jeans favored by the qasba's middle-class youth. The Regar children's excited behavior was likely indicative of less training in the disciplines of the schoolroom, where the first lesson taught is how to sit, that is, how to submit their small bodies to an ideal of order (doubtless inherited from the British; see Kumar 2007:25–48).

When I initially inquired what the name "Bindi" signified, people told me that the gate once led to a village called Bindi that "no longer existed." As it turns out, Bindi village still does exist in Jahazpur *tehsil* (subdistrict). The 2011 Census records it as inhabited by seventeen families with a population that is 94 percent Scheduled Tribe.[20] Although Bindi is not numbered among the twelve hamlets incorporated into Jahazpur municipality, it shares with them a preponderant Mina identity. Yet not that long ago, before Independence when Jahazpur belonged to Mewar, Bindi was a "revenue village," defined as an administrative unit of the smallest order. At that time, members of the ruling Rajput community lived there, doubtless in order to collect taxes and perform other low-level administrative functions. Even in its heyday, and despite its giving its name to one of the three qasba gates to the exterior, I suspect we might safely presume that Bindi was never a plum posting.

Looking out from Bindi Gate you can see the old fort on the hilltop. Turning inward you find that those neighborhoods nearest to this gate belonged to leather workers (SC), lathe-turning woodworkers, and boat-men (the latter both categorized OBC, "other backward classes"). Among these communities, unlike the former butchers with their reputation of collective improvement, it seems only a few of their members have pros-pered in these changing times.

The Kir (boatmen) keep boats in their street as emblems of identity (and these are still in occasional seasonal use as for harvesting water chestnuts). Kewat is their dignified caste name, after the fabled boatman from the Ramayana epic who took Ram, Sita, and Lakshman across the river when the three divine beings made their way from the palace of Ayodhya to their fated forest exile. New bridges and dams combined with draught would be the main combined causes of decline for the traditional work of boatmen. The lathe-turning carpenters (Kairathi) have seen their business markedly dwindle with the lowered demand for wooden implements, including toys, for which the town of Jahazpur was once well known (Census of India 1994). Several Kairathi families moved away from Jahazpur, having sold their homes to Sindhi merchants who now populate their neighborhood, I was told. In 2011 there were just two active Kairathi workshops infused with the sense of an accomplished yet moribund artisan identity. I say moribund because fathers deliberately were not apprenticing their sons but rather devoting familial resources to training the new generation for alternative careers.

Leather workers retain neither mementos (as the Kir do their boats) nor active workshops (as the Kairathi still possess) that would bring to mind their own stigmatizing past work of tanning hides. Many have gone into construction. A fair number of leather workers are government servants and have ascended to middle-class status, at least economically. Affirmative action (called "reservations" in India) supports higher percentages of gov-ernment service jobs for members of SC communities, but some appear more able to find advantage in these programs than others. I found, when interviewing persons close to the bottom of the old ritual caste hierarchy, expressions of gratification that much had indeed changed, and simultane-ously of anger that change was maddeningly incomplete.

This is not a book about social organization, social hierarchy, or power. I will not make a list of all the castes that live in Jahazpur, nor could I with total accuracy even if I wished to do so. No chapter here is devoted to compiling or analyzing the many statements about social hierarchy that in fact I did record. Mostly I recorded them because Bhoju Ram, who assisted in about two-thirds of my interviews, inserted into most of them routinely, and without my ever requesting that he do so, one or more queries about caste. I privately brooded over what seemed to me to be his tiresome fascination, or his old-fashioned sense of what might be significant. References to caste in the interviews would have been far fewer had I been the only one asking questions. In my interviews with women, where I controlled the lines of inquiry, there is almost nothing about the birth-given social hierarchy. When the conversation departed, as it often would, from my own directed interests it followed theirs: domestic politics, neighborhood quarrels, food.

Sumit Guha has recently suggested that "caste's religious strand has frayed away but the one binding it to the exercise of power is thicker than ever" (Guha 2013:211). Guha and others see caste today as something akin to ethnicity. I appreciate that turn in the recent literature on India's social hierarchy. Basically it lays stress on inherited identity as it infuses sense of self and as it is used instrumentally in relation to others both politically and professionally. Such active uses of birth-given identity or rank certainly are among the circumstances of life in contemporary Jahazpur.

Bhoju is my collaborative research partner, not an assistant paid only to do my bidding. I therefore held my tongue and respected his interests. Indeed I thought it might represent an integral feature of the village-to-town transition that I seek to highlight in these pages that Bhoju, himself a participant in that transition, thought in terms of caste when living in a place where it had genuinely lost certain kinds of salience. People in Jahazpur readily, and for the most part unhesitatingly, respond to questions framed in a language of caste with answers similarly framed. It is not that the caste framework had become alien to them. But it is, I would argue, not their first way of looking at things. Only very rarely did an interviewee initiate this topic.

Throughout this book I make observations using the language of caste. When I write in Chapter 3 about Santosh Nagar, I talk about a Brahmin woman and her status as a self-proclaimed ritual expert, often but not always valued by the women from agricultural communities who predomi-nated in the groups that gathered around her at collective rituals. When I write about processions in Chapter 4, I speak of the leather workers' strug-gle to be included in the Jal Jhulani parade and the rather anticlimactic if satisfying result: normalization of their participation (as if the resistance had been more knee-jerk than of any heartfelt discriminatory depths). When I write about the market in Chapter 8 I emphasize roles played by former butchers and former wine sellers, and it seems to matter who they are "by caste." Caste identity literally leaps out at a stranger; here as throughout much of Rajasthan, caste names are used as last names, includ-ing Gujar, Khatik, Kir, Mina, Regar, Vaishnav, and so forth (see Pandey 2013:208–10). But caste is not the dominant subject of my book, and I would venture further to argue that caste is not the dominant subject of life in contemporary Jahazpur.[21]

Bindi Gate, by evoking the old revenue village and the contemporary struggles of leather workers, carpenters, and boatmen, leads us in two direc-tions: outward to the fiscal bindings of town with larger units of governance including taxes and benefits for the poor; inward to the intersections and interactions of discrete but variously integrated communities, to the histor-ies of political and ritual struggles for power and dignity, and to the ways that governance enables, obstructs, or ignores these struggles.

Mosque Gate: Pluralistic Passages

An archway traditionally bestows honor and respect, creating a passage simultaneously conferring and confirming status. We see this easily in the plentitude of temporary cloth arches set up to welcome the Ram Lila pro-cession, a distinguished visitor, or a wedding party. Mosque Gate is an internal gate. It never served to segregate the Muslim population but rather to mark a sacred area before the doorway to the mosque and thus to set apart and to honor the mosque itself.[22]

We learned from Mahavir Singh (one of just two Rajput interviewees) that long ago the Rajput neighborhood also had an arched gateway, as did a few other neighborhoods belonging to more important merchant and Brahmin lineages. With the decline of residents most invested in maintain-ing them, these structures had been torn down when it became expedient to make way for additional construction of more useful edifices. Small but vividly blue, Mosque Gate, in contrast, was in fine condition during my stay in 2010–11. On revisits, I noted that the old deep blue gate I had always thought very attractive had been allowed to deteriorate, while an imposing, tall, new Masjid Gate of stone blocks was constructed.

A number of persons, when pressed to list the characteristics of a qasba during both recorded interviews and casual conversations, would begin with a single defining attribute: diversity. This comprised a multiplicity of castes and secondarily of religions. One of the hallmarks of urbanization is diversity; and with diversity arrives the necessity of pluralism. This observation would certainly be deemed a truism in urban studies. However, here I follow the lead of Gérard Fussman, who codirected an Indo-French collaborative investigation of history and culture in Chanderi, a qasba in Madhya Pradesh state. Nearly the same size as Jahazpur, Chanderi, like Jahazpur, has a mixed population of Hindus, Muslims, and Jains. I summarize Fussman's points in a condensed paraphrase: The passage between a village population and a town population entails a veritable rupture corresponding to the transformation from a population which is relatively homogeneous and an economy which is essentially pastoral or agricultural, to a population and an economy which have become much more diversified, and where commerce, manufacturing and political-administrative functions all play roles of more or less increased importance (Fussman et al. 2003, vol. 1, 67). Places such as Jahazpur, and other North Indian qasbas including Chanderi, present this "veritable rupture" on a smallish scale and thus perhaps with particular vividness. Just to run your eyes over the styles of clothing visible at Jahazpur's busy bus stand, or worn by those peopling its crowded market streets, is to observe a diversity that is locally so run-of-the-mill as to attract no notice whatsoever.

Only the foreign outsider finds the scene striking and wonders at the proximities of men in Western shirts and pants, some bareheaded, some capped; some bearded, some clean-shaven; other men in dhotis or kurta pajamas, some heads adorned with Rajasthan's characteristically bright red or multicolored turbans. Women's dress also varies by class and age and religion: some in saris, many in long skirts and blouses covered by the Rajasthani *orhni* or "wrap"; many in kamiz-salwar, which are worn by Muslim women of all ages and among Hindus and Jains by younger, unmarried teens or young women returned to visit their natal homes; a sprinkling of upper-class teenage girls in stylishly fitted jeans and T-shirts. The latter reflects not just urbanization but the influence of television. Most adult females still keep their heads covered, but it is not uncommon to observe a few on any given day who are bareheaded, and readily to conclude they might be teachers, or perhaps visitors from a larger city, NGO workers, or representatives of local, regional, or state government.

Thus a visible everyday mix encompasses rural/urban; Hindu/Muslim; and an array of differences in caste, class, and profession. Do these differences play out in mutual engagement and enrichment, or in fissure, abhorrence, and violence? Throughout most of Jahazpur's history, it has been the former. The plural nature of Jahazpur was one of the reasons I was drawn to study it. Jain families, here as elsewhere, are successful in business and influential in local politics. Jains add to the diversity of the qasba, but it is the large Muslim population that distinguishes Jahazpur from most Rajasthan towns. As is the case throughout Rajasthan, Hindus are the majority in Jahazpur. But whereas in the state as a whole, Muslims average around 8 percent of the population, inside the walls in the oldest part of Jahazpur qasba I regularly heard estimates as high as 40–45 percent. In the 2011 Census data for Jahazpur municipality, the official breakdown is 73.05 percent Hindu; 25.39 percent Muslim, and 1.45 percent Jain. Given that the municipality includes the all-Mina twelve hamlets, these high estimates for the qasba itself are not terribly exaggerated.[23]

Mushirul Hasan, in his literary and historical study of qasba life in the eastern Uttar Pradesh region during the colonial era, particularly celebrates *qasbati* pluralism. He writes that in North Indian qasba culture, "Besides differences and distinctions there were also relationships and interactions. . . . The stress is therefore on . . . religious plurality as the reference point for harmonious living" (Hasan 2004:27, 31).

Jahazpur Muslims are divided into various groups, far from homogeneous in terms of ancestry, social class, attitudes, and reputed behaviors. The majority belong to a jati-like community called Deshvali or "of the land."[24] They are understood to be locals who converted to Islam in the Mughal period; many said this took place during the time of "Garib Navaz," the famous Chishti Sufi saint of Ajmer who lived during Akbar's reign.[25] This conversion likely took place during that same era in which the name change, Yagyapur to Jahazpur, was inscribed.

In summer 2007 we interviewed a distinguished Muslim citizen of Jahazpur, who was then seventy-two years old. Bhoju asked him, "How many generations have you resided in Jahazpur?" He replied that his community had been there for six hundred years. He said that Muslims had not been in Jahazpur when it was first settled but came during the Mughal period, under the emperor Jahangir in 1602 CE. He estimated that eighteen or twenty generations of his family's forefathers had lived in the town.

Both Hindus and Deshvali Muslims tended in interviews for the most part to downplay the differences between their respective communities' practices and character. Both stressed shared roots, shared lineage names, shared cultural traditions, and a long-standing mutual regard.[26] Middle-class Hindus often said of Deshvali Muslims: they are "like us."[27] If asked to elaborate, they pointed to two factors: landownership and parallel customs.[28] (For example, before a wedding among Hindus the first invitation goes to Ganesh; among Muslims it goes to the saint, Garib Navaz. Thus, in both cases, the invitation initiating an auspicious event goes to an enshrined and revered persona—as both Hindu and Muslim interviewees explicitly noted.) Of course Hindu and Muslim interviewees did emphasize evident noncontentious distinctions such as festivals celebrated or the ramifications of internal divisions (or lack thereof).

A class factor entailed by "sameness" discourse is evident.[29] When middle-class Hindus say that Deshvali Muslims are "like us," they mean they are solid, propertied citizens, businessmen, and people with an obvious stake in the peaceful and prosperous life of qasba trade. The category Pardeshi Muslims is often contrasted to Deshvali in essentializing discourse: they are viewed as rootless potential troublemakers lacking stable sources of livelihood. The propertied versus indigent divide does not in reality align with the Deshvali/Pardeshi distinction, however. Among the Pardeshi Muslims are families possessing considerable land both inside and outside the walls. Some Pathan families were historically a kind of nobility whose ancestors probably played roles under Muslim rule similar in function to Rajput hakim under Hindu kings. Other Pardeshis are of a lower economic status. An example often given to me in this regard was that Pardeshi women roll *bidi*s (locally made cigarettes) for a living; there were always a few such women sitting on the street visibly engaged in exactly that work. But certainly not all of Pardeshi Muslims are poor. Neighborhood is another factor used to classify Muslims prone to disruptive behavior. I heard it said again and again that the Muslims who live around the crossroads known as Char Hathari ("four markets") are unruly and quick-tempered, spoiling for a fight, so to speak. Yet both Hindus and Muslims often testified—Hindus ruefully and Muslims proudly—that all Muslims have a special unity within religious contexts: they eat and pray and vote together, although the different Muslim communities do not intermarry.

One Hindu man, Bhairu Lal Lakhara, explained to us why Hindus are disadvantaged by the unity of Muslims. Although the similes he employed ("Hindus are like dogs but Muslims are like pigeons") were unique within my interviews, the ideas expressed—that Hindu unity suffers from multiple fissures because of caste divides, but Muslims are all for one and one for all—were extremely common and often expressed by Hindus and Muslims alike. Bhairu Lal had a way with words and spared no one in his social commentary; he is the same person who defined the middle class to me as a "camel's fart" hanging between the sky of wealth and the earth of poverty. Here is how he characterized the difference in unity between Hindus and Muslims:

> Muslims just say Bishmillah ["in the name of God"], and then eat together. And if you fight with one Muslim, then ten more will come to support him. But among us [Hindus], people will say: "That's a Mali, that's a Brahmin, that's a Gujar, that's a Kir, that's a Carpenter," so no one will come to your aid. The Butchers are separate; the Sweepers are separate. But they [Muslims] have unity. Hindus are like a pack of dogs; if you throw them one piece of bread, they will fight each other over it, and even kill each other. Muslims are like pigeons: if you throw a handful of grain, they all will peck it together.
> [Bhoju Ram for my benefit, spelled it out even more clearly: "The dogs would rather lose the bread and kill each other; but the pigeons happily share."]

Muslims, in spite of belonging to named groups that operate very much like Hindu jatis in terms of marriage, replicated this discourse of their superior unity and egalitarianism in the context of religion.

For example, Sariph Mohammad Deshvali—a dignified, successful businessman in his prime—discussed internal differences among Muslims with Bhoju Ram and me. Bhoju put to him a question about Pardeshi Muslims, asking Sariph if the Deshvalis transacted "daughters and feasts" with them: that is: did they intermarry and did they co-dine?[30] Sariph answered without hesitation: "Not daughters, but we do share food." He spent a fair amount of time telling us about the different Pardeshi communities, all of whom, like the Deshvali, are endogamous.

Then, spontaneously (that is, without any prodding from either me or Bhoju), Sariph went on at length to emphasize lack of discrimination among Muslims at religious events.

> When people are praying, there is no difference, all the Muslims are together. At Id [for example] the time for prayer is fixed for 1:30 and everyone will be standing; suppose the *maulvi* [esteemed scholar or teacher] comes a minute late, he can't go in front he has to stay behind, but if a poor person comes early he will stay in front; there is no special respect.
>
> Once we were reading *namaz*, and a minister of the Rajasthan state government, a Muslim, came to join us, and he stood in the back. No one said "here is a minister." Even though he was standing in the sun, no one took care to give him room. And he didn't say anything either, he did not ask for room, for a place in shade. He stood there in the back, in the sun. There is no discrimination among persons.

What may divide Jahazpur Muslims (although this was in my presence rarely discussed) is religious orthodoxy, rigidity, or strictness—attributes wrapped up together in the Hindi word *kattar*. A number of persons from both communities used this word to describe certain Hindus as well as certain Muslims, but it was more often used for Muslims. The term *kattar* seems to hold implications of embracing global, acultural Islam, and stricter application of many rules. For example, I heard Deshvali Muslim women use it, disapprovingly, to refer to those Muslims who promoted stricter veiling practices.

Here is one usage supplied by a highly educated (Hindu) Mina man, who lived in a nice house outside one of the twelve hamlets but commuted quite some distance to teach college; he succinctly unites the two main elements of class and strict religion that people say make some Pardeshi Muslims prone to troublemaking: "The Deshvalis get along [with us] because their culture is like that of the Hindus and they have land and business (*kheti dhandha*), so they think about that. But the Pardeshi—they have neither land nor business, and they follow Islam very strictly [literally: "they are kattar"]."

Not long after the November festival (*urs*) of Jahazpur's main Muslim saint, Gaji Pir, my husband and I went shopping for shoes. A bearded young shopkeeper we encountered on this excursion told me he had heard that I had attended the urs (word gets around, Jahazpur is village-like in that way). To my discomfiture, he lectured me (partially in Hindi and partially in passable English) on his views that such events were the culture (*sanskriti*, using not the English, but the Hindi term) of India and not "true Islam." He told me he had personally stayed away from the urs, and that he preferred always to pray in the mosque. His views were not at all the norm in Jahazpur, I should emphasize. I bought the shoes but brooded over encountering such views unabashedly articulated in the heart of Jahazpur market.

Elsewhere in South Asia, some Islamic leaders have critiqued visits to saints.[31] Yet all evidence showed the majority of Jahazpur's Muslim community highly invested in the celebration of their miracle-working *pir* (A. Gold 2013). All other Muslims with whom I conversed, whether in an interview situation or casually, honored Gaji Pir with enthusiasm. Many loved to tell story after story about his miraculous boons.

I persuaded Bhoju (who was acutely sensitive to any potentially delicate or offensive topic when dealing with Muslims) to ask one Deshvali community leader, a professional educator, whether there were any Muslims in town who objected to the practice of revering the tombs of saints. He answered, emphatically, "There are no such people in Jahazpur; it is Jahazpur's good fate [*shobhagya*, a Sanskrit word] that there are no such people here *yet*." His "yet" (*ab tak*) reflected an awareness that elsewhere on the subcontinent this might not be the case and that Jahazpur itself might not be spared the arrival of these views.

Jahazpur is by and large a successfully plural place, with a strong Muslim community and an important multistranded sense of commonality among Hindus and Muslims in terms of possessing shared history and traditions as well as contemporary interests in keeping the peace. Among *Shiptown*'s thematic gateways, Mosque Gate stands for my conviction that Jahazpur qasba is a place where strongly held religious identities coexist not just in mutual tolerance but in mutual regard. It also stands for what Hasan and Roy (2005) call "living together separately." The new Mosque Gate looks much like an Arabic gate and may speak of this separation in the language of stone. But it also speaks simply of community pride, of the urge to build and display one's identity, which Jahazpur's Muslims, Hindus, and Jains all have in common. Thus the imposing proud structure of New

Mosque Gate and the egalitarian humility of the idgah may be held in one thought, as all of one piece.

Hanuman Gate: Ecological Passages

Hanuman Gate leads beyond Nau Chauk outside the qasba walls in the direction of Gautam Ashram, a retreat belonging to a Brahmin lineage used as a site for social and religious events. There, it is said, one can still see and decipher an inscription referring to the site as Yagyapur, although a painted signboard for the ashram normally obscures the old lettering. There is also an old temple to Hanuman here, accounting for the gate's name. Not far from Hanuman Gate is a Muslim saint's tomb, as well as a separate Muslim shrine of the type known as *chilla*—not a tomb but rather the location of a saintly person's ascetic practices, especially fasting. Jahazpur's chilla is dedicated to Gagaron Baba, whose well-known tomb in another city Bhoju and I had visited in 2006 (A. Gold 2013). The chilla's wall and the ashram wall are contiguous. When Jahazpur's chairman set out to redirect the gutters and keep sewage out of the Nagdi River, at least as it flowed through the town, objections made by the communities attached to the two sites were among the difficulties he encountered. The new gutters flowing with pollution would have to pass uncomfortably close to the boundaries of sacred sites—ashram and chilla—a situation ultimately ameliorated by the construction of a wall (see Chapter 6).

Hanuman Gate, through which Bhoju and I passed each time we were on our way to update the river's ever-changing story, serves to evoke environmental issues. More than that, it evokes the unity of human life as bound, in an ever-fluctuating but permanent condition of mutual interdependency, to a geophysical and natural environment. Hanuman as divine monkey appropriately confuses nature/culture binaries and adds an element of uncalculated power (Lutgendorf 2007).

For about two months of my research time Bhoju and I obsessed together on the Nagdi River's plight. It was definitely the longest (though not the sole) single-mindedly dedicated phase of my Jahazpur fieldwork. Yet I had never intended to study ecology in Jahazpur. The river itself was not on my agenda, nor was it in my line of sight when I began fieldwork. Because of the garbage I didn't actually want to see it. We came upon the struggle to save the Nagdi in a roundabout way, through listening to tales of local politics. Years earlier, an interest in small-scale ecological successes effected by divine power brought me to Jahazpur. This was long before I had any interest whatsoever in urban ecologies writ large. On Jahazpur's hilltops are two well-protected "sacred groves," each surrounding a shrine, Hindu and Muslim, respectively. Malaji, a regional hero-god of the Hindu Mina community, is housed in a dazzling white temple. Near the fort is the revered tomb of Gaji Pir, a Muslim saint who was also a warrior, eye-catching with its glowing aquamarine wash. Jahazpur's hilltop shrines are important sites of religious power and community which are lovingly tended.

Stories and practices associated with environments under divine protection offer some promise or potential for imagining benign relations with the natural world (Centre for Science and Environment 2003; Kent 2013; Gold 2010). Taken together, river and hills reveal the thoroughly inter-locked nature of urban landscapes with twenty-first-century environmental issues. Hanuman, the monkey god, and the real monkeys that range through Jahazpur seem appropriate mascots for passages into and out from endangered ecologies.

Window Gate: Ethnographic Passages

Window Gate provides an apt metaphor for my own fieldwork practice, which often involved choosing those passages that were small, unheroic, without fanfare (as I never wished to call attention to myself).[32] We found Window Gate only when directed there. No parades march through it, nor indeed could they.

How did I encounter Jahazpur? I recorded about 140 interviews. I took so many photographs I cannot even attempt to count them. I drank, by my estimate, more than fifteen hundred cups of tea at other people's houses, not counting the tea we brewed at home. Anthropologists are consumers and contribute to the economy as well as fattening on sugary hospitality. Mostly, Daniel and I did our shopping in Jahazpur qasba. We patronized the fruit and vegetable vendors at the bus stand almost daily and bought supplies of spices, oil, sugar, raisins, and so forth from shops within the qasba. Soaps and toothpaste, bangles and braid holders, slip-on shoes for winter and rubber thong sandals for the rainy season, cough drops and vitamins galore, a shawl and a sweater and a cotton-stuffed quilt for winter, a cooler (our biggest market purchase) when the hot season rolled around. So many lemons, so much garlic, cases of soda water!

We subscribed to the Hindi *Rajasthan Patrika* with its Bhilwara District insert full of local color; it was delivered every morning along with a half kilogram of dairy milk. We hired a cook for a while. She was an angry young woman and eventually quit without warning (in spite of the whole neighborhood's outspoken conviction that we overpaid her outrageously). But before she left she taught me some things I needed to know.

Sometimes the routine of fieldwork took second place to hospitality. We were visited by one of my graduate students whom everyone mistook for my son; to make matters more confusing he was followed not so many weeks later by my actual son with his fiancée (but we told everyone she was his wife); then my niece and great-niece; my husband's two sisters and one brother-in-law; my younger son; and a whole busload of Syracuse students (who only stayed one afternoon). Thus we made a bit of an impression on Jahazpur; pretty much every female visitor, no matter what her age, was inappropriately dressed by Jahazpur lights.

For about the first eight months of my time in Jahazpur I felt so privileged, so lucky. Except for a terrible worry about my sister's health that began in November, I was perfectly happy. Released from the classroom, from dull and dulling meetings, from all academic obligations—those are the things I was glad to be without. What was I glad to be with? First, to have Bhoju's family around the corner, for they are like my family. Second, to have embarked on a vast project, taking me back to my dissertation research days when I lived in Ghatiyali; to know that anything that happened was worth writing down, that every conversation held gemlike glimmers of the unattainable whole; that even if I couldn't keep perfectly straight who lived in which house and who was married to whose brother, I was nonetheless absorbing a whole new world of sociability.

My voice will not vanish from the chapters that follow. Window Gate opens into every chapter. For this introduction to my ethnographic practice, I need to say a little more about its collaborative nature and its composition. Over the past thirty years Bhoju and I have crafted, recrafted, and published accounts of an evolving relationship at once working and familial (Gujar and Gold 1992; Gold and Gujar 2002; Gold, Gujar, Gujar, and Gujar 2014). Although professional and familial motifs have intertwined in our relationship from the beginning, both in Bhoju's mind and in my own the mode of our connectedness has increasingly become one of kinship. I am part of Bhoju's family now as he is part of mine. Madhu and Chinu take these conditions for granted, having known me since birth as their paternal aunt (Buaji). In 2010–11 they too became graceful, part-time producers of ethnography (see Chapter 3).

How do we negotiate this odd union of kinship and research? I expect it sounds much harder than it is. Familial relatedness and intellectual relatedness have in common an intimacy and an interdependence that is at once psychological, emotional, cognitive. As family we exchange gifts, we worry about one another, we chide one another, we ask personal questions, we quarrel, we forgive. As research collaborators, we labor tediously to get details right and exalt in shared discoveries.

By his own account, Bhoju's orientations to matters such as caste rules of commensality remained rooted in the rural community that had formed and nourished him and on which he still depended for crucial social solidarity. This led to some discomforts with our new research endeavor.[33] It would go without saying that Bhoju's experiences of caste and religious difference in Jahazpur should contrast strongly with my own. Sometimes we argue openly about these matters, and sometimes we brood silently but palpably. Friction is the word that comes to mind, and in highlighting tensions resulting from our disparate viewpoints, I argue that such friction is fruitful—that dissonant, alternative perspectives may yield enhanced understandings.

One source of friction between me and Bhoju derived from my enthusiasm for documenting Jahazpur's pluralistic culture. The qasba's significant Muslim population was to me one of the most important pieces of my study, and I found Jahazpur Muslims, most of them, welcoming with an almost overwhelming hospitality. If Bhoju had his ingrained doubts about Muslims as a collectivity, fortunately all his negative thoughts were impersonal. When it came to interacting with individuals or families he was able not only to present a smiling face but, it seemed to me, to relish discovering a varied religio-cultural universe so close to home.

Bhoju closed a written account of our ethnographic collaboration in Jahazpur with the following words, chastening to me. (Small capitals denote a change of script: words that stand out on the original page from Bhoju's Hindi composition because they are written in the English alphabet.) "In conclusion: In this kind of work, the ASSISTANT has a more important role than the RESEARCHER, because if the RESEARCHER makes a mistake or asks

Figure 9. Window Gate, showing latrines and Shiva Shrine, 2015.

a question that really shouldn't be asked, no one MINDS all that much because after all she is a foreigner, and there are a lot of things she doesn't know. But as for the ASSISTANT, he must think a whole lot and every single question that he asks should take into account the local atmosphere" (Gold, Gujar, Gujar, and Gujar 2014:350). It seems important to recognize the validity of Bhoju's conclusion.

I explained to Bhoju on my 2015 visit that I was using Window Gate to represent ethnography. He immediately "got" my metaphor. Reading my mind, he suggested we take my picture there. So we revisited Window Gate, and I received a fresh lesson in the selective nature of memory. There was much nearby this small opening I had failed to retain since the last time I was there in 2010: an old shrine to Mahadevji; a neem tree; decaying garbage; vital pig life; and—I wonder how I missed it?—public facilities for men and women, of which Jahazpur qasba had a lamentable shortage. Possibly the weather or the wind was different the last time we were there, but on this day in February the place reeked. Bhoju, who is especially sensitive to odors, became nauseated. We had to duck into the conveniently nearby homeopathic dispensary (another institutional setting of which I had no previous inkling). There the attendant cheerfully informed us that no qualified homeopathic physician was currently posted to our medically challenged municipality. He nonetheless unhesitatingly selected a bottle from dozens lined up on the shelves behind the counter and unceremoniously applied a few drops of something or other straight onto Bhoju's tongue. Whatever the potion was, Bhoju started to feel better and we proceeded on our way. However, I never posed at Window Gate, and I wouldn't especially want to pose there anymore.

I felt not only chagrined but embarrassed that the Window Gate smelled bad: this is decidedly not the association I intended to make with ethnography when I first conceived this chapter. Of course I could contrive an evocative theoretical point along the lines that human beings are embodied creatures; bodily functions unite us while cultural approaches to bodily functions divide us. Such truisms could even be seen as standing for the subject of all anthropology. But embodiment, however valid a condition of ethnographic work, was not the point I originally intended to have Window Gate signify for me. Rather, it was that my vision through however many windows is of small scale and limited scope. That point holds. What my 2015 revisit impels me to add is the need to keep all the senses—the "gates of the body," as the Bhagavad Gita calls them—engaged in fieldwork.[34]

Chapter 3

Colony

Suburban Satisfaction

We also produce knowledge in a mode of intimacy with our
subjects. Hence ethnography as a genre seems to me to be
a form of knowledge in which I come to acknowledge my
own experience within a scene of alterity. . . . In being
attentive to the life of others we also give meaning to our
lives or so I feel. . . . So ethnography becomes for me a
mode in which I can be attentive to how the work of very
ordinary people constantly reshapes the world we live in.
(Das 2015b:404)

Fieldwork is life itself. (ca. October 2010, author's
optimistic email to colleague)

Suman [my neighbor, chiding me for speaking as if we lived
in the qasba] "This *isn't* Jahazpur, this is *two km* distance
from Jahazpur, this is *Santosh Nagar!*" The truth! (30 April
2011, author's journal entry)

Having introduced Jahazpur qasba and looked both ways through its gates,
grand and small, I now turn my back on those historic portals for a chapter
and portray the place where I lived, ate, slept, and got to know my neighbors. What I did for large parts of my days when I wasn't occupied with
research and/or shopping forays into town will also emerge. Whether hanging out my hand-washed laundry on the roof, chatting with women or kids

on the roof or in the street, taking tea with a shopkeeper when their business was slack, or watching TV with Bhoju's serial-addicted daughters, I
felt no qualms in asserting I was conducting valid fieldwork. But there's
always a catch, and here is where ethnographic self-doubt lurks and
clutches me: I lived outside the walls. In a way, my Santosh Nagar life felt
organic and real, while my more formal "research" life—recording interviews, documenting hectic religious processions, photographing sites of historical importance, observing practices of commerce, and so forth—always
made me feel a bit like a poseur.

This chapter has several related aims, but all are thoroughly embedded
in the residential colony of Santosh Nagar, and all are inflected by
gender—my own, my helpers', my neighbors', my friends'—all of us female
(discounting Bhoju Ram, who was rarely present when I was hanging out
in Santosh Nagar). Women's roles, preoccupations, and limitations are not
the entire content but certainly compose the ballast of this chapter. My
portrait of Santosh Nagar cannot claim to be wholly balanced. Much of
what I say about the place comes through the mouths and experiences of
women.

If this seems an unjustifiable skewing in a book that is after all about
Shiptown and not about women, I have two rationales. The first of these is
simply experience. The Santosh Nagar life I shared was largely life as experienced by women. This extended to my similar dependence on men for any
transportation other than my own two feet. The second rationale for this
chapter's focus must give away in advance one of its main conclusions. This
is that men who live in Santosh Nagar believe they live in Jahazpur, while
many Santosh Nagar women feel that they do *not* live in Jahazpur. It was
April, well over halfway through my stay, before I finally admitted to myself
that Suman (as cited in one of this chapter's epigraphs) was as usual correct
in her insistence that I recognize that neither she nor I actually was a
Jahazpur resident.

It took me that long to hear what these women were telling me: that it
was foolish to ask them how they liked living in Jahazpur when they did
not actually live there. Why was I so dense? I suppose because I knew I
was doing an ethnographic study of the town of Jahazpur. My neighbors'
distinction between qasba and colony was peculiar to their gender, with its
limited mobility. The men of Santosh Nagar were far more integrated into
town life for a very evident reason: they could jump on their motorbikes
(as Bhoju did multiple times every day) and be at the bus stand or inside

the qasba walls in just a couple of minutes, negligible time, no distance at all. Women in these parts still didn't drive or bike.[1] To get to the qasba women and girls must either walk or be passengers, dependent on male drivers: husbands, brothers, and fathers. If there were no husband, brother, or other trusted grown male around to ferry them, they might easily walk to town in nice weather, and get there in about ten to twelve minutes. But rain (which produced mud), cold, and heat all rendered this walk less appealing at various times of the year. For those who had small children in tow, of course, the distance was magnified at any season by the weight or whines of an infant or toddler.

It is not a long or difficult walk between Santosh Nagar and the bus stand, but women have their modesty, their vulnerability to think about every time they go out. Girls prefer to go in pairs or larger groups if they do walk. And there are spaces they rarely enter. I was really shocked when early in my stay, I had to mail something, and I still didn't know my way around town very well. Bhoju's middle daughter, Chinu, an educated college girl, accompanied me to the post office. I sensed an aura of nervousness in her normally poised and confident demeanor; later she told me she had never before been there! In my own subsequent trips I rarely saw other women inside the post office; certainly there were none working there. Old behavioral constraints die hard; every public space offers a challenge, an unwritten rule or a rule no longer posed blatantly but built into habitus. Going to the post office would hardly brand a woman as brazen or out of control; still you rarely see women in the Jahazpur post office. This is quite unlike Jaipur, Rajasthan's capital, where not only many of the patrons but many of the postal workers are themselves female. Thus it bears noting as weighing on the village side of qasba life.[2]

This chapter has three sections with particular aims. In the first part I aim to characterize Santosh Nagar as colony—a different kind of place in contradistinction to the qasba, although intrinsically connected with it. Second, I aim to bring to life fieldwork days spent in the context of Santosh Nagar, and especially to describe the ways that Madhu and Chinu Gujar, Bhoju's two elder daughters, helped me learn. Madhu and Chinu "officially" worked for me on and off during my fieldwork, assisting me in getting to know the neighborhood women, including scheduling and conducting interviews. Together we probed the dynamic intersection of gender and place in a relatively newly settled neighborhood. How do women in such a new kind of place reinvent some traditions, choosing styles in which to enact stability, or even to break free (if covertly) in some limited fashions? That is, how are changing gender roles in changing times produced in a very particular kind of setting? Here, acknowledging inspiration from Doreen Massey, and using language borrowed from her, I describe a ritual and translate a ritual narrative to get at some crucial fragments of the whole.[3]

The final segment of Chapter 3 explores the rather different ways a different young woman taught me about life in Santosh Nagar. This was Suman, whose voice and views are present in *Shiptown*. Her judgments of me and of her surroundings had a strong impact, if a gradual one, on my subtler understandings. Suman lived between my home and Bhoju's and often detained me as I passed. She asked me many questions, while actively resisting being a subject of my research. In spite of her deliberate recalcitrance vis-à-vis my formal fieldwork, Suman became a force in my mind; her voice often echoed in my head, and was transcribed in my field notes.

What Kind of Place Is Santosh Nagar?

> Santosh Nagar seems like a place of many random paths
> crossing; what makes a neighborhood? what gives a feeling
> of neighborliness? (11 August 2010, journal)

If you don't count Chavundia (once numbered among the twelve hamlets but now more like a *mohalla* or qasba neighborhood, in spite of being outside the walls), Santosh Nagar is Jahazpur's oldest and most populous "colony."[4] *Colony* is a loanword from English, used to refer to a planned suburb or housing development. Santosh Nagar was both and neither.[5] It was neither distant enough, nor bounded enough, from the center of town to feel like a true suburb; and it wasn't planned enough to feel like a "development." Some referred to Santosh Nagar as *basti* (a broad term applicable to any human settlement), but it was never called a neighborhood (mohalla). Those were inside the qasba.[6] In Jahazpur municipality's electoral rolls, Santosh Nagar counted as Ward #3 (among twenty wards all told). Our elected ward member was a politically savvy Khatik, Babu Lal, who won easily in the 2010 election limited to Scheduled Caste candidates. At the far end of Santosh Nagar where I lived there were just two SC households: one *mochi* (shoemaker; originally refugees from Pakistan) and one *dholi* (drummer, from inside the walls).

The rather bland appellation Santosh Nagar (Satisfaction City) was bestowed at some relatively recent point in time. Santosh Nagar is a straight shot from the center of Jahazpur. Its fuzzy boundary begins just past a large complex of government offices (all those that had previously been located at Nau Chauk), somewhere around the Muslim cemetery. This proximity to a graveyard is why the locality was initially known as Bhutkhera (Ghost-ville), a designation still used by many old-timers who live in the qasba. Bhutkhera was the area's name when no one resided there (except for the dead). Santosh Nagar as a populated colony came into existence gradually over the past thirty years through a combination of officially authorized land auctions leading to deeded ownership, and squatters' encroachments that, once a house has been constructed, appear thus far to be seldom if ever challenged.

The colony has mostly grown up along both sides of the main road. Between the graveyard and the last homes of Santosh Nagar were lateral expansions on multiple cross streets which rarely stretched more than a block or two on either side. At the tail end where we lived were a few homes which, their owners seemed eager to tell me, had been built well before the neighborhood itself existed, as well as many that are newer, gradually filling in what had been empty space or empty plots.

Mohan, a Rajput matron whose marital family had moved to Santosh Nagar at an early stage in the neighborhood's development, told us that when they purchased their home, about twenty-five years ago, "there was nothing between Santosh Nagar and Jahazpur; the *thana* [police station] and *tehsil* [subdistrict headquarters offices] weren't there; the first thing was the Jats' house, and the rest was *plots." Daji (the Jat patriarch) confirmed that he had purchased his plots and begun to build on them in the 1980s.

Saraswati Sindhi, who lived right across the street from Bhoju Ram's family, told us in an early interview that at the time of her wedding, when she first moved to her in-laws' house in Santosh Nagar, "there were snakes and scorpions, and rats." She elaborated: "From the post office, on this side, it seemed exactly as if it were a jungle, there was nothing, there was no electricity. Now there are streetlights, there weren't any of those either." Affirming her observations, I asked unnecessarily, "So there has been a lot of change?" She answered emphatically, "Yes, it was complete jungle! But now it has become a basti (settlement)."

Seeing a good opening in this description to get at local history, I said, "I heard this place was called Bhutkhera." Saraswati, who made no pretense of appreciating her place of residence, answered, "For me, even today it is *still* Bhutkhera. When they started selling plots here, they named it "Santosh Nagar," so it would strike people as good." (She digressed then from local history to speak scornfully of how only weak-minded people, unlike herself, were afraid of ghosts.)

Kalu Singh, the retired Mina who had returned to Jahazpur after an adventurous working life and whose views I cited in the introduction, described Santosh Nagar before he built his house. He said that thirty-five years ago, "you couldn't even get here, there was no road, nothing! There was only jungle, and thorn bushes; Bhils would gather wood and sell it for fuel. When there was still royalty in Jahazpur, horses and camels belonging to the rulers grazed in the jungle right here where Santosh Nagar is today." The Bhil are an ST group that historically lived off of forest products.[7]

As it approaches the end of the colony where Bhoju's family lived and where my husband and I resided, Santosh Nagar Road becomes known as Ghanta Rani Road, for once past town it leads a few kilometers farther to the regionally famous goddess shrine of Ghanta Rani (Valley Queen)—a place I had first visited in 1981 when studying regional pilgrimage. Ghanta Rani was near enough that her Jahazpur devotees told me they sometimes made round-trip foot pilgrimages, barefoot, in a single day. On monthly dates special to the goddess, jeeps and trolleys overflowing with pilgrims passed by on their way to Ghanta Rani. Her annual fair drew huge throngs of devotees.[8]

Just beyond Santosh Nagar, a few minutes' walk further in the direction of Ghanta Rani, another housing development, already named Shiv Colony, is coming into being. Plots had been surveyed and sold, and by the time Daniel and I left in June 2011, a few houses were going up. But many of the plots had been purchased as real estate investments and remained empty as late as 2015, perhaps indicating that Jahazpur was not growing as fast as some expected. Another reason given to me for the slow pace of Shiv Colony becoming populated is that investors, or speculators, were biding their time, convinced that the price of land would only go higher. Still, some families have begun to settle there, and power and water hook-ups are available for the new plots.

During our fieldwork year, Dan and I liked to stroll through and beyond Shiv Colony in the cool of the evening. Once past the empty plots or scattered construction sites, where sometimes a worker greeted us, we encountered only goatherds and shepherds who daily take small flocks out to forage, ranging across the uncultivated, rocky grazing lands that characterize the landscape on this side of Jahazpur qasba: a source of fodder, firewood from thorny mesquite, and little else.

Bhoju bought his home in Santosh Nagar in 2007. The first time I visited, that same summer, when all the interior paint was new, small representations of Ganesh, the god of beginnings rendered in bright orange paint, were still visible above every doorway in the house. They had been painted for the ceremonial inauguration of the family's new lives as homeowning townspeople. Three years later, at the beginning of August 2010, my husband and I settled in a rented flat just one street over from where Bhoju's family lived. We had agreed with Bhoju's suggestion that we rent in this area and not seek housing in the heart of Jahazpur qasba, a decision finalized in a single day that profoundly impacted my fieldwork and shaped this book, for better or worse. Bhoju had scouted potential rentals in advance of our arrival. He conducted us to three or four possibilities the day after we reached town. All of these were within a few blocks of his own house.

The overriding, important reason for staying where we did was to be close, a neighbor, to Bhoju and his family. I could see their rooftop from my rooftop and this pleased us all. At this time all three of Bhoju's daughters, not yet married although their engagements were fixed, lived in Jahazpur while pursuing their education. One son was in boarding school (which he disliked) not far down the Devli road. The youngest son lived with Bhoju's wife and mother in their village home in Ghatiyali. Except during the protracted season of the wedding (Chapter 7) these three significant family members were not often present.

There was one more reasonably weighty justification for positioning myself outside the walls while studying the qasba: physical and psychological comfort. It was much easier to find commodious rooms and relatively more (if far from absolutely) private space by settling in this newer area where plots and homes were simply larger. In terms of ethnographic work, privacy is not always a desideratum; my earlier fieldwork experiences were often richly abetted by exposure, permeability. Having an unintrusive nature, not at all well suited for a career in anthropology, being intruded upon by others is actually good for me. However, my husband, whose company I dearly value, had come with me. He was finishing a book manuscript and needed a quiet place to work, a long day's journey from his main research site in Gwalior, Madhya Pradesh (D. Gold 2015).

Figure 10. View of rooftops and street where author lived in Santosh Nagar;
woman carrying firewood; motorbikes.

Dan and I resided in our Santosh Nagar flat through the middle of June
2011, for the better part of a year. We had two inner rooms with doors—
one our bedroom and the other a shared study with two small writing desks
obtained locally, and two desk chairs purchased on an emergency run to
Jaipur when we realized our aging backs were in deep trouble. We had one
Internet card and it only worked on Dan's machine, and then with a slow-
motion quality that felt like the virtual equivalent of walking in rubber
boots through a sea of molasses. Our accommodations also included a
small kitchen with sink and shelves, in which we installed a typical two-
burner stovetop fueled by a gas cylinder (normally rationed but magically
obtained for us by friends through channels into which we discreetly
refrained from inquiring). We also had a sitting and dining space with two
plastic chairs, a plastic coffee table, and a small fridge. Unlike the two side
rooms, this central sitting space was semipublic. A large metal grating covered most of the floor, and directly beneath it was our landlord's front
hallway, allowing the passage of air, and of course sound. On both sides of

this ceiling/floor courteous discretion on all our parts limited visual intrusions, but we had no way not to hear one another's arguments and smell one another's cooking. Our sitting room also offered the only passage to a shared rooftop strung with all-important clotheslines in daily use by all of us. From the roof Daniel and I had access to our own "latrine-bathroom," two separate spaces next to one another each with its designated bucket, and water on tap from the rooftop tank where it would (under auspicious conditions) be pumped up every other afternoon when the town supplied water to public and private faucets.

The three-generational family with whom we shared our space, and to whom we paid our rent, consisted of five adults and two children, a boy and a girl, whose ages at the time were around six and five respectively. My unfulfilled yearning for grandchildren meant that I never minded hearing them repetitively recite their school lessons in a charming singsong lilt. The adults were a retired teacher and his wife; their son and his wife (whose first child was born after our time living there); and their divorced daughter, mother of the children, who together with her brother and father worked in a small store they owned. Sometimes two additional married daughters, each with two somewhat older offspring, came to visit, and at those times the noise and rowdiness level could get overwhelming. But we grew very fond of the boy and girl who regularly lived below us and who would bring up our milk and our newspaper each morning, melodiously and exuberantly announcing their arrival by calling, "Auntie-ji!, Uncle-ji!"

In contrast to the more homogeneous neighborhoods in the congested heart of Jahazpur's old walled center, Santosh Nagar is a locality with a radically mixed population. Castes are mixed: persons from the top, middle, and lowest realms of the Hindu ritual hierarchy live in Santosh Nagar, including priests and butchers, shopkeepers and drummers, herders, farmers, and artisans. On one street with which I was familiar, right across the main road from our own street, three houses in close proximity belonged respectively to a Brahmin, a Rajput, and the neighborhood tailors mentioned earlier who belonged to the SC Mochi or shoemaker community. The Khatiks (butchers by hereditary identity) are clustered at the other end of the colony, closer to the bus stand and the qasba, forming Santosh Nagar's most homogeneous area caste-wise. Judging from the few interiors I saw in that part of Santosh Nagar, these were upwardly mobile, middle-class Khatiks by and large.

Economic classes are mixed: Santosh Nagar residents pursue a variety of livelihoods: some hold salaried government positions; some run small businesses; others might be shopkeepers, truck drivers, or day laborers. At our end of the street a wealthy patriarch, a self-made businessman, owned four huge houses, one for each of his four sons; he was building more for his grandsons. Origins and years of residency are mixed: recent migrants from the surrounding countryside in pursuit of economic and educational opportunities live next door to families deeply rooted in Jahazpur town, who have shifted to Santosh Nagar to escape uncomfortably close quarters, both physical and interpersonal.

Religious identities in Santosh Nagar are distinctly less mixed. Predominantly Hindu, Santosh Nagar's population did include several Jain families. While the vast majority of Hindus belonged to families rooted in the immediate region, there were also a few whose immediate forebears had migrated from Pakistan around the time of partition. There was one family of Sindhis who held themselves apart from other Hindus in various ways including dress (even adult women wore kamiz-salwar rather than Rajasthani outfits).[9] I interviewed several women in the Sindhi family, as well as several Jain women. Interestingly, although Hindu, Sindhi women like their Jain neighbors spoke of themselves as different, and explicitly expressed their sense of lack of community. Nonetheless, the same individuals regularly joined other Santosh Nagar women's rituals and in that sense were well integrated. No Muslims had moved to Santosh Nagar. Jahazpur's well-off Muslims possessed considerable property inside the qasba and nearby farmland outside of it. Possibly they had no need for the kind of added space that attracted Brahmin and merchant families, as well as former butchers, to shift from cramped quarters within the walls to more spacious dwellings in this colony outside the qasba. Or there may be deeper limits to residential pluralism than were ever articulated to me.

Many of my neighbors in Santosh Nagar were financially secure but far from affluent. They were at a far remove from that cosmopolitan middle class that ostentatiously consumes global brands. However, many did possess motorcycles, color televisions, and fridges.[10] One thing that struck me was how carefully the people I knew cared for their possessions, protecting them from the constant accumulation of dust and cleaning them diligently and frequently. Summer heat was intense, but air-conditioning was not practical in Jahazpur due to power cuts as well as architectural design. Many homes in Santosh Nagar did possess "coolers"—large, noisy machines that created powerful blasts of blissfully chilled air in a very limited space and had to be frequently fed with water (often in short supply). Dan and I purchased a small one on wheels at the peak of the hot season but it was of disappointing efficacy. We had to take turns positioning ourselves directly in its air flow to benefit from it.

While I was living there, the bourgeoisie of Santosh Nagar were just beginning to acquire "inverters"—large cells capable of storing enough power when current flowed to keep some fans and lights running for up to six hours during electricity cuts. Usually cuts were not that prolonged.[11] At night, of course, it was easy enough to see who had one of these, and to desire to join that privileged company (although we never did). On my three post-fieldwork visits, I observed that inverters had rapidly proliferated—a substantial investment that doubtless pays off, improving quality of life in multiple ways. Bhoju was motivated to acquire one largely to prevent computer crashes, as well as avoid the hassle of intermittent darkness; his TV was not hooked up to it. I noted in other households that inverters keep the television going for those who do not want their favorite programs interrupted.

If rural and town lives intersect commercially inside the walls, in Santosh Nagar the meeting of town and village was most evident in domestic configurations. I met many village-born persons who lived there. While quite a few of these were women moved by marriage, others were men moved by jobs or business opportunities. All those who had recently shifted to Jahazpur maintained strong connections with rural origins. While it was an exception not the norm, there were a few women (among my acquaintances, notably Saraswati Sindhi from Kota and Asha Jat from Ajmer) who had grown up in more urban areas but whose marital lives deposited them in this backwater. They both articulated interesting and distinctive perspectives on the qasba and its suburban periphery (Gold 2014b).

I learned so much by living a woman's life in Santosh Nagar, I must acknowledge in advance that when I write about the qasba in later chapters, my insights into the gendered nature of experience are more limited. It isn't just the disproportion in numbers of interviews, although that is striking: I have about forty interviews recorded with Santosh Nagar women, and not more than a dozen with women inside the walls, where my female helpers had fewer connections and where it was far easier for Bhoju Ram to make appointments with men. The difference in interview numbers hardly reveals the real difference based on everyday encounters and experiences—a difference beyond reckoning.

Gendered Days, Gendered Methods, Gendered Visions

> The girls think of their studies, of relationships, of child
> marriage and love marriage and *nata* [remarriage]; they all
> have their eyes on the prize of "sar-vis" [service, that is, a
> job] without a lot of faith but with a lot of hope and I don't
> know, Karuna's word, aspiration.[12] Yes, aspiration. this
> generation is doing tuition, coaching, big time. almost as
> their parents are doing *vrats*. spend money for the future
> and the future is to succeed in the competitive
> examinations, to get scores that put you in the running for
> the next competition. a girl whose marriage has gone bad
> may be returned to the world of education. a girl who never
> married must find her match in the world of education. (23
> August 2010, journal)

As related in the preceding chapter, Bhoju and I began to work almost immediately after my arrival in order to gather some foundational knowledge about the town that would help me start to focus in, to transform my unwieldy subject of identity and place into manageable chunks. At this early stage, when I knew virtually nothing, anything I learned was useful. When I was not out with Bhoju and not at my desk alone, I was in the company of women.

Given Bhoju's taxing schedule and my wish to gather women's viewpoints, it made sense to both of us for me to hire his daughter Madhu (whose schedule at this time had relative flexibility) to work with me when Bhoju was otherwise occupied. Madhu and I did considerable research together from August through October. Chinu began assisting me after that, when Madhu was preparing for a crucial examination and simultaneously ill with a diagnosis of typhoid fever requiring a strict regimen of diet and behavior. From the middle of December to the middle of April neither Madhu nor Chinu was much available due to the compelling preoccupations of both their weddings (in late January) and their schooling (ongoing). As is common, they both did return home after their marriages, and we did work together again, sporadically but very fruitfully, in the hot season.

Madhu and Chinu in 2010 were innocent of prior fieldwork experience. Madhu had recorded some interviews in 2008 with fellow college students under her father's close supervision. Chinu had done nothing in the way of research. Both young women were somewhat reticent in interview contexts but at times could be surprisingly proactive. For me, fieldwork in their company was often more relaxing and social rather than intense and businesslike. Visiting female neighbors, I learned much just from observation: body language, home decor, clothing, and the ways interviews lapsed so readily into gossip. I watched the atmosphere in a room change when a male person joined a previously all-female company, and noted how this differed in nuanced ways according to the ages and kinship relations of all present. Formal interview content was often secondary.

When I worked with Madhu and Chinu the linguistic situation shifted. Inexperienced and reticent, they left it to me to formulate questions. Because they required me to articulate my own questions, these interviews stretched my language skills to their fullest extent. I felt inadequate but also in control. Because of all our time together as a family over the years, Madhu and Chinu had no problem with my accented Hindi. Thus if the interviewee couldn't fully understand me (or the other way around) one of them would chime in and explain. These interviews thus proceed in an elementary language, my language. In certain ways, when I review their content, I see a usefulness in this simplicity; I confess to enjoy not having Bhoju taking the lead. I am also acutely aware of how my language level limits the depth to which we are able to probe any given topic.

When we were interviewing Madhu's and Chinu's friends and fellow college students among our neighbors, we all spoke Hindi and not Rajasthani. From time to time, however, my young female assistants would contact a female neighbor who was not educated. Reacting to my American accent, a few women were stymied, resulting in occasional embarrassing miscommunications in first conversational encounters. One declared, on tape: "Even if I am born again, in my next life I still won't understand your speech!" Once an unschooled woman becomes accustomed to the way I talk we are able to converse—me improvising in a mix of Rajasthani and Hindi, she responding in Rajasthani slowed down and sometimes minimally Hindi-ized for my benefit. I have for many years conversed fluently in this fashion with Bhoju's nonliterate wife, Bali, and eventually did so with a number of unschooled Jahazpur women, all but a very few of whom were Santosh Nagar neighbors.

For a jointly authored article on the role of the research assistant, Bhoju, Madhu, and Chinu each wrote about their experience. Bhoju of course had a *longue durée* view of our collaboration; his daughters discussed what for them was a new experience.[13] Madhu and Chinu both wrote about the difficulties they had at the beginning, especially when interviewing nonliterate women. Madhu stresses the hurdles of explaining our purposes: "Talking with some of these women was difficult even for me. Before they would even answer, they asked me so many questions: 'Who is she? What kinds of things does she want to talk about with us? And what is she going to do with the things she learns from us?'" Chinu notes similar problems and speaks also of becoming flustered herself.

> It was easy to talk with educated women and get their answers. But it was difficult to talk with women who were totally illiterate. Those women would always begin by asking us more questions, questions such as, "Why are you doing all this?" and "What if some kind of confusion results from this?" It was very difficult to explain things to them. Actually, when I first began working with you [she wrote the essay addressing me in the second person], I myself became extremely muddled in front of people: "How will I talk with them?" But more recently this perplexity totally vanished, and now I can easily converse with anyone.

Regarding research practice and its rewards, one thing that we all had in common was true enjoyment of learning. As did Bhoju, his daughters too repeatedly employed the Hindi word *jankari* as they described their work with me. Jankari can mean "information" but is commonly translated as "knowledge."[14] For me, fieldwork as a quest to obtain information also involves rarer and subtler transformative moments—fusion-like moments when information becomes knowledge and, as is the case with chemical fusion, energy is produced.

Both young women made efforts to create an atmosphere conducive to the flow of information that would be for my work a valued knowledge —that is, jankari. While they found this most taxing with uneducated women, they also began to realize that such women might provide the most satisfying or original material. For example, there was the interview with the old drummer woman whose language was difficult for me to penetrate as it was not just Rajasthani but a quaint, flowery, bardic Rajasthani. We asked her the usual questions about Jahazpur's festivals. Later when transcribing the tape, Madhu noted that when I had asked how long a certain festival had been going on in Jahazpur (a question to which most responded, "one hundred years" or "four hundred years" or " a very long time"), this old woman declared, "since the creation of the universe." Somehow this gave us a particular and shared delight. For Madhu I believe it was a moment when she suddenly appreciated as invaluable her maternal heritage, the oral cultural worlds of her mother and grandmothers. Educational priorities force young women such as Madhu and Chinu to race as fast as they can in the opposite direction of their unschooled mothers' traditions. Working with me certainly did not deter them from that determined course, but it did foster appreciation for the older generation's verbal arts.

Both young women in their own writing stress two different but related subjects that were of particular interest to them while working with their Aunt Ann: learning about working women and learning about women's rituals. Regarding our interviews with working women (a category I introduced), I note that both young women emphasize economic independence. This was particularly striking to me because they lump together sociologically low-ranking vegetable vendors or seamstresses with esteemed, salaried teachers. In other words, they took into their own modes of appraisal a commonality residing in earning capacity cutting through what are normally steep divides in local society. In this regard, Chinu writes, "Some do tailoring, some have beauty parlors, some work in shops, and some have teaching jobs. These women are not dependent on their in-laws or anyone else!"

Madhu and Chinu composed their statements about fieldwork looking back on that experience over a year after their weddings. And Madhu, who was older and possessed of greater life experience, commented more fully: "I also helped interview some businesswomen who had their own professions or trades. These included a seamstress, several beauticians, teachers, vegetable vendors and so forth. Such women do not have to be dependent on their in-laws. They do their own work themselves. Along with this they do the housework, and they also pay attention to their children's education." Madhu thus observes that earning is not exactly the same thing as independence.

About our work on rituals, Chinu wrote: "In order to learn about vows, most of the time we talked with those women who had the most enthusiasm for keeping them, and who in general were most interested in worship and recitation of religious texts. From talking with these women, I learned a lot about the practice of worship and religious storytelling, and I heard a number of stories." With Madhu and Chinu's help I was able to gain insights into women's ritual and storytelling worlds as they flourished in Santosh Nagar, and also to look more broadly at how neighbors create communities in various physical spaces.

A Santosh Nagar Women's Ritual:
"That Throwntogetherness"

On Sunday, 5 December 2010 (Dark Moon of Margashira), three women bearing worship trays quietly gather, late one morning, in a spacious private courtyard in Santosh Nagar. The courtyard lies close to the outer edge of our neighborhood. Out here, as already noted, a few houses actually predate the neighborhood's existence. These were homesteads in the jungle built by ambitious or foresighted persons involved in agriculture, business, or, as was the case with our hostess's late husband, the manufacturing of *chuna* or lime. I have come to join the three women, each in the final year of a three-year vow to fast monthly on the dark moon, for their worship. Their collective performance of this worship has been a recurrent event for over two years. All three women are between forty and fifty years of age and live in Santosh Nagar because their marital lives (that is, their husbands' working lives) deposited them in this neighborhood years ago.

Chinu, who at the time was an unmarried first-year college student in her late teens, accompanied me. We brought my small digital recorder to capture the stories that would be told as part of the ritual. Chinu was not fasting but she did participate in the prayers. Our hostess, Santok, was a wealthy widow from an agricultural community with no deep roots in Jahazpur. Our ritual expert was Madhu-Didi, a cheerful Brahmin housewife whose in-laws lived in a village but who resided in Santosh Nagar because of her husband's employment. Many Santosh Nagar women called her Madhu-Didi, for big sister, and I will follow that practice to distinguish her from Madhu Gujar. The third participant, another close neighbor, was Prem, in whose life sorrow has provoked unusual devotional fervor. She belongs to an ST (Scheduled Tribe) group, populous and politically powerful in this region, although only a few reside in Santosh Nagar.

A mixed-caste group of neighbor women worshipping together was not uncommon in Ghatiyali, the village where I did all my earlier ethnographic research. However, as I gradually discover, the lives of these Santosh Nagar women thrown together through domestic proximity and devotional predilection are distinctively inflected by the time and place: the second decade of the twenty-first century and the eclectically mixed "suburban" colony where they live.

The household where we gathered was doubly unusual. Not only was it the sole private home in Santosh Nagar containing its own small temple; but this open-air temple dedicated to Lord Shiva also houses not just the usual figures of Parvati, Ganesh, Skanda (Kartikkeya), and Nandi ranged around a central aniconic Shiva lingam (an assemblage found at small Shiva shrines throughout the region), but a fifth: the large marble bust of our hostess Santok's late husband, Makhanji. As I learn later, the bust has been carved realistically to resemble his photograph. Thus the former owner of this property, reputedly one of the first settlers of Santosh Nagar when it was still known as Bhutkhera, is enshrined as a revered ancestral spirit.[15]

Although I had been living in Santosh Nagar since August, not much more than a block away, I had never been in this compound before. However, I had already visited Madhu-Didi several times. Her home was nearly adjacent to the house where my husband and I rented our flat. She and I could wave to one another from our respective rooftops. I had not previously met either of the other two women. Of course, I heard the sounds of twilight service emanating daily from the temple and had told myself to investigate.

I was engaged in research on abstractions, difficult to encounter on the ground: identity, locality, belonging. Compared with pursuing these ineffables, nothing seemed easier than pushing "record" at a women's ritual and sitting back to enjoy the stories.[16] I felt as if I were happily slipping into a familiarly comfortable research role. Moreover, with my back to the anomalous temple, this scene with its open cooking hearth and livestock was deceptively reminiscent in sight and scent of a spacious village courtyard.

The dark moon fast the three women had undertaken is called Tin Panoti vrat or "Three-Panoti vow," a vow that protects from undesirable planetary emanations.[17] Madhu-Didi volubly explained to me the vow's major features. For three years on every dark moon (that is, once a month), the person who has made this vow must eat only a specific designated grain: barley in year one, rice in year two, sesame in year three. The practice requires a total fast before the puja; even after it, no grain other than the specified one for the year may be consumed until the following morning.

As is the case throughout much of Northwestern India, the region's present-day staple, its twice-daily, filling fare taken with cooked vegetables or lentils, is whole wheat flatbreads. To eschew wheat is thus a major break in eating routine. Moreover, although you are allowed sugar or spice with your grain, salt is prohibited for those participating in this vow. This month the dark moon has fallen on Sunday, and I am told that those women who also fast for Shiva every Monday (two of the three present), will not eat a normal meal until Tuesday.

Among Jahazpur's reasonably solvent households, as far as I have been able to observe, women's vows such as these do not mean going hungry. It indeed frequently struck me during my time there that such vows, although certainly requiring self-discipline and demonstrating self-restraint, also provide opportunities for variations in a somewhat monotonous diet (for example, fruit and nuts normally viewed as luxuries and reserved for visitors are consumed guiltlessly on vow days), and creative cooking (sweet potato halva, for example). I know this because during the course of the year neighbors and acquaintances frequently offered me special foods prepared for their fasts (allowing me, undeservingly, to savor this culinary variety). Today's worship trays feature sesame candy (*gajak* or *tilpatti*), which will be offered to the deities, and of course become *prasad* (blessed leftovers) to be shared by all present.

The women circumambulate the Shiva shrine eleven times and then move to another side of the courtyard to perform a brief but tender worship of one of the healthiest basil plants I have ever seen—it is as big as a bush. The tulsi plant is regarded as a goddess and addressed as Tulsi Ma or "Basil Mother." Finally we seat ourselves for the dark moon worship. Santok, our hostess, announced just then that she would prepare tea, but Madhu-Didi with the combined authority of her Brahmin status and ritual knowledge suggested waiting until the final prayer to the *lungya* before starting the tea. Santok agreed, adding that she would make masala chai, with pepper and cloves, and that she would throw some down as an offering to this *lungya*—a term I might hazard to translate as the "dissolute fellow," but I think "creep" is a possibly more appropriate colloquial equivalent. As I would discover, the final truncated story, really no more than a rhyme and a prayer, is directed to this creep, an enigmatic figure I encountered in my earlier work by another name: *lobhya*, "greedy one."[18] The creep's essence, in a nutshell, is that he seeks illegitimately to co-opt for himself the fruits of women's vows and must be pacified by designating as his due a modicum of regard and a small offering of grain (and today, it seems, tea).

Madhu-Didi then began to tell the ritual stories. Before arriving at the lungya, she narrated the standard number of three tales dedicated to true divine beings; all three were totally unfamiliar to me. Unlike the main story-teller I worked with in Ghatiyali village, whose performative art was lei-surely and who made sure her audience was fully engaged and responsive, Madhu-Didi rattled off worship stories in Rajasthani at breakneck speed and almost without inflections of voice. Normally I can follow women's stories, even in regional dialect, as I am so familiar with the genre and benefit from the traditional performative style in which the teller checks frequently on whether her listeners have followed and understood her. Today I am crestfallen to find I can do no more than catch a few words: cow, king, vow. Apparently, Madhu-Didi related exactly the same stories every dark moon and they are performed by rote for the divine rather than the human audience.

A few days later I sat down with Chinu and Madhu to listen to my recording and to translate these tales into standard Hindi. All three of us were surprised at how charming the stories were. Both sisters were sensitive to and appreciative of the tales' messages about gender and power. Here is the first story (always the most significant for the day's ritual):

Once there was a king who went out to survey his kingdom, riding on his horse. From the road he noticed a cow grazing in his barley field. The cow was doing the dark moon vrat, the "*tin panoti vrat*," and on this day she could only eat barley. That is why she was in the king's barley field.

The king started to chase the cow out of his field. But then the cow began to speak. She said, "I am doing my *tin panoti vrat* and today I can only eat barley. That is why I am here. But I won't do much damage, I'll only eat a little."

Even though the king heard what the cow said, he chased her away. Because he chased the cow away, she cursed him: "Because you have abused my vrat, the moment you dismount from your horse you will turn into a donkey!"[19]

Well the king stayed on his horse and rode on his way.

[To condense: *The king has similar encounters with talking cows who are in the second and third year of the vow, in his rice field and in his sesame field. In each case, the outcome is the same: he chases them out of the field and they curse him to become a donkey.*]

After receiving the same curse three times, the king began to worry, thinking to himself: "Cows don't usually talk, so how did they start talking today? Who knows, maybe this curse from Cow Mother will come true."

So, still on horseback, he decided he had better find his queen. He thought, "Only she will recognize me even if I *do* turn into a donkey; nobody else would know who I am."

The king rode into his castle grounds and asked where his wife was. They told him, "She has gone to her parents' home."

Immediately he rode to his in-laws' place and asked them to send his wife back to him. They requested that he dismount, because they wanted to serve him chai and food. His in-laws welcomed him cordially, assuring him, "Of course, we will send our daughter with you, but meanwhile please dismount from your horse so you can relax in comfort."

But he refused to do this. He thought to himself [with embarrassment], "How can I tell them I was cursed by Cow Mother, and that if I get off my horse I will turn into a donkey?"

But his wife's brother grabbed his hand and pulled him off the horse and just like that, he became a donkey.

Then everyone started talking excitedly: "He used to be a man, so how did he become a donkey? How did this come to pass?"

They asked around for someone who might be able to explain this unfortunate turn of events. One person, a learned Brahmin (pandit), knew just what had happened. He explained to the king's in-laws about the Tin Panoti vrat, and how the king had abused the cow's vow, and how Cow Mother had cursed him.

This same learned Brahmin also knew a remedy for the king's plight. He told it to them: "If some woman who keeps the Tin Panoti vrat will pray, 'God, please let my vrat's fruit go to him,' he will become a man again."

So they made inquiries all around the village to see who was doing this vrat. Well, the high castes were not doing any vows at all!

But the Bhil [ST] and Regar-Chamar [two different leather worker communities, SC] were keeping many vows.

When they asked just who was currently performing the Tin Panoti vrat, it turned out there was one Regar [leather worker] woman who came and said, "I am." But, when they explained the situation to her, she set conditions: "I won't give the king the fruit of my vow unless his wife, the queen, comes to my house and eats a meal there. If she does that, only then I will give him the fruit of my vow." When the queen heard this, her first thought was: "How can I possibly do this?" But then she reconsidered, realizing that to help her husband was the most important thing. So she accepted the Regar woman's terms.

It was the dark moon, and the final day of the Regar woman's Tin Panoti vrat. On that very day the queen came to the Regar woman's house to eat.

The Regar woman had cleaned her house, and made nice arrangements for the queen and her attendants to sit. She set out the food before them. Just as the queen extended her hand to eat, the Regar woman grabbed her hand and stopped her from eating.

She said, "I don't want to spoil your honor and be the cause of people gossiping and saying you ate at a leather worker's house. I just wanted to see if you were willing. You have come to my house, that is what is most important. No royal person ordinarily would even enter my house, but you came and sat down for a meal. Just showing me this respect is enough to enhance my dignity.

She continued, "Today I will give you the fruit of my *tin panoti vrat*. So she sprinkled the donkey with water from the worship jug, and he became a man again.

After that, the king and queen together both undertook to keep the Tin Panoti vrat.

[concluding prayer]: "Just as that queen protected her husband, please protect me."

However fanciful, the story of the fasting cow reveals quite a lot about women, gender, and society in provincial Rajasthan—about effort, challenge, and accommodation; about negotiation and agency. The two educated young women, my willing helpers, displayed an indulgent affection for the speaking, fasting, intrepid cow in the story and her effective curse of the dense, autocratic but ultimately vulnerable king whose well-being turns out to be doubly dependent on the grace of women. For them the stories (perhaps like Frank Sinatra songs or Humphrey Bogart films for my generation in the USA), come from their mother's world laden with meanings somewhat quaintly packaged but of ongoing appeal.

The story's messages chime clearly at several levels. First, it shows that both gender and caste hierarchies are ultimately false—a typical lesson from the world of bhakti or devotion.[20] Second, it stresses not just that devotion matters but that self-disciplined beings accumulate power, again a common theme in popular Hinduism. This power is capable of enhancing well-being explicitly of others but also of those who accumulate it, although this latter goal may be muted. The lungya/lobhya must be acknowledged even as his greed is checked and derided: to seek the fruits of vows solely for one's own purposes is a disapproved endeavor. I have always supposed that in acknowledging the "creep" one acknowledges sub rosa inclinations impossible to deny. Third, the story—perhaps disappointingly from the perspective of outsiders looking for emancipatory theology—gives a strong nod to the importance of reputation, of maintaining one's place in society whether high or low, of rendering what is due to conventionality even while acknowledging that it is based on false, invidious, discriminatory premises. The leather worker woman simultaneously challenges the rules of purity and hierarchy and acquiesces to their twinned regime. The queen will do anything to help her husband, and her courageous willingness to break eating rules is admirable because it is in the service of her marriage. The story thus manages both to convey socially subversive messages and to recommend acquiescence to status quo caste and gender roles.

Although I never asked her more about the story, over the eleven months of my fieldwork I did conduct several interviews on various topics with its teller. Madhu-Didi is a vital, energetic woman in her prime, channeling a great deal of energy into two particular passions: religious practice and handicrafts. Aware of being less educated than some other Brahmin women, she was nonetheless self-confident and authoritative. Madhu-Didi's extensive religious practices included hosting large groups of twenty neighborhood women or more at her home for prayers on fast days more popular than Tin Pinoti—such as Tij and Karva Chauth (both fasts having to do with ensuring husbands' long lives; see A. Gold 2015). She also devoted much time and effort to producing all kinds of handmade decorative items, including beaded and gilt flower arrangements and bright embroidered bedcovers.

Madhu-Didi took an evident leadership role among Santosh Nagar's middle-caste women. There was a bit of noblesse oblige about her manner when she was sitting among groups of women from the farmer communities—Gujars, Jats, Minas—most often as the only Brahmin in the room. But she was also a down-to-earth lady, putting on no special airs. Just like her middle-caste companions, she was clearly more comfortable speaking entirely in Rajasthani rather than the schoolbook Hindi of the educated, and she obviously enjoyed her participation in frequent women's gatherings on auspicious occasions in the neighborhood, whether to celebrate weddings, housewarmings, or babies.

Both Santok and Prem had suffered tragedies in their lives. Santok's husband, a successful entrepreneurial businessman and farmer, had died suddenly (presumably from a heart attack), and her adult son had his own problems. Prem had lost one of her four sons to a mysterious disease, and the child's terrible suffering, although now many years in the past, had evidently left deep psychological scars. Prem told us she had learned about the Three-Panoti vow from Madhu-Didi, her neighbor, declaring she had known nothing about it beforehand. She stressed her total reliance on the other two women in matters of ritual practice. Santok expressed decidedly less deference. She told us she had been doing various vows her whole life and claimed to have learned nothing from Madhu-Didi. She nonetheless saw, and stated frankly, that there was a virtue in having a Brahmin woman conduct the worship. She told us straightforwardly that giving cloth to Madhu kept various sins from sticking to the giver. The example she gave me was the sin of stepping on insects by accident and causing their deaths.[21]

Such braided communities of women are the essence of what I am calling (after Massey 2005:141) that "throwntogetherness" in Santosh Nagar. Arguing in an earlier essay against a static and constricting view of place, Massey observes, "what gives a place its specificity is not some long internalized history but the fact that it is constructed out of a particular constellation of social relations, meeting and weaving together at a particular locus" (1994: 154). While some approaches to place have seen it as static, conservative, confined, and gendered female, Massey proposes that space, which she does not oppose to place, is imbued with unfinished narratives—

or, to use her language, a "simultaneity of stories-so-far" (2005:9). Massey's feminist position is intrinsic to her views of place as dynamic, relational, and storied.[22]

Ritual and devotional practices both collective and individual seem to help many Santosh Nagar women find and keep their footings and their bearings in a context where many old certainties are up for grabs.[23] Rituals create solidarities that spill over into other arenas, even if the most radical egalitarian messages from devotional narratives might remain unrealized. In the story a Regar woman, member of an oppressed community, first exemplifies spiritual parity but second endorses adherence to rules of stratification once she has made her point about the need to be blind to them. In Jahazpur, unfortunately, I did not record stories told by Regar women themselves. However, during earlier research in Ghatiyali I did gather a few tales from that community which were far more blistering in their angry assault on discrimination; in these narratives reversals of high-born advantage may have permanent, violent outcomes (Gold 2008a).

Through their neighborly, place-making arts, Santosh Nagar women actively engage, assess, and improve their conditions of life. Santosh Nagar women, especially those between their late teens and early thirties, find themselves in circumstances quite different, although not radically disjoined, from those of preceding generations. It is upon these already shifting sands that these female neighbors are able to forge solidarities and sustain or transform identities in often subtle ways.

Suman: The Voice in My Head

> I'm getting to know my neighbors. Since arriving we have shared an invasion of gorgeous grasshoppers, eye flu, the joys of a good rainy season, ripe cucumbers and roasted corn. One young married woman who lives next door has little education but a keen mind. As I pass her several times a day, she detains me, offering friendship and posing some very hard questions: why would I want to leave my family and live so far from them? what will I get? what will she get? My answers thus far have not satisfied her or me, but I hope to offer better ones at the end of eleven months.

(Author's letter from the field, composed eleven weeks into
an eleven-month stay in Jahazpur; published in the
Fulbright newsletter)

Years later, I still find Suman's questions difficult. In spite of those troubling, unanswered questions, she and I forged a tenuous friendship. In this
section I consider what part this friendship has played in the emergence of
Shiptown.

Santosh Nagar women often congregated in small groups on the stoops
outside their front doors. One particular group was positioned right
between our rented flat and Bhoju's home. Inevitably I took this route
multiple times in a single day. At the core of a shifting cluster of women
and kids were two sisters-in-law with four small children (two preschool
girls and two infants, a girl and a boy). These women tended a home-based
flour mill located in a room facing the street. Business was sporadic at best,
leaving them with time on their hands. Suman, the younger of the two, was
about twenty-five years old with no more than a grade-school education.
Outspoken and deeply curious about the world, Suman had a subtle sense
of humor, veering to irony. At the beginning she truly was the sole person
in Jahazpur to probe my motives as a researcher. With her beautiful open
smile and her lilting, girlish voice, she demanded I explain myself for real.

In time, Suman became an eloquent source of casual insightful commentary on the social world whose patterns I was trying to learn. Often she
would blithely compare her world with what she could gather of mine.
Suman steadfastly refused to be interviewed, yet her words—perhaps
because unrecorded—echoed frequently in my head and often found their
way to my thoroughly stream-of-consciousness journal entries. We never
once made arrangements to meet, but I recollect experiencing acute stings
of disappointment on those days when her door was closed. Such stings, I
learned, were at least partially reciprocated. If I had been gone a week, as
sometimes happened, she would reveal a bit of longing on her part by
rebuking me for deserting my usual route. It wasn't until my first revisit in
2012 that she invited me into her house for tea.

Suman's voice and views, her judgments not just of her own society but
of my presence there, are integral to the fabric of *Shiptown*. If Madhu and
Chinu, her age-peers, are coproducers of this book, it may be that Suman
is its muse. In this final segment about gender and neighborhood, I explore
why and how a person wholly peripheral to formal research practices may

become crucially central to emergent understandings. I acknowledge emotional as much as intellectual factors involved in these ephemeral, casual but nonetheless powerfully resonant encounters. I realized rather late, with what was doubtlessly deficient self-awareness, that some of my emotional engagement with Suman must come from my being a person with sons but no daughters, and no grandchildren whatsoever. Moreover, Suman was the same age as my youngest son.

I suspect that to Madhu and Chinu, Suman represented not just a recalcitrant potential interviewee but a female fate they had narrowly escaped themselves: married as a young teen, a mother before twenty, with career options thus foreclosed in a way still normative for rural Rajasthani women. In the brave new world of the twenty-first century a major assault on such inevitability for girls was in the air and on the ground, as more and more young women from the middle castes pursued education and the rainbow's end of a job, with determination. Madhu and Chinu were wholeheartedly committed to that assault and rightly proud of it. They observed my enchantment with Suman a bit perplexedly and could not fathom it.

Because of Suman's perpetual presence, and her unsettling mix of straightforward naiveté with a perspicuity that could be quite subversive, I began to think of her as the "Greek chorus" for my fieldwork. What did I mean by this? That she commented on the action, in summary, pithy ways that furthered my understandings about the world I was trying to gather up into my notes and photographs, through my pores and feelings as well as ears and eyes (Wikan 2012).

Names and naming matter. As a field-worker (and in the classroom, the playground, the academic conference, and so forth), I have always been excruciatingly, embarrassingly bad at remembering faces and therefore at putting faces together with names. This has been a lifelong handicap from which I have suffered almost as much as from having no sense of direction. Now add age: In Jahazpur in 2010, I was already deaf in one ear and becoming increasingly myopic—afflictions which only exacerbated cognitive recognition deficits I have had all my life.

Suman's face, early in my Jahazpur stay, became perfectly familiar to me, but I had trouble with her name. No one introduced us; and I didn't get it down in writing as would have been the case if I had done an interview with her. My uncorrected original journal entries refer to her in more than one erroneous way. I have corrected these errors in the journal excerpts included in this chapter, but to recapitulate their sequence reveals

Figure 11. Portrait of Suman.

the coming into focus of this young woman who gradually became important to me and to my ethnographic work.

When I first arrived in Jahazpur Suman had a babe in arms named
Neelam. Someone must have pointed and told me, "That is Neelam," and
I was confused and thought the young mother's name was Neelam. So my
first journal entries call her that. Like many people in Rajasthan, Suman
had two names: a recorded "school name" and a nickname used by family
and any who have everyday familiarity.[24] Suman's nickname, Samud, was
hardly euphonic, but it was how everyone referred to her, including unre-
lated neighborhood women, most of whom did not know that her name
was Suman. My journal at times employed a reliable route by referring
to her as "Neelam's mother"; but that submergence of a woman into her
reproductive history went against my grain, as did calling her "Mast Ram's
wife." At times I mention Suman and her sister-in-law Maya together as
"the Vaishnav neighbors." In Rajasthani folklore the wives of two brothers
are a fabled pair, often spoken of in hyphenated fashion: *dorani-jethani*.
Suman is the *dorani*—the younger brother's wife.

Listening to Suman

The best method of showing at once Santosh Nagar sociability and the role Suman played in my fieldwork is to use journal extracts, interspersed with explanatory and interpretive commentary. These extracts are unedited except to correct typographical errors in spelling and to replace wrong names with correct ones.[25] I offer them in chronological order.

We arrived in Jahazpur on 5 August 2010. The first reference in my field journal to Suman appears about six weeks later.

25–26 September 2010
I also showed my album [a purse-sized photo album with pictures of my family and home in it] to everyone. I had it in my purse for the Vaishnav girl, younger than Madhu [I compare her to my collaborator Bhoju Ram's daughter], who sits on the stoop with her baby day after day after day. She thinks I should pine for my family but . . . I tried to tell her what email was but she really didn't have the concept.

27 September 2010
This young woman, Madhu's age, I feel she is my conscience. She says to me all the things I need to think to myself:
"Don't you miss your children?"
"Don't you miss your family?"
"When you live in a house like the one in the picture, why would you come here? How can you like this house?"
"Why don't you drink the tap water? We drink it!"
"If I let you talk to me what will you do with it?"
(to this I had an answer): "I will make a book."
"You will get something for it?"
"Yes, I guess."
"What will *I* get?"
I attempt directly to ask her what I can do for her. She says she is joking, but she has penetrated the whole plight of the selfish ethnographer; the conscience. She is my conscience. Eli's age [my youngest son], with a baby, sitting in front of her house and thinking thinking thinking . . . .
I cross her path, by accident, and she thinks about me.

"How can I live when I only take roti once a day?"
and
"Is it possible that the children in America speak English at such a young age?"

By now of course the whole neighborhood knows that we have hired a woman to make us Indian food, but just one meal a day; we cook for ourselves (without bread!) in the evening. To Rajasthanis a meal without bread, however nice it might be, is not actually a meal; it might even be considered a fast.

The question about children able to speak English was one I often got in my earlier village research. Among the rural, less educated the idea that English was purely a school-taught language still prevailed. I include this comment in no way to mock Suman's ignorance but rather to highlight what to me was an extraordinary and unusual contrast between her innate sensibilities, which were so stingingly acute and perceptive, and her naiveté about the wider world for which only her lack of access to education was responsible. I must also acknowledge that this discrepancy was doubtless one source of her charm.

Yet she is very very smart, penetrating, insightful, frightening to me in the way she cuts through the crap.
Suman. What can I do for you??????????

The string of ten question marks following those closing words of my journal entry is surely melodramatic, perhaps expressive of a lazy or contrived postcolonial angst.

The truth is, Suman needed nothing from me. She was happy in her marriage; she had plenty to eat; and while child care and housework certainly kept her busy, she was not overworked, looked very healthy, and usually was cheery. It seemed to me that her only unsatiated hunger was of the mind. She was always looking around for something interesting to feed a restless intelligence. Luckily for me, I passed through her field of vision regularly and she couldn't resist the invitation my presence held: to find out more about the world beyond her quiet town street, her remote village childhood. Glimpses of that world in truth are what she did get out of our relationship. If these were surely less exciting than those readily available on television, they must have been more intimate and real to her, as she elicited them in a personal relationship.

26 January 2011
I stop at the Vaishnavs. Suman's baby, Neelam, cries at the sight of my face, sucks her thumb, stares, and finally stops crying. Suman quizzed me about my job in the U.S. [She listened to my description of my work as a professor; I did my best. Then she delivered her punch line]. Suman says [prettily, sassily]: "*Hamari ek hi naukari: rat ki* ["ours is just one job, the night-job"].
Everyone laughs.
"It is the most important *naukari*," she adds. "They say you in America are trying to stop your population, to make it less; and here we are doing everything to make it greater." [more laughter]

Joking around about sex is daring, but Suman uttered these playful words with her baby in arms and an innocent face. With them she also delivered some astute cross-cultural commentary.

24–25 February 2011 [I had four months left.]
but the specter of return is there
the idea that I will not pass Samud every day or see Neelam with her thumb so firmly jammed in her mouth
last night Samud joked about it, getting Neelam married, and how she would do the *phere* [wedding rounds] with her thumb in her mouth.
Samud, fearing my loneliness [Dan was in Gwalior], yesterday offered that I could sleep with her
my chorus
my reality

Where did that possessive pronoun come from? I was moved at her concern for my well-being because so often she seemed to find me an object of sheer intellectual curiosity. Now I detected gut sympathy. In provincial Rajasthan, a woman of any age hates to be left alone. As I free-associate in my journal, I don't make the rather obvious link between Suman's expression of care for me and my sudden dismay at the finite nature of my residence in her vicinity.

15 March 2011

Suman: she resists when I say that the hot season will be hard for me; she says, "It is hard for me too"; I realize I am only parroting what others say to me; she thinks differently.

Wherein lies this difference? If I could name it, I would have the precise source of my being so taken with Suman's company and words. She began our relationship by interrogating my reasons for being there; now she asserts her own themes and rejects the pedestrian comments of others. In this particular case she insists on shared embodiment. Rather than asserting, as everyone else did, "The hot season [to which *we people* are accustomed] will be very hard for *you*," she simply holds that it is hard for one and all. Suman thus gently but unmistakably chides me, even shames me, for imagining myself of any more delicate a constitution than other humans of Jahazpur.

Suman normally doesn't speak of caste, and women from all kinds of communities will stop to chat with the group in front of her house. Assorted children will also congregate, listen a while, and disperse to their play. We were having a conversation in the street about the upcoming Holi festival and I decided to take advantage of the children to ask them about the festival here in their home neighborhood. Most of the answers were general and predictable: People throw colors, burn Holika at Gandhi Maidan (the neighborhood assembly ground).

15 March 2011

One little girl says, "People drink *daru* [liquor]."

Samud says, "*Your* people might drink daru but my people don't."

I say, "What *samaj* is she?" knowing the answer in advance: Khatik [former butchers, SC].

The Khatik girl holds to her story; "Yes, daru" [she insists with no embarrassment].

I like her tough little face.

Thus Suman delivers a lesson in difference and identity. She does want me to get things straight. And her insistence also affords me the chance of confirming my impression of the Khatiks, which is that they wear their identity, even when among higher castes, without any discomfort.

After Holi, Suman's household holds a *dhundhana* (protection ritual) for both brothers' new babies: the elder brother's son and Suman's daughter.

20 March 2011
The babies squalled a lot; the little boy got all the attention and also the silver ornaments. Neelam, my thumb sucking sweetheart, got new clothes. . . . Suman jokes with me: that Neelam will give up sucking her thumb when she goes to her *sasural* [in-laws' home].
The jokes about sasural-going are frequent.

Unexpectedly, one of the old women present became possessed by Neelam's grandfather's spirit; people asked questions of this spirit. They asked if they had made mistakes. They asked why Suman only gave birth to daughters. I couldn't understand the answers given by the *bhav* [possessed person; typically a bhav blurts out speech that may be slurred or distorted], but their earnest questions brought home to me how troubled the family was by the need for the virile Mast Ram to produce a male heir. And I think about Suman's important "night-job." She made a joke of it, but it is also a burden and a worry that the ancestors are implored to relieve.

There are many other references to Suman and Neelam from my year of Jahazpur journals. Mostly they have to do with the kind of highly trivial everyday interactions already exemplified here. However, two more bits hold larger significance.

In the last month of my fieldwork, the height of the hot season, Suman's husband had entrusted to her the task of supervising the construction of a wall on some farm property not too far out of town. She was intensely engaged in this project. In the middle of June an unexpected and violent early monsoon storm hit Jahazpur hard.

15–16 June 2011
the aftermath of the storm
nukshan [destruction, damage]
Suman told me that the wall on which they had spent 25,000 rupees had blown down, was totally destroyed, a total loss; she had been supervising its construction and all that was left was the gate;
she said she was alone and she and Neelam wept together

her husband had gone to a funeral [in another place]
she said it was *kismat ka lila* [the inexplicable play of fate]
she said "we don't kill ourselves when we lose a human being so we
can't kill ourselves over this," but [added that] her soul was sad.
And she said that she had been joyful over the way it looked; she
was sad I didn't get to see it
It may have been the first thing [beyond home, kitchen and child-
care] over which she had charge; I've never, I realize, seen her serious before. With me she is always joking.

This episode made me aware of Suman's ambition as well as her cosmology,
two aspects of her being with which I had not much previous contact.

Not long afterward came the day of my departure from Jahazpur. When
I went to bid her farewell, Suman displayed one last time her uncanny
capacity to discomfit me sweetly—by calling attention to the disparities
between our lives. This day it was our skewed mobility: "Why do you get
to see the whole world," she ruefully remarked, "when I haven't even seen
Bhilwara!" But then she added a reflective footnote: "Well, I vomit if I even
drive twenty kilometers." Although these words haunted me, I was never
sure how to interpret Suman's comments on my final day of residence in
Jahazpur. Would she like to trade places? Or did she honestly find comfort
in her circumscribed world?

More than a year later, on my first post-fieldwork visit, 23 December
2012, I easily found Suman in exactly the same location. She was pregnant
again.

23 December 2012
Things I must not forget:
My visit to Suman yesterday, I show her my photos of *Amrika*
[deliberate use of Hindi pronunciation] and she exclaimed predictably at the snow ("you wouldn't need a fridge") and at the immod-
est clothes of all the women at my son's wedding—from [my
daughter-in-law] Sarah's aunt to Sarah herself in her lacy see-
through wedding dress.
She thinks my house is good. She notes the distance between houses.
There is something that makes us enjoy one another's company.

I had no notes at all about my meeting with Suman in the winter of 2013,
when I found her the glowing mother of a healthy baby boy. I had brought

her a bracelet, not expensive, but of the type called "friendship bracelet" that was sold by the company my daughter-in-law worked for, catering to youthful tastes. We sat in Suman's kitchen, not on the stoop, and it felt just like old friends catching up on news.

She had about her that sense of completion that, in spite of my wish not to accept it, I can't help but notice in the mothers of sons—especially those who had daughters first! There was a palpable if elusive transformation. Was it a transformation from a feisty, impish femininity to a more fulfilled maternal glow? Certainly she had gained self-confidence. The subtext was: "I did what everyone wanted me to do and I need not be nervous anymore about who I am."

I promised to come again but I was only there a few days and had so many visits to make that I failed to keep my promise. But such promises were never part of our relationship—always free-floating, unplotted, spontaneous. When Suman and I met in 2015 I brought small gifts for her children and for Maya's. Suman exclaimed at the bond between us, and attributed it to the love (*prem*) within her soul (*atma*). I was deeply moved. She and Maya, barely skipping a beat, next grilled me about birth control methods, right down to the best brand of condom.

Power of Proximity

To close this chapter with its double intentions to portray the gendered nature of my fieldwork and the gendered experience of place in Santosh Nagar, I try to analyze what is different between what I learned from countless casual chats with Suman, and from my forty-some recorded and transcribed interviews with other women in my neighborhood. These interviews ranged from superficial and/or awkward to deep, rich, and illuminating. Some developed into intense engagements and complex conversations with three or more women participating. The recorded interviews direct beams of light onto specific topics such as marriage, gender roles, shopping, shrines, schooling, jobs, aspirations. From Suman, I have gathered instead sporadic sparks, bright but momentary: expressive reactions, emotions, critiques. With the interview texts, I select passages from abundant and often repetitive possibilities; I can juxtapose several women's comments on one subject, and show continuities or discontinuities across discrete chunks of discourse. With Suman, a few words contain worlds; they seem precious to me.

Even though interviews of the kind I conduct are never actually scripted, the interview situation itself has a structure. It is mechanically framed by the on and off of the recorder; and it is verbally framed with the preliminary queries: "What is your name? What was your birthplace? How long have you lived in Jahazpur?" The situation with Suman was unscripted, always improvised, and without the skewed power dynamics of even the most relaxed interview situation. It was, after all, Suman who beckoned to me, who put questions to me. If not, I would have walked right past. It was she in fact who initiated the relationship from which I benefitted so much, but which she controlled and enjoyed. I would like to believe that my friendship with Suman was more mutual, less extractive, than interviews.

A slight young woman, she was a presence for me, not just on the street but in my mind. If friendship is for anthropology a bridge between worlds (Grindal and Salamone 2006), and intimacy may be considered as a feminist methodology (Pratt and Rosner 2012), I might locate the pleasure Suman and I took in one another's company somewhere within or between these two related notions. There was an easy delight for me in the casual nature and everyday content of our exchanges. I loved having someone who was no more, and no less, than a neighbor: not an entry on my spreadsheet, not a digital file to be cataloged, transcribed, possessed. Each recorded interview was a kind of burden requiring accounting; also of course each was like "money in the bank." My light-hearted conversations with Suman were a mode of everyday sociability differently valuable.

Suman's singularity lay in her refusal to let me be an anthropologist first and a human being second. She had astute understandings conjoined with deep-seated unarticulated yearnings. In terms of actual "stuff," it may be I learned little from Suman. And yet when I write about women in particular, but also about neighborhoods, space, community, identity, and the ascending value of education, I know I draw from her views. In 2013 Suman showed me that she had put the one photo with us together into a framed assemblage of her family members. She told me with some pride that visitors from elsewhere often pointed to me and asked, "Who on earth is that?" or "Why is she there with your family?" Thus I discover, late in the game, a strand of evident desire to be different—it pleases Suman thus to display a foreign friend; I'm also touched by this inclusion. Suman's voice, unrecorded, echoes in my head and in these pages; my picture resides in her frame. The novelty of my friendship with Suman also contrasts with the taken-for-granted, decades-old kinship I have and cherish with Madhu, Chinu, and their whole family.

The following chapter, "Streets," moves deep into the qasba, where historically chartered proximities also have their consequences, sometimes harsh and sometimes surprisingly replete with affection. Readers will likely find it a rather abrupt transition from the intimacies of Santosh Nagar to the experience of processions that fill the streets inside the walls and spill through to surrounding spaces including the bus stand. These processions, along with other more stationary fairs and displays, demonstrate relationships to place quite other than those negotiated by clusters of women. Public pageantry, however chaotic it may seem when in the midst of it, involves orchestrated efforts by event organizers who belong to committees and must execute fund-raising and arrange for extensive material preparations, including the ever elaborate light decorations, street cleaning, arches, and canopies. They must muster musicians, singers, and other performers; for the physical prowess demonstrations there must be weeks of training and practice. The government in its turn has to muster the forces of control: various uniformed men and women belonging to police and border patrol and assigned the task of "keeping the peace."

In my everyday life as an anthropologist in Jahazpur, especially from September through December 2010, I expended a lot of my personal energy attending to the energies that public expressions of religious identity produced, as well as those behind-the-scenes energies required to produce such expressions. I wanted to understand not just what happened while parades were moving through the town but how they were organized and what people thought about them. I probed delicately but persistently into the histories of tension associated with festival events. Readers lulled by the peaceful, slow-paced trivial pursuits of everyday life in Santosh Nagar will now follow me into the band-blasted scenes of parades. The transition is made easier for all of us in that my first festival was Krishna's birthday and it was not a parade but a gorgeous light show.

Chapter 4

Streets

Everyone Loves a Parade

Janamashtami, Krishna's birthday, arrived on 2 September in 2010. It was my first experience of Jahazpur's exuberant displays of public religiosity. None that followed it left me so intoxicated. From our colony of Santosh Nagar, many people strolled along in groups composed of friends or multi-generational families. Everyone happily answered the sociable query, "Where are you going?" with two words: "*jhanki dekhna*" (to see the *jhanki*). It gave me a simple sense of belonging to repeat this phrase. Jhanki are scenes or tableaux, whether constructed with cardboard or living human bodies, depicting the divine play of Lord Krishna.[1] Janamashtami involved no procession except that of the viewers, who moved along at a pretty good pace from one stationary scene to another, and whose clothing revealed a thorough mix of town and country as well as festival finery. Krishna's birthday party could be enjoyed without the (to me) painful blaring of one or more amplified bands which I would soon learn were insepa-rable from most religious processions.[2]

I was awestruck by the way that lavish light decorations on temple ex-teriors and cloth-covered walkways—fabricated arcades that channeled the viewers from one jhanki to the next—transformed the spaces I was just beginning to recognize on daytime fieldwork and shopping excursions, ren-dering them totally unfamiliar once again. Every Vaishnavite temple in town glittered magnificently. The festival also featured extraordinary pag-eantry. Inside a school building beautiful children, costumed and made-up, posed to represent well-known exploits from Krishna's childhood and youth.[3] The same scene was replicated in multiples so that as many children as possible had a chance to participate.

This chapter, its title only partially ironic, has a dual aim: to explore through ethnography and memory two different but related areas. Based on observations in tangible realms, I describe ways festivals take religion and identity outdoors to public streets and squares. Less tangibly available, but certainly not without external manifestations, are the workings of pluralism and its discontents in the qasba and its environs. Thus this chapter sidles up to pluralism through the lens of public religion, or more precisely of public cultural performances that engage and demonstrate religious identities. I seek also to uncover the tensions, both subtle and gross, that are at times associated with public religion. Historically in South Asia festivals have been linked not only with amiable relations among communities but with occasional virulent outbreaks of violence, and this is true, in a mild way, of Jahazpur as well.[4]

Hence a major aim in this chapter is to portray both tension and peace. I attempt to evoke these at the intergroup and interpersonal levels, using a subtler palette, in a more nuanced fashion, than I was able to achieve in the limited venue of an earlier anthology chapter (Gold 2014a). I include here ethnographic "resonance": slight impressions recorded in my informal field journal that document or bare my raw responses to unspoken tensions and affections. Processions or parades offer a ready entry into these issues because they are bright, loud, and frequent and because they actively if temporarily transform city spaces inside and outside the walls, laying claim to them. In this chapter I shall move back and forth between pleasures and anxieties spanned by public religion in Jahazpur, and between my ethnography based on "being there" in the present, and interviewees' accounts of the past.

My earlier published essay on pluralism in Jahazpur saved the worst for last and discussed Jahazpur's past experience of *danga* (riots) after emphasizing all the dazzling or deafening pleasures, harmonies, and goodwill of the town's present festivals. I reverse that order here. After introducing the phenomenon of public religious displays, I speak of muted tension in the present, contrasting the ways Bhoju and I interpret it. I turn then to the troubles that, significantly enough, began in 1947 and recurred in the mid-1980s—another fraught period of history in modern India. The last substantial segment samples sparingly observations of public religion in Jahazpur during my fieldwork period. In concluding I discuss ongoing ways and means of peacekeeping.

I have found it useful in thinking about Hindu and Muslim relationships in Jahazpur to combine two rather different definitions of pluralism, both of which, while seeming to speak of all societies, not insignificantly emerge from ethnographic and historical research in South and Southeast Asia. One economically elegant view is proposed by Michael Peletz, who defines pluralism succinctly as "difference accorded legitimacy" (2009:7).[5] The other is "living together," which Shail Mayaram has explored extensively in the context of Ajmer, a large Rajasthan city not too far from Jahazpur (Mayaram 2005). In Mayaram's words, living together comprises "shared imaginaries and grammars that are rooted in everyday perceptions of being in the world" (2009: 9).

"Rush Hour of the Gods"

In Jahazpur public religious expressions such as Krishna's birthday— whether fairs, festivals, or processions—all transform everyday places into special sites and sights. They transform visually through the use of light displays, festoons of tinsel, banners, and arches. They alter the experience of place aurally through vocal and instrumental music as well as rhythmic chorused chants. Additional expressions of conjoined devotional feeling and identity may include the distribution of sweets, dressing up in new clothes, tossing flowers, being sprayed with perfumed water. Thus the senses are engaged in multiple fashions, composing a predictably polysensuous experience of a festival day in Jahazpur as elsewhere. Above all, there is an emotional or devotional transformation that happens by introducing emblems of spiritual power, abstract or iconographic, into public space. The most awesome processions all involve such a charged exhibition of power moved just for a day from interior to exterior—whether it is the glittering *taziya* representing an historical moment critical to Islamic history; or the Hindu gods in their very splendid chariots hung with artificial flowers; or the image of an austere Jain Tirthankara seated in a simple golden vehicle.

Processions traverse town streets, temporarily claiming place with feet, flags, and crowds. Of course the number of participants in any given festival varies enormously, depending on its reputation and, it goes without saying, on the communities engaged by it. Processions are opportunities for embodied expressions of collective identity. The Jains, for example, as a prosperous minority all dressed alike for their major fall procession day.

Although their numbers were small, they stood out in their bright designs and homogeneous colors.

While some processions have their origins long ago in Jahazpur's colonial and precolonial pasts, others are relatively new. Moreover, many of the older processions and celebratory events have become significantly more elaborate in living memories. As reported in Chapter 3, the delightfully emphatic Kamala told us that Jal Jhulani Gyaras (Water-Swing Eleventh), the most ambitious and widely attended of the town's Hindu processions, had been going on "since the creation of the universe"—a possible exaggeration. We heard frequently, however, that the number of chariots (*bevan*) participating in Jal Jhulani had dramatically increased over the last few decades, resulting in insufficient space on the banks of the reservoir for bathing all the images in one place. The community Ram Lila was instituted in living memory, and newer still is the opening procession honoring the Tulsidas Ramayana as sacred book. Muslim elders explained to us that the Gaji Pir urs had been taking place for maybe half a century, but that it was not so splendid until fairly recently when a new committee took over the arrangements, raised additional funds, and began to spend more freely on its grandeur.

At the very close of 2010, in late December, a second urs took place to honor the saint to whom Jahazpur's chilla near the Nagdi River was dedicated. As did Gaji Pir's urs described later in the chapter, this additional urs involved a parade, complete with ascetic performers and musicians called from elsewhere to perform qawwali (a stirring genre of Islamic devotional song). Jahazpur residents recollected such an urs from their childhoods, but it had not been celebrated in about a decade. The year I lived in Jahazpur saw the first ever Hanuman Jayanti parade (by which time in the calendar cycle I had turned my attention to other topics and was content to admire Bhoju Ram's photos after the event).

In India's twenty-first century, Jahazpur is far from unusual in its expanding and expansive public religious expressions. It was tempting during the first months of my fieldwork, which coincided with an especially hectic season of fall holidays, to expend energies and attention on nothing but the constant streaming spectacle: parades, collective rituals, attendant commerce. Meera Nanda discusses this phenomenon with staunch secular disapproval in an unrepentantly polemical book. Nanda dubs this "the rush hour of the gods" (2009:63; a phrase she borrowed from a 1967 work by Neil MacFarland about postwar Japan).

Nanda's observations are consonant with my own in Jahazpur with two very important modifications. First, based on my Jahazpur experience, I would question her assertion that some forms of a politically backed Hinduism are inevitably the major perpetrators and beneficiaries of these phenomena. In Jahazpur it is not just Hinduism that is on display. Where other South Asian religions coexist with Hinduism, as is the case in Jahazpur, they also have increased displays and increased claims on public space. Hindus, Jains, and Muslims (as well as many subgroups, including caste lineages and reform sects) are all avidly engaged in producing public festivals that annually increase in cost and splendor. The municipality provided certain basic services for any public religious event, including street cleaning, route marking, and power for the lights. One can't help wondering what the limits might be to this ongoing proliferation. I also modify Nanda's argument that these elaborate or excessive displays are fundamentally intertwined with processes of globalization (influenced by media and economic flows). While this is partially true of Jahazpur, it is also clear that celebrations are rooted in local circumstances, and I suspect this would often be true elsewhere.

My ethnography of processions also differs from that of Eva Ambos and William Sax, who make a rather categorical claim, insisting that "processions are public, embodied displays of political authority. They articulate political and religious power and authority by 'staging' them in a public display in which people and objects move, or are carried, along routes of special significance. . . . The order of the procession is the order of society, along with its hierarchy and its power relations, and by publicly embodying this order, processions create and strengthen it" (2013:27).

I would never deny the work of politics and hierarchy; readers will see plenty of both in this chapter. But there are other factors at work, or play, as well: desire for blessings, enjoyment of entertainment pleasures, even the creation of beauty—an aesthetic stretching from the lovingly meticulous adornment of divine chariots and taziya to the lovingly extravagant dressing up of one's own children. The latter practice crosses all community boundaries. As Chapter 8 will testify, all merchants of ready-made clothing listed Diwali and Id as their best seasons. I prefer not to trivialize these matters nor to subordinate them as epiphenomenal to power. If there are a few festival organizers and attendees with purely political maneuvers in mind, I imagine there are far more participants who genuinely relish the chance to offer a banana, or a few rupees; to lose themselves in devotional song (whether qawwali or bhajan); to leave their chores and jobs for an interlude of holiday pleasures; to seek a blessing.

I also must alert readers to the necessary understanding that in actuality not everyone loves a parade, or loves public expressions of religiosity. Besides those who are enthusiastically involved in the performance of public rituals on festival days, and they are this chapter's central focus, there are others who follow various gurus and paths, embracing quite disparate teachings. Whether such alternative teachings stress an inner meditative life, social uplift, or both, the groups gathered around them might eschew some of the very activities that others most enjoy and value, including the public displays to which this chapter gives pride of place.[6]

One very recent addition to Jahazpur's holiday extravaganzas (one I chose not to examine in detail during fieldwork or in this book) is the Garba dance, vaguely understood to be an import from Gujarat. Garba is performed during the fall Navratri or "nine nights" of the goddess. Most of the participants are middle- and upper-middle-class school children and youth. When we interviewed a renouncer-priest associated with Jahazpur's Narsinghdwara temple, he spoke scathingly of Garba: "It is all *dikhavana* [for the sake of show]. . . . They drink and dance at the Garba, it is mischief (*badmashi*) . . . boys and girls dance together, and they wear skimpy clothes; it is not in our culture! They think, 'Let's go and show that we are *devotees.*' But what are they really?" His implication was all too clear, and his question required no response from us.

I had gone only one night to see the Garba and it appeared quite innocent and well chaperoned to me. My husband, Daniel, who did video shooting there on a different night, agreed that he observed neither drinking nor any kind of misbehavior. But that is beside the point. The priest's attitude revealed a persistent strand of Hindu thought that disparages external practices and displays of religiosity. Regarding festivals in general another interviewee, a Hindu householder, said: "In the old days, we expressed our inner devotion with our traditional celebrations. But these days, we are spending money whether or not we are devoted, to put on a show. It used to be faith (*shradha*) and devotion (*bhakti*). In the present, those feelings are there, but people also think: 'I want to do something in order to show something.'"[7]

One or more of the three of us—Bhoju, Daniel, and I—followed eleven processions during the months of August through December 2010: Jal Jhulani Gyaras (18 September; Hindu); Anant Chaturdashi (22 September, Jain); Agrasen Jayanti (8 October, Jain lineage); opening of Ram Lila (8

October, Hindu); Ram Lila procession to burn Ravana on Dashera (17 October, Hindu); urs of Gaji Pir (24 November, Muslim); RSS (Rashtriya Swayamsevak Sangh; 5 December, Hindu social/political); procession to mark a new priest's possession by Tejaji (16 December, Hindu); Gayatri Parivar *kalash yatra* (17 December, Hindu social uplift); Muharram (17 December, Muslim); urs of Gagaron saint's chilla (29 December, Muslim). All of these involved extensive tours of the town, although the routes taken were not identical.

The course of such exhibitions is literally and deliberately halting. They move forward; then stop to perform song or spontaneous, inspired dance or exhibitions of physical feats, or simply to give devotees time to admire displays and make offerings; then move along again. Only the Muslim processions for the two urs included outside hired performers—notably the *malang*, practiced ascetics who displayed fearsome but evidently painless body piercings. Moreover, at the urs itself were two outside qawwali groups hired from elsewhere. These were exceptions. For most Jahazpur processions and associated events, local talent prevailed.

In all cases, the progress of a procession involves slow passages. Bhoju and I would walk along with them for a time, retreat to a shop for a cup of tea or a rooftop for a different view, and then rejoin without any sense of having missed anything and without any danger of falling behind. I followed the entire course of the processions only for Jal Jhulani, Dashera, Gaji Pir, and Muharram. I watched chunks of all but three of the others. On 8 October I had to be in Jaipur so Bhoju documented the Jain and Hindu processions that day on his own. And I couldn't bring myself to attend the RSS procession, but Bhoju and Daniel went.[8]

An old friend, Shiv Lal Mina, who is among other things a successful speculator in the local real estate boom, lives in a village not far from Jahazpur. When I exclaimed over Janamashtami's splendor, his response was to tell me that Jahazpur's public displays were particularly elaborate because of its unusually large Muslim population. This, he said, inspired competition (he used the English word) between Hindus and Muslims. Festivals are also, as already mentioned, occasions for formal displays of physical prowess, referred to as *akhara* by both Hindu and Muslim communities. Hindu and Muslim parades also at times feature more impromptu youthful "sword rattling," particularly a patterned type of slogan shouting that young men perform, almost jumping with their hands in the air. I was struck by how the body language and the sound rhythms of Hindu and

Muslim youth were nearly identical even though the slogans themselves praised different beings.

Resonance

Uni Wikan (2012) suggests that ethnographers need to rely in part not just on observations and verbal exegesis but on resonance "beyond the words," to intuit meanings that are not necessarily embedded in language. She stresses the importance of feeling and of using one's own sensibilities to learn nonverbally.

My journal entries can be soaked in emotion. Normally when I write academic prose I filter it out, probably wisely. Here, riskily, I shall present original journal notes reflecting my own internal experience of two Jahazpur processions. Remember that for me, already in my sixties, these days out in the streets, in the proximity of crowds soaked in amplified sound, are physically exhausting days of sensory overload. I would usually return to our living space half dazed and more than half deafened (for I only have one good ear and the vibrations from the amplified band music often left me literally, and frighteningly, unable to hear at all for several hours after I got away from it).

I would force myself to go through the mechanical motions of uploading photographs from camera to laptop, then try to give them the minimal preliminary order, making files for the main stations of the parade (Nau Chauk, bus stand, and so forth). Later, at leisure, when rested, Bhoju would help me label individual images. I also forced myself to do the keyboard equivalent of scrawling some cryptic notes to myself. I would not dignify this activity by claiming that I wrote field notes. But I did jot key things so as not to forget—reminders for specific topics I needed to cover on the next day. That is what happened with Dashera.

On the tenth day of the Ram Lila, the theatrical rendition of the epic tale of Ram's victory over the demon Ravana, who has kidnapped his wife, Sita, the actors process to the outskirts of town where Ravana will be defeated and burned. The Ram Lila procession had once been the occasion for a stone-throwing incident, as I will relate later in the chapter. This year, however, it was formally welcomed by one of the Muslim committees who—in a fashion completely similar to that of several Hindu groups—erected a fancy cloth and wire archway. Their sign used distinctively

Urdu words, although written in the common Indic script. It read: "Gaji-community Society heartily welcomes you," and was signed by two Muslim businessmen, both of whose names revealed that they belonged to Pardeshi, not Deshvali, groups as I might have expected; one was Pathan and one Mansuri. With that much background, I offer raw resonance. I jotted fragments on 17 October, the day of the events; then on the morning of 18 October I wrote the following, still very rough impressions. These are as much filled with my inner life as with the world I am trying to observe.

notes on Dashera jalus (procession) 17 October 2010 made the next day, 18 October
When we began I was in a kind of ecstasy, the charm of the actors, the hustle to get out of the temple, the unexpected rain; there did seem genuine anxiety about being late and I only recollected later the whole police and timing thing and the need to pass through [mosque gate] before the call to prayers . . .

But the truck with Ram, Laskhman, and Hanuman on it seemed so charming;

and the crazy old man with the backpack dancing his devotional energy was also nice and the Darbar Band was not so loud . . . .
So we processed; but then as the border of "Pakistan" [as some Hindus refer to the Muslim neighborhood] approached, the young people began chanting; Bhoju told me they were chanting about the temple [in Ayodhya]—which turned out to be a false assumption on his part
when we got closer [we realized] they were chanting:
chandan mala [garland of sandalwood] something Raghunath something . . . .
anyway it was an innocent chant but it sounded like the kind of chant people do in aggressive protests.
Bhoju was tense; he transmitted it to me; we were right in the neighborhood where the so-called danga (riot) took place, char hathari; it was years ago; these young chanters would have been little kids [Doing the math after the fact I must amend this to: not yet born]; they were all "under 24"

Figure 12. Dashera procession passes through Hanuman Gate; chariot carrying
embodied deities Ram, Lakshman, and Hanuman on their way to defeat
and burn the demon Ravana.

then we came to a Muslim welcome arch [a cumbersome but light-
weight structure of cloth and wire]
I saw it shaking
I was afraid the Hindus were pushing it over disrespectfully
I felt like weeping
but in fact they were moving it aside, as they had later to move other
arches [from Hindu organizations], so the truck could pass through.
It was set aside.
. . . .
yet the tension was in the air, and then it dispersed,
and then there were fireworks, and then Ravana burned and then
we went home
but my own state of mind was altered, I can feel the tears even now,
the reason is that the charm of Ram's story, the fable, the legend,
the sweet delight of victory; all of it has been corrupted somehow

hopelessly by the true forces of evil who are not Ravana at all but the politicians exploiting the emotions of the people and the people's love for their mythic narratives. This grieves me almost beyond endurance
back at Bhoju's house, the girls hadn't even gone out; they had instead fixed another delicious meal, and everyone watched the ravanas from all over the country burn on TV.

One thing that is revealed here is something about the influence of rumor (Brass 2003)—that is, Bhoju's nervous misinterpretation of the chant certainly was a factor in compounding my fear and imbuing the shaking of the welcome arch with ominous implications.

Another journal entry harks back to my distress at Dashera even though I wrote it almost two months later, on 24 November, after the first day of the three-day urs for Gaji Pir, the most important Muslim saint (although not the only one) buried in Jahazpur. I was emotional during this procession *not* because of communal tensions, which seemed genuinely nonexistent. Rather, I had heard that the Muslim community had just lost a daughter, a college girl, to "fever" (malaria? typhoid?). Somehow I put together my recollected distress from the Dashera tension with my distress on this day and in some ways attributed both the distress and its alleviation to the collective effervescence that is the essence of public religion.

24 November
Twice in the context of processions I have been suffused with grief. Why?
In the Ravana procession it happened when the Hindu youth moved the Gaji arch . . . then, yesterday, when I heard of the 21 year old girl student's death from fever, fever! in Udaipur hospital; she had gone from one hospital to another, and died in Udaipur, the daughter of someone well-to-do in the Muslim community
my heart quailed!
I felt there couldn't be a celebration; they were in the cemetery; now they are in the streets [as it was expressed to me]; I wanted to weep . . .
but then the band the crazy sword play the masses of excited kids; all of it took me into another place
is that what it's for?

to forget grief
Gaji Pir fought without his head[9]
is that what humans must do to stay alive in the face of intolerable
loss that is the human condition?

I find myself willing to bare these written scraps not in the least to imply
that they offer an undistorted portrait of community relations in the qasba.
Nor do I imply that my private universalizing reflects Jahazpur residents'
own understandings of the purpose of festival. Rather, I stress an outsider
position here. What these entries may be able to convey are a soft-minded
foreigner's momentary sensings that reach, as Wikan puts it, "beyond the
words."

At Dashera I know that the unspoken tension was not imagined; others
confirmed it later as disturbing even while quickly brushing it off as fleeting
and inconsequential. At the urs, the community was aware of their loss,
some having come from the funeral rites. Not one person spoke to me of
that sorrow during the procession; not even when I eventually gave up
trying to stay in a gender-free zone and joined the women wrapped in
shawls to relax and listen to qawwalis.

I argue that both these sensings—of Hindu resistance to Muslim cor-
diality and of grief set aside to celebrate a saint's death anniversary—which
is called, literally (figuratively?), a "wedding"—offer insights dependent on
my being there, in the streets, absorbing the intense ambiance both physically and psychologically. I might therefore trust these insights as I trust my
skin, which is permeable, vulnerable (and at times develops minor cancers
caused, I am told, by the sun).

Dissonance

In a recent article focused on Bhoju's and my particular collaborative
chemistry, we considered not just the satisfying moments of fusion and
discovery but also those moments when we rub each other the wrong way,
producing friction. There were occasions in Jahazpur, when we would dis-
agree, sometimes fiercely. I argue that such friction can be generative of
new understandings (Gold, Gujar, Gujar, and Gujar 2014).

One of two main areas in which we saw things differently was that
of intercommunity relationships expressed in public religion. In an earlier

publication I have testified to a festive and benign pluralism (Gold 2014a). Bhoju more readily found tension. I expect both of us are right some of the time, and that in our excesses we may correct one another through a kind of generative friction.

In discussing research in Jahazpur, Bhoju frequently uses the word *mahaul*, which translates as "atmosphere," and he characterizes Jahazpur's mahaul as one of tension:

> [He writes]: In Jahazpur as a research field, whether you take a social perspective or a political perspective, there are many differences you must take into account. It is a *sensitive* research field. In Jahazpur, whenever there is any public festivity, whether Hindu or Muslim, there are always arrangements for both the police and the army to attend the entire event. No disturbance ever actually happens, but there is an atmosphere of tension that remains. Both of the major religious traditions hold very elaborate festivals and celebrations; these are done in a competitive spirit because these groups feel a kind of rivalry and try to outdo one another in their festivals.
>
> . . . .
>
> There are multitudes of processions and they all take place in an atmosphere of competition and tension. (Gold, Gujar, Gujar and Gujar 2014:348)

My own essay on fall festivals in Jahazpur, titled "Sweetness and Light: The Bright Side of Pluralism in a Rajasthani Town" (Gold 2014a), was explicit in taking a brighter view. There I also mention police presence, but I describe it as muted, almost gentle. The following passage specifically treats the [Hindu] festival of Jal Jhulani Gyaras, when chariots process from every Vaishnavite temple in town to the water for a bath and home again. This is one of Jahazpur's most ambitious Hindu festivals.

> I heard that ours was the second best procession in the district. The feeling was good. People told us that when the lead chariot passed through Mosque Gate it could have been an opportunity for tension, but it was not. . . .
>
> The omnipresence of police at festivals is due to our town's official classification as "sensitive" (*sanvedanshil*): a place where trouble

can happen. Yet in such spectacles I have found both formal and
informal indications of living together. . . . This does not mean that
[qasba culture] is invulnerable to rupture.

As already related, it was Bhoju's own close friend Shiv Lal Mina who
used the English word "competition" in talking to us about how splendid
were the spectacles displayed in Jahazpur's public religious celebrations.
While Bhoju gives a negative spin to this, discussing in one breath "competition" and "tension," for me such rivalry seemed positive, amiable, sport-
ing. I responded to Bhoju's use of the term "competition," citing Shiv Lal's
comment and concluded in the article that "each community works harder
and spends more to create vivid spectacles. Others we questioned confirmed this more or less friendly rivalry understood to result in a public
good (eye candy)." I also observed that Bhoju and I while acknowledging,
"the same circumstances, the same police, the same possibility of rupture,"
present these elements differently when writing separately (Gold, Gujar,
Gujar, and Gujar 2014:349).

So shall I ascribe my nonverbal sense of violent potential at Dashera to
Bhoju's dark apprehensions? I suppressed these deliberately, if not exactly
consciously, in my earlier essay on festivals. Nothing is more contagious
and too often unfounded than fear in a crowd. But there is also a matter of
susceptibility: after all, we had been interviewing about danga.

Stones in the Pool of Love

As far as we are willing to give credence to collective memory, Jahazpur
was historically a place where *prem* (love) prevailed between Hindu and
Muslim. Elders from both communities readily and eagerly spoke of mutual
regard and of shared cultural histories. But the sense of rupture was also
regularly expressed. As one old Hindu man put it: "In the past, Muslims
and Hindus lived like brothers; they had affection (*prem bhav*) for one
another, but now it isn't like that, a stone fell into this love." He was not
alone among seniors in proffering a nostalgic narrative of love. I use the
term "nostalgia" not to imply deluded romanticization but rather to imply
yearning, though the two may be inseparable. I believe these speakers
because of the unguarded looks I saw cross their rugged faces, the ways

their eyes lit up, the ways their voices were infused with some surge of emotion. This too is resonance.

That "stone" in the pool of affection was the impact of danga. *Danga* is the term everyone employed when speaking of either two or three painful moments of Hindu-Muslim friction universally viewed as blemishes on qasba history, wounds that had closed over but left scars. *Danga* means "riot," but I never heard the English word used, which seems somehow significant. Only two of the three danga had involved actual destructive action, but the first, in dramatizing the possibility of trouble where there had been none before, was paradigmatic.

Conflict's imbrication with festival is widespread, taken for granted. Yet I also need to emphasize Jahazpur residents' insistence on their basically pluralistic, peaceful community, a community persisting in spite of past ruptures and present instances of tension. In this segment I probe the remembered past, examining divisive, even violent moments that intersect tangentially or crucially with public festivals. Many historians of South Asia have documented the ways processions in diverse localities have often provided flashpoints for violence. The admixture of crowds and heightened emotion evidently provides a volatile chemistry. (Durkheim was on target about certain things.) Jahazpur is no exception.[10]

More than a decade ago, a number of political scientists based in the United States turned their attention to communal violence in India. Among them, Ashutosh Varshney was perhaps the most influential. The specific puzzle Varshney addressed was why some places are able to keep the peace while others, under pressure, erupt.[11] Varshney analyzes data across contexts to think about which urban conditions might be conducive to peacekeeping and which render a town or city more susceptible to outbreaks of violence between religious communities. Some observations about Jahazpur mesh pretty well with some of his suggestions. I judge Jahazpur to lie on the more auspicious end of the violence-prone/peace-prone continuum. Jahazpur had, and still has, plenty of "everyday forms of engagement" (Hardgrave 2001:97) linking Hindus and Muslims. And, as we have seen in passing, Jahazpur possesses in good measure what some call "cross-cuttingness"—a business world in which Muslims and Hindus are thoroughly intermeshed (Laiten 2001:101).

There is still a limited amount (less than in the past, I was told) of intercommunity socializing at life cycle events and holidays. Muslim shrines, especially Gaji Pir, are respected, visited, and prayed at by Hindus.

Given the strictures of their theology, Muslims may be more reticent about respecting the unseen powers that people the Hindu world, but I gathered a few bits of evidence that at least some do, some of the time (albeit the less educated).[12] The Ajmer shrine of Garib Navaz, several hours' journey from Jahazpur and located in the heart of a densely populated, traffic-clogged city, was named by Hindus and Muslims alike as a very important regional pilgrimage site, a must-see.

To the best of my knowledge Jahazpur had no "associational forms of engagement" (Varshney 2002) established in the qasba that predated the governmental peacekeeping processes imposed after the disruptions of the 1980s, to which I will turn briefly at the close of this chapter. In Varshney's schematics, where associations already were in existence along with every-day engagement, their presence augured significantly for a community's ability to deflect and control outbreaks of interreligious enmity and vio-lence, to nip them in the bud.

In Jahazpur there is overlap, not overly competitive, in the market, where Hindu shops dominate. For example, there are Muslim-owned businesses—including grocery stores, shoe stores, bangle sellers, photo studios—purveying goods that overlap with those marketed by Hindus. In addition, Muslims are the only source of cotton quilts and pillows (locally made) and run the only store fully dedicated to the kind of sparkling or colorful trim that Rajasthani women love to sew onto their wraps (the Garib Navaz Gota Center). The vast majority of mechanics and tire repair experts lining the Devli road are Muslim.

I turn now to episodes when the delicate fabric of living together wore thin in Jahazpur. In addition I relate the more obscure story of an old murder case as presented by one Hindu and one Muslim. This case was also connected, after the fact, with festivals and serves to show how eco-nomic tensions may get tangled with religion; yet even retrospectively, nar-rators tend to keep economic motivations quite separate from religious surroundings.

Proto-Danga at the Time of Partition

Depending on who is speaking, Jahazpur town experienced two, or three, danga. We gathered many confused reports of both dates and causes for these so-called riots. According to some, the town's troubles begin, significantly enough, in 1947. We recorded interviews with approximately twenty-five persons who told about Jahazpur's two well-remembered danga from the 1980s; only four mentioned the 1947 event. They were all Hindu men, all over sixty, from different communities and positions in the social hierarchy.[13] Those who brought up 1947 used the word *danga*, but it was not a riot by definition in any telling. Yet, although there was no actual fighting, not a single physical encounter and no destruction of property, this event augured something. It marked the first occasion when anxious enmity between Jahazpur's two major religious communities was publicly, collectively experienced.

Prabhu Lal Soni (interviewed 31 December 2010) gave one of the fullest accounts of the occasion, which he had witnessed as a child. Bhoju asked him, simply, "Was there a riot [*dango*, the Rajasthani form of the noun] in 1947?"

> *Prabhu Lal Soni*: Yes, a riot happened (*dango ho gyo*). Here is how it happened: there was a temple, still is today, near Kalyanji Well; and there was a pipal tree near that temple. So the Muharram procession was coming, and the *taziya* was built kind of tall; so they cut [a branch] off of it [the pipal tree].
>
> *Bhoju*: Did they ask for anyone's permission before they cut it?
>
> *Prabhu Lal Soni*: So, it was the king's agent (*hakim*).[14] He gave them permission; he was standing right there while they cut the branch. [He added parenthetically, for our benefit as persons who wouldn't have lived in that era:] Just like these days we have a magistrate and a tehsildar, at that time there was a hakim.
>
> Then the townspeople thought, "Oh no! they cut the branch of the temple tree!" [Bhoju clarifies: "The rumor went around."]
>
> Then they sent five drums up to the top of Malaji's hill.[15] And when they started to beat the five drums at Malaji, then the people of the twelve hamlets [that is, the Mautis Minas; see Chapters 4 and 5], from all around, got the idea that there was some terrible danger in Jahazpur. So they came quickly toward the town. They came running. Some had spears, some had sticks, some had rifles, some had swords and axes—but they all

came running. Everyone assembled at Chavundia Mother [the
goddess temple at the foot of the hill, tended by Mina priests].
    And the hakim [the one who gave permission] was very
upset, realizing that there was now a terrible danger.

Note the echo of the words "terrible danger"; first for the surmise of the
Minas that there must be a dire reason to beat the drum; then again for the
realization that comes over the hakim as he considers that he may have
personally been responsible for unleashing here, under his watch so to
speak, the possibility of Hindu-Muslim violence, which at this time is happening in a fearsome fashion at flashpoints throughout the subcontinent.

> *Prabhu Lal Soni*: The Muslims fled. They went up and over Gaji
>   Pir's hill and fled into the jungle (on the other side).[16] Every
>   one of them left their homes and ran, no one remained, not
>   even a child!
> *Bhoju*: So the drum was beaten, and the Minas came, and then the
>   Muslims ran away?
> *Prabhu Lal Soni*: There were some police, the hakim was there, and
>   at first they prevented the Minas from entering Jahazpur. But
>   the Minas declared, "We shall either die or kill!" (*mar jaenge ya
>   mar denge*). And they also announced throughout the town
>   that Hindus should not wear caps, but *pagari* (small
>   turbans)—so we know who is Hindu. And Hindus should not
>   wear pajamas, they should wear dhotis—so we know who is
>   Hindu and who is Muslim. No Hindu should cover his butt
>   with pajamas, he should wear a dhoti! [Presumably this advice
>   was spread via the town crier, an official position in those days
>   before Twitter, that usually went to a member of the Balai
>   community (Gold and Gujar 2002: 120–21).]
>   I was very small, but we children were all watching. A whole
>   lot of people came. There was such a long line of Minas. They
>   came in from Hanuman Gate and went into the market all the
>   way up to Galgatti; and then they started to move toward the
>   Muslim neighborhood.[17]
> [The entire bazaar is spanned by this line of Minas with weapons
>   who have entered through Hanuman Gate, and proceeded
>   through Nau Chauk, and Delhi Gate into the qasba. To a qasba

child, from an artisan caste, albeit Hindu, the sight of all those Minas with weapons was doubtless impressive if not downright scary.]

But then the hakim presented himself in front of the Mina leaders. He prostrated himself, putting his head at their leaders' feet, at the feet of the Minas. He touched their feet and implored, "Please don't go in their neighborhood, I am begging for forgiveness! What happened, it happened, now please don't do anything."

To appreciate the story's drama at this moment, readers must realize that abject pleading, physical prostration, self-blame, and humility are all behaviors totally out of character for a hakim, who is normally haughty and commanding.

> *Prabhu Lal Soni*: The Minas answered: "We won't do anything but we want to go to the temple and look at the pipal tree." So they came to the temple and saw it [only a branch had been cut after all] and came back to Nau Chauk.[18] And the hakim arranged for them to eat *karhi puri* [karhi is a thick nutritious sauce made with buttermilk, chickpea flour, and spices; puri are deep-fried breads served at feasts, thus special], and so they ate that meal, and returned to their homes in the twelve hamlets.
>
> *Bhoju*: So who had that food prepared for them?
> *Prabhu Lal Soni*: The Hakim Sahab.
> *Bhoju*: Was that the first time anything like that happened?
> *Prabhu Lal Soni*: [emphatically] Yes, the first time!
> *Ann Grodzins Gold*: Before this there were no problems?
> *Prabhu Lal Soni*: No, there were absolutely no problems before this.
> *Bhoju*: It must have been the *tension created by partition.
> *Prabhu Lal Soni*: Marsab [respectful address to a school teacher], the times had changed (*jamana badal gaya*)!

Prabhu Lal Soni related this account with the vivid and doubtless selective memories of a child who has witnessed rare and disturbing events. Thus we learned from him that in 1947, just around the dual critical juncture of Independence and Partition, Jahazpur experienced, for the first time ever, a Hindu-Muslim disturbance. I use that bland word deliberately. The tale has something of the quality of a fable. Perhaps significantly, it involves both of the hilltop shrines—Malaji which is Hindu, but ST Hindu; and Gaji Pir belonging to local Muslims—that frame Jahazpur as a plural place (and that continue today to serve as tree-protecting powers; see Chapter 6).

To recapitulate the story: it was Muharram, and the Muslims were processing with their taziya, as they do today. Taziya represent shrines dedicated to the martyrs Hasan and Husain, who are mourned during the entire month of Muharram in the Islamic calendar. This month culminates in various parts of the Muslim world in processions bearing elevated replicas of the martyrs' tombs. Jahazpur Muslims universally identify themselves as Sunni. Muharram is an important occasion for them, but it is celebrated without those displays of mourning, weeping, and self-flagellation that are associated with Muharram when Shi'a communities perform it in other parts of India and elsewhere.[19]

I don't know what the taziya looked like in 1947. Today it takes the form (from top to bottom) of a huge orb paneled with different colors of glass, mirrored and sparkling, raised over a square or rectangular base, often with multiple layers which looked vaguely to me like the stories of a house. These included an accessible open receptacle for offerings (fruit, cash, flowers, boxes of incense, and so forth). Many decorations, especially artificial flowers, adorn the taziya. While taziya are explicitly defined as "replicas" of the tombs of the Karbala martyrs, these Sunni taziya in Rajasthan have little of the funereal about them.

In 2010 Bhoju and I observed the first Muharram quite exhaustively, staying with the procession from its departure from Nau Chauk in the early afternoon into the dark evening, when it culminated in a farmer's field designated as Jahazpur's "Karbala"—the site of the deadly siege and battle—some ways out of town.[20] By then the huge crowds had dwindled to very few, among whom I was the sole female. In 2013 I was not engaged in research, but I happened to be visiting on the day of the taziya's procession for the second Muharram and got to see it once again.[21] On both occasions I noted that some members of the procession go in advance of the taziya itself, carrying large forked prongs to raise up electrical and telephone wires that would otherwise impede the progress of the colorful, mirrored orb. Thus I have a clear visual image of the tall taziya's way being prepared from above as intrinsic to the procession's progress.

Figure 13. Taziya in procession at Muharram; wires must be lifted
to enable its passage.

As we just heard, in 1947 it was not a power wire but the branch of a
pipal tree, sacred to Hindus, obstructing the taziya's path. A hakim, local
agent of royalty, thoughtlessly gave official permission to Muslims to cut
the branch (an action he soon came to rue).[22] According to all tellers, after
this violation of Hindu religious sentiment, the Minas—whose recent shift
to settled lives as farmers had evidently not obliterated their former role
as fierce fighters, whether guards or highwaymen—resume their martial
identities in this apparent emergency. Upon hearing the drum, or multiple
drums, sound from the top of Chavundia hill, the Minas pour into town,
bearing as weapons whatever tools they could quickly put their hands upon;
Muslims flee.

There is an evident glitch in the logic of this narrative sequence because
if Muslims had truly emptied their neighborhood, as Prabhu Lal Soni
insisted they had, the hakim's extreme nervousness would seem inexplicable. He might have feared looting and a subsequent cycle of repercussions,
or feared the Minas would give chase to the fleeing Muslims. Or this story

may be replete with fantasy and/or hyperbole. Still, we know that something happened in 1947 that was the first stone in the pool of love, an intimation of tension.

Terrifying reports of deadly Hindu-Muslim conflict all around the nation must have reached Jahazpur via radio and newspaper. These would account for the hakim's own terror and his willingness to prostrate himself and cough up money to feast a great crowd of uncouth and doubtless lean and hungry farmers. For the first time ever a specter of violence loomed in Jahazpur's small and hitherto peaceful qasba. Times had indeed changed.

In Chapter 2 I briefly sketched the composition of Jahazpur's Muslim population and pointed out that the Deshvalis were happy to speak of their similarities to Hindus, from whom they knew they sprang. Particularly disturbing in the recollections we recorded of this 1947 proto-danga was the emergent use of sartorial identity markers, elaborated in Prabhu Lal Soni's account.[23] His childhood memories, like all memories, were doubtless selective and influenced by retellings across the years. But hearing the shouted instructions to Hindus not to dress like Muslims clearly impressed him and stayed with him. The vividness is persuasive and seems to mark a moment of psychological rupture. We surmise that at least males belonging to the two different religious communities in the 1940s did not necessarily always distinguish themselves from one another in their dress; otherwise there would have been no need for such directions to be articulated.

1984 and 1989

There was not another serious disturbance between religious communities in Jahazpur for about thirty-five years. Two incidents in the 1980s left the town reeling and stigmatized right into the present. Jahazpur today is still labeled a sensitive (*sanvedanshil*) area where peaceful relationships among groups requires constant orchestration through various government interventions, to which I will turn at the close of this chapter.

In 2010 it had been over two decades since Jahazpur had experienced any major disorder. Yet I was struck by how vividly collective memory lingers, with a bad aftertaste, even if many got the dates and precise details wrong. A local journalist, Dinesh, the son of a retired journalist, helped me to organize contradictory oral accounts into an orderly list. Jahazpur citizens have experienced danga involving property damage, police action, and the imposition of curfew just twice in a way that impacted everyday life on a memorable scale. These episodes occurred in 1984 and 1989. The 1984 event was not directly connected with a festival; the trouble in 1989 involved both Muharram and the Ram Lila procession on Dashera. Significantly, casually elicited oral histories often placed both "riots" from the 1980s in a festival context: that is, multiple interviewees associated the 1984 disturbance with a procession, even though it actually was precipitated by what may have been an accidental injury at a local cricket match, or simply an unruly boy's bad behavior. The story of the photographer's murder, also related below and also set in the 1980s, shows how narrative links may be forged between festivals and tensions even when the precipitating event has nothing to do with religious identities.

In the 1980s the Hindu right was attempting with considerable success to stir up trouble everywhere in the nation with the accelerating Ramja-nambhumi movement.[24] Thus, as in 1947, so in the 1980s the historical context was a time of heightened national tension between religious communities. Without external influence it seems unlikely Jahazpur would have experienced such trouble, but clearly the town was not immune.

The dangas that took place in Jahazpur in 1984 and again in 1989 both resulted in memorable police action and administrative crackdowns: beating of perpetrators and enforcing of a curfew that was true punishment for all Jahazpur citizens but especially for shopkeepers, Hindu and Muslim alike. Shopkeepers explicitly stated that even today the aftermath of these quarter-century-old troubles continues to have a lingering impact on local business.

In 1984, a Muslim boy injured a Hindu boy in the course of a cricket game; both teams were mixed. Rumors spread and were distorted; disturbances followed, resulting in significant property damage and a curfew imposed on the town. The most detailed and I believe the most trustworthy description we elicited came from Dinesh. Here is his account:

> So in 1984, in Gandhi Maidan [open field where various events take place, located in Santosh Nagar] some boys were playing cricket; the teams were mixed, there were Hindus and Muslims on both teams. But a Muslim boy struck a Hindu boy, with a sword (*talvar*) [who knows what he was doing on the cricket field with a sharp weapon] and nearly cut off half his arm. That boy was taken to the hospital; he needed ten or twelve stitches.

Rumors ran through the town: "His hand was cut, his hand was cut," and so the gossip spread.

People started to gather, groups of Muslims and of Hindus; and they started to scuffle with one another, inside the city, whenever one group saw another group.

This was after the boy was hospitalized.

Hindus started to beat Muslims. A few people were wounded in the fight. Then some started to set fires.

And those Muslim stores in Hindu neighborhoods and those Hindu stores in Muslim neighborhoods were broken into and looted. . . . After this there were two or three days of total curfew. After three days they gave relief for a few hours a day so you could go out and shop and return home. That partial curfew continued for another five or six days.

And the secretary of the municipality was terminated from his job and other officials were suspended. They weren't doing a good job putting out the fires or controlling the danga. The police beat the journalists, and the journalists protested! The police were not local, and they beat anybody who came their way. After five or seven days, little by little, the atmosphere (*mahaul*) cooled down.

Our interviews often reached the painful subject of Jahazpur's danga by a somewhat circuitous route. I quote here from a conversation with a Brahmin shopkeeper, Sri Krishna Niketan (known to us as "Lovely" after the name of his store). We began by speaking of the Garba dance, mentioned earlier, a nightly event throughout the Nine Nights of the goddess (Navaratri) festival which was currently in full swing. It took place just outside the Hindu temple known as Ashapurn Mataji (Wish-Fulfilling Mother), located right on the edge of Jahazpur's Muslim neighborhoods. As already indicated, the Garba was not totally approved of in Jahazpur by some conservative Hindus. Bhoju wondered out loud if the temple's location on the edge of the Muslim neighborhood had drawn any objections from local Muslims, as the music for all nine nights was terribly loud.

Lovely, evidently a fan of the Garba, replied emphatically: "No, not in the least! Muslims also come to watch it!" He added that at Id and during the entire month of Ramadan, Muslims use loudspeakers all day and Hindus don't object, so why would Muslims object to just nine nights! He reiterated with emphasis: "We both use loudspeakers and nobody objects."

Bhoju then inquired, "These days it is so peaceful, but has it been that way ever since 1989?" Lovely's answer reveals his interests as a merchant and his nature as an even-tempered man.

Exactly! because people were beaten so badly, and curfew was imposed. Now everyone knows what kind of punishments you get for misbehavior, so no one does anything.

In 1989 there was a curfew, and even Ratan Lal Thambi, the MLA [member of the legislative assembly], was beaten by the police because they had no idea who was the MLA! It happened that he came out of his house and they started to beat him!

At that time he lived in the market. . . . He was from Pander and just renting in Jahazpur. So he stepped outside and the police grabbed him and beat him!

Yes, there was a danga, but in Jahazpur no one beat one another; no murder, no knife, and they call it "danga"; nobody hit anyone; no one even slapped anyone—but still they call it "danga"! [uttered with a combination of regret and sarcasm] But really it was just some shops; Hindus set some Muslim shops on fire and Muslims set some little shops belonging to Hindus on fire. So they set these things on fire. And then there was a curfew.

There was no murder, no violence, there are no records of a single person injured or murdered.

Jahazpur is a very old city and a dharmic place and it was once called Yagyapur.

It seems important to note that Lovely, in evoking Yagyapur, evokes not pitilessness but dharma—that is, morality.

It is again from Dinesh that we heard the most detailed and coherent description of the 1989 danga. It seems there were two distinct confrontational moments both involving annual festival processions: Hindus carrying bricks as part of the nationwide Ramjanambhumi movement tangled with the taziya procession; later Muslims threw stones at the Ramayana procession as it traversed their neighborhood at Dashera. Eventually stores were burned (but never within the main market) and again a severely enforced curfew was imposed.

Then in 89 the Ramjanambhumi matter had become very intense (*tez*). They were doing brick worship in Gautam Ashram.

And after the brick worship, Hindus were carrying bricks to their homes. This was at the same time that the Muharram procession was taking place.

So in the evening, near Takiya Mosque (located just inside the qasba gates), there was a confrontation.

But elders from both sides came and calmed down both sides, and things were peaceful.

However, a few days later came the day of Dashera. And on that day, the procession was on the way to Barah Devra to burn Ravana. When they reached the crossroads (Char Hathari) Muslims started to throw stones at the procession.

The riot began in that very place. Muslims threw stones down from their roofs, and Hindus threw them back.

The police and the administration just watched, as if they were watching a show!

After that, just outside Hanuman Gate, there was a cabin [a small shop] belonging to a Muslim, and the Hindus set it on fire.

And after that, Hindus went in different directions, in small groups, and everyone started fighting with one another, and the riot spread.

In the night, some Muslims threw hand-bombs [home-made hand grenades] at Hindu houses.

And someone opened fire; and one bullet struck a wall and ricocheted back and hit a Brahmin in the head, and he had to go to the hospital in Ajmer. This happened near the Kalyanji temple. So the bullet hit the wall of the temple. After that curfew was imposed.

After that there was always tension. At every holiday, people remained nervous. The curfew lasted for five or six days, and customers from outside Jahazpur took their business elsewhere.

Readers may be startled, as was I, that Dinesh's account contradicts the often repeated theme that no one hurt anyone and not a drop of blood was spilled. Not one other interview among the twenty-five mentions a gunshot. Even here the bullet is described as hitting a wall directly and a person only indirectly.

Prabhu Lal Kairathi was an old lathe-working carpenter. He had this to say about the 1989 danga:

Ten or fifteen years ago, there was a *danga*. The police beat the rioters so badly that they still remember; they have new skin on their butts; the beating broke their skin so badly that even now it hasn't fully grown back! Nowadays there is peace.

The police beat Hindus too. The riot happened in Char Hathari on the day of Dashera. Muslims threw stones at the Ramayana procession. [This corroborates Dinesh's basic outline.]

None of the elders participated! But the new generation are hoodlums. They are the ones who caused the trouble. But at the time of the disturbance, everyone was punished, whether they had committed a crime or not. The police beat everyone and there was a fifteen-day curfew . . . people lost business for a month!

In the many accounts we heard of 1984 and 1989 details were often quite fuzzy. No one named instigators. In fact, the only name of a living person that came up repeatedly in multiple tellings was that of a powerful, near legendary (although still living), and widely hated local political leader, Ratan Lal Thambi. Whether carelessly, or falsely believing in his own immunity, Thambi, as the story went, happened to step out his front door at the wrong moment, breaking the curfew. He was roundly beaten by the police who apparently neither knew nor cared who he was.

Noteworthy is that many accounts of police action emphasized merciless beatings of perpetrators and innocent bystanders. The police punished Muslims and Hindus alike. The police succeeded in demonstrating effectively that the government would not tolerate violent expressions of communalism and that it was on no one's side but that of civil society.[25]

In conversing with another Brahmin, Kailash Pancholi, Bhoju began by asking him about the welcome arch the Muslims had put up for the Ram Lila/Dashera procession (the one that had been shaken and had shaken me). Bhoju queried Kailash as to whether this arch was evidence of Muslim goodwill. He responded:

Kailash: The troublemakers are not *all* the Muslims, just 1 or 2
  percent, who are prone to anger, and they are all young men.
Bhoju: Deshi or Pardeshi?
Kailash: [avoiding the labels] They are the people who live around
  Char Hathari: they are the troublemakers!

Kailash highlights the distinction between most Muslims and the few prone to anger. He went on to characterize the majority of Muslims using not just neighborhood but civic involvement and education, stating, "The ones who live near the mosque, they all want peace, and they are ward members. Literate people always want peace." (If only this were true, I have to exclaim, from the cynical place of the USA in 2016.)

Following up on what others had told me, I asked Kailash about the bad impact of danga on Jahazpur market. He agreed:

> *Kailash*: People read this in the newspaper, and they think that
> Jahazpur is the kind of place where there are always riots. But
> really nothing happened here! What happened? No one even
> slapped anyone. No one was wounded, there was little damage.
> Nothing really happened!
> *Bhoju*: I heard someone's arm was injured.
> *Kailash*: Yes, but there has never been another event like that. And
> that happened on the playing field! Nothing like that *ever*
> happened in the town. Still, fear remains, spread by the media.
> The media people make too much of it, they bring it to
> prominence.

A Muslim government servant who worked in Jahazpur tehsil offices spoke of Jahazpur's reputation for danga, in terms quite similar to those employed by Hindu interviewees:

> *Nazir*: Whenever any kind of issue arises in Jahazpur, then the
> government helps protect Jahazpur. This is the thing: Jahazpur
> has a bad reputation (*badnam*) but still it is protected
> (*mahphuj*). Jahazpur had so many *danga*, but no one even
> slapped another person! Some think this is Gaji Pir's blessing.
> There has been no terrible destruction, just some stores and
> cabins were burned.
>
> Yet our reputation has been so tarnished, in the newspapers:
> the news even reached Delhi. Even so: no one even slapped
> another person! *Danga Danga Danga!* It is all badnam.
>
> All right, some mischievous people live here, and they set
> some things on fire, but in terms of fighting (*larai*): there was
> no fighting here at all.[26]

Bhoju: Jahazpur must have a good *kismat* [fate] when it has
    experienced several dangas and no one except the police ever
    beat anyone!

Nazir [affirming, repeating the familiar phrase]: Not a drop of blood
    was spilled!

Note that the enshrined warrior-saint Gaji Pir is evoked as a peacekeeper.

A Muslim auto mechanic and tire-repair man, whose business depends
on Hindu customers, was quite matter-of-fact about the impact of danga.
He was very clear about the role of disreputable people, although he does
not identify them as belonging to either religion or to a specific neighborhood, as many Hindus did.

In '84 it was minor (*choti moti*), but in '89, it was heavy, the one
about the Ravana procession. At that time people had such an attitude; and there were "bad elements," HS [history-sheeter] types
involved.[27] So we [Muslims and Hindus] stayed away from each
other. But after two or three or six months everything goes back to
*normal (vapas normal ho jata hai).

At that time in peoples' minds some tension would remain, they
might think, "this is a Muslim store so I won't go there," and Muslims might not go to Hindu shops, so we had this kind of thinking
for a few months . . . and then it went back to normal. [He added
perhaps by way of explanation of this speedy recovery]: You see, 90
or 99 percent of those in the mechanic and puncture line of work
are Mia-bhai (Muslim).

He didn't need to finish the thought which would of course have been:
"Therefore our customers, dependent on hard-worked motor vehicles
which take a beating on the local roads, can hardly avoid coming to us."
There was also a long history of amiability, of crosscutting local economies,
wrapped up in "normal."[28]

Many shopkeepers were less sanguine than this mechanic and felt that
in general their businesses continued even today to suffer from Jahazpur's
reputation as a place where there had been and might once again be trouble. Perhaps because Jahazpur's dangas had scarcely involved deliberate
bodily harm, the commentary I elicited on them often focused on the
imposition of curfew (some people told me they didn't even know the

meaning of the word "curfew" before these events) and the consequent long-term damage to business. As one man put it, dangas are bad for *dhandha* (business), and on this precept Hindus and Muslims are in full agreement.[29]

Thus merchants lamented that during the curfews imposed in the 1980s their regular customers from outside Jahazpur had gone elsewhere (Devli, Pander, Shahpura) to do their shopping and simply never returned. This attribution of causality stretching back decades struck me as an improbable conjecture (especially when paired with much commentary, elicited in interviews about the town that were not danga-specific, on how Jahazpur stores stocked a "lower standard" of goods). But whether or not the perception had validity is irrelevant. More significant is that the stain of being known as a danga-prone area pains Jahazpur businesspeople and has evidently led to a kind of defensive discourse. Except for a few who may desire trouble for ideological reasons, peace is the preferable mode. A series of minor episodes in 2001 involved damage to two of Jahazpur's peripheral Muslim shrines and a fire in the mosque of Pander, another comparably sized qasba not far from Jahazpur. But these were rarely named as danga. Nothing at all has happened since then, but at times, as we have seen, the atmosphere can be tense.

Another 1980s Tale: The Photographer's Murder

Support for the claim that class trumps religion emerges in the story of the photographer's murder, inflected differently by two different tellers, one Hindu and one Muslim, both highly dedicated to their respective religions. Set in the 1980s—the same period of time as the two danga—this story helps us see in panorama social, religious, and economic differences and the ways that religious festivals, Holi and Gaji Pir's urs, may be backdrops as much as motivating forces for the ups and downs and twisting paths of individual lives and dramatic local events. By pure happenstance, we recorded two relatively detailed accounts of this crime. It involved a Brahmin Hindu murdered by a poor Muslim, although not at all on account of religion.

This tale may grip the imagination of Jahazpur people in part simply because murder is very rare here. The tale becomes embellished in distinctively different ways depending on who the teller is. What is interesting is that while religious identities are definitely salient, the crime's motivation was purely economic. Religion gains some significance in the story only in the murder's aftermath. Yet a landscape of temples, shrines, festivals, and miracles is perhaps more than a backdrop, containing elements crucial to the drama and its denouement.

I will give condensed and paraphrased versions of the story, first as told by Nazir, a Muslim man in his fifties, a qawwali aficionado and a government servant; second as told by Ram Kishan, a Brahmin temple priest who had reached the age of eighty. Both men set the story within their own life histories.

Nazir's Version

Nazir knows how to spin wonderful yarns and his faith in Gaji Pir is boundless. He began by emphasizing his personal connection with the victim, a Hindu friend who had made him a ritual brother. As for the murderers, they were from a lower-class neighborhood and a poor family, although their grandfather was a well-known and, as far as I could learn, well-respected wrestler. The boys had plotted not murder but robbery, deciding to lure the photographer up to the fort and steal his camera. As Nazir told it, the event happened shortly before the time of the Hindu festival of Holi and a day or two before Gaji Pir's urs. He dated it around the time of the Bhopal disaster (1984). Not insignificantly this was the same year as Jahazpur's first major Hindu-Muslim disturbance, as just related. Nazir expressed his deep sympathy with the murdered boy's family and his empathy with their rage and desire for justice. He described how the Hindu community printed flyers and posted them around town, advising all Muslims to flee: "Muslim, brothers, you should get out of Jahazpur, empty it, or we will play Holi with your blood."

Nazir's narrative then shifted to the scene of Gaji Pir's hilltop shrine during the urs festival. With communal tension running very high in Jahazpur due to the murder, police had given permission for the urs to take place, but only to fulfill ritual needs and not with the usual festivities. According to Nazir, and doubtless an exaggeration, "there was a policeman on every step" near Gaji's shrine. The DIG (Deputy Inspector General), a high-ranking police official, was seated outside the saint's tomb, and a qawwali group from Madhya Pradesh was performing, thus defying the injunction to minimize the urs. Someone heard the DIG muttering, "These

Muslims are doing what they want whenever they want." Just after saying these things, he fell into a faint. Our narrator went into the *mazar* (tomb-shrine) to get some blessed water which he sprinkled on the DIG's face. As soon as the officer regained consciousness, he immediately wanted to enter the mazar. He had first to remove his policeman's hat (explicitly because it displayed symbols of India's secular republic that he could not lower before any divine being).

Nazir provided the penitent DIG with a handkerchief to cover his head (as all must do when entering a mazar). Inside, this Hindu policeman prayed to Gaji Pir, begging forgiveness for his former rude statement and simultaneously making a request and a promise: "Tell us who did the murder. I won't let a drop of Muslim blood be shed in Jahazpur but I want to know who is the killer, give me a sign."

What happened next is a little vague, but it seems that the DIG was wandering in town the next day, and it came to his attention that a letter without a stamp or a return address had arrived, addressed to a home in the more disreputable Muslim neighborhood. The police, who had instituted surveillance at the post office, opened the letter, and in it was all the evidence they needed: one of the criminals had written from Ajmer city about disposing of the stolen goods. The culprits were identified and apprehended. The DIG went back to Gaji Pir's shrine to express his thankfulness and vowed a lifelong dedication—not only to revere the saint but to protect Jahazpur's Muslim community.

Ram Kishan's Version

Ram Kishan, over twenty years older than Nazir, also had personal memories of the photographer's murder. He and his brother were the third generation in their family to serve as worship priests for the Jahazpur fort's Vaishnavite temples. (Indeed Ram Kishan attributed his good health at age eighty to a lifetime of walking up and down the steep hill.) He told us that on the day of the murder his brother actually ran into the three young men—that is, the victim and the two who planned to rob him—and asked them what they were doing up at the fort. As Ram Kishan narrated it, his brother, who was going about his priestly duties, told the youths to go back down as he was about to lock up the buildings. One of them retorted, "O Brahmin, get out of here or we'll kill you." Ram Kishan's brother was frightened; he proceeded to do his temple service and went straight home. Ram Kishan added that his timid brother's claim to be locking up was invented as a nonconfrontational ruse to convince the unwelcome intruders to leave; in fact there were no locks (nor are there today).

Disturbed by this encounter with a meddlesome priest, the two aspiring robbers brought the photographer down from the main fort to the freestanding goddess temple, slightly beneath it. There, they urged the photographer to take some pictures. His camera was the old-fashioned kind where in order to shoot pictures you put your head beneath a curtain. While the unsuspecting young man's head was under the curtain, one miscreant came up from behind and choked him. They took his equipment and fled.

Ram Kishan went on to describe the discovery and arrest of the criminals; his story converges with Nazir's on two points only: one, a piece of mail from Ajmer led police to the house of the culprits; two, a high-ranking police official from outside of Jahazpur was involved, although in this case it was a member of the "CID" (Crime Investigation Department) rather than a "DIG." The rest of Ram Kishan's story has some thoroughly unique features: the CID disguised himself as a fakir and wandered in the Muslim neighborhood; when he sat down with the killer, the killer became possessed by his Brahmin victim and cried out in the voice of that dead boy, "O, Yar [pal, friend], don't kill me, let me go, let me go!"

Moreover, Ram Kishan told us that there was a Muslim witness, Saddiq, a businessman, who testified to seeing all three young men eating sweets together before going up to the fort. Ram Kishan's brother, of course, would also have been a witness, having exchanged words with the criminals. But we heard nothing about whether or not he came forward. Possibly he was both frightened and ashamed of his failed effort at an intervention that might have saved a life.

These two versions of a quarter-century old crime story reveal nuances of intercommunity amity as well as tension, negotiated on the hilltop in the setting of the fort and of the dargah, as well as down in the town. Nazir evokes the urs as a scene of truth, while Holi, notoriously chaotic, is one of threat. Gaji Pir's rapid miracle, at once a punishment and cure, converts the Hindu police inspector not to Islam but to sincere reverence for the local pir's powers (shared by many Hindu residents of Jahazpur). Moreover, the DIG's reverence toward the pir leads him to feel more warmly toward Muslims in general. The Brahmin priest by his own account makes an effort but is unable to exert any influence on the young men or to alter their murderous intentions.

Nazir's telling sets the detective's action in the context of the urs and shows Gaji Pir's capacity for both punishment and grace; essentially the saint is a force that must be reckoned with on the side of intercommunity harmony. Ram Kishan's account resorts to spirit possession as the key to locating a criminal. Both narratives thus demonstrate the ways that invisible realms of power assist in bringing justice into the mortal world. The tales also demonstrate collaboration across lines of difference between members of a respectable, middle-class business community. Just as in the memories of Jahazpur's riots, it is the poor Muslims who live around Char Hathari who emerge as the villains of the piece.

In addition, these stories show the ways that categorical othering—"these Muslims"; "O Brahmin!"—serves to create dangerous, even threatening divides. By contrast, individual human relationships—"my ritual brother"; "Saddiq, a businessman"—recognize fellow human beings and serve in some ways to decategorize individuals or to expand individual identities beyond mere religious affiliations. I would add incidentally that it is much like that today: personal friendships cross all kinds of boundaries while categorical thinking is often, although not always, divisive and negative.

I turn in the final substantial portion of this chapter to less fraught moments, to the festival everyday. There are so many festivals and parades in Jahazpur that this phrase, the festival everyday, is not an oxymoron, especially if you add to the big community-wide events treated in this chapter countless private celebrations that also take to the streets. These latter might include arrivals or departures of grooms, or of brothers bearing gifts, or of lineages celebrating a deity specific to just a few families, or of corpses on their way to the cremation ground or the graveyard depending on their religion, and so forth; it becomes utterly run-of-the-mill to encounter small processions when going about one's own business. Eventually it became that way for me, as for other qasba residents. Moreover, to resume the theme stressed at this chapter's opening, an urge toward identity visibility is evidently on the rise. In the following section I will focus largely on just three major festivities and what they might reveal about Jahazpur's public religiosity, including some divides that are social more than religious.

Tejaji Tenth, Water-Swing Eleventh,
and Gaji Pir's Urs: Festival Moments

> The procession, in short, does not *re-enact* a story that is
> already finished, but rather *keeps it going*. And in so doing,
> it momentarily fuses or brings into phase the otherwise
> divergent and unsynchronized life trajectories of individual
> participants into a unified tale of belonging to this place.
> (Ingold and Vergunst 2009:9; emphasis in original)

Tenth and Eleventh

The tenth and eleventh of the bright half of Bhadrapad were both major public festival days in Jahazpur. Even if we agree on the randomness of their contiguity (upon which everyone insists), by taking a close look at these consecutive days we can still learn something about diversity and possibilities for, as well as obstacles to, pluralism just within Hindu traditions. When in 2010 Bhoju or I asked people in Jahazpur to comment on the relation between Teja Dashmi and Jal Jhulani, few had much to say. Some asserted that the crowds who attended Tejaji's fair came mostly from the surrounding villages while Jal Jhulani was more attractive to Jahazpur town residents.[30]

Educated townspeople insisted that Tejaji was a *lok devata* (folk deity) and therefore not *bhagvan* (God).[31] While they might make offerings to Tejaji, they ascribed to him a definite lower rank in the scheme of things, which is both a cosmic scheme and a sociological one. Lok devata may be petitioned for assistance with specific human problems in ways that it is not appropriate to petition Bhagvan. They are, moreover, accessible and able to give advice through divination and possession.[32] The discourse of folk deity versus God strikes me as urban overlay dismissive of rural devotional sensibilities. In my years in Ghatiyali village I found that rural devotees worshipped regional folk hero deities including Tejaji, Ramdevji, Pabuji, and Dev Narayan, or one of the many mother goddesses, as all-powerful supreme beings. Devotees accept Ramdevji and Dev Narayan as Vishnu. Diverging theological notions can become profoundly relevant for contested moments in the history of Jahazpur's Jal Jhulani procession.

Tejaji, however, was not identified as a form of Vishnu and had his own celebration. On 16 September Bhoju and I went into town to see preparations for both the Tejaji Tenth fair (Tejaji Dashmi) and Water-Swing Eleventh (Jal Jhulani Gyaras). At the water reservoir where the gods would be bathed on the eleventh, a whole team of Harijan women, on the payroll of the municipality, were cheerfully cleaning up. Another crew of workers made sure that the water itself was cleared of debris and choking plants.[33] The next day I noted a giant truckload of all this muck passing through Santosh Nagar on the way to being dumped somewhere beyond the residential area.

At the bus stand, where the Tejaji fair would take place, the ground was nicely swept; the fruit and vegetable sellers had moved their portable stalls to the sides, and ropes of tinsel were strung overhead. At his stall close to Tejaji's shrine a crippled tailor was very busy sewing pennants for devotees to offer Tejaji. These were advance orders. On the day of the fair he was still turning out banners, smaller ones, for those who had an on-the-spot impulse to make such a gift to the god known for snakebite cures and who was a source of knowledge pertinent to many other human difficulties.

On the morning of the Tejaji fair, 17 September, we made a quick trip to the shrine well before crowds would gather to be present during the divination. At this time I observed many middle- and upper-middle-class Jahazpur residents (easily distinguished by their clothes) coming to make their offerings, have a quick *darshan* (vision of the deity whose shrine was newly painted and decorated for the fair), and take their leave. When Bhoju and I returned to the shrine in the early afternoon, the scene was beginning to be packed with crowds from the surrounding villages.

Whether urban or rural, each person who came to make an offering to Tejaji brought what Bhoju called in English "one diet." A god's diet consists of a bit more than food, but mostly it is indeed composed of the ingredients for a simple, homey meal. There would be enough flour for one person's bread, as well as dal, spices, and clarified butter, and a package of incense. A diet offered to Tejaji also should include a small pitcher or plastic bag of milk, destined for the snake enshrined separately but adjacent to Tejaji's own altar, near a hole in a tree—a hole in which I was told a real snake resided.

Offerings, some on trays and others in plastic bags but all containing versions of the "one diet," came thick and fast. I watched in amazement as women thrust steel trays over the shrine fence and eventually received their own efficiently emptied platter back into their hands; how did the shrine attendants begin to tell these apart when so many were whooshing back and forth? Women who belonged to the shrine priest's family concentrated exclusively on sorting the offering materials and paid no attention to the oracles coming from several possessions happening at the shrine.

One of the main issues addressed at length by Tejaji's possessed priest had to do with a cow shelter in a nearby village that had been raided by thieves who planned to sell the cows to butchers. According to the *bhav* (the priest possessed by an oracular divinity), a punishment of drought had been inflicted on the perpetrators' home area. The rural crowds listened with intense interest to all this, which would have been less compelling for those qasba residents who had visited in the morning. Outside the shrine was another lively world of more mundane transactions; Tejaji's fair included a temporary market for clay pots and metal utensils.

My field journal closes with these words: "What I want to remember is Shiv Lal [Bhoju's friend from the village of Gadoli] saying to me today: 'India is a strange country; the people are poor but the gods are rich' (*log garibi; devata amir*)." He was actually not commenting on the abundance of food given to Tejaji but rather on the spectacular finding of a treasure of wealth in a South Indian temple that had been all over the news media.[34] Still the two were hardly unconnected as I saw it, given how many meals had been presented to Tejaji that very day.

On Saturday, 18 September, Hindus in Jahazpur celebrated Jal Jhulani Gyaras, or Water-Swing Eleventh, a regionally widespread event but not everywhere as elaborate as it is here. In Jahazpur it is a major celebration in which thousands participate. I heard that ours was the second best procession in the district. Jahazpur's own citizenry formed the bulk of the crowd.

Shravan Patriya explained the festival to us as a seasonal one, saying, "Now the month of Bhadra is almost at an end, the water reservoir is full, the crops are ripe, and for this reason, out of happiness, we take God for a bath." Jal Jhulani, like Janamashtami, is basically a Vaishnavite holiday and it is linked in several ways with Janamashtami, which came a little over two weeks earlier.

As is often the case at major festivals, several things happen simultaneously. As the divine vehicles (bevan) are assembling, there is an akhara or physical prowess display at Nau Chauk. (There will be another, also at Nau

Chauk, at the Muslim celebration of Muharram). We went out early and were able to observe some quiet preliminaries, before the crowds and tumult. Inside the Kalyanji temple, we saw the bevan arrive carrying the Vishnu known as the Kilewala (the one from the fort). The two chariots, one from the hilltop and one from the town, stayed there in repose for quite some time. People belonging to the temple neighborhood were able to enjoy peaceful darshan and to make more personal offerings. These would be the lead chariots in the big procession.

Soon the bands began, and before too long I wanted to escape the noise for a while, so we hurried to Nau Chauk and watched the displays of physical prowess. This included stick fighting, twirling of wooden weaponry, and a delightfully comical-serious virtuosic slicing of bananas that are laid on young boys' lower abdomens. Later the akharas lead the procession, and one by one the bevan join it until the streets are crammed and one loses track of how many there are.

The police seemed at ease and even smiled. On Jal Jhulani, I felt that I could see beyond their uniforms to their own village origins; they know how to behave respectfully at a festival. There was more than one band playing, and one of them was the Gaji Pir Band, which plays for both Hindu and Muslim events. Sometimes we were behind or even beside the parade; sometimes we squeezed through and went ahead. We shot pictures from different rooftops. When the procession finally reached the water reservoir, just as dusk fell, we were able to see the boats bearing the gods launched toward the island where the images would be bathed, away from crowds of onlookers.

Linking Jal Jhulani Gyaras back to Janamashtami, where this chapter opened, are the *bandarval*—strings of leaves or flowers hung over doorways that signify an auspicious event, especially the birth of a child. People put them up for Janamashtami to celebrate Krishna's birth; people take them down at Jal Jhulani, the day of baby Krishna's first bath, his *navan*. Like any sacred objects they must be cooled after they have served their ritual purposes, and hence they are thrown in the same reservoir where the gods are bathed—that very body of water that the municipality devoted so much energy to clearing of garbage before the festival. As night fell, the water was clotted with plastic bags, which bewildered me until Bhoju told me that these bags contained all the newly discarded bandarval—too sacred to deposit in any ordinary trash.

After the boats came back ashore, the refreshed images were replaced in their chariots for the return ride to their respective temples. This is when blessings become available. People push to have a chance to pass beneath a bevan or to get their children under one. Arati, the circling of an offering tray with a flame, is done to honor the divine passengers; the flame is passed around and transmits grace to worshippers. Temple priests who accompanied their images are active in all this. Bhoju and I both had our faces painted with sandalwood, but I could not tell you which bevan's priest rendered us this blessing.

In conversations about Jal Jhulani, definitely Jahazpur's most complex and ambitious Hindu procession, we heard little about religious difference and far more about the establishment of a negotiated sharing of space among different caste communities. Altogether in 2010, as we learned later, there were twenty-six temples and twenty-three chariots involved in the procession. Joining last and peeling off to return home first were two chariots belonging to SC communities: the Khatiks' Satya Narayan and the Regars' Ramdevji. I have written elsewhere of the Khatiks' victorious struggle to build a Vishnu temple in the heart of Jahazpur in the 1980s (Gold 2016). Once they achieved that, it was less difficult for them to join Jal Jhulani because their temple's deity was indisputably Vishnu. Moreover, the Khatiks were doing well economically, transitioning to middle-class housing, income, education, and habits and achieving these successes on their own terms and in their own style (see Chapter 8). Historically, Khatiks were traders of live animals as much or more than they were butchers of dead ones (in spite of the caste name). The Khatiks were part of an urban economy and had never been incorporated into the patron-client (*jajmani*) system, which had provided stability even while sustaining hierarchy.

Regars, by contrast, had been near the bottom of the client groups, stigmatized by their obligations that included removing dead animals and tanning their hides. They long ago opted out of this demeaning work, but an enduring stigmatization associated with it still clung to them. They also lagged behind the former butchers in economic and educational success. The majority of Regars, I was told, have entered the labor market in the area of construction. I met one who was a very prosperous contractor, but he appeared to be an exception. There were quite a few Regar educators in Jahazpur, both teachers and administrators. By contrasting the Regar community's progress with the Khatiks', I do not in any way imply lack of

capacity for achievement. Rather I observe that different histories of work
may result in different outcomes for different groups even when both share
the history of oppression united with current advantages now glossed as SC.
The reservation system, designed to uplift the formerly oppressed, brings to
both communities similar benefits from government programs.

A merchant, Suresh, whom we interviewed on 7 September 2010, just a
month into fieldwork and not many days before the Jal Jhulani festival was
to take place, articulated past objections to Regar participation. He told us
with confidence that the Regars would not bring out Ramdevji because "he
is hardly God; he is a folk divinity (*lok devata*) and that is why they should
not bring out his chariot."[35] He told us that about three years ago, when
the Regars first took out Ramdevji's chariot, "the atmosphere was very hot
and there was a lot of tension." Note that the words, *mahaul bahut garam*
"the atmosphere was very hot" along with the reference, in standard Hin-
glish, to "ten-shun" are the exact same phrases and words used to describe
situations when Hindus and Muslims are at odds. Suresh's narrative continued: a Regar lawyer had obtained legal permission for Ramdevji's chariot
to join the procession. This, Suresh stated, is after all a constitutional right.
Hence the Regars, with a strong police presence in place, joined the parade.
Their chariot would join two minutes behind the others, but this did not
seem to mar the satisfaction of Ramdevji's devotees.

Ganesh was a bright-eyed, quick-tongued, and vigorous older Brahmin
who loved to participate in Hindu processions. Here is what he had to say
about Ramdevji joining Jal Jhulani: "Ramdevji also comes, but they bring a
stone, a Salagramji . . . *not* the murti of Ramdevji! The Khatik have Satya
Narayan and the Malis have Lakshmi Narayan and there is Char Bhuja
from the bazaar: they are all Vishnu. The Chipas (cloth printers), just like
the Regars, bring a *salagramji*." Now a salagramji is a smooth oval stone,
considered to be an aniconic representation of Vishnu that may be worshipped as Vishnu's "form" (*rup*). Such stones are commonly found in
Vishnu temples. Here the message, the high-caste party line, appears to be
that an image of a folk deity such as Ramdevji could not be treated as
Vishnu. So, bring a stone.

Having conducted these interviews before the day of Jal Jhulani, Bhoju
and I were amazed, and both of us were thrilled if perhaps for different
reasons, when we looked into the Regar bevan in the midst of the festival's
joyful tumult. There was the murti, the image of Ramdevji himself. I was
happy that the downtrodden were having their day; Bhoju I believe took

pleasure in finding that the complacent upper-caste men who had spoken with such authority were thus proved in error.

During Jal Jhulani Regar men were shouting:

as long as the sun and moon will remain
Ramdevji, your name will remain
jab take suraj chandi rahega
Ramdevji apka nam rahega

The shouting of slogans is significant. As I have already observed, when young men jump up and down with their arms in the air and shout slogans, those are the exact moments when the atmosphere gets "hot."[36] For the chants often hold meanings both assertive and challenging: the chanted slogans of Hindus and Muslims challenge by asserting dominion. Ramdevji's slogan, however, simply asserts his eternal glory.

Urs

About four months later, one of the major events for Jahazpur's Muslim community took place: the urs (death anniversary) of Gaji Pir. Gaji Pir's tomb is the oldest of Jahazpur's hilltop buildings. The story goes that a Hindu king had embarked on construction of the fort. But he was frustrated as the work accomplished each day was undone in the night. Then, as Ehsan Ali, a passionate devotee of Gaji, put it while walking us around the shrine and its environs: "Gaji Pir came into this king's dreams and said, 'First make my place.' So that king caused Gaji Pir's tomb to be erected, and only then was he able to build the fort." Gaji was a warrior beheaded in a battle in the rather distant city of Chittor, but his body kept fighting, they say, until he reached Jahazpur (Gold 2013:317–18). Jahazpur's landed Muslim community holds a copperplate deed to the shrine and its surrounding land.

Gaji's urs is a major three-day extravaganza in Jahazpur's annual festival cycle. It involves a town-wide procession, a fair at the foot of the hill, two nights of devotional singing up at the shrine itself, and much else, culminating in blessing the large assembled crowds with the saint's rose-scented, power-infused water. While I had seen village versions of almost all the Hindu festivals I found in Jahazpur, this was my first real urs.[37]

Shortly after the urs, carrying a long list of questions, Bhoju and I interviewed two Muslim educators, sitting in a school office inside the qasba.
They were both reserved and dignified, speaking now and then in an Urdu
too chaste for my comprehension but perfectly intelligible to Bhoju Ram,
whose vocabulary of recognition includes countless Urdu words he never
uses in speech. We asked about the organization for the urs and were told
that a committee had been doing the work for about thirty years and taking
care of the finances as well. (They added that the municipality pays for
street cleaning and marking as well as supervising the route arrangements.)
Both men agreed that while in the past "it was just a custom people needed
to do," for the last ten to twelve years there has been more effort put into
the urs, and it has been celebrated with more splendor. My journal on the
day of the procession recounted my experience viewing these displays:

> the performative feature of this procession, besides the chadar, flags
> and trays with roses, was a group of hired guys, who looked very
> rum to me, who played with swords and put them in their eyeballs
> and through their cheeks (with no blood)
> this was freaky the first time; one person told me not to get upset,
> it was all their power of illusion, that we see "only that which they
> want us to see"

Our conversation with the two teachers about the urs touched on this
very point regarding the ascetic performers, known as *malang*. These teachers echoed my fellow spectator using nearly identical language. They said
that the malang do not really hurt themselves, but "you see what they want
you to see." Bhoju, using my camera, had taken an amazing photograph of
one of the malang apparently stabbing his own eyeball. Bhoju argued that
"seeing is believing" and added that we could see in the computer exactly
what we saw with our own eyes. How could the computer be deluded?
However, the two men still held that no bodily injury actually happened,
insisting that the malang "do *sadhana*" (here they did employ a Hindu term
for spiritual practice) and admonishing us that should ordinary people like
ourselves try to duplicate their feat "we might die or put out our eye."

We also discussed the *chadar*, that is, the beautiful bedspreads or sheets
that are offered to Gaji. The most splendid of these are usually purchased
in Sarwar or Ajmer but there is no requirement, those are just places where

such things are available in high quality. The urs began with a major procession on day one that included the malang performing in the streets and at stopping places along the route. It also featured the most gorgeous of the bedspreads to be offered to Gaji, which was carried by several persons, spread open, and became a receptacle into which observers and participants tossed offerings of coins and notes. Eventually the procession flowed up the hill to Gaji Pir's place. My journal records: "Up at the shrine I am pushed underneath the chadar [coverlet], to press my head against the tomb of the saint; my sleeves get dirty and I don't even notice. I am given prasad of halva and a rose; the old man is worried I won't eat it, but I already have it in my mouth after giving half to Bhoju who eats his also. The rose I must save." There is a kind of fervor at the urs that is infectious. I did save that rose and I can still see in my mind's eye where it is safely stored among fieldwork memorabilia.

Some stayed at the mazar that night for the performance of *milad*.[38] Bhoju and I decided to save ourselves for the second night, when the qawwali performers would play. A cold rain was falling and we were far from the only ones rushing down the stairs as quickly as we could to head home. Our interviewees explained to us that the first night's performance, the milad, involved a fixed "syllabus" that they followed. This, they said, included verses in praise of Mohammad and of Allah. "After that, the people from our society who have done good works" are praised, and finally "respect is paid to everyone." We missed all that, and I regretted it.

The next day (25 November, Thanksgiving in the far away USA) was important; there was no procession; everything happened up at the shrine and mainly had to do with qawwali. My quick journal entries describe my own experience:

> but although I went without really wanting to go, I loved being there, loved the rock fest feeling of it;
> there was such a party atmosphere.
>
> . . . .
>
> When the Indore group was playing, no one paid attention, but when the Delhi group finally started to perform, it must have been after midnight, people became rapt; their music was great and their style was engaging; I imagine them joking about Jahazpur. arriving hours late for their gig. but once they are up there they are fabulous.

Figure 14. Author stands between women and police, Gaji Pir's urs
(photo by Bhoju Ram Gujar).

on the way down, in the early hours of the day we were passed by
the fat jeep of the fat [Congress] politician, Dhiraj Gujar, on his way
to the urs this late.
Bhoju was not surprised to see him!

Bhoju asked our teacher-interviewees about why there was always a passage
kept clear between the qawwali performance and the tomb. In spite of the
major crowds, no one was allowed to use that space. Here is what they said:
"Gaji Baba is sitting there and he comes and goes and listens to the qawwali
so no one comes in his way. We are going there because we think his soul
is alive, if he were dead why go? That is why we bring flowers, perfume,
green things." On the last day we went back to Gaji's hill around 3 p.m. At
the bottom of the hill was a small fair in full blast, featuring hand-powered
Ferris wheel and merry-go-round, all tended by itinerant "carnies."
    As Bhoju and I walked up the stairs, it felt as if we had arrived at the
right time, because the stairs were crowded; when we reached the top the

ladies' seating area was already packed. I ended up initially positioning myself behind four policemen. There were more qawwalis and one more performance by the malang. My journal:

> Does that guy have some kind of plastic contacts on over his eyeballs???? Bhoju smelled marijuana and said they were smoking it, just like Shiva's devotees; they seem pretty stoned. Maybe around 4 pm Ehsan beckons Bhoju into the mazar;
> women can't go and cameras can't be used
> they take off the chadar and wash the saint, the headless fighter [Bhoju told me later]
> the sprinkling with rose water
> the tying turbans on distinguished guests
> the collection of donations and giving of receipts
> the man who tells us his miracle stories while a crowd gathers round
> four hours of urs
> Bhoju scores us prasad
> when I am sprinkled with rosewater (so very like arati and charanamrit combined) I feel emotion I feel this headless warrior's dua [blessing]

Keeping the Peace in Jahazpur: Viable Pluralism

> Although it is essential to research places where conflict is endemic, it is equally important to see the day-to-day life of a place where tension and conflicts are managed productively. (Bigelow 2010:239)

> "Peace," in this sense, should not be envisioned as merely the absence of violence but rather as a process which is constantly ongoing. (Heitmeyer 2009:118)

> But the focus on syncretism sans conflict amounts to taking only half a step. And this is so because our concentration on inter-communal goodwill and harmony, though necessary, leaves the field of sectarian strife as the special preserve of sectarian and "communal" historians. Mine is a

> plea for essaying non-sectarian histories of conquest and
> conflict. (Amin 2015:8)

Local government exerts multiple pressures to ensure that Jahazpur remains danga-free. In Jahazpur today, the organizers of every procession must not only obtain permission from the police but submit their route in writing, in advance. They also are required to hold a pre-event "good feeling" (sadbhavana) meeting involving leaders from all communities and focused on maintaining civility and order.[39] Just in case such negotiations prove unsuccessful, at every single festival there is a quiet but alert and visible uniformed police presence armed at different levels depending on the occasion.[40]

We asked one participant in the *sadbhavana* process, a respected and prosperous shopkeeper, to describe it to us. This was an informal, unrecorded conversation. He told us that a CLG (Community Liaisoning Group) ideally should have a member from every community.[41] These members should be literate. Meetings precede any major religious function. The examples he gave were Muharram, Jal Jhulani, Holi, Diwali, and Dashera—all but Holi are occasions involving processions.[42] When we asked him if meetings were held before Jain processions he said no, adding tellingly that there is no need because "Jains do not shout slogans and in their minds is no intention." My own visceral sense of the slogan shouting as critical to the generation of tension is thus confirmed by government practice.

Generally, while there may be thirty people invited, the meeting held in advance of any given event will be attended by about ten to fifteen. There should be representatives from both Hindu and Muslim communities. Officials from local government, both civil service and police, are also invited, and these include the Subdivisional Magistrate (SDM), the Tehsildar, the Circle Officer (CO), and the Circle Inspector (CI). Elected ward members who form the municipal government are also called, and they will come if they anticipate any problems in their ward. At the meeting, administrators exhort everyone to avoid tension. They go over the route and ask if anyone has objections to the route or the timing. They instruct Hindu parade organizers, for example, to turn off their loudspeakers if prayers are taking place when they are near the mosque. Ideally a Hindu procession will wholly avoid passing the mosque at prayer times. Members of the committee who attend the meeting are charged with responsibility to keep the peace and to alert participants if they are making any mistakes. Those motivated to join in the peacekeeping process include the head person for every society with shops in the market, people with status and influence. Journalists are also invited.

Our interviewee added that when any celebration includes displays of physical prowess (as do Hindu Jal Jhulani and Muslim Muharram), separate permissions are required because such displays mean the presence of weapons; otherwise weapons are forbidden. The police always are armed with sticks; depending on the occasion there may also be several with guns; usually there are two carrying tear gas. A fire engine is also kept at the ready.

A route may change if any potential confrontation can thus be averted. In December 2010, for example, the Gayatri Parivar, a Hindu reform group with a small Jahazpur constituency, decided not to take their procession, which happened to fall on the same day as Muharram, to the major gathering place of Nau Chauk, although it was in their original route plan. That morning the taziya (brought out the night before) was at rest in Nau Chauk, awaiting its own parade to commence later in the day. As it was expressed to us, the Gayatri Parivar organizer did not wish to "*disturb the taziya."

Jahazpur, because of its "sensitive" classification, gets extra attention not just at festivals but at any moment deemed potentially tense. The government shut down the market twice in anticipation of trouble related to nonfestival events, trouble that never even slightly stirred. To be treated this way bothered some Jahazpur citizens. These two occasions were the much-vaunted announcement of the high court's judgment about Ayodhya (30 September 2010) and the World Cup cricket finals (30 March 2011) when India played Pakistan. As far as I could tell from chatting with diverse neighbors, no one cared much about what happened in Ayodhya—it seemed to them like a thing that had certainly mattered in the rather remote past but no longer did. Santosh Nagar neighbors, and a few of Bhoju's friends explicitly told me they were more concerned with educating their children and enjoying some middle-class comforts than with the fate of that patch of ground in Ayodhya. Many resented the media hype, and the aftermath of the much vaunted "three-piece judgment" was decidedly anticlimactic (an excellent outcome).

Unlike Ayodhya in 2010, the 2011 World Cup mattered enormously. A few Hindus muttered in advance that Muslims would certainly celebrate if

Pakistan won and predicted darkly that this would enrage Hindus. Yet among Bhoju Ram's acquaintances in the qasba I saw Muslim and Hindu friends avidly and peacefully enjoying the game together. In the market large groups of viewers clustered round many different stores' television sets to watch the match. Shortly before the end of the game, police instructed all the viewers to hurry home and forced shopkeepers to lock up their stores. I heard after the fact that when India won, a small victory parade had traversed the market in defiance of police orders and without incident. The next day some of Jahazpur's citizens expressed indignation at police repression. I heard several people assert that if the prime ministers of the two countries could have watched the live game together and behaved with civility, as indeed they had, surely the people of Jahazpur could have watched it together on television.

This indignation at Jahazpur's stigmatization as a place of potential trouble is perhaps best summed up in a comment from Shravan Patriya, retired journalist and amateur historian with a passion for truth. He commented, rather mildly but pointedly, "There isn't all that much tension in Jahazpur, but there is tension in the mind of the government (*sarkar*)." While town residents may not welcome all precautionary procedures, most do appear to understand the need for most preventative measures.

In the conclusion to her excellent book *Sharing the Sacred*, focused on a community that had stayed peaceful even through the torments of partition in violence-ridden Punjab, Anna Bigelow suggests that the need for institutionalized peacekeeping in no way negates the beneficial conditions of informal interchange and interpersonal relationships. I think her point helps to illuminate what the required *sad-bhavana* meetings accomplish in Jahazpur. I also must acknowledge what the elders say: those who lament the loss of *prem* or love between communities imply that an institutionalized "good feeling" (*sadbhavana*) cannot truly fill the hole caused by the stone that fell (that is, the two danga), displacing perhaps with its weight a corresponding volume of trust.

If I think back to the shaking of the welcome arch at Dashera, I might imagine first that the arch itself was intended by Muslim elders to evoke that lost era of prem. But it was a mere representation and, materially as well as symbolically, a flimsy one. Thus to hot-headed Hindu youth who had just been aroused by shouting Ram's slogans, it might have seemed a provocation rather than the welcome that was intended. When they shook it with force and barely restrained hostility they were not in touch with what it symbolized; they did not possess shared memories of the deep pool of love before the stone fell.

Only the very elderly today like to reminisce about a time of pure love and fully cordial sociability among the town's Hindus and Muslims. I was moved by the old men and women from both communities who evoked that love with a swell of feeling in voice and facial expression. Certainly such memories can smack of a "good old days" nostalgia. But I would like to value their truth. Younger people in my experience are edgier, more suspicious, products of a more dangerous era. Nonetheless, the majority of Jahazpur citizens of all ages are habituated in multiple ways to a plural social universe, to shared commercial and residential spaces.

This chapter has attempted to examine Jahazpur's homegrown brand of pluralism through several lenses including ethnographic resonance, recollected harmony, past conflict, and present negotiated peacekeeping. I have also tried to highlight the existence of multiple lines of difference, to show not only fissures but well-knit tissues that create an overall picture far more complex than a focus on nothing but religious identity would suggest.

In introducing a recent and excellent anthology, *Muslims in Indian Cities*, Laurent Gayer and Christophe Jaffrelot write that acknowledging "interactions and cultural cross-fertilisations does not imply to engage in a romance with syncretism" (2012:13). While I would never aim to engage in a (deluded) romance, I want to acknowledge along with Gayer and Jaffrelot some of the subtler modes of living together. These are elements of the everyday that Veena Das, citing Bhrigupati Singh, has called "agonistic belonging of Hindus and Muslims as neighbors in the same local worlds," (Das 2010: 395) or Mayaram has described as "practices of co-living" (Bhuyan 2013).

I summarize some formal and informal ways of enacting peaceful pluralisms observed over nearly a year's fieldwork in Jahazpur. Constitutionally secular India's laws hold sway in Jahazpur, and we therefore find formal evidence of pluralism as granting legitimacy. The municipality, for example, cleans the streets and chalks the routes and pays for lights for all religious celebrations—whether Hindu, Jain, or Muslim—in public spaces. Hindu leaders scrupulously attend every Muslim event, both those scripturally chartered such as Id and those associated with local Muslim saints such as the two annual urs. This too is a form of granting legitimacy, even if it is equally blatant and self-interested vote-seeking behavior.

Alongside such evidence are those subtler forms of pluralism evoked by Mayaram's questions: "Are there shared imaginaries and grammars that are

Figure 15. Moment of spontaneous affection between two elderly gentlemen (thoroughly unaware of the camera), identities proclaimed by their dress on a day of two processions, Hindu and Muslim.

rooted in everyday perceptions of being in the world? What are the practices that we might see as making possible Living Together, enabling us to capture at least some of the fluidity and diversity of social formations we encounter in urban spaces?" (2009: 9).

Festival and everyday examples demonstrate a shared culture, a shared commercial world, a modulated, shared aesthetic. Even the shouting of assertive slogans with different words but similar gestures and rhythms—as young men perform at both Hindu and Muslim events—reveals, however ironically, shared modes of asserting commitment to separate identities. Festivals reveal shared grammars—from the sparkling new clothes worn by children, to the omnipresent balloon sellers and snack vendors, to the seeking of physical blessings by going under the divine chariots at Jal Jhulani and the taziya at Muharram.

Outside of festival time we encounter many small examples of shared material worlds. In Hindu living rooms the TV is often located near framed pictures of deities; in Muslim living rooms it is located near framed pictures of fruits and flowers. Hindus keep basil plants on their roofs and worship them as the goddess. Muslims keep basil plants on their roofs because they are medicinally useful. We had one delightful interview with a Deshvali Muslim comparing Hindu and Muslim wedding customs. Parts of weddings are the same, with modulations such as differently adorned grooms who arrive on identically adorned horses. Parts are parallel such as the Muslim practice of delivering the first wedding invitation to a Sufi pir's tomb while Hindus deliver it to Ganeshji, the god of beginnings. Parts, of course, significantly diverge: Muslim brides and grooms do not sit together until after their union has been sealed with a legally binding contract. Hindu couples joined together circle a sacred fire at the culmination of their marriage rites, a culmination effected in Muslim traditions by the signatures and accompanying prayers. Yet the surrounding festivities including multiple lavish meals are common across all Jahazpur marriages.

In the next chapter I turn to look at Jains and Minas, two Hindu groups that are major players in the political economy of Jahazpur municipality. Both are deeply rooted in the same space even though they could strike a superficial observer as belonging to alternative universes. Their religiosity, for example, takes highly disparate forms. Besides worshipping Malaji, who is a Vaishnavite vegetarian type, Minas tend the fierce mother goddess often bright with red and sparkling adornments, who is understood to desire and consume offerings of beheaded goats and country liquor. Jains revere impassive white or black stone Jinas, victors over the self and its desires who are understood neither to desire nor actually to receive anything as they require nothing. Every story I heard that linked Jains and Minas startled me; such stories form the centerpiece of Chapter 5.

Chapter 5

Depths

Minas and Jains Inside, Outside, Underground

> Jahazpur is a kind of a sheltered spot (*sharan ki sthali*); the
> Jain people found shelter here, the Minas also found shelter
> here, it has always been a sheltered spot. (Interview with
> Deepak Pancholi, journalist, 2 January 2011)

Whenever Bhoju and I queried interviewees as to who might have been the earliest settlers of Jahazpur territory, both Jains and Minas were commonly and consistently named, usually in a single breath. In this chapter we turn to the depths of the past, to the intimations of history falling drop by drop from "the pot of time" (Reza 2003). With "depths," in the case of Jains, I allude to the literal underground from which an ancient Jain past occasionally resurfaces, reshaping the present. In the case of Minas, I evoke a people who might once have lived metaphorically underground, that is, beyond the purview of the state. For centuries, Minas belonging to the Jahazpur region were more often than not "illegible"—to employ James Scott's phrase (1999). The adjective suggests not invisibility but modes of life that resist categorization and governance.

Because of our shared predilection to stay away as much as possible from the homes of the affluent, powerful, and proud, Bhoju and I learned more about Minas in the first months of our research than we ever did about Jains. Later, when researching the market (see Chapter 8), our Jain interviews overtook in numbers, but never in richness of content, those with Minas.[1] The full extent of Mina and Jain overlapping and partially interwoven pasts remains inaccessible to an everyday ethnographer of the contemporary.[2] I cannot lead readers through a chronological, linear account of Jahazpur's past. I am not that kind of scholar, and I believe Jahazpur is not that kind of place. Much of Rajasthan's recorded history is presented through heroic tales of Rajputs battling one another and/or battling Muslims. This chapter looks at two groups whose significance has drawn less scholarly attention; moreover, in the case of the Minas, in particular, it is a far less documented significance.[3]

In this chapter I strive to render my portrait of contemporary town life more robust by revealing some ordinary and extraordinary intersections of two disparate, equally pivotal communities. Positioned midship, so to speak, concluding Part I and leading toward Part II, "Depths" contemplates and recapitulates everyday complexities in a pluralistic small town as these are served up in stories and storied artifacts of past times. Contemporary fieldwork such as mine provides stories about the past—movements, intersections, fusions that live in memory and sometimes in materiality. Such stories, whether volunteered or elicited, are often fragmentary and at times conflicting. Even events from the 1980s, as we saw in the preceding chapter, may be retold from different and divergent perspectives, remembered or forgotten in different ways. It is therefore not surprising that accounts of what might have happened several hundred (or thousand) years back must be received as meaningful narratives exposing patterns or configurations of significance, while there is no way to test for facts or truth value.[4]

Had I merely studied the market, the buying and selling that is Jahazpur's economic foundation, I might have seen one picture only: savvy educated merchants catering to the simple, gaudy tastes of barely literate peasants, and fleecing them when possible. Had I merely studied local politics in the present I might have seen the Minas (or at least their thick creamy layer) organized and victorious, over merchants as well as Brahmins. Luckily for me, Bhoju Ram had friends in the twelve hamlets, and from them we were able to gather how much more there was to Minas than the covetous, dazzled, calculating eyes of peasant shoppers or the agile, successful, strategic political leaders. We met among Minas dedicated agriculturalists, high achievers in government service and business, devotees of Mataji and Malaji, and even a published author of local history (Mina et al. 2009).

Throughout this chapter I normally and self-consciously speak, for convenience, of Jains and Minas as if these were internally homogeneous categories, which they very evidently are not. My justification for a heuristic shorthand—one that elides both conceptual and sociological distinctions and in some ways participates in "essentializing" processes—is a simple one. When Jains and Minas are juxtaposed as communities—whether in terms of religious practice, historical roles, occupations, dress, or other traits—commonalities within each large category outweigh multiple, nuanced, internal differences.

In addition, this chapter is often guilty of conflating Jains with merchants. If many Jahazpur Jains are indeed engaged in trade, there are certainly merchant groups, in class and caste, who are not Jain—Maheshvari and Hindu Agarwal, for example. But my conflation is consonant in some ways with local discourse. Typically in Jahazpur conversations, speakers who are not part of the merchant class will casually refer to those who are as *baniyas* (shopkeepers, moneylenders) or *seth* (merchants). Another term for merchants, usually restricted to Jains and more respectful than *baniya*, is *mahajan* (literally "great person").[5] *Baniya*, *seth*, and *mahajan* are not exactly caste names; rather they indicate class and profession. But all are sometimes used in place of a caste name, to answer a question such as "who is so-and-so?" by indicating membership in a class and caste status.[6] Those thus designated would be presumed to be either Jain or Hindus of a Vaishnavite persuasion. These have in common vegetarianism and aversion to the consumption of alcohol.

Most of the Minas in the twelve hamlets belong to the Mautis lineage, associated with devotion not only to the goddess but to their own regional hero-god Malaji, who has some Vaishnavite traits and is known for his protection of living beings (Chapter 6). A larger population of Pariyar Minas, and many other numerically smaller Mina lineages as well, are spread throughout this general area. At times, Pariyars are mentioned by name in secondary sources in ways that distinguish them from other lineages including Mautis. Such particularities are, however, diffused when we consider that Minas abide by the common North Indian Hindu marriage rules requiring lineage exogamy for multiple generations (conventionally seven, although I am given to understand that these rules may be bent, especially in recent years). In my experience, women generally retain a sense of identity with their own fathers' lineages; and children grow up with some allegiance to their mothers' people. To identify any village as "all Mautis" (or "all Pariyar," etc.) is to recognize only the paternal lineage, along which land inheritance normatively passes. Other elements of community heritage such as lineage deities, stories, ritual practices, and so forth are transmitted through generations by women.[7]

Some minimal known parameters of pertinent local history: Jains built temples in this region of Rajasthan, conservatively dated to around the twelfth century CE.[8] Later, perhaps in the fifteenth and sixteenth century, some Jains from this area carefully buried sets of exquisite stone images and presumably migrated elsewhere with plans to return. Minas are described by a visiting British colonial officer in 1820 as the "sole proprietors" in Jahazpur and its environs. In between those eras, of Jain flight and Mina predominance, various external regimes both Hindu and Muslim held sway here, at least on the record, as related in Chapter 2. It is unclear how much control rulers who were not physically on the scene actually exerted. It is also unclear exactly when Jahazpur/Yagyapur as a place took on the identity of market town, where Jains as merchants would have played an important part.

There is no historical evidence to link those long-ago Jains, who buried their images with reverent care, and the Jains of today, who have been central to qasba economy in the recollected past. No one sought the ancient images; all the finds were accidental, and the finders, as far as I know, were never Jain themselves. What we do know is that Jahazpur's present-day Jains feel that they live on particularly hallowed ground (*atishaya kshetra*).

Jains as traders are, and ever have been, quintessentially urban.[9] Most local Jains belonging to Jahazpur municipality today are solidly middle to upper-middle class. Besides owning businesses large and small, their numbers include bankers, lawyers, government employees, and comparable professionals. Today the majority of Minas appear to be well-rooted as rural. However, appearances can be deceiving, and everyone asserts that once, not too long ago, the Minas lived inside the qasba walls. It does not take more than a couple of generations to establish significant affective roots. Most local Minas living in Jahazpur municipality express a genuine sense of belonging to the landscape of the twelve hamlets. Many are farmers. However, when visiting the hamlets we also met politicians, teachers, drivers, military personnel, and policemen—all holders of salaried positions—who nonetheless choose to live rurally. They do live in nicer, more recently constructed houses than those in which ordinary village people resided.

Using stereotypes, one might juxtapose Minas as "children of nature" attached to the countryside with Jains as urbanized merchants; Minas as goat-sacrificing, goddess-worshipping, martially able farmers with Jains as renouncer-worshipping, nonviolent traders. Such rough and readily available stereotypes do not of course describe reality but caricature it; just as does a successful caricature, they may exaggerate salient features. An examination of Minas and Jains, peasants and merchants, interacting with one another may serve to shed light on an ongoing multistranded intertwining of rural and urban economy and polity—in other words, to illuminate this book's central topic.[10] In Chapter 8, where my focus is the market, we see the shopkeeper/customer relationship that seems to unite these two groups forever in an almost affectionate if eternally combative or sparring mutual dependence. My limited aim in this chapter is to explore how these two demographically, economically, and politically significant communities crucial to Jahazpur's identity, both past and present, have been intertwined in ways that may seem peculiar but that make local sense for reasons that will gradually unfold.

I first characterize Rajasthan's, and Jahazpur's, Minas, drawing from secondary sources, field notes, and interviews. I then sketch an established Jain presence in Jahazpur. The third, purely fieldwork-based segment of this chapter uses one worshipped image and two local legends to portray Jains and Minas in startling configurations, unpredictably joined at the hip. I speculate briefly on how these two communities, in cohabitation, inflect the distinctive nature of Jahazpur as place and as passageway between rural and urban lives.

Starring the Minas

Long ago there were not any great kings [maharajas] here, just Minas, and they fought a lot. (Interview with Mahavir Singh, one of our very few Rajput interviewees, a journalist by profession, 2010)

Jehajpoor Sept. 28 [1820]
The population consists entirely of the indigenous Meenas who could turn out four thousand *kumptas* or "bowmen," whose aid or enmity were not to be despised. . . .
Throughout the whole of this extensive territory, which consists as much of land on the plains as in the hills, the Meena is the sole proprietor. (Tod [1832] 1978:539–40)

Census figures for 2011 show over a quarter of Jahazpur subdistrict's population numbered among the Scheduled Tribes, and Minas are evidently the vast majority in that category.[11] Although an official ST designation may often suggest aboriginal peoples with liminal status in village economy and society, Minas of this area have long been well integrated into agricultural and pastoral modes of production as well as Hindu practices. In this regard they are unlike the Bhils (of whom there are few in and around Jahazpur). When I first worked in adjacent Ajmer district of Rajasthan in 1979–81, even those Bhils counted among the village population were known as forest people and associated with gathering honey and supplying herbal medicines. Minas, by contrast, were readily incorporated into the core of village society, often referred to collectively under the umbrella term *kisan log*, which included other farmers and herders: Gujars, Lodhas, and Malis. Each group of course had its distinctive community traditions.

Rajasthani Minas' tribal (ST) identity has to do not with their way of life but rather with their being understood as original inhabitants, true natives of the region (Hooja 2006). In recent years a substantial educated elite has emerged among this area's Minas. Educated Minas have taken advantage of reservations accorded to their ST status, and in and around Jahazpur large numbers of Minas are in government service as teachers, police, and army personnel. Moreover, Minas hold many elected offices in local and state governments. Jahazpur has had a Mina as chairman (mayor) for over two decades.[12]

In the murky but recollected past—as told by Mina and non-Mina alike—Mina men served rulers (whether great kings or petty princes) as guards and soldiers. Sometimes they operated as bandits (either working independently or, as we occasionally heard, sharing their loot fifty-fifty with local regimes). Minas' presumed exodus from the qasba to the twelve hamlets, about which we gathered various theories, is ultimately attributed by the Minas themselves to their acquisition of farmland granted to them by overlords who were either rewarding their service or deflecting their depredations.

Minas continue today to inhabit Jahazpur qasba as a political and ritual space. The Minas are staunch devotees of Malaji and the goddess, and two of Jahazpur's most important temples belong to them. By belong, I mean that while members of any community may come to worship there, it is Minas who serve as priests and who are custodians of agricultural lands deeded to the temples. In the case of Malaji, few besides Minas are drawn to worship. However, in the case of Chavundia Mataji's temple, there are worshippers from every community, some regulars and others who flock here and swell the crowds during festivals special to the goddess such as Navaratri. Minas were named in our interviews with shopkeepers, especially vendors of cloth and clothing, as preeminent among the customers in Jahazpur market.

Colonial Accounts

Multiple sources from colonial times repeat some patterned stereotypes about Minas which may be rapidly summarized in paraphrase. Minas are lawless, independent, handsome, healthy children of nature, touchingly flattered by gifts and courtesies. Minas are equally a force with which anyone aspiring to rule over, or profit from, this region must reckon.[13] Some among the British appeared to admire the Mina character and note the possibility of co-opting their bodies and courage to colonial purposes. Colonel Tod, for example, comments on Mina potential to be molded or cajoled into useful subjects, were they treated with respect (Tod [1832] 1978:539). In his personal narrative of 1820, besides declaring Minas to be "sole proprietors" of the region around Jahazpur, as cited in the epigraph, Colonel Tod speaks of his travel from Jahazpur to Kujoori in these words:

> October 2 KUJOORI
> My journey was through a little nation of robbers by birth and profession: but their *kumptas* (bows) were unstrung and their arrows rusting in the quiver. . . . I found these Meenas true children of nature, who for the first time seemed to feel they were received within the pale of society, instead of being considered as outcasts. (Tod [1832] 1978:541).

Tod also notes in passing the Minas' allegiance to Ghanta Rani, testifying it seems approvingly to their religiosity, as opposed to their brigandry: "The outlaws of the Kiraar, though they sacrifice a tithe of their plunder to 'our Lady of the Pass' (Ghatta Rani), have little consideration for the idlers of the plains" ([1832] 1978:542).[14] Ghanta Rani's shrine remains a major regional pilgrimage site, a place I have visited many times between 1980 and 2015 (Gold 2008b). A magnificent new hilltop temple was completed in 2012 with much fanfare. While people from many communities helped raise funds for this endeavor, Minas took the lead, and the current priest in the new temple is Mina.

The *District Gazetteer*, compiled by K. K. Sehgal in 1975 but doubtless based on past iterations, contains testimonies from other British officers who, like Tod, expressed ambivalent views of the Minas, tempering critique with measured approbation. Sehgal cites Sir Henry Lawrence, who in an 1855 missive had this to say: "The Minas were accustomed to plunder all around and to defy their own rulers as also the Governments. . . . Every adult Meena in a score or so of villages is or has been a robber. The tribe is naturally lawless and many of these villagers have little alternative but to rob, steal, or obtain service. There is not an appearance of anything whatever having been done to reclaim the people, or even to give them a motive for good conduct." (cited in Sehgal 1975:56–57). Sehgal adds that Sir Lawrence was convinced that "Minas were energetic for good, as they were for evil, and that they might easily be redeemed" (1975:57).

Henry Schwartz's observations in this regard are pertinent: "While colonial sources frequently mention a Mina propensity to thievery, or general disregard of the rule of law, Minas are rarely essentialized as unredeemable reprobates in the ways that other so-called 'criminal' communities sometimes were" (2010).[15]

The *Imperial Gazetteer* of 1908 refers in similarly dualistic language specifically to Pariyar Minas of nearby Bundi: notorious robbers who have settled down, joined the British infantry, and been converted to the side of good conduct, that is, of the colonial power.

> In Būndi State and in the rugged country round Jahāzpur and Deoli, which is called the Kherār and belongs to Būndi, Jaipur, and Udaipur, are found the Parihār Mīnās, who claim descent from the Parihār Rājputs of Mandor. They are a fine athletic race, formerly notorious as savage and daring robbers; but they have settled down to a great extent, and the infantry portion of the 42nd (Deoli) regiment (or the Mīnā Battalion, as it was called from 1857–1860) has for many years been largely composed of them. (*Imperial Gazetteer* [1908] 1989:36)

In one of our early interviews, a knowledgeable Mina in Borani also referred to the Khairar region in reference to his community's history:

This whole area is called Khairar and no English came here [that is, were able to come]. Whenever the King of Udaipur came here, with his army and his horses, they would stop at the Banas River, and not cross it. The king would come but not the army. The Minas knew he was on his way. The Mina *patel* (leader) would greet the King at the Banas. And the king himself would come without his army. The Minas guaranteed the king's security and protection.

Another Mina elder contributed to the same conversation:

Once, the Bhil people rebelled against the Maharana and he sent a letter to Jahazpur, and from here the Minas went to help the king in the war, and they won the battle against the Bhil for the Maharana, and he gave a golden bracelet weighing a half kilogram to the patel.

As an additional reward, the Maharana granted the Minas of this area permission to put Singh as their last name. This was written on a copper plate and given to the Minas.

In these interesting accounts we see the Minas representing themselves, accurately I believe, as their own masters, subject neither to the Rana nor to the British colonizers, and as freewheeling mercenaries of a special sort. They were willing to back regimes with their military prowess if rewarded not merely with wealth but with respect.

In Chapter 4's oral history recounting the qasba's first interreligious tension in 1947, we encountered collectively the Minas belonging to Jahazpur municipality's twelve hamlets. Minas were characterized there as ready and willing to fight, but also equally ready and willing to lay down their improvised arms and enjoy a good meal when an authority figure treated them respectfully and was thus able to persuade them to eschew violent intentions.

S. H. M. Rizvi's slim ethnographic volume on the Minas, based on late twentieth-century fieldwork in a region not too distant from Jahazpur, is the best attempt I have seen to depict Rajasthan's Minas from a sociological point of view. Rizvi observes here, articulating what seems to me to be a self-evident truth but rarely seen in print, "Coming to the people of Rajasthan one finds that a lot has been written on its palaces women and kings but no author has ever attempted to delineate the social history of Minas"

(1987:7).[16] I am not the one to accept Rizvi's challenge, but I concur fully with his main point. Rizvi also notes:

> The social history as collected from the oral traditions prevalent amongst Minas definitely appears to be contrary to all that is recorded by the British Colonials. . . . The maligning of Mina character associated them with various social evils had been detrimental to their socio-economic development. The declaration of Mina as a "criminal tribe" might have been a political strategy of Rajput and British rulers to dissuade this militant tribe from reclaiming their areas lost in the hands of the Rajput chiefs. (Rizvi 1987:29)

One of the more understated, subversive interview statements in our collection, confirming Rizvi's view, was enunciated by the very aged Hira Lal Mina (a resident of Pancha ka Bara), who said, "The Rajputs turned the Minas into thieves; they would shoot them; they were killed in the day by the Rajputs, and so they had to earn their livings at night." Bhoju and I couldn't help smiling at this turn of phrase from an eloquent speaker who simultaneously acknowledged and justified his community's illegal activities. We smiled in spite of ourselves because thievery is a Mina attribute much joked about; the charge of violence committed against the Mina community is of course serious.

Madhu Tandon Sethia's excellent historical study of Bundi and Kota, regions adjacent to Jahazpur, describes tensions between Rajputs and Minas dating back at least to the fourteenth century. At that time, Hada Rajputs successfully "marginalized" Minas' position in the region. Sethia adds, "This paved the way for new agricultural settlement in the areas dominated by the Meenas. It does not mean that Meenas lost their hold on the land completely. They continued to live in the region as peasant proprietors and were in a dominant position in scores of villages." She concludes tellingly that Minas "could never be completely pacified" by the ruling Hada clan of Rajputs (2003:219).

Local Lore

Most Jahazpur Minas live today outside the town proper in one of the twelve hamlets, where they are demographically dominant.[17] Local lore

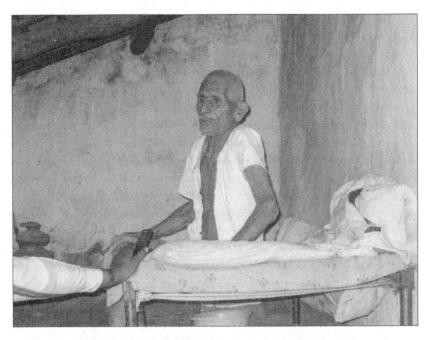

Figure 16. Hazari Lal Mina telling local histories.

holds that they formerly resided in town and later decamped. One shop-keeper informed us early on that there was once a Mina neighborhood "but now it no longer exists. But their *hathai* [meeting place] is still there. When they gather to make annual offerings to their ancestors, then afterward they convene at this hathai." We heard the same again and again.

My interview texts and diary entries, to which I now turn, offer some glimpses into the twelve hamlets, but I retain my focus on the presence/absence, or absent presence, of Minas in the qasba. As for the hamlets, during my fieldwork year they represented a world with which I was and was not familiar. That is, because of having done so much fieldwork in villages, the physical layout of the twelve hamlets, streets and inner court-yards, made me feel nostalgically and pleasurably at home. Yet I knew that Mautis Minas' culture and history had distinctive qualities. It was not nec-essarily the same as the culture and history of Ghatiyali's farming families, including its Mina farmers. I had to curb my sense of comfortable familiar-ity and pay close attention.

Most of our forays into local Mina history were made by seeking out aged Mina men with reputations for knowledge. Bhoju was able to locate them through his excellent connections in the twelve hamlets. These connections had been forged in part because of Bhoju's status as school headmaster in Pancha ka Bara, one of the hamlets. Still more helpful were his close friendships with several successful Mina professionals who worked in and around Jahazpur, doing business in areas such as life insurance and real estate. These men lived in their ancestral multigenerational joint family homes in nearby Mina villages including some that belonged to Jahazpur municipality and others that did not. In either case, their homes and lives were in some ways object lessons in the union of rural and urban.

Whenever we found a knowledgeable Mina person from whom we elicited local history, I would be repeatedly impressed, thinking that these unwritten Mina histories were as detailed, dramatic, complex, intrigue-ridden, full of internecine rivalry and genealogical complexities as those of the much-studied Rajputs. Local Mina history had played out on a small scale in terms of territory and left little in the way of written records. I struggled to follow long, meandering accounts of long-ago events related in rustic Rajasthani often from nearly toothless mouths. Bhoju and I spent many long hours trying to transcribe and translate these recorded interviews, telling ourselves it was worth the time and effort. We also had to acknowledge that much remained opaque and fragmented. Corroboration across speakers only emerged in a few cases.

I was struck whenever visiting the twelve hamlets by meetings with returnees. These were Minas who had traveled the country, and sometimes the world, as soldiers or officers in the Indian army. After retirement, they settled contentedly back into their villages, cultivating crops, enjoying roasted corn, delighted to show a foreigner their favorite spots of natural beauty as well as their local temples.[18] While some of our Mina history interviews were with nonliterate elders in the twelve hamlets, several of our most fruitful conversations were with Mina educators and retired military officers. The distance between them is only a generation, or two at the most.

One recurrent theme in my journals is the ways that local landscapes are incorporated into Mina lore and the pride and pleasure that Minas of the twelve hamlets took in their densely storied landscape: the rocky hills of Sailadanta (Porcupine Teeth); the legend of Bindhyabhata (Pierced Rock). The latter was said to have held one end of an acrobat's tightrope stretched all the way from the remote Jahazpur fort. On one of my revisits,

Figure 17. Gol Hathai (Round Meeting Place); where Minas from the twelve hamlets gather once a year in the qasba neighborhood where they no longer reside.

spanning the winter break of 2013–14, Bhoju and I took a climb into the hills around Vindhyabhata. High on the hillside was a year-round water source, miraculous in origin, called Bhim-lat or "Bhima's Kick." The Mahabharata hero, the strongest of the five Pandava brothers, was said to have created the pool when he and his family were wandering here during their forest exile and felt thirsty. No one could plumb the bottom; seven brothers tied their seven turbans together and still could not reach it, we were told. Our guide was a retired army officer, aged but intrepid and spry; he was surely over seventy and walked with a cane. He was so determined we should see the pool, he led us on a precarious climb that no old man (let alone an aging anthropologist in slip-on sandals) ought to have taken. Indeed, I halted short of the desired view, handing my camera over to braver souls.

Two main topics integral to elicited local histories are closely interrelated. The first is the out-migration of the Minas from Jahazpur; the second is the Minas' ongoing claims on a ritual place within the town. At the center of these narratives is the Gol Hathai or "round meeting place." In what is now a Muslim neighborhood, the Minas' Gol Hathai sits in a state of apparent disrepair and disuse. I was deeply disappointed at my first sight of it. So many people had mentioned it as a landmark, I was expecting something far more striking. I recorded in my 13 September journal entry: "I still have trouble matching stories with places; the Gol Hathai of the Minas was perhaps the most anticlimactic . . . and yet it figures in local geography; the Minas are here, but they're not here." Many persons referred to the Gol Hathai as evidence that the Minas once had lived in this neighborhood, now largely Muslim.

Once a year, at Diwali, the chips and cracks covered over with a nice cloth, the Gol Hathai is briefly reclaimed as part of the Mina community's protracted and multi-sited ritual, paying respect to their ancestors. Ram Dayal, another retired military man, who lived in Ghanti ka Bara, was a regular participant in the Mautis Minas' annual rituals for their forefathers. Ram Dayal described a whole sequence of places visited during these rituals, including the Gol Hathai: "We go every year to the Hathai to do *chant bharna*. First we have a meeting at Chavundia, and we worship the goddess; then we go to the Hathai; and then we go to our Char Bhuja temple near the Kalyanji temple where the deity's chariot is kept; and then we go to our small Hathai near Sitala Mata. And then we come back to Chavundia and there is a water tank there called Chantola, that is where we make our ancestral water offerings." Thus Minas reenact their qasba history, keeping alive in collective memory a move from the area around the Gol Hathai out to Chavundia (and eventually beyond).[19]

To make annual ritual water offerings to the ancestors (*chant bharna*) is not unique to Minas. Most Hindu communities perform such a ritual around the festival of Diwali. Each group does it differently, at a different time of day or a different specified body of water.[20] Mautis Mina practices, however, are especially elaborate. With ritual movements they mark specific spaces inside and outside the walls that hold significance for their particular history.[21]

The Minas have a Vishnu temple in the qasba to which Ram Dayal refers in his description of their Diwali rite. It is just a short distance from the Kalyanji temple, a major Vaishnavite site tended by Brahmins. While scores of interviewees had mentioned the Gol Hathai as evidence of Mina presence in Jahazpur town, only a few had thought to tell us about this small temple. Neither Bhoju nor I were aware of it until the day of Jahazpur's grand Jal

Jhulani festival when all the Vaishnavite gods are processed to the water reservoir.

As related in Chapter 4, we sat for some time in the Kalyanji temple, watching their respective priests lovingly adorn and worship the two lead chariots (Vishnu from the fort, who was known as the Kile-vala, and Kalyanji) before the parade would commence. Just before that moment of departure arrived, these two were joined by the Mina chariot. The Mina Vishnu temple turned out to be located just down the street, and we went later to explore it. Although its exterior was unprepossessing, enshrined within was a beautiful four-armed Vishnu. It is telling that the Mina chariot comes third, just behind what are known as the "two lead chariots," among twenty-three all told. That means it was likely one of the original deities to have been paraded and bathed on Jal Jhulani, a festival that has steadily expanded, as we have seen, so that now even formerly excluded communities such as the Khatiks and Regars participate, bringing up the rear. Minas, as already noted, serve as priests at most local goddess temples including Chavundia Mata, arguably the most important. While it would be fair to say that Mina identity is far from primarily Vaishnavite, they nonetheless play an important part in this long-established, town-wide festival that includes only deities associated with Vishnu.

How and Why the Minas Moved Outside the Walls

16 September (about six weeks into fieldwork)
Yesterday I did ordering and lists of questions in the morning which was helpful; I proudly gave Bhoju a print-out of my list of "four theories" why the Minas don't live in town:
1. They moved from the town to the small hamlets so they could more easily be thieves and no one would see their loot. [e.g., one person, a shopkeeper, told us wryly, "They got tired of answering questions such as 'where did you get that goat?'"]
2. Some converted to Islam and stayed in town, no longer to be known as Mina but becoming Deshvali Muslims; those who remained Hindus moved out to the hamlets to escape the threats of the Mughals. [Some Deshvali Muslims share lineage names with some Minas, although there is not a perfect match.]
3. They were rewarded with agricultural land by the royal family whom they served as guards/soldiers; once they had the land, little

by little, they moved out to work on it and thus the hamlets formed; this is the way villages come into being as population grows in a particular place.

This one has now been elaborated in that it has been related to the closing of the town gates at dusk . . . if they were out working their land, they couldn't work late as farmers sometimes need to work, and still get home. . . . the obvious solution to make their homes "outside the walls."[22]

4. The Minas *never* lived in town; they just came into town then as now to do the rituals to their ancestors.

Without saying anything Bhoju took a black pen and crossed out #1, the "thieves" theory, telling me later that it wasn't good to have it lying around for fear someone would see the paper on his desk.

I was quite taken aback by Bhoju's abrupt action; I had never previously seen him treat a typescript of mine, however ephemeral, in such a cavalier fashion. (A respect for the printed word remains powerful in these parts.) The funny thing is, there was one sole Mina who regularly frequented Bhoju's home, who might conceivably sit down at Bhoju's desk and read the papers lying on it even if they were in English. That was his dearest friend, Shiv Lalji, another school headmaster and prosperous speculator in real estate. I had more than once heard Shiv Lalji himself joke about his community's past as bandits. On reflection it is easy to see, as we know very well in the United States, that to joke about one's own maligned identity is not the same as having others, especially foreigners, put such aspersions down on paper.

Members of the Mina community most commonly provided the third cause on my list as the main reason that Mina families, at least those belonging to the Mautis lineage, had quit their old neighborhood inside the walls to settle one or another of the twelve hamlets. It is hard to be a farmer and live inside the walls. Here is how Ram Dayal Mina described an aftermath of the move, as recollected by one of his own forebears. He uses the term "Darbar," which I have in the past translated as "Court." In this region of Rajasthan Darbar often refers to a person of preeminent power, usually a Rajput. Here I imagine it refers to one of the Rajput agents of power delegated to serve in Jahazpur on behalf of remote Udaipur. "So the Court called him [my forefather] back and asked him why he didn't want to live in town. He replied, 'You have these gates and they are closed and this is a problem: The gate not being open late at night or early in the morning, and our agricultural work being outside the walls.' Hearing these reasons, the Court agreed, and they [Ram Dayal's forefather's family] began to live in Chavundia."

Chavundia is the closest to Jahazpur proper of the twelve hamlets. Although outside the walls, it nowadays feels more like a town neighborhood than a hamlet. The cluster of houses and businesses has grown up around the goddess temple from which it takes its name. The Minas' other main deity, heroic Malaji, is at the top of the hill accessed from Chavundia. Eventually families that had moved from inside to Chavundia moved still further into the countryside, where more land was available, until all twelve hamlets were settled.

Another Mina elder related a similar story. His own forefathers had lived near the Gol Hathai, "but little by little our population grew, so then we came out to Chavundia. We had some fields that were further away; our land was in the direction of Sarsia and Nagola; but we sold it and moved all in one direction; into the twelve hamlets." He added, "At that time, the land was empty, lying there, so our forefathers opened it." Bhoju explained to me that the land would have been grazing land (*charagah*, jungle). In this context, the phrase "to open land" means that they plowed it for the first time.

Bhoju enquired about the move outside the walls: "Did it change your culture?" The answer to this came as a rather strong dismissal of any such suggestion: "There is no special difference: the way we live inside so we live outside. People live according to their community; they keep their own traditions, there is no change. In the past there was plenty of room in Jahazpur; so people used to move in because there was space, but now they are moving out." In speaking of the Minas' collective move out from the qasba into the twelve hamlets, which happened many years back, this man made light of it: a short move that did not alter their identity. He seems here to associate the short migration with the way that many of our neighbors in Santosh Nagar explained their move out from qasba to suburb as a simple need for more living space.

Yet it strikes me that the Mautis Minas' collective transformation into agriculturalists, living on their own land and cultivating it, did mark a significant shift in orientations and identity. The elaborate ritualization of their ongoing connection with a qasba neighborhood, as performed annually at Diwali, seems to me evidence of this.

We have no knowledge of where the ancient Jains who vanished from Jahazpur went, after securing their exquisite, revered images safely underground. In contemporary times, Jahazpur's Jains are a restless, highly mobile community. There are neighborhoods in the qasba named after whole lineages that no longer live here. Jain families seeking more compatible surroundings or better business opportunities continue to move, generally to larger urban areas. But those who stay in Jahazpur have the strong sense of belonging to a special place.

Jahazpur Jains

> Nemi Nath came out of the ground in Jahazpur, and for that reason we call this area *atishay kshetra* [hallowed ground]. (Interview with Bal Kishan Jain, teacher, 26 September 2010)

My interactions with Jahazpur's Jain community were, as already indicated, relatively scarce. I remember once thanking our Jain neighbor profusely for informing me about an important upcoming Jain procession. "Who else would tell you?" she bluntly responded. The implication was clear: only Jains know about Jains. During that procession I did notice many Jahazpurites going about their market business but showing little interest in the procession: "The Jains are doing their thing . . . but it doesn't concern us," seemed to be an attitude, and it struck me because it contrasted with spellbound onlookers at both Hindu and Muslim public religious events.

In Jahazpur town today live both Digambara ("sky-clad") and Svetambara ("white-clad") Jains, categories derived from a well-known split that took place during the early centuries of the religion's formation in India. From the iconographic traits of most emerged images in this area, it seems clear enough that the ancient Jains who lived around Jahazpur, perhaps a good millennium after that split, were predominantly Digambara.[23] Moreover, the ongoing flurry of fund-raising, temple-building, web site action initiated by the most recently unearthed cache of images in the heart of the qasba, is also very much a Digambara project (see the Epilogue). Within Jainism are additional complex divisions which, although salient in

Jahazpur practice and society, do not fall within this chapter's limited scope.[24]

Jain interviewees regularly referred to the first major split in Jain identities, represented by separate temples. To the question, "How many Jain temples are there in Jahazpur?" a Jain man responded: "There are two: one Digambar; the other is Oswal or Svetambar." He went on, however, to elaborate another major bifurcation in Jain dharma between those who practice image worship and those who do not. But he added that all of Jahazpur's Jains, whether Digambara or Svetambara, identified as *murti-pujak*. This term designates Jains who ritually respect images of the twenty-four Jain teachers—called *Tirthankaras* ("forders" of the ocean of existence) or *Jinas* ("victors" over the body and its passions).

All kinds of people in Jahazpur were quick to say that Jains had lived in this place from ancient times, or even that they were the very first to settle here, in part because of the already noted phenomenon: Jain images, intact and often exquisite, keep emerging during excavations of Jahazpur land. I heard repeatedly from Hindus of ancient Jains' wisdom in burying and thus securing their images—purportedly on receiving the news of fabled iconoclast emperor Aurangzeb's approach.[25]

Lined up in a side room of Jahazpur's rather cramped Digambara Jain temple are a row of beautifully carved statues of standing tirthankaras, naked as is typical of Digambara images. All these, which I first saw in 2006 and photographed again in 2010, had been found beneath the town during various construction projects. Another Jain image, a seated one and therefore less evidently belonging to either Digambara or Svetambara, had found a home in the Juna Char Bhuja temple due to its placement being disputed (A. Gold 2013). These statues, a striking material presence, are understood as signs of dramatic changes that took place long ago. They also denote present-day transformations as their reappearance is a result of the town's expansion and prosperity. They serve to provoke speculation on history and place.[26]

Here is how one Jain man explained the whole phenomenon:

It was the rule of Muslims: Babur, Akbar, Shah Jahan . . . Aurangzeb. He wanted to spread the influence of his religion, he tried to destroy Hindu and Jain dharma. All the Hindu and Jain temples in India, he tried to break them. Hindus wanted to fight and they died in the

battle to protect their dharma. Jains don't like to do battle, according to their religion; so they thought, "When better days come, we
will take them out." So with proper ceremonies they buried them,
so that no harm would come to them, and they fixed them in such
a nice way. But as it happened they did not live to see better days;
all these people died and no one knew where the images were. They
buried them to protect them; they were all buried upside down.
When people dig to build a new home, they find them.

Hindus were prone to stress Hindu folly or bravery in thinking they
would fight and save their images, versus Jain wisdom or cowardice in
hiding theirs and fleeing according to their doctrine of nonviolence. One
Hindu man with deep roots in the town gave this interpretation:

The Jain images are not broken because they hid them in the
ground. You see, Jains don't fight. The Hindus didn't hide their
images, because they intended to fight. But the Jains found ways to
protect them, because their religion is nonviolent. So they ran away.
They ran away and nobody knew where they had buried the images.
So nowadays, when foundations are laid for new buildings, Jain
images come out. Some of them are as deep as eight or nine feet
underground, but when they dig foundations these images emerge.
They are not broken.

Another Hindu, the young journalist Deepak Pancholi, provided the
most detailed elaboration on Jahazpur history:

Jain dharma came here, after the time of the Guptas [normally
dated 320 to 550 CE], and they built their temples and monasteries
here, at that time when the Gupta era ended and Jain dharma was
on the ascendant.

And because of the Nagdi River the Jains came here to bathe and
they accepted it as a sacred place, and then they settled here and
began to live here. And the kings of Jahazpur protected them
and helped them and they had their temples built here.

After the Guptas there were lots of Jains, and then they heard
that the Mughals were coming and destroying temples. [Well over a

millennium would have elapsed between the Guptas and the Mughals.] So in advance of the Mughals' arrival, they took all their images out from the temples and buried them in the earth.

There is a line: from the hospital to the Harijan Mohalla to Galgatti, in that area whenever you find a buried image you find a stone pillar next to it, to protect it. And the images were all buried upside down so they would not be harmed. The pillars are laid on their side, over the images, to protect them.

Some people thought there must have been an earthquake, but I don't think so, because of the way they were arranged: it was systematic. And also they put a coat of clay on the images so insects and other things wouldn't harm them, like chemicals. Sometimes they might break because of temperature change, but they [the images' surfaces] were protected with clay.

I learned of recent out-migrations of Jains, evidenced by the names of neighborhoods in the qasba. In 2011 we interviewed Mohan Das Vairagi, who lived in a qasba area called Natiyon Neighborhood (Natiyon ka Mohalla). He explained that this was a Jain lineage, but that "now there are no members of that lineage left on the street." Only the name remains. He told us, "There is nobody left, there is only Agarwal, Mahesvari, and Osval [all merchants]; Vairagi and Parasar [Vaishnav and Brahmin lineages, respectively] who live in this neighborhood, but it is still called by its old name—just like Jahazpur's name used to be Yagyapur." This analogy is poignant because it is misconstrued. The name Natiyon has endured as a term of reference, while the name Yagyapur has not. But I knew what he meant; the depths and shallows of the past are revealed in names.

Stories of Stone and Flesh

If Jains and Minas are the oldest inhabitants of this region, as everyone in town agrees they are, how should we envision their ongoing interrelationship? In what ways is its dynamic foundational to qasba life? Identity, religion, and power slip, collide, merge, repel, and reconfigure. Early on Bhoju and I began to realize that the apparently separate paths of Minas and Jains were oddly and complexly intertwined in Jahazpur's past. The oddness of these linkages should serve to reinforce our portrayal of a local politics of negotiated pluralism in Jahazpur, one in which ideals and pragmatics interact.

I turn to stone images and orally transmitted tales of conflict and rebalancing as media through which to observe configurations, if shifting ones, of Mina and Jain interactions in Jahazpur's self-defined character as a plural place. I focus on three sets of objects or episodes involving images and what they represent, ritual processes, and politics. These are, first, Matolai Mataji: a Hindu goddess shrine tended by a Mina priest but acknowledged by both Jains and Minas as incorporating an ancient Jain figure; second, the annual buffalo sacrifice to Chavundia Mata from which it is said prasad was once regularly sent to a Jain home; and third, the sati stones said to be merchant women who "became sati for Minas."

Image and Temple Pass from Jains to Minas

That the most ancient Jains, who left their images so carefully buried, preceded the Minas in settling Jahazpur (or rather the terrain on which Jahazpur would come to be) was implicit in many conversations. One of the Jain men we interviewed explained his own view of Jahazpur's ancient history, without referring directly to the Minas' installation of the goddess Chavundia: "The grandson of Emperor Ashok accepted Jain religion, and from that time there was a Jain area in Jahazpur. . . . The whole region was Jain.[27] . . . On the step well at Barah Devra [Twelve Temples, just on the edge of Jahazpur] you can see a Jain sign, and near the Ayurvedic hospital is a pillar that is a Jain pillar."

A broad consensus held that the building housing Chavundia Mataji, which today belongs to the Minas, had likely been built by Jains. The Minas, we were told, found it empty after the Jain exodus. As Hindus, people explained, Minas felt that a sacred place without an image was "inauspicious," so they installed their goddess, whose powers are revered throughout Jahazpur Hindu society today.[28]

To the question, "Who built the Chavundia temple?" a Vaishnavite merchant interviewee responded, "I think it might have been a Jain temple, and the Minas took it over. Who can fight the Minas? The mayor and *sarpanch* [head of the panchayat] are all Minas, so nowadays no one can oppose them." Bhoju became increasingly intrigued by the ways Jain spaces had been usurped by Minas.

Bhoju asked Deepak Pancholi, who spoke with much authority, "What about Chavundia temple? It looks old." Deepak replied:

Yes! It seems like this temple goes back to the Gupta era. Perhaps there were some other images in it, originally; but it was empty and the Minas installed their own image [of the Goddess].

Maybe the Jains made this temple and took out the images and buried them; and the temple had remained empty. It seems as if the temple was not built for Mataji [the Hindu goddess now installed there]. It could date back to the time of the Jain sect (*sampraday*).

This presumption about Chavundia was strongly reinforced by reference to another shrine we went to see in Matolai, one of the twelve hamlets not far beyond the town, yet with a totally rural feeling about it. Bal Kishan Jain had told us about an image there, saying, "There was a Padmavati Mata, near Matolai." He said that the Minas accepted the mother, but did not call her Padmavati. Ram Dayal Mina also told us about this image, saying she was "Savan Mata who is called Padmavati by baniyas."[29] Bal Kishan added that he had brought the issue up with a Mina leader [in the twelve hamlets], who had responded in no uncertain terms: "Please leave this matter alone, you will never be able to take her!"

Bhoju was fascinated, and I never could resist an excursion. In Matolai we found a small goddess shrine, a very simple structure akin to thousands which dot the landscape of this whole region. However, Matolai's image proved to be unusual indeed. It appears as a jina (a Jain renouncer figure) sitting on the head of a more typical Rajasthani goddess. This intimate merging of divergent religious imagery produces a strange visual effect.[30] We found a Mina shrine priest nearby, in the guise (as I put it to myself) of a village shepherd. He was in fact herding sheep with the lax attentiveness the job requires. As it unfolded, he was a member of the same family that served as priest in Chavundia Mata's big urban temple in town. He and his brother traded posts every six months. At another time of year this seemingly utterly rural person would be at the busy town temple, while his brother, presumably, shifted to more laid-back sheep duty.

Matolai's image with its strikingly blatant fusion (or dissonance) tells a story. Moreover, because of the connection between rural shrine and urban temple evidenced by a single priestly lineage among the Minas tending both, we may reasonably connect the fusion of Hindu goddess and Jain

Figure 18. Matolai Mataji.

renouncer imagery in Matolai with the purported Hindu appropriation of the larger temple. Thus a profound link going back many generations between Mina shrine priests and formerly Jain images and structures is demonstrated. At some point in history, after the departure of an original group or groups of Jains, Minas who inhabited this part of Rajasthan took over or took care of structures and images the departed Jains had left behind.

Several Jains we interviewed averred in so many words, whether about the temple in town or the image in the hamlet, "We'll never get it back, not from the Minas." They readily acknowledged the physical and equally the contemporary political strength of Minas, and their own disinclination to create friction. They explicitly stressed that the Jain character is essentially nonviolent and noncombative. As one Jain explained it to us, his community has no enmity (*virodh*) with anyone, "not even Muslims." His implication would be that if there were no enmity with Muslims, surely there would be none with the Minas who were after all Hindus. This is why, as we heard in the previous chapter, Jain parades need not take peacekeeping measures in the way required of other communities' processions.

From the Mina perspective, years of worship and service make the difference. Their attachments were devotional. It is worth noting a similar if far more recent story surrounding the Jain image now residing in the Vishnu temple (mentioned earlier in this chapter). Here the tale has living witnesses. I heard that when Jains tried to remove it, the truck broke down; or perhaps the statue could not be lifted. From this kind of devotional perspective, one which refers to miraculous powers inherent in the images, the word "appropriation" is quite incorrect; rather the images themselves have agency and they respond to human emotions of love and human actions of faithful care.[31]

The Head of a Sacrificed Buffalo Calf Passes from Minas to Jains

In interviews with persons from multiple positions in the caste and class hierarchy we heard repeatedly that in the old days (and possibly even recently although the contemporary reality was disputed), the Minas annually sacrificed a male buffalo calf to the goddess Chavundia Mata. After the sacrifice, the head of the calf would be carried on a platter to the home of the "*chaudhary*."[32] When we asked who this was, the answer was

Mahajan—an esteemed Jain merchant (only one interviewee put a name on one of these chaudharys). This generic chaudhary, we were told, would place his hand on the sacrificial head and then have it given "to eaters"; according to some, more specifically, these eaters were the Regars, leather workers connected with the chaudhary by hereditary patronage links. Some specified that it was a Regar who delivered the head.

The ethos of Hindu or South Asian practice at all levels insists that prasad (literally divine grace) cannot be refused (Gold 2008a). Hence the touch on the head before distributing to "eaters." It was clearly a symbolic acceptance of the prasad, an acknowledgment of the goddess and her devotees as possessing a power to be recognized by all, even by a paradigmatically vegetarian Jain. By definition Jains would never be "eaters," and they are legendarily opposed to animal sacrifice—an opposition that lies in some ways at the heart of their religious identity in Rajasthan (Babb 2004). Thus to deliver to the door of an esteemed Jain person the prasad from an animal sacrifice offered to the goddess was sheerly and significantly ceremonial. Some tellers give it that spin: the Jains were receiving their due and it was a respectful if distasteful process. Others make it definitely an act of subversive defiance, a gesture of respect that was also an insult.

There was something about this tale, which we recorded from Minas, Regars, and one Vaishnavite merchant, that seemed to me to convey an uneasily negotiated copresence of Mina and Jain communities, commonly accepted as the two original populations. We were too polite to ask Jains about it, and I have reason to believe they would have ignored or dismissed such a query. A Jain leader, at least from the perspective of the present, could hardly be thrilled to open his front door to the sight of a bloody buffalo head on a tray. To bring it would seem on the part of the Minas a gesture of deference but simultaneously of disrespect, a ritualized power play. The goddess Chavundia herself plays a role here, as we will see, for we heard of occasions when the sacrifice was stopped, and she rapidly punished those who stopped it. Ultimately they had to agree to restore her annual *pada*, her buffalo calf.

In recent years the general tide of public opinion in India has turned against animal sacrifice, and the practice has been outlawed in numerous localities.[33] The story of the annual buffalo sacrifice to Chavundia Mataji looms importantly in the town's history, at least among Mina elders, for it validates the balance of power between their goddess and the vegetarian baniyas, and it stresses that Mina traditions continue to hold sway. Several stories about attempts to stop the practice of sacrificing a buffalo, and a goat with it in many tellings, were located in the past—one clearly in the time of kings, others more recently. All told, while we had about fifteen interviewees who spoke about an annual sacrifice in Jahazpur, we never were able to nail down exact dates and details: when, why, and how it had been banned and then reinstated. The legal situation is fuzzy as well.

Ram Dayal Mina told it this way: "In the time of the Darbar there lived one Bhavar Lal Chaudhari [a baniya]. And after the animal sacrifice (*bali*), they took the head of the buffalo calf on a tray covered with a red cloth to his house. But now the people in the town don't like it; for the past twenty years, they are not sending the head." Bhoju asked why the Minas sent the head of the calf to the chaudhary, who was after all neither priest nor medium. Ram Dayal answered:

> Their forefather [that is, the Baniya chaudhary's forefather] was a great devotee of the Mother. Yes, he was a devotee; and he was the one who paid the cost of the calf, going back to the time of the Maharajas.
> [So he gets the *prasad* or blessing but doesn't eat it.]
> I have seen myself the head of the goat or buffalo, being carried there, and their Regars, they would take it. But nowadays, no one says, "Here is your *pada*."
> [If we did] the Baniyas would be angry, and they no longer pay the costs either!

Chagan Lal Regar, an educated professional of the leather worker community, gave the following account to us when we interviewed him at his home in Chavundia:

> The name of this neighborhood comes from the goddess, and her special temple here. It was built in the time of the great kings. Before the rains they would perform a sacrifice, offering her a goat and a buffalo calf. They used to do it every year, but now they do it every other year; this year they did make the offering. And the head of the calf they would take to the chaudhary and he would put his hand on it and place five rupees on the tray, and then give it to the Eaters.

Notice that he does not say "give it to us." In the past Regars served the high castes and would have readily accepted this prasad; but a man like

Chagan Lal, who holds a high position in the education department and owns a grocery store as well, dis-identifies with those Regars of the past.

Ram Kanvar Sarraph (a Hindu Agarwal merchant very involved in Jahazpur civic efforts) also talked with us about the buffalo sacrifice to Chavundia.[34] He said, "They used to do the *bali* and take the buffalo head to the chaudhary and he would put his hand on it." Bhoju asked him, "Who was the chaudhary?" and the answer was simply, "A mahajan." Bhoju continued to probe: "Is this tradition still going on?" Ram Kanvar answered directly, "Yes it is, but it is not done openly, it is done secretly."

Hira Lal Mina, eighty-five years old, talked about the annual animal sacrifice to the goddess. "In Asarh, the first month of the monsoon, people of Jahazpur offer in sacrifice one buffalo and one goat. They would take the head of the buffalo to the mahajan chaudhary [head person among the Jain merchants]. And the chaudhary gave it to the Regars [leather workers]. But [he reemphasizes] it went first from the goddess to the chaudhary."

We heard several confusing stories about attempts to put a stop to this sacrifice, set both in the colonial era and in the present. Hira Lal responded to Bhoju's questions about such an attempt by telling a story that clearly dated to the past, pre-1947, when the area was still officially ruled from Udaipur. Here is what he said:

Yes, they stopped it for one year. The hakim [king's agent] stopped the animal sacrifice. His subdistrict was Itunda. He would come here riding on a camel or a horse. But [after he stopped the sacrifice] that hakim would fall off of his horse. And the women of his family became possessed as if by ghosts or witches. Everything of the hakim's and of the merchants' was spoiled.

So they had to do something about it. They decided to ask Chavundia Mataji what was happening; so they offered *dhup* [ghi on smoldering cow dung] and the bhav came [the priest became possessed by the goddess].

They asked her what was wrong.

She said, "Why did you stop my bali?" And so they started it again! They sent riders into the twelve hamlets to call the Mina leaders. And everyone was afraid: "Why is he calling?"

But some leader came to [the neighborhood of] Chavundia and told them: "A miracle! the hakim's family is ill!" They called the bhav and she said: "Why did you come here, you wretch, the one who stopped my balidan [sacrificial offering]?"

They dragged him here unconscious, and he said "My women are all ill," and she [the goddess] said, "All will be well if you start my bali again."

Now, it seemed we had found an explanation for why this long-ago chaudhary received the head as prasad: because his household allied with the hakim was afflicted, along with the hakim. Afterward, his family undertook to pay the expenses for the ritual. Therefore he would by custom, as the patron of the sacrifice, receive the choice prasad.

From another, equally senior Mina, Hazari Lal, we heard a slightly different account of the dramatic moment when the animal sacrifice was first stopped and then resumed. This seems to be the very same story that Hira Lal told us. But Hazari Lal followed it up a bit confusingly with another narrative from more recent times in which the impudence to the Jains is made quite explicit.

As Hazari told it:

There was a ruler whose name was Kesar Singh. He forbade the *bali*. After that, what came to pass? All the queens started to play like witches! Kesar Singh was on his way to Itunda, on horseback. A wild boar came out of the bush, and the king fell off his horse, and he heard the queens in the palace shrieking. So they went to the temple and they called the bhav and the bhav asked, "Why did you call me?"

And Kesar Singh said, "My queens are playing" [that is, have become possessed].

The goddess said, "You ought to know better! Why did you stop my balidan?"

So, after that, he started offering it again.

Then there was another event that happened much later. Once the Minas were sacrificing a pada and some baniyas reported to the police, and the police grabbed the Minas. Then all the Minas in Chavundia got together, and after the police left, the next day, they gathered and gave another bali to Mataji. Because the police had come and prevented the bali. They said, "Yes sir we won't do it!" But they took the very same pada and sacrificed it, the very one that the police had saved. And they called some Regars to skin her, and they took all the meat in a bag; they took it to the houses of the Baniyas; and they called, "Hey Honorable Merchant, Please come, how much cooked vegetables do you need?" ["*Hey Sethji, aiye! kitni sabzi chahiye?*"]

And after that they collected all the expenses for the sacrifice from the baniyas: the cost of the calf, and the labor of the Regars. At that time, they would take the head to the Mahajan, and he would put money on it, and then they would take it elsewhere.

Who knows, maybe he [the Seth to whom the presumably unwelcome prasad is delivered] is the very one who made the complaint to the police.

Bhoju and I both tried to probe why the head was sent to the baniyas to begin with. Hazari Lal's answer was this: "It is *lag*, a system from old times; the system of the Regar bringing the head on a tray." *Lag* is normally understood as a gift denoting respect, not insolence.[35] Hazari Lal told us that the "kitni sabzi" ("How much cooked vegetables?") episode happened during his lifetime, less than sixty years ago.

These narratives, mostly but not exclusively told by Minas, contain subtle and not so subtle digs at the Jains. The stories make it clear that the Jain chaudhary is leader at least partially on the sufferance of the Minas, and of their goddess who must be worshipped according to Mina, not Jain practice. None of this was made explicit until Hazari Lal Mina added the "kitni sabzi" story, in which muted antagonism becomes blatant performance, provoked by attempts to put a stop to the sacrifice (changing the balance of divine and human power). By attributing the victory to the agency of the goddess herself, no one loses face totally. The Minas are glad enough to follow her orders; the Jains are cowed into acceptance by her immanent punishing power. However doubtful we may find the chronology and specifics of these tales, massed together they suggest an orchestrated if uncomfortable sharing of place between Minas and Jains of the qasba, who have long lived in one another's company. Here the relationship is negotiated by Chavundia Mother.

No one could really tell us when or if the annual sacrifice had ceased. Some said it hadn't been done in years; some said it was done on the sly every other year; some said a calf had indeed been sacrificed this very year.

There was, however, agreement that the head is no longer delivered to the home of a merchant.

Jain Women's Sati Stones Pass Honor to Mina Heroism

There is one more story of Mina and Jain relations to be considered. We heard it only from a few elderly Mina men. It expressed blatant disrespect for Jains, but also posited extremely close relations between the two groups. Among the many sati monuments in Jahazpur there are stones known as the *chaudhari ki sati*. It is a truism that Jains would not go to war. So how could Jain satis exist?[36]

These sati stones, we were told, honor Jain women who "became sati" for Mina warriors. As the simple tale, devoid of details, went: after their husbands had ignobly fled, these Jain women's honor was threatened. Who came to their rescue? It was Minas, who fought to the death to defend the abandoned wives of Jains. Hence the "Jain women became sati *for* the Minas." Kishanlal Mautis Mina told us the tale, beginning with the material evidence of the sati stones: "Near the step well are the *chaudhari ki sati*. These were wives of the Jain chaudhari family. The Mughals were attacking, threatening their honor; and their own husbands ran away. And Minas killed the Mughals, but they themselves perished in the battle. And so the Baniya ladies, five of them, became sati for their Mina defenders [whose lineage was Mautis]."

As Kishanlal bluntly put it, "There was no one else to protect them. But the chaudhari don't say 'these are satis for Minas'; they say it is Ghorla Brother's image."[37] Bhoju added as we typed our notes, "They are ashamed." The Jains in my experience are proud, not ashamed, of their commitment to nonviolence. But abandoning women in need of protection is of course another matter.

How Jahazpur Folds Minas and Jains into One Place

In August 2010, a few short weeks after my arrival, there was an election in Jahazpur for the town council. The chairman position was contested by seven candidates, all female as required by the state's affirmative action measures. Victorious was Kali Mina, whose husband, Gaiga Ram, had already served several terms as chairman (one of these already under her name). Gaiga Ram was widely appreciated as a government official who would get your work done without jerking you around—or as the Hindi idiom has it, dragging you. Maybe for his troubles, he would take something, but his demands were not unreasonable and his actions efficient. In short, he practiced a kind of "corruption without tears." Jahazpur had reelected him again and again for these reasons. I knew none of this, having only recently breezed into town. I talked some women friends into voting for a Brahmin woman lawyer. I joked about liking her symbol "kap-plet" (cup-plate) but what I actually especially liked was that she was running on her own qualifications, not to be the puppet of a literate husband. I made this clear and it was evidently well received. However, after my candidate lost, these friends reproached me; they would have preferred to have backed a winner.

Shortly after the election we interviewed some Minas in Borani about their political power. My journal from 22 August 2010 notes, "The Minas from Borani, one of the twelve hamlets, credit their leader [Gaiga Ram, and of course they are his allies and kin] for bringing electricity and other improvements to the twelve hamlets. Otherwise these things were in the center only."

In Borani we had spoken with several Mina men at once. One told us this: "In Jahazpur [qasba] they had electricity in 1963 but there was no light in the twelve hamlets until 1990; and no *nal* [water taps] either." The second man elaborated:

Before we didn't even know what *nagar palika* [municipality] meant. No one was taking care of us. All we knew was that if we needed kerosene or sugar we had to go to the town hall (nagar palika), or if we needed an ST certificate. But we didn't know about development and we didn't know what they could do for us; just the ration card. No one told us that facilities were available to the villages. We had the same ration as people in the town, but we had no conveniences (*suvidha*) whatsoever.

It was not until the era of Mina leadership, then, that amenities that had long been enjoyed "inside the walls" came to the twelve hamlets. Bhoju asked the Mina men, "What do the people who live inside the walls think about this?" One of them answered, "They are extremely jealous, because after we elected our own chairman we got light, we got roads . . ."

Our interviewee went on to note that there were 3,500 voters living in just four of the twelve hamlets—Borani, Bindhyabhata, Pancho ka Bara, and Lala ka Bara—all within a four kilometer area. This is a dense population in a small area. He added that there are 4,700 voters all told in the twelve hamlets. This would not give the Minas a clear majority. According to Bhoju, who as a headmaster assisted in the census of 2011, Minas make up no more than one-quarter of the voting public in Jahazpur municipality. But according to unrecorded viewpoints on local politics, as summarized by Bhoju Ram, "They all get together. Another reason is that there are many persons belonging to many different castes and so they are divided. But Minas keep together." In other words, like the Muslims as characterized by Bhairu Lal Lakhara (Chapter 2), Minas too are pigeons, not dogs.

Like all places, Jahazpur qasba is steeped in histories; these are plural histories because it is a fundamentally plural place. In this chapter I have attempted to sketch some materially evident, orally narrated elements of a dynamic qasba society. I have tried to highlight the links between two groups that on the surface would seem quite disconnected from one another. I did not intend to paint a comprehensive portrait of either the Mina or the Jain communities, as my knowledge is inadequate to do so. Rather, this chapter aimed to show how in present-day Jahazpur, as well as in some past eras, these two highly disparate groups have arrived at various modes of mutual accommodation. And these modes extend well beyond their everyday interactions as merchants and shoppers; or in these democratic times as members of the public and democratically elected leaders (a turning of the tables in some ways). The Jina-goddess hybrid image is revered, if largely by Minas. Might there have been a time when Jains' devotion to, or fear of punishment from, Chavundia Mata made them respect that buffalo head as prasad? Were the Mina warriors who gallantly defended the Jain ladies truly chivalrous? These things must remain mysterious, and the stories themselves blur with time.

PART II

Ecology, Love, Money

Chapter 6

Questioning Landscapes

Of Trees and a River

The hills and the river, respectively set above and flowing through the municipality of Jahazpur, are geophysical attributes of the landscape intrinsic to the town's social and cultural identities. They provide contrasting cases of environmental protection or restoration. To explore their situated histories illuminates the fluctuating constitution of persons and communities generated by a fluid, emotional interpenetration of self and place. We encounter variations in how forcefully this interpenetration may serve to generate care for the environment. Under some circumstances it appears to entail powerful motivations for direct action; under others breaks, ruptures, interruptions happen and care in the form of nostalgia or regret comes dishearteningly to seem like its opposite: indifference. But Jahazpur's experiences in these areas, and accordingly my own, demonstrate that at times paralysis resulting from a sense of helplessness may well be a reversible condition.[1]

As related in Part I, my first visit to Jahazpur as a research scholar had nothing to do with the qasba in all its religious and commercial vitality. Rather, I was following a trail blazed by Bhoju Ram, who wanted to show me the sacred grove on top of Malaji's hill. We had together been studying the phenomenon of Rajasthan's sacred groves on and off since the late 1980s, and we had spent the better part of the 1990s researching and writing oral histories of deforestation in the region. In short, we had trees on our minds.

In contrast to the friction occasionally provoked by our divergent views of caste and religion, a focus on environmental protection was an opportunity for Bhoju and me to work together with enthusiasm and total harmony. We both passionately seek evidence of positive efforts, of elements in Rajasthani culture that may be harnessed in the service of the earth. It consoled us both if we found ways, however small, to promote environmental well-being. Bhoju's tree-planting projects at several schools where he worked had been gratifying. In one case I had been able to fund his efforts, writing them as an educational initiative into a fellowship budget from the Spencer Foundation. Bhoju created original curriculum materials in an effort to inspire rural children to value and protect trees (Gold 2002).

In Jahazpur, Malaji's devotees required no outside intervention to inspire their tree protection efforts. Members of the Mautis Mina community were united in wishing to keep the hillside grove intact and donated generously, according to their means, to the shrine committee's efforts. Bhoju and I wrote about this grove together, with him taking the lead authorship (Gujar and Gold 2007). Thanks to Bhoju's original ethnography, Malaji's case supplied me with a powerful argument about the ways that rationalized tree and bio-diversity protection might be religiously motivated yet in no way dependent on faith in miracles. Moreover, local religious efforts on behalf of trees were not dependent on "saffron" politics (M. Sharma 2012). Jahazpur's other religiously respected, tree-covered hillside is not Hindu: Gaji Pir's tomb stands atop a hill just as densely wooded with old-growth trees as Malaji's.

In 2010–11 I was no longer particularly interested in sacred groves and my original project had no focus on ecology either. I had a whole new topic: the small town. Bhoju and I had not intended to get involved with the condition of the Nagdi River. Rather, it presented itself to us with full-blown fascination, by chance or fate, as often transpires in fieldwork. We ran with it, not only because of our predilection but because it was a topic about which everyone had something to say. The people of Jahazpur directed my studiously averted eyes to the Nagdi's present plight and told me stories of its previous charms. They eloquently recounted the river's travails as provoking struggle and sorrow. Since the time we turned our attention to the Nagdi, in the fall of 2010, this small river's tale has had so many twists and turns that we have twice published accounts of its unfinished story with thoroughly different endings (Gold and Gujar 2011, 2013). In this chapter, we report one more new and promising development. The river's story flows on.

Discrepancy

I perceived a discrepancy between the two flourishing groves of indigenous trees on protected hilltops and the dwindling river clogged with trash and filth. Sacred groves are "set apart" (to evoke Durkheim's still apropos definition of the sacred) from populated areas; in Jahazpur's case, they are set above it. Although it takes only a few minutes to climb the stairways leading up from different parts of town to reach one or another of Jahazpur's hilltop shrines—Malaji's temple or Gaji Pir's tomb—these shrines and trees are not located in the midst of humanity, as is the river. The growing town's residential and commercial areas have spread across the river but not up the hillsides.

Naveeda Khan elegantly describes a riverine setting in Bengal as "a domain of localized interactions" and points to noninstrumental "entanglements" that twine humans and landscapes together in all kinds of ways (Khan 2015). In Jahazpur's very different scenery, both protected trees and degraded rivers exhibit such multistranded meshing with the communities of people that care for and depend on them. Yet one attribute of rivers, their constant motion, renders them fundamentally different from the rooted.

When Bhoju introduced me to Malaji's shrine, over a decade back, I was still a scholar of nothing but the rural. At that time, biodiversity conservation—within which sacred groves were a small focal area—preoccupied much environmentalist thought. I came to the river in 2010, having recently repositioned my ethnographic work in a town and my academic orientations within urban studies. By then, as scarcity stories increased and water tables sank, water as topic and crisis had risen notably at the larger intersection of global environmental studies with South Asia.[2] Jahazpur's still-forested hills might seem to belong to a different discourse world, if not a different era, and to stand visibly for effectively protected nature. By contrast, Jahazpur's Nagdi River epitomizes a characteristically citified messiness—actual and conceptual, sociological and geophysical.

I elaborate separately on the contrasting ecological and social situations surrounding the trees and the river. These lead me eventually to reconsider observed discrepancies, dissolving a portion but pointing to some residual validity.

Protected Trees

The two wooded hilltops overlooking Jahazpur town are both sites of powerful presence: the Minas' Malaji and the Muslims' Gaji Pir. Both hills are covered with *dhokara* (*Anogeissus pendula*), a species that had dominated

Figure 19. Gaji Pir mazar and mosque; dense trees on hillside; fort ramparts to left.

this region through the first half of the twentieth century, before radical deforestation (Gold and Gujar 2002). These days it is mostly found only in the groves (*bani*) surrounding shrines.

Malaji is located atop the hill called Chavundia, after the goddess mentioned in Chapter 5, who is installed in a temple at its foot. The view looking down from Chavundia hill reveals a stark contrast between Malaji's tree-filled dominion and the more distant, barren landscape. The Mautis Minas, as explained earlier, are the dominant Mina lineage in Jahazpur municipality, where they maintain a prominent place both in politics and pageantry. It is they who tend and attend Malaji's temple. Malaji's efficacy in tree protection is embedded in a larger social and religious complex, including narrative traditions performed as songs.

Equally protected and equally embedded in a locally rooted religious community's lore is Jahazpur's other wooded hilltop, upon which Gaji Pir's enshrined tomb (*mazar*) resides, not far from the crumbling and deserted fort. Gaji's tomb is equally a storied place (see Chapter 4). Both Malaji and Gaji Pir are sites of profuse miracle stories, annual fairs, and everyday devotional practices.

Bhoju was drawn to learn about Malaji not only because of the notably green hillside but because of the way that Malaji's narrative traditions intertwined with those of the Gujar divinity, Dev Narayan.[3] He initiated independent research on Malaji in the early years of the century, and with his wife, Bali Gujar, he participated in a Malaji foot pilgrimage in August 2005. This pilgrimage is an annual event drawing ever-increasing participation and commencing with a major procession through the qasba. I have never walked along with them but have twice been able to attend the opening ceremonies and send-off for Malaji's foot pilgrimage.

In 2003, my first visit to the temple and grove on Chavundia hill, we photographed the shrine and hillside and interviewed Ram Swarup Mina, a key figure in the shrine's management. In Gujar and Gold 2007 we sketched Malaji's legendary life history, traced back about a millennium. Bhoju and I suggested in this article that the religious complex around Malaji drew its vitality and efficacy from a conjunction of narrative, ritual, and collective action. We also pointed out the importance of sites on the earth's surface to Malaji's biography, emphasizing again that reverence for places associated with a divinity's experiences—such as birth, battle, encounter with a holy person—infuse the material world with significance. The religious energies that went into protecting Malaji's grove on Chavundia hill emerged from a reverence that included not just trees but plant and animal life in many forms, as well as geological formations.

In general, Malaji's devotees find it meritorious work to protect the forests they view as sheltered by their chosen deity together with the birds and animals that live in them. As Bhoju put it, in his eloquent Hindi prose, "Believing service to living beings to be the greatest virtue, the Mautis Minas' selfless service to Malaji *becomes* protection of the natural environment" (my translation and italics). Note the deliberate wording here: protection of the environment is not the Mautis Minas' aim; rather it is a side effect or consequence of their true aim, which is serving their worshipped divinity and all associated plants and creatures. This service, which expresses their religiosity and their identity, *becomes* protection of the environment. Here is how they organized this efficacious protection.

About thirty years ago, on 16 July 1986, a committee was formed on behalf of the Mautis Mina in the twelve hamlets in order to oversee the development and care of Malaji's Jahazpur shrine. According to Ram Swarup, this measure was taken due to concern that Malaji's grove was threatened by the town's expanding population, Among this population there were doubt-less many who would not have heard of a god named Malaji; Bhoju himself had not known about Malaji until he started spending time with Jahazpur Minas. Since the committee's formation, each household among Mina fami-lies in the Twelve Village area around Jahazpur was to take regular turns sending one person to patrol and protect the forest belonging to Malaji. Every day of the year, two volunteer guards make their rounds, and the managing committee keeps track of whether or not a designated person arrives for his turn to patrol the hill. If someone who has been assigned a date does not show up for it, the community fines him 101 rupees. Other fines were estab-lished for owners who allowed their livestock to stray into the grove and for lopping branches or cutting wood from Malaji's grove. These fines are posted for all to see at the foot of the stairway that leads up to the temple.

What is striking about the Malaji model of sacred grove management is that it unites ongoing claims for a deity's miraculous power with a thor-oughly systematic and rationalized mode of landscape protection. Ram Swarup told us, as an afterthought it seemed, that if someone harms the forest and yet cannot be identified, then the community prays to Malaji, and Malaji punishes him. In adopting their pragmatic mode of tree protec-tion, the Mautis Minas did not shed their religious orientations but rather deployed them. Many scholars have noted that, when religiously protected groves lie near urban areas, regional population growth can threaten, dam-age, and ultimately destroy a deity's protected greenery. What Malaji's case reveals is that devotees are capable of establishing effective protection when it becomes necessary.

What motivates Malaji's devotees to donate their scarce time and resources to the collective project of sustaining their hillside's greenery? Bhoju and I argued in our earlier publications that this has something to do with the ongoing potency of their deity's life narrative as it celebrates his miraculous and valorous deeds, embedded in local landscapes. It also has much to do with the strength of the Mautis Mina population in the region, a strength that, as we have seen, is primarily demographic and polit-ical but is also rooted in common understandings of the Minas' primeval presence here and their consequent ST status. Not insignificantly, when the Mautis elders assemble within Jahazpur, whether for political or religious purposes, they seat their dignitaries and honored guests before a painted backdrop featuring idyllic natural scenery.

Gaji Pir, Jahazpur's other wooded hilltop shrine, houses a Muslim saint. The story of Gaji Pir, historically embedded with the specificity of emperors' names and dates, turns out to be of a genre frequently associated with regional warrior deities: the headless horseman.[4] Jahazpur's shrine is the resting place of the warrior's body (his head is elsewhere) and of his horse and his dog. Other open-air saints' tombs have accumulated around Gaji's *mazar*. As Chapter 4 details, Gaji's annual urs, a three-day festival in his honor, makes Gaji's followers visible to all of Jahazpur, much as the annual Malaji pilgrimage procession does for Malaji's Mina devotees. Both these elaborate processions traverse the heart of the qasba. Moreover, bystanders can make offerings in both cases: Malaji's procession includes a portable shrine, and for Gaji an ornate coverlet serves as a receptacle for cash.

A rich repertoire of miracle stories are volubly produced by devotees of Gaji Pir. These range from deathbed cures, to giving babies to the barren, to visions of moving lights, to locating thieves (as recounted in Chapter 4). Hindus as well as Muslims seek help from Gaji Pir. On the stairs going up to Gaji's tomb, at least twice in my research year, and once previously in 2006, I met the same old Hindu couple of the Soni or goldsmith community, who had climbed these stairs regularly for decades according to a vow they had taken in gratitude for the birth of a son, now an adult (A. Gold 2013).

A few years before commencing fieldwork in Jahazpur, but after we had documented tree protection in Malaji's grove, I asked Bhoju casually if devotees of Gaji Pir also took turns patrolling for wood thieves, their hill being equally green. He replied at that time, somewhat glibly it seemed to me, "They don't need a guard, because the Muslims are afraid of Allah and the Hindus are afraid of communal trouble." During my residence in Jahazpur in 2010–11, I came to believe that this understanding is more or less the way things work. Jahazpur, however urban, remains a place that consumes fuel wood and fodder, testifying of course to its rural elements: cooking on fire and cherishing fresh dairy products. Firewood gatherers sally forth every day, to return with bundles gleaned from various areas on the outskirts of town. Goats graze on the hillsides. Yet the groves of trees surrounding both Malaji's and Gaji's shrines remain inviolate, neither cut for firewood or timber nor lopped to feed animals. Goatherds graze their animals near the fort but refrain from lopping.

Any local person may visit these two hilltop shrines, no matter their religious identity, and pray for boons or general well-being. But Mautis

Minas take special responsibility for Malaji, as do most of the town's Muslims, Deshvali and Pardeshi alike, for Gaji Pir. Minas and Muslims are equally deep-rooted communities understood by all to be integral to local history as well as forces in present-day electoral politics. However, because the vast majority of Minas reside in the twelve hamlets, they lack the constant presence that Muslims possess. Perhaps Malaji's trees would indeed be depleted were it not for the patrol system. Minas acknowledge that their motivation for organizing the tree-protection rotation was provoked by a sense of endangerment to the trees. The main Muslim residential neighborhood is right at the foot of Gaji Pir's hill. It would be hard to get away with wood thievery. Moreover, there is universal respect across all town communities for Gaji Pir's potency. Thus no guard has been necessary.

Between my first encounters with these two hilltops and my fieldwork year in Jahazpur, drivable dirt roads were cut into both sacred hillsides, funded by the broad communities of devotees. These roads slashed right through the beautiful groves. Such glaring gashes in the natural scenery of the wooded hillsides offer a visual rebuke to romanticization of the union of religion and ecology. In fact the wish to make the shrines accessible to aged or disabled persons trumped regard for the beauty or intrinsic natural value of the groves.

I never asked members of either the Muslim or Mina communities if they themselves minded the sacrifice of trees for road as I was hesitant to undermine their evident satisfaction with having achieved access. Intended not only to assist devotees unable to climb stairs but to facilitate the transport of building supplies required for shrine improvements, the roads remind us that the protection of trees on these hills isn't about nature, biodiversity, or sustainability per se. It is about devotion to revered powers and places. The beauty of a landscape may be a valued side effect of devotion and is often understood as proof of power, but it is not the highest priority for worshipers.

Degraded River

In the winter of 2010–11 Jahazpur's mythic and polluted Nagdi River became a passionate obsession for Bhoju and me. How this happened was an accident of fieldwork. We were interviewing a man of Bhoju's acquaintance, after hours, in the municipality building or Nagar Palika. We heard from him, in passing, that a former elected ward member, Bhairu Lal Tak, had once gone on a "hunger strike until death" to protest the Nagdi's condition and demand that the government take action. Because I have always fiercely shied away from the role of critical outsider, I had until this moment simply closed my eyes to the ugliness of the trash-burdened river. Learning of passionate activism on the part of a local citizen propelled us into a single-minded if meandering pursuit of the river's history and future.

It took some time before we were able to arrange an interview with the hunger striker, Bhairu Lal Tak, but because he loomed large in my coming to appreciate the relationship between Jahazpur and its river, I will describe that conversation first. It took place in his lovely backyard garden, where I learned first of his interests in herbal remedies, including aloe vera. Bhairu Lal turned out to be not only an audacious local politician but a man who had pursued many ventures in his life. His unusual career moves had included motorcycle mechanic, restaurateur, and poultry farmer.

Bhairu Lal told us that the aim of his hunger strike had been to force the state government to pay for a cleanup of Jahazpur's Nagdi. He readily described his actions to us in detail. As a result of his first hunger strike, he told us, a state irrigation minister had pledged one crore seventy-two lakh rupees to undertake the necessary work. However, local politicians, not wishing our hunger striker to get credit for the cleanup, prevented the plan from going through. Rather than leading to unity for the sake of the natural environment and public good, the ultimate outcome was a stalemate of political egos.

Still determined, Bhairu Lal embarked on a second hunger strike. After three days, he was hauled to the hospital in the night and fed intravenously against his will. He escaped from the hospital but, disillusioned, abandoned the struggle. We asked him about his hope for the future of the river. He responded fervently that only the *upar-vala* (the one above, God) could clean the Nagdi now, by sending a huge downpour. Thus he pushed the problem beyond reach of human effort. Notable for his highly public effort, Bhairu Lal Tak was not the only person in Jahazpur to have expended personal energy to undertake actions on behalf of the river.

At the Nagdi Bandh (dam) one day, Bhoju and I encountered by happenstance a well-to-do man, a seventy-nine-year-old jeweler, Prabhu Lal Soni. Committed to open-air bathing as a principle of health, he told us that he came every day to the reservoir since the Nagdi had become too polluted. Later we sought him out and found him eager to relate his own past attempts to save the river. Prabhu Lal Soni told us that over the course of five years he wrote reports to the subdistrict and district headquarters as well as to Jaipur; he wrote to past and current members of the Legislative Assembly and chief ministers, but none of them responded. About four years earlier, he had succeeded in persuading an environmental minister on tour to have a look at the Nagdi. The first thing she said was, "I don't have enough balance [funds] to clean it." However, she had described a solution: destroy the check dam, dredge the riverbed, redirect the gutters. This prescription for a remedy was repeated by more than one interviewee. But where were the funds?

If the Nagdi was a natural resource, useful to Jahazpur people in their everyday lives for cleanliness and ritual, they also appreciated it aesthetically. Nagdi memories are endowed with wonder and affection. Sajjan Parasar, in her eighties and with an old-fashioned charm to her speech, told us that the Nagdi was so clean in the old days that "even if the water was up to your waist, if you dropped your nose pearl you could see it at the bottom—the water was that clear!"

Bhairu Lal Lakhara gave his age as sixty. He spoke of a time when people bathed regularly in the Nagdi and "the water was clear as glass." Then, "there was no shortage of water, there was lots of it—but little by little it was all finished—little by little by little." His voice as he stretched out this phrase bore witness to the whole sad story of environmental decline.

By the time Bhoju and I interviewed retired lawyer Shankar Lal Mandovara Jain, we were over a month into a quest to understand the Nagdi's plight. The lawyer was of a social status higher than most of the people upon whose doors we felt free to knock. But Bhoju knew him because both of them were at times active in the Gayatri Parivar (a reform Hindu group stressing caste equality and social action).[5]

I summarize a few critical moments in the interview, which in one man's voice tells much of the story we heard repeatedly from many others. Shankar Lal said that the river was originally holy, that temples were built along its banks, and that the first big cause of its demise was the dam, constructed in the fifties. "After that the flow of the water was stopped and then the filth started to collect."

He described his childhood memories predating the dam, when he would jump into the river from the branches of a big tree on its banks.

Bhoju asked incredulously: "Was it that deep, that you could jump?"

The old man's answer: "Yes, it was very deep under the tree but now because of the government's neglect (*upeksha*) and the apathy (*laparvai*) of Jahazpur people the result (*pranam*) is the end of the Nagdi." Bhoju affirmed this statement by recalling the human excrement he and I had recently observed on the steps leading down to the river.

A conversation followed about the failure of politicians to fulfill campaign promises regarding the cleaning of the Nagdi—no matter which party they were. "Who is listening to us, Mar-sa?"[6] Shankar Lal asked rhetorically.

Near the end of our formal recorded interview I articulated the problem that had been bothering me. I said, "All of Jahazpur is troubled by the condition of the Nagdi but no one thinks that it is possible to change it!" Shankar Lal replied, "That's the truth! And even if someone *wants* to do something they cannot do anything. Only the government can manage such a big project." He told us how the Gayatri Parivar had tried to start a movement (*andolan*) in which members would themselves volunteer manual labor to remove trash from the river. Attendance went precipitately down from one day to the next. We agreed with Shankar Lal that it would require a large machine to dredge the riverbed properly; this could hardly be accomplished by human hands no matter how dedicated people were. It was at this point, very near the end of the interview, that the lawyer supplied a proverb: All our efforts amount to no more than a cumin seed in a camel's mouth (*unt ka muh me jira*).

I thought this metaphor, a proverb for futility that sounds conventional rather than exotic in Rajasthan, where a camel's maw is not an unfamiliar sight, captured a crucial aspect of ecological problems facing human beings the world over in the twenty-first century. The hungry camel with its gaping mouth and large teeth can't even taste a tiny seed, however pungent, let alone be satiated. Individuals and small groups, no matter how moral and motivated their desires to redress environmental damage, experience a sense of insignificance when they confront multiple causalities of rapid ecological degradations. Bharat Singh Kundanpur, who was minister for the Public Works Department of Rajasthan when I met him in 2011 and had previously been minister for Rural Development and Panchayati Raj, read our preliminary account of the Nagdi's story (Gold and Gujar 2011) and pronounced with feeling, "Oh, there are a thousand Nagdis!"

Writing of Kathmandu's Bagmati River and its travails in the first decade of the twenty-first century, Anne Rademacher emphasized that the

"degraded river scape . . . was produced at a nexus of cultural and biophysi-
cal processes" (2011:16); her study meticulously tracks and traces these.
Many of Rademacher's observations resonate with everything Bhoju and I
encountered, on a smaller scale, in Jahazpur. Interviews with Jahazpur residents, as already exemplified, revealed a strong sense of overwhelming factors beyond their ken and control. Such a sense haunts many ecological
struggles all over the globe.[7]

However, Jahazpur's Nagdi possesses one unusual advantage over many
other polluted rivers worldwide: there are no upstream polluters—neither
industrial nor urban. The immediate sources of gross filth afflicting the
Nagdi come from the town itself. Of course this circumstance does not
obliterate factors beyond control of local citizens—notably weather and
groundwater extraction. But it certainly enhanced the people's potential to
take successful collective action and to assume responsibility.

Unlike India's major sacred waterways, the Ganga and the Yamuna,
which have the status of goddesses, Jahazpur's Nagdi River was never dei-
fied. It might have died without generating any great theological paradox.[8]
However, the Nagdi does have its mythology, bound up with Jahazpur
town's origin legend: the snake sacrifice (Chapter 1). The river's origin is
attributed to snakes' blood flowing out of the fire pit, or to the course taken
by a wounded, bleeding, primal female snake as she slithered to safety.

Not that long ago the river reputedly possessed two special properties,
some said miraculous and some said chemical. First, Nagdi water dissolved
bones within three days. For this reason, all Jahazpur's cremation grounds
were constructed on the banks of the Nagdi, where people also bathed to
remove ritual pollution after cremating their dead. People would put all
bone remains from the cremation ground in the river. No one went to
Hardwar or Gaya. Today undissolved bones are visible in the dry river bed,
a sign of the times.

Second, there were three constructed *kund*, pools or ponds, for bathing.
These still existed as structures in 2010–11 but they were totally dry. People
told us that in these pools the water was warm in the winter and cool in
the summer. Our interviews included many statements that these properties were the inexplicable result of divine natural power (*kudarat, karamat*);
others attributed them to fluoride, phosphorus, or most frequently and
authoritatively, sulfur. On a very brief visit in February 2015, to my complete astonishment, one of the kund was full again and we saw someone
bathing in it, again appreciating its temperature as different from that of

Figure 20. (*below*) One of three small pools for bathing (*kund*),
all totally dry year-round in 2011; (*above*) after Nagdi River cleanup,
pool once again filled with clear water, 2015.

the river. This was the result of recent interventions by Jahazpur people on behalf of the river.

Lacking all expertise in civil engineering, Bhoju and I gathered a list of multiple causalities for the Nagdi's degradation using our customary ethnographic method: asking and listening. Although the river's decline began half a century ago, the first decade of the twenty-first century had witnessed the most dramatic change. Five factors rang through more than thirty interviews as common knowledge.

1. *Dam.* Under Mohan Lal Sukadiya, Rajasthan's chief minister between 1954 and 1971, the Nagdi Bandh was constructed in 1959, creating a reservoir upstream from Jahazpur. Except in drought years, when it is much depleted, this reservoir remains a lovely place. Some Jahazpur people go there for bathing, washing clothes, and religious purposes, but due to its location outside the town, only persons with motor vehicles or plenty of spare time would resort to it with regularity.

2. *Taps. Nal* means faucet or water tap. In the mid-sixties the state government installed the first public water taps in Jahazpur. The municipality now maintains free public water taps in every neighborhood (supplied from tube wells, not the river). These taps supply water for home use, making life infinitely easier. Those who can afford to pay may obtain their own private connections. Interviewees stressed that the nal itself was a major causal factor in the Nagdi River's deterioration, because it increased the use of water in houses and therefore a greater volume of dirty water poured out of home drains into gutters. In the past, most people neither bathed nor washed clothes at home, because it was less arduous to do these things near the river or a well than to carry water home.[9]

3. *Gutters.* Inextricably paired with the nal but enumerated separately by interviewees are the dirty gutters. Water from houses drains into gutters that empty directly into the river. It seems they always did. However, the input and impact was far less before the nal. Moreover, middle-class persons have installed indoor flush latrines with septic tanks out of which imperfectly treated sewage eventually flows into the same gutters.

4. *Trash.* Jahazpur lacks a town dump. A horrific accumulation of plastic bags and other nonbiodegradable debris clogs every gutter in town, and much of it ends up in the Nagdi, choking the river itself. The shift from clay to plastic cups at tea stalls was mentioned by many.

5. *Drought.* Encompassing all the rest and noted by every single interviewee is that lack of good heavy rainfall in this region in recent years has

Figure 21. Wastewater and trash flow toward the Nagdi River, 2011;
since then new gutters have rechanneled wastewater.

diminished the river's volume and flow, exacerbating all the other
problems.

Two other causes, less commonly listed, particularly exemplify the complexly varying nature of causalities around the Nagdi's deterioration.

Groundwater depletion. Besides what is piped to Bhilwara industries,
there is unrestricted tube well usage for agriculture in the vicinity of
Jahazpur. Throughout Bhilwara district, according to a 2008 report, the
groundwater level was either "overexploited" or "critical" (Government of
India 2008).

Encroachment. With the river's shrinkage, its former land, public land
in perpetuity, has been put to use by the wealthy and the poor and by two
religious institutions. Encroachment was a factor we were slow to realize
but in some ways presents the knottiest moral problems (as affirmed in
Rademacher 2011). Crops grown where the river once flowed are for some
poor families their sole source of livelihood. Besides landless farmers'
encroachments with the plow, there were also two religious institutions that

had gradually expanded their boundaries into the Nagdi's riverbed. A few interviewees alluded to this situation as a major problem, vaguely hinting at the possibility of inflamed communal tensions if river restoration should result in loss or damage to these shrines. The logic of this worry escaped me, as both shrines would feel the impact and all persons, no matter what their religion, suffered equally from the Nagdi's current condition.

Whether communal tensions were taken into account or dismissed as trivial, it was clear that the compounded factors contributing to the river's demise produced a situation few felt able to alleviate. Nonetheless, Shankar Lal was hardly the only person in Jahazpur to try to do something, to "make a difference" as the American cliché would have it. While I would never label the populace "apathetic" as had the discouraged lawyer, it was clear that most of those with whom we talked in 2010–11, like Shankar Lal, counted their dedicated efforts as failures (Gold and Gujar 2013).

After our investigations had yielded considerable, although far from total, understanding of the river's plight, Bhoju and I each composed and published in two different NGO newsletters, in Hindi and English, respectively, short and polemical documents about the Nagdi's condition. We were striving for a new kind of activist position and prose to give our research at least a bit of real-world meaning, to feel we were making some small contribution to Jahazpur's well-being (Gujar and Gold 2011; Gold and Gujar 2011).[10] Realizing that we both possessed similar yearnings to participate in such an effort was a hopeful revelation. In our preliminary write-up Bhoju and I had concluded that it is difficult to sustain individual or collective action in the face of a massive array of discouraging circumstances on every scale. This was hardly a revolutionary insight, but it was the best sense we could make of a bad situation.

Bhoju and I had the satisfaction of allowing ourselves to imagine, without concrete evidence, that our work might have had an impact on local governance when, not long after Bhoju distributed copies of his Hindi piece around town to various concerned persons, Jahazpur municipality's acting chairman, Gaiga Ram Mina, decided to launch a project to construct new gutters, redirecting wastewater. This was his fourth term in office and, while every candidate for chairman generally included the need to clean the river in a platform of promises, effective action had never followed. Gaiga Ram began by finding undesignated funds and using them immediately to begin to construct new gutters. The gutter-construction process proceeded in fits and starts, often frustrating and demoralizing. Now, over five years down the road, the chairman's initiative appears as a solid and critical step toward the Nagdi's present and strikingly improved condition. The river may not be "saved," but it is visibly transformed. I briefly recount some signal moments along the way to this improvement.

Gaiga Ram had assured us that by the end of March 2011 half the work would be completed, predicting that the people of Jahazpur would then get behind the project and contribute to it. I left Jahazpur to return to the United States in June of that year; when I visited briefly in December 2012 there had been no further progress. Half was indeed complete. What about the rest? Two different reasons were offered for the halt. One was simply that funds were depleted. The other had to do with religious sentiments. The route of the new gutters would carry dirty water, pollution both literal and figurative, too near the encroaching Hindu ashram and Muslim shrine.

In May 2013 Bhoju was elated, writing to me that the work on the gutters had not only recommenced but significantly progressed. The issue of religious objections had been solved by building tall walls to shield both ashram and shrine from direct sight of the gutters. The municipality was funding this work from brisk sales of land plots. I was able to conclude our 2013 article with tentative optimism and praise of local government's efficacy (Gold and Gujar 2013).

And yet, when I arrived in Jahazpur in late December 2013, just half a year after Bhoju's burst of hope and several months after our article was published, despair over the river's future seemed to have set in more deeply than ever, although only a small stretch of new gutter remained unfinished. I was not doing research, just chatting. Some acquaintances confided their conviction that even if the gutters were finished it wouldn't really help; nothing would really help. As if to confirm this bleak view, I saw that both the actual riverbed and the spanking new cement-lined gutters displayed about equal amounts of trash.

Late in 2014, however, a different flurry of "save the Nagdi" energy swept through Jahazpur, as I learned from my Facebook friends' posts. A *shram-dan* (labor donation) day drew many participants, young and energetic, who pulled globs of muck from the river and posed doing so for photos later posted to Facebook. About a week later other photos, including some Bhoju himself took, showed the water looking cleaner than I had ever seen it. I learned later that not all this was achieved by human hands. A machine commonly referred to as JCB (a brand of backhoe) had been used to dredge the worst stretch of riverbed. People acknowledged the need for additional dredging but meanwhile were donating labor to sustain the improved cleanliness and flow.

I have done nothing that could be called research in relation to this new initiative. But in February 2015 I chatted, photographed, and observed. What is interesting to me is that this campaign defines itself as an enterprise launched "without help from the administration." Posted right next to the shop of one of the major organizers is a large computer-generated multicolor poster vivid with different typefaces to get its message across. It advertises the cleanup effort and offers the mobile numbers of its main proponents. A translation follows.

"Get up, wake up, and don't stop until you achieve your aim!" [well-known saying of Swami Vivekananda]

CLEAN NAGDI CAMPAIGN

A heartfelt appeal!

Beloved citizens of the town

Without help from the administration, the New Youth have launched the Nagdi River cleanup campaign.

Participate in it with your body, mind and wealth

and receive spiritual joy.

Come: Donate your labor!

The time for Labor Donation is every day from 6 am to 7:30 am

To collaborate, get in touch with:

[Eight phone numbers are listed here.]

Now, Citizens of Jahazpur, wake up from your deep sleep and fully dedicate your body, mind and wealth

A special appeal to the town's Guardians of Wealth, philanthropists and esteemed donors[11]

Respectfully, from the Youth Action Branch, Jahazpur

I suggested to Bhoju that we show up at the river one morning but tell no one of our intentions. Frankly I expected no one would be there. It was after all more than three months since the initial labor-donation call was issued. Surely enthusiasm would have waned. As it happened, we found four men there, ages I would guess between early thirties and forties; each of them was from a different community. None was from the formerly stigmatized group that normally cleans the town streets and extracts crud from the water reservoirs before ritual occasions. These were middle-class men, not afraid to get their hands dirty, united by their interests in a clean environment and a cleaner, more progressive market in Jahazpur.

In one of my last 2011 interviews, when I was working on the market not the river, I spoke with a woman, Chanda Soni, who operated a beauty shop out of her own home on a qasba side street. We got to talking about the state of the Nagdi. She declared: "If the Nagdi is cleaned, then perhaps Jahazpur will become the way it was at the time of Yagyapur. That is how people know Jahazpur, because of the Nagdi. So if it goes bad then there is no meaning to Jahazpur." Such an understanding may underlie this new market-oriented cleanup campaign (although I stress this is my speculation, not something articulated by any of the men we met at the river).

The sign's wording hints of obvious Hindu orientations, because of the unreferenced but immediately recognizable quote from Vivekananda, other mythological references, and the twice-repeated turn of phrase, "body, mind, and wealth," familiar from Hindu prayer. Still, one of the four men we met dedicating morning hours to clearing scum and debris from the Nagdi was a Muslim.

Place, Identity, Religion, Ecology

I have examined here in detail two contrasting ecological tales from Jahazpur, tales involving largely different swaths of the same population. Why in this small community is tree protection a more linear success story than river restoration? While both the hills and the river belong to Jahazpur, they are different kinds of places, engaging different segments of the town. Their maintenance entails different behaviors. Moreover, the town's growth has had more impact on the river as Jahazpur spreads around it, with nowhere to dispose of an ever-increasing burden of nonbio-degradable trash. On the hillsides, population increase, and perhaps increased prosperity as well, have impinged in the form of new roads cut through the sacred groves to provide better access to the shrines. Beyond those differences inherent in the geographic situation of hills and river, I turn to other signal factors. To understand the contrasts between tree protection and river restoration requires an examination of the ways aesthetic sensibilities as well as emotional and religious attachments influence behaviors toward the environment.

1. Each of the two protected, forested hilltops "belongs" to a unified community, a relatively homogeneous subset of Jahazpur's highly diverse population. To negotiate the river's full protection takes alliances crosscutting not just religion but caste and political party affiliations. In the developments of late 2014 described above, such alliances began to form. Limited inquiry suggests that they are at least partially inspired by the interests of stakeholders who wish to sustain and improve the physical surroundings of Jahazpur market without relying on the state.[12]

2. It is far easier to catch and punish individual tree poachers than it is to stop (treat, rechannel, dispose of) the flow of wastewater and garbage from an entire municipality. The wastewater flow may be successfully rechanneled, but the garbage has nowhere to go. As the November 2014 cleanup proved, muck can be extracted from the river and conveyed beyond the town limits, where it becomes for the time being inoffensive, at least to humans. However, if the Nagdi and its banks continue to be default dumping sites, the current improvement will be difficult to sustain.

In examining these discrepancies I have attended to the inchoate assemblage of meanings and motivations glossed as religion. These played a positive role in the case of the trees, but appear at times to have hindered the cause of the river. Two elements are most relevant here: identity and devotion. Religious identity is evidently critical to the success of tree protection in Jahazpur, but many considered it an impediment partially responsible for repeated failures in efforts to keep wastewater out of the Nagdi River. Devotion has played a positive role in the case of the trees on both hilltops; in the case of the river it has not figured (unless as absence).

The negative force of religion in the case of the river was twofold. First, both Hindu and Muslim communities initially opposed the new gutters because of their attachment to sacred places that were imperiled by the proximity of pollution: a kind of divine NIMBY. This opposition was dispelled by the barrier walls, but it left a sour association of religion in opposition to environmental improvement. Second, although Jahazpur sustains a working pluralism, as described in earlier chapters, it seems that motivating identities (our river, our town, our health) have been difficult to transact across religious boundaries. As participation in the Youth Action campaign suggests, this may be changing.

Conspicuous during my fieldwork and ever increasingly, an evidently large proportion of Jahazpur citizens' energies and resources have poured into the construction of new religious structures: edifices that proclaim a strong, proud identity, prosperous donors, and dedicated devotees. Such projects pull together both motivating strands just noted: identity and devotion. Hindus, Jains, and Muslims are all building, and the results are highly visible. Issues of visibility linked with identity are also at play in the contrast between protected trees and degraded river. Under what conditions does religion become a motivating force in the interests of environmental care? The answer may be when a community's visible identity is bound up with the landscape. Natural beauty is understood at once to be a sign of divine presence and to be pleasing to deities. In addition, the protection of a shrine's natural surroundings must be within community members' capacity to sustain.

The case of the two hilltops reveals just such a positive convergence. The groves surrounding sacred places testify to the greatness of revered beings, whether gods or saints. Just like expensive building projects, they proclaim success. Minas and Muslims keep their wooded hillsides forested for the same reasons that they and others engage in temple or mosque improvements. Another important factor to stress is pride in competency, the rewards of achievement (versus humiliation in failure and futility). Regarding cleaning the Nagdi we heard in 2010 from different discouraged activists who had decided the task was beyond their capacity: "only the government can do it" or "only God can do it." People shy away from hopeless causes, understandably. By contrast, regarding the protection of the grove on Malaji's hill, Ram Swarup bragged that the devotee-guards mustered by his committee were far superior to the government forest guard.

The desire to have a visible emblem of immediate community, whether it is a sacred grove or a new temple or mosque, appears to be more powerful than the sense of value in a natural resource as a common good that is not linked to any particular group. We saw this in the case of the Nagdi, where the river's deterioration profoundly affected public well-being in multiple ways and a diverse population cherished memories of its past beauty, yet collective action had seemed out of the range of possibility. In 2014, the call to "citizens of Jahazpur" implied a unity across religion and caste differences. I am fully aware that the incorporation of Hindu figures and figures of speech into the rhetoric of this appeal undermines its universality. Nevertheless, a sense of civic duty does seem to have emerged at present, unclouded by religious difference although certainly associated with the middle class. In appraising the energies that helped restore the river's cleanliness in 2014, I speculate that the identity of shopkeeper (or stakeholder in the market) has rallied participants.

Chapters 7 and 8 dive into realms of family and business that might seem disconnected from the landscape, or rather that reflect the kinds of projects compelling enough to obliterate attention to environmental problems: taking care of the family and earning the wherewithal to do it properly. By way of transition to Chapter 7, I hazard a few points of intersection. People spend enormous energies to launch their children into the householder stage of life with all its material requisites and a huge dose of blessings; emotions are culturally prescribed but also highly real. Viewed as a cultural performance, a wedding is another way to celebrate identity. And in Jahazpur, while much of this celebration is visible only to invited guests, there are some public elements to it: light decorations, music, and a few associated processions and brief rituals that take place in the streets. Elements of nature are not totally absent from the overwhelmingly cultural and social project of a wedding. For example, the wedding of three young couples that I am about to describe included a pot of Ganges river water representing a fourth bride. This river water—contained, sacred, feminine—reminds us of continuities between the geophysical and the social. The water pot went through all the same rituals as the brides. I paid it little attention, yet when I look back now I recollect that container as a token of divine nature held in the midst of a major social extravaganza.

Chapter 7

Teaching Hearts

A Triple Wedding

My Poem About the Wedding: Sparkling

I always require
things sparkling
the brides' mother says
sequins called stars
massed weightily upon her own dress
sparkling sparkling
even the gods cannot resist
let alone a young girl
the leash, the knot
that too gleams with
tinsel trim
the girls keep it at their waists
the boys take hold.

This world is made of cloth
and when it fades and shreds
that finery takes new birth
as grocery bags.
[composed spontaneously in late January 2011; the only complete
    poem I wrote during fieldwork]

The Wedding's Poem About Me: Insults for Ainn-Bua

Daniel-sahib is oh so handsome! (*rupa-rupalo*)
but his wife is *no beauty!*

Her house is full of spiderwebs,
her cooking-hearth is broken,
all full of cracks.
When she rolls out roti
they aren't even round!
Unsalted dal,
stones in her sauces,
filth in the bright white buttermilk.
Better not to marry at all!
[performed by the brides' mother and her companions during
    bawdy dancing on the morning of the wedding day]

Between these two pieces of poetry; between my voice and voices of Rajasthani women, my foreign gaze and their amused return stares; between the
personal and the collective, the private and the public, the desire for goods
and the desire for love, the everyday toils of domesticity intertwined with
the passions and pleasures that add up to matrimony; between the glossy
bright beauty of brides and grooms and the predictable fading and tarnish-
ing of all flesh; between the rigid requirements of gender roles in marriage
and the startling realization that these may at times be turned upside down,
I attempt to write the wedding.

"The wedding?" you wonder.

I mean the wedding of my dear friend and coauthor Bhoju Ram Gujar's
three daughters on 23 January 2011, just about midway through my fieldwork time in Jahazpur.

"And please enlighten us, just whose hearts are being educated? Is it the
brides'? the grooms'? the parents'? the Americans'?"

All of the above.

Contexts, Pretexts, Backstories

Three sisters—Madhu (Hemalata), Chinu (Lalita), and Ghumar (just plain
Ghumar)—ages twenty-four, nineteen, and seventeen at the time—were
married to Amit, Shaitan, and Om Prakash, respectively. Amit and Shaitan
were brothers from the village of Thavala.[1] Omji (as he was called) came from
Jamoli. The grooms were not much older than their brides. No last name
change was entailed. Most Gujars in Rajasthan use their caste name as a
surname rather than a differentiating *gotra* or lineage name, and most Gujars

in Rajasthan marry Gujars. So it was at this wedding. Whether or not these young women thought of themselves afterward as belonging to their husbands' lineages was something we discussed but with indeterminate results.[2]

Except for the eldest, Amit, the grooms had been chosen by the brides' long-deceased grandfather when they were small girls. Their late grandfather, Sukhdevji, had arranged these marriages without consulting the parents, let alone the children. His aim, I surmised from various clues, was to forge connections for his much-loved granddaughters with trustworthy, land-owning families who shared his devotion to the deity Dev Narayan.

About a week after the wedding's successful conclusion, Bali, the brides' mother, reminisced about how she had learned the surprising news of her middle daughter's engagement. She described this during our long and rambling recorded conversation with Munni-bai, the barber's wife.

> *Bali*: I didn't even know the old man had given the betrothal! We
> were at a feast, and there were some elders there, and they
> called Chinu [then a small girl] over to them. . . . [I asked]
> "Why are you calling her?" They gave her clothes. [I asked]
> "Why are you doing that?" *That* is how I learned.
> *Ann*: Were you angry?"
> *Bali*: No.
> *Ann*: Why didn't he tell you?
> *Bali*: I don't know.

Munni-bai commented, "In the old days, people accepted what the elders did. In the old days, they didn't ask." And actions from the "old days" have results right into the present.

The betrothal of Madhu, the eldest daughter, to Shaitan's elder brother Amit was a much more recent development in the wake of a wisely broken earlier engagement to a military man who proved unconscionably demanding. Amit also had been previously engaged, which is the only reason he became a possibility. Well into the twenty-first century, it is rare to find either gender of Rajasthani Gujars unmarried in their twenties. Madhu and Chinu were close and gladly embraced the idea of residing in the same in-laws' place. They consoled Ghumar, who would have to go alone, by reminding her that Jamoli was a much shorter distance from home.

I obviously played no part in any of these arrangements. Yet it is possible that my presence affected the matter of fixing the date. Moreover, Bhoju told me somewhere in the midst of it all that his enhanced income that year due to institutional funding channeled through my research grant helped him to pay for the elaborate and costly event. Would different choices have been made without Fulbright money? For example, might they have skipped the stage, which was after all just for show. The brides much desired it, but it certainly added to the cost of the whole affair and was not a part of family traditions on either side. I will never know for certain how and in what ways my presence and my grant affected things. I am sure only that the impact was relatively minimal but likely more than nothing.

Readers should be forewarned that the wedding of Bhoju Ram's daughters is hardly typical. Just the rarity of educated Gujar girls makes them already exceptional. Add that their father has spent time in the United States and been research assistant to various foreigners, and you are still further from the norm. Yet, however changed he was by his cosmopolitan experiences and disciplined ethnographic practices, Bhoju remained fully embedded in his own society. He cared deeply for his family's status and reputation. While he was in some ways aloof from his own community and critical of other Gujars' failures to seize the advantages of education, he held his Gujar identity in high esteem.

Beyond the courteous care that he took whenever possible to invite me to observe important moments, or even participate in them, Bhoju did not act as research collaborator during the most intensive weeks of the wedding period. The role of father of the brides was so utterly taxing and exhausting, he could not possibly do anything else. He ceased working for me after the first week of January, and as the occasion drew near, by mid-January, he also took leave from his "day job" as headmaster of the government middle school in Pancha ka Bara. For both Bhoju and his wife, Bali, this was an intensely demanding and engrossing period of time culminating in a singularly important event in their public and private lives as members of various communities and as deeply dedicated and loving parents.

No wedding planner was for hire in these parts. Bhoju needed to arrange for the Brahmin priest who would do the astrological charts known as *lagan patra*, the two Ganesh installations ("small Ganesh" and "big Ganesh"), and conduct the culminating "rounds" (*phere*) of the sacred fire. Also necessary were the services of a barber and his wife who by caste and experience were ritual experts with more work to do than the priest. Far more than rituals needed to be organized. A short and not exhaustive list of nuptial necessities might begin with two I first observed and recorded:

fixing up the house and buying gold for the brides and grooms and the mother of the brides as well. The assembling of dowry goods was a huge responsibility and financial outlay, and it took months of effort.

Further, Bhoju had to contract with caterers for the feasts and make sure that all the culinary equipment would be ready when the time came; he had to make decisions about menus and ensure that all ingredients would be available. The wedding required a tent, a stage, a photographer, and a videographer. In addition, there were the accommodations and bedding for guests, the light decorations, the music, the horses for the grooms to ride; the beautician for the brides, the cloth, clothes, and more clothes—not just for the couple but for many other extended family members involved in the event.

Then there were invitations to be printed, addressed, and delivered. In these provincial areas, sending an invitation by post is not socially acceptable; they had to be hand-delivered, and Bhoju Ram undertook some of this himself. He also found friends to delegate and sometimes sent his sons. The need for such personal attentions made the mustering of friends' assistance a serious aspect of the wedding process, especially for a man without brothers such as Bhoju. He had a few reliable helpers. For years in advance of his own need Bhoju had always made sure to help his friends at similar junctures in their lives (as he would again in the future). He did call to Jahazpur some remote relatives from his father's village, where he had never lived, so that his birth lineage would be represented. Their presence was important, but they were not all that useful for the wedding work.

Bali was just as busy as her husband, if not more so. She was a veto-wielding consultant on all the dowry purchases and in general on any clothes, cloth, and jewelry that was required. Besides sharing in all the crucial decision making on big purchases, she had her own domain for which she was solely responsible. She personally selected the spices and had them ground to make sure the flavor of the food (to be professionally prepared) would be the best. As did Bhoju, Bali needed helpers with wedding work, especially for the singing. This would have been no problem at all in the village, where Bali had many friends and was known as a powerful singer and gracious hostess. A bartering of mutual aid exists among women as it does among men. This was a challenge for Bali in Jahazpur, where she simply had not spent a lot of time and Gujars were scarce. In Santosh Nagar there was just one other Gujar house. Nonetheless, Bali was able to muster enough neighbors to perform as soon as it became ritually necessary. If the initial tunefulness of this mixed-caste group, unused to singing together, left something to be desired, their harmonizing noticeably improved over several days. Eventually many Gujar kin from villages arrived and gleefully took over.

During my doctoral research in Ghatiyali, in the 1980 hot season, I had made a major effort to track two different weddings—one of a Brahmin groom and the other of a Rajput bride. I attended and recorded myriad singing sessions, rituals, processions, and feasts associated with these two high-caste marriages, as well as dropping in occasionally on other wedding-related events among farming communities, Mina and Lodha. I documented worship of the rolling pin, the grindstone, the compost pile, the ancestral spirits, and so forth. I followed the procession with pots from the potters; I saw the full-grown Brahmin groom bend to give his mother's breast that hasty token suck before riding off on horseback. (Among Minas and Lodhas there were grooms so small they might still be nursing.)[3]

At the doorway to the bride's home before the wedding ritual, I recorded the *toran marna* songs with their explicit references to the groom's mother's genitals (or lack thereof) and her predawn amorous trysts. At the groom's home I attended, but was forbidden to record, the *tutiya* or rowdy sexual jokes and songs indulged in by the groom's female relatives after all the men had departed. I never published any anthropological analysis of those 1980 weddings as full events, as transformative life cycle rituals, or as performances of gender—although they were all those things. A very small percentage of the songs I recorded, those for which I felt my translation secure and which held poignant messages about women's lives and desires, found their way into my publications on gender and expressive traditions. The explicit insult songs (*gali*) were a major source for one essay on female sexuality (Raheja and Gold 1994:30–72). But the hard truth is that I felt my anthropology woefully inadequate to the vastness of Hindu marriage rites.[4]

In Santosh Nagar in 2010, when Bhoju Ram announced that a date had been fixed at last for his daughters' weddings, it might have presented an opportunity to redeem myself as an ethnographer of Hindu marriage. However, although I approached the complex, multifaceted event with committed fascination, my goal was not to document all its elements. If I had to articulate my anthropological aspirations around this Santosh Nagar wedding, I would say they were to soak up, through every pore, its ambiance. I saw it as an elaborate, prolonged cultural performance through which identity, modernity, rurality, cosmopolitanism, tradition, innovation, social class, kinship, and gender roles were proclaimed, respected, revised, and improvised. I also came to some appreciation of the many forms of desire expressed through weddings. The wedding was about divinity and humanity; it was about love and money; it was about family and friends; it was about gender and beauty; it was about sex and procreation. I wanted to feel and be able to transmit these diverse aspects without the compulsion to record every detail or to ask too many questions.

The wedding presented me with an unusual cluster of tangled research and ethical dilemmas that were at once academic and emotional. I love this family as my own and have known all three of the brides since they were small. I have no daughters, and I felt a deep affection and admiration for these remarkable young women. In the case of Ghumar, the youngest, I was there at the time of her much-lamented birth (as the third daughter in a row) and have been credited by her parents with her being named Ghumar (a Rajasthani dance) rather than Ghani ("too many," a name that in the 1990s was not uncommonly given to a third or fourth daughter born in a family without sons; see Gold 2001). I teased the three of them in the months before the wedding, telling them quite truthfully that they reminded me of fairy tale princesses—so virtuous and diligent; obedient and intelligent; charming, cheerful, and beautiful. As Chapter 2 relates, Madhu and Chinu both worked with me sporadically as research assistants by helping me to conduct and later transcribe interviews, mostly with our Santosh Nagar neighbors (see also Gold, Gujar, Gujar, and Gujar 2014).

I kept my field notes and photo logs obsessively but told myself I would never be able to write about this wedding. For how might I properly describe an event so intimate, which was a singularly dramatic watershed in lives I cared about so much. Sometimes I felt almost ecstatically incorporated: pulled in by the brides' female kin, at age sixty-four I learned to dance. Sometimes I stared glumly at the ever-growing, elaborate dowry display wondering why three lovely, intelligent, and well-educated young women needed to arrive at their in-laws bearing such gleaming props to enhance their worth.

It is quite customary for the transition to in-laws' homes to be gradual. Following the January wedding all three brides returned to live at home for most of the duration of my stay, even resuming their pre-wedding style of dress. All three were still studying: Madhu preparing for competitive examinations, Chinu attending college, Ghumar completing her higher secondary education. So it happened that, after the fact, Madhu and Chinu even participated in research endeavors around their own nuptials. The brides and their mother helped me to translate a few songs, to log ritual action in photographs, to interview the barber woman who officiated at most of the complex women's rituals as well as the beauty shop owner who did the sisters' makeup.

Constrained by the linear necessities of prose but aiming to provide something of a kaleidoscopic ethnographic perspective on the prolonged ritual-social-emotional-material process that was the wedding, this chapter adopts three different modes: (1) *experience* (a blurry swirl of impressions recorded and presented as raw field notes); (2) *chronicle* (a patchy but sequential recounting of selected ritual and social events, occasionally elaborated on the basis of subsequent interviews or conversations); to create an accurate chronology I follow dated photographs (most of which are not reproduced in this book) and journal entries (some of which I cite); (3) *interpretation* (musings on dowry, compost, town and country counterpoints, and associated transformations of the heart, body, and market).

Experience

The wedding was polysensory and deeply emotional. Sometimes, after long, intense hours of what anthropologists traditionally call participant observation (involvement in an event), I would sit at my laptop in an unusual posture, leaning back, my eyes closed, my fingers bumping breathlessly over the keyboard, letting the words flow out as quickly as possible the way you would write down a dream.

I am the kind of person who reacts neurologically, viscerally, to prolonged intense social interactions and exposure, and all I am capable of after hours and hours of being out there are such fragmented jottings. I made no attempt to organize, neither to sustain chronology nor to compose systematically and describe in detail. Later, over the next day or two, another set of notes would emerge, striving for all the qualities these first dreamlike keyboard scribblings lacked. But sometimes these phantasmagorical field notes convey the most, if by most I mean valence, or power, or what mattered. (The segment of Chapter 4 titled "Resonance" also includes similarly raw fragments.)

Here is the sum total of what I typed in a few stolen moments on the wedding day and what I added/inserted into these jottings the next morning

while still in a sleep-deprived daze. Minimal explanatory material is given
in brackets.

Sunday 23 January *Shadi* [wedding]
In the morning I wander into Bhoju Ram's house in search of my
petticoat, right into the women's bawdy songs and dances at 10 a.m.
or earlier;
They [older Gujar women from the village] are taking over, and
some of the younger women seem slightly not [ok] with the joyful
sexuality but no one can stop the old Gujaris, and they sing my galis
[insults with sexual innuendos].[5]
and I dance with them, first I have my photo taken, but later I dance
for the sake of dancing.
the drum makes you move
the twirling is easy
there was also a puja, sandya puja? I need to know whose puja!
it was in the front of the angan, not by Ganesh

. . . .

so the wedding day, today
the girls are having their last beauty treatment
[inserted on the next day in italics]
the result of which was that when they arrived for the stage program
their faces were unrecognizable and yet I felt a pang of grief right then,
perhaps because they were transformed, the transformation of the wed-
ding, their bodies and their gold
and soon I will dress
and the barat [grooms' parties] will come
and the stage program will take place
and
and
and
break in time; next morning
the food
the dirty dancing of the young men
the *i-stej* [attempt to reproduce Rajasthani pronunciation] as photo
op
the *phere* [marriage rounds] which started with another Ganesh ritual and the tying together of the hands

Figure 22. Groom and members of his party query the author about her country's
practice of love marriage (photo by Joseph C. Miller, PhD).

Ghumar turns, "ghumo!"
the women sing about the rounds
the pandit jokes a little
it is hard to stay awake
and we leave at 3:30 a.m. . . . it isn't over until 5:40
then the dowry exhibit and the departure of the stuff
but the girls go to Banjari ka Devji, as married girls, still together[6]
and then the morning there is more food at the nohra [means an
area where livestock are kept but here refers to a large enclosure
belonging to the rich neighbors that Bhoju's family is using for wedding feasts]
the sad news that a boy from Ghumar's sasural is killed in an accident so they delay her departure
the departure of the other two
the ritual weeping
last night the young men, the two grooms and their friends, grill us
about love marriage

when we say that in our country it is all love marriage, we had one
ourselves, they clap
and they say it should be like that here
and I say love will grow in this kind of marriage
and they clap again
their masculine displays of dancing, extreme
crotch thrusts
is it only Bollywood influence?
rubbing against one another, sitting on one another's laps
the girls who knows what they were doing while I was with the boys
but when they arrived in their clothes and make up they were not
recognizable
the stage program was totally directed by Iqlaq[7]
the wedding of daughters; emotions of loss I've never felt or shared
before
Raji, bonded to me, two old ladies.
[Raji is the grandma, the Dadi; actually, she is twenty years older
than I am.]

From these fragments coalesce a few inklings regarding my ethnography
of what I romantically but truthfully labeled in all my computer files *sundar
shadi*, "beautiful wedding": The things I highlight or repeat are clearly the
things that lodged in my sensibilities, drugged as they were by overstimula-
tion. These were the way my three princesses' bridal makeup made it difficult to tell one from the other; the dirty dancing in separate localities by
the women and the men; and the grief of departure. I retain a few shreds
of traditional anthropological identity, for example: "I need to know *whose*
puja." I wonder at my own surrender to participation: in dancing, in weeping. The wedding as a whole could not be wholly taken in by one person,
and I was distraught that I could not be everywhere at once. I would
become absorbed in each event and then shake myself into the realization
that other things were going on elsewhere.

Chronicle

The date for the wedding was not set until October 2010. From that time
on I paid avid attention to the accelerating preparations. In the weeks

following the main events I spent a lot of desk time obsessively arranging photos in orderly sequence, with dates. I used not only my own photographs but Joseph Miller's and the hired photographer, Iqlaq's. On the basis of these ordered photos along with disorderly journal entries, I offer a skeletal chronicle of wedding proceedings. My incomplete chronicle should deliver a sense of the ritually, materially, socially, and emotionally dense event that is a Rajasthani wedding. In addition, it reveals multiple ways that town practices and village traditions were alternating currents in this very particular event. These currents interweave, interact, and give rise to improvisation.

With big intervals between them, the first events are social and economic preludes, investments, commitments.

28 October 2010 Having come to the decision to hold the wedding at his current Jahazpur home rather than his ancestral Ghatiyali house, Bhoju hires a workman to tile the kitchen walls.

18 December 2010 Bhag Chand Soni, Bhoju's jeweler friend, makes a house call with his catalogs and some samples of ornaments; the three brides-to-be, their mother, and a girlfriend drawn in as consultant together pore over all of it; ordering gold is a serious once-in-a-lifetime business.

23 December 2010 Bali undertakes the preparation of spices for the catered feasts. She sorts a vast quantity of whole red peppers on the roof, explaining that the types endow vegetables and lentils with subtly different tastes. Caterers will do all the cooking, but they have advised her to provide the spices herself if she wants her feast to have the most exquisite and memorable flavors (which, we will all agree afterward, it definitely did).

26 December 2010 Sitting on the roof in the winter sun, the young women sew "falls" onto the saris purchased for the wedding (including mine); I never knew a sari required such a thing. The fall is a strip of extra cloth sewn to the edge of the sari that will hang down; its purpose is to weight the garment so it falls properly.

2 January 2011 The two bridegrooms from Thavala, Amit and Shaitan, come to town to be measured by Bhoju's own tailor for the gifts of clothing that Bhoju is providing them. Bhoju takes me to meet them and we sit together, somewhat awkwardly, at Jahazpur's best sweet shop (the only one with a few tables and chairs). I liked them; they were lacking the arrogance of grooms, but they were not too bashful either. At first we ate carrot halva together in silence. I told them I had known Bhoju's family since before Madhu was born. As they loosened up a bit, it ensued that they knew all about me. They ask if Eli is coming, referring to him as my *bhaya*, an affectionate term for a son of any age. I took their pictures. They did not come to the house and did not get to see their future wives.

8 January 2011 I had been excited to show my photographs of the grooms, imagining the brides would just be dying to see them. But the young women initially disappointed me, skillfully feigning lack of interest. Several days passed until, under the pretext of Madhu's friend Surekha's burning curiosity, they asked me to bring my laptop and display the grooms. Liberated by Surekha's unabashed interest, the modest brides-to-be allowed themselves a surge of fascination.

Ritual activities commenced about twelve days before the wedding.

12 January 2011 Bhoju delivers the first invitation to the deity Ganesh. With several options in Jahazpur's vicinity, he choose the Ganesh at Barah Devra, which offered a relatively secluded and peaceful atmosphere.

14 January 2011 The Brahmin priest who will conduct the wedding comes to the house for the first time to install Ganesh in the family home shrine; this is known as the "small Ganesh" installation (*sthapana*).

Later the same day, the *lagan* is ritually prepared (and sent to be delivered to the grooms). Fragments from my very lengthy journal entry highlight this important juncture in the wedding process:

> Damn! the first complicated brahminically conducted ritual I've seen in years! Bhoju is bouncing around with anxiety at the beginning, but then it all settles into writing on the big posters the matched horoscopes. This [executed with calculated precision] takes time.
>
> Daji [our rich Jat neighbor] is also supervising [with his usual air of commanding authority oddly enhanced by his being so hard of hearing he is quite unable to attend to other people's opinions]. Daji told me I should let the pandit do his work and *then* take pictures, and I ignored him feeling that sometimes it is truly useful to have people assume you might not understand what they say. [Two can play the game of being deaf; if a family member had asked me not to photograph I would have immediately acquiesced; but Bhoju's family is well schooled in the habits of anthropologists and love the resulting pictures too. Daji understandably doesn't get ethnography; he has the attitude, very familiar to me from my work

over the years in rural Rajasthan, that completion, never process, is the only correct condition for the record.]

One of Mohini's sons is there [that is one of Bhoju's only sister's two sons]. Who are the other men? I have to find out, I do not know.

One is Bali's *batija* [brother's son], a great lad who talks to me like a human being instead of like an idiot, and who explains to me that next to Ganesh is Diyari—yes Diyari! the family ancestress lineage deity. [I approve this recognition of the female line.]

[Next]: The writing and folding of the three lagan [poster-size horoscopes purchased blank in the market and completed for each couple by the priest]; each has a pocket made in it; into these three pockets are poured all ingredients from the three saucers prepared for each of the grooms. The saucers contain not only ritual items, sweets and grain, but new silver rings. Once filled, each is further folded into a nice little package and then tied up with LOTS of *laccha* [multicolored string used for rituals] and finally, finally each packet tied with laccha is placed in the lap of a bride.

The girls who until now have been busy elsewhere [ignoring this plighting of their fates by male authority] are called over only for this. They sit demurely, cross-legged, and a packet is placed in each virginal lap. I want so badly to take this picture but somebody with a big ass blocks my view. Gone, lost . . .

The little packets are removed [from the girls' laps] almost as soon as they are set down, and off they go with the two hired barbers to the grooms' respective villages.

Bali tells me later, when I go back for the heavy oily puris and the watery spicy dal, that when the Barber gets to the groom's house the women will sing galis [insult songs]—insults of the Barber!

Somehow, during all of that, the Small Ganesh *sthapana* is also done; it seems to me it is done in the middle. That is: First the writing of the lagan; then Ganesh sthapana; then the packing of the lagan.

There is more men's work, but meanwhile women start silently to come in the door for the first singing session. [These are neighbor women from Santosh Nagar, all different castes!] The first song is so totally unharmonic and ugly and not like a song at all that I despair, but they start to work together, to harmonize; it is not the women with whom Bali usually sings, and they haven't of course rehearsed, but they start to get their groove.

The women get *gur* [unrefined brown sugar] in newspaper packets to take home with them. Madhu-Didi, the [one] Brahmin neighbor seems a little too bossy but she is also full of earthy fun.

A long long day from cows to kites to weddings.[8]

An extract from our postwedding interview (31 January 2011) with Munni-bai, the barber's wife, gives some sense of the significance of these protracted rituals:

> *Ann*: It seems as if you do a lot of work . . . can you tell me about the special work of the barber?
>
> *Munni-bai*: First, for any wedding, the program begins with the priest and the barber. Because the first work is the *lagan*, written by the priest and delivered by the barber. Only then can the wedding begin. If the Brahmin is a bit of a dolt, then we are able to tell him what to do.

The lagan is understood to be the moment when the die is cast irrevocably. It is followed by the first singing of *bani*—"songs for the princess-bride" performed in the girl's home. (In the groom's home the women sing *bana*—"songs for the bridegroom-prince.")

I left Jahazpur for a day after the lagan to meet my son Jonah and his fiancée, Sarah, and bring them back to our home. They were officially engaged and therefore quite interested in weddings. The two of them were able to attend some of the events on 18 and 19 January, and they both appear several times in the final wedding video, sitting on the floor, watching, or in Sarah's case, dancing.

18 January 2011 Women and girls enjoy dancing at the brides' home in the evening. My journal notes the genres of women's songs performed, including *bani* and *kanyadan*. While older women were singing traditional songs in the central sitting room, the girls in the bedroom dance to pop tunes played on a mobile phone. I observe that the young women are "radiant as brides should be," that all the women are joking and high energy, and that Bhoju himself as he addresses his invitation cards has "a glow of achievement."

This is also the day of the Big Ganesh sthapana. Moreover, relatives from elsewhere are beginning to accumulate. Bhoju's mother, Raji, arrives from the village, accompanied by his youngest son, Sandip. Mohani, Bhoju's elder sister who is Raji's only other living offspring, Mohani's married daughter Kamalesh, and Kamalesh's own daughter all join the soon-to-be-overflowing household. I pay attention to Raji, whom I've known since 1979. I write in my journal: "Raji says she's ninety and isn't as deaf as she makes out to be; ninety withdraws from the world (like my own mother at that age) and feels the cold, getting the sweater caught on her thick silver bracelets [as she dons it]; Raji, her life's work soon over."[9]

19 January 2011 Sitting at the Ganesh shrine, the three human brides and the fourth bride, a pot of Ganges water. This water pot will be ritually married along with the young women, so there are four brides, considered more auspicious than three. All the brides have charm bracelets tied on their wrists that won't be removed until after the wedding. Gathered women receive bracelets too, and I treasure mine. The bracelets are called *dorara*. They dangle symbols of auspicious wifehood: a lakh bangle, a cowrie shell (crudely rendered in plastic).

That evening comes the worship of the compost pile (*rori puja*). The women go in a small procession to a compost pile belonging to neighbors and bury an iron nail there—a ritual whose symbolism will be explored in the final section of this chapter.

The days 22, 23, and 24 January are packed and chaotic. There is too much going on for a blow-by-blow account. Moreover, I have house guests: first Jonah and Sarah, then Bhoju's first American friend and employer, Joe (Joseph C. Miller) with his wife Renu Rajpal whose family lives in Jaipur. Still drawing on the same sources of photos and field journal, I offer a more condensed narrative, highlighting just those fragments of the wedding that attracted my vulnerable heart, my anthropological eye, or both.

On 22 January light decorations transform Bhoju's street and home, showing the world that a wedding is taking place here. They include a big Valentine heart pierced by an arrow. Catered meals begin to be served to accumulating family members and others. Dan and I partake of these increasingly sumptuous meals.

In the daytime, women bring new clay pots. Were they in a village they would go to the potter's house, worship the potter, worship his wheel, and carry the pots back to the house, singing. Here in Shiptown, there are no potters—at least there are none who turn the wheel and make pots. About

Figure 23. Wheel worship in Santosh Nagar.

an hour's drive away in the village Gadoli, however, there remains a significant population of working potters. One of these men is called to Santosh Nagar; he delivers the pots required for ritual use in the wedding, and
he himself accepts the traditional "worship of the potter," for a potter is a
creator and sometimes addressed as "Prajapati."

There is no potter's wheel, yet that too must be worshipped. The
women, carrying their trays of offerings, consult among themselves quickly,
and then squat down by the wheel of a jeep parked in the street. I am
completely confused initially but snap plenty of pictures in total bafflement.
I wonder to myself, because there is no one to ask at the time, everyone
being involved in the ritual, whether it might be that contemporary weddings would include the worship of a car. I have seen cars worshipped more
than once, to inaugurate their use or [at Diwali] to respect them as a form
of shakti or female power, but usually attention is given to the hood, not
the wheel!

Later I learn that the car wheel is simply a stand-in for the potter's
wheel: the roundness, the ability to turn in circles, are all that matter. This

is a prime moment of improvisation or bricolage (an after-the-fact anthropological light bulb). In the move from village to town, such things will happen. The compost pile was borrowed, as nearby neighbors with spacious property did have one; the potter's wheel was improvised. How adept the women are at determining what to do; substitution is an ancient practice in Hindu ritual, after all.

After the ceremony, at the neighbor's house, the pots are carried to the home of the bride, where they will reside in the shrine where Ganesh has already been installed. One pot is adorned with the heavy silver belt (*kalankti*) that was once an important part of a Gujar bride's gifts from her family; these modern girls will never wear such a belt, but the pot at their wedding still does.

Later that day the bride's mother puts a pot on her head, this one a pot of welcome, as she goes to greet her brothers who have brought the *mayro* from her natal village. *Mayro* is a Rajasthani word for gifts brought by a married woman's brother at rituals conducted in her husband's home. The women sing mayro songs as they walk down Santosh Nagar road—a whole set of songs that speak of a sister's anxiety: her brother is asleep, he has overslept and won't get there on time, he might be stingy, he might have just forgotten, when will he come? The songs also provide the brother's responses as he assures his sister that he is on his way and bringing all that she might wish.[10]

The mayro expresses an enduring bond between a woman and her natal kin—a bond materialized, as are so many kinship ties in this region, through the medium of cloth. While appreciating its sentiment, I have in my long fieldwork career privately judged the mayro to be the most tedious of all Rajasthani customs. Not just weddings but other major life cycle ritual occasions include a mayro. Members of the culture cherish it and never rush through any of its pleasing moments. This night we sit for hours while the drum beats and one presentation of clothing after another takes place including outfits gifted to me and Daniel and to Joe and Renu. The mayro goes on and on, everyone bundled up in shawls and chilled in the winter night air.

I keep my eye on Bhoju's mother, worry about her as my journal records: "Raji seems distant but now and then smiles a true smile, reminding me of my mother, old age a remote country where it is lonely, but sometimes she comes back to the world of cloth." I also worry about Bali, who is keeping a Chauth Mother fast because the day before the wedding

Figure 24. Clay wedding pot adorned with a silver belt of the type Gujar brides once wore but no longer desire (photo by Joseph C. Miller, PhD).

as it happens has fallen on one of the four Chauth Mother puja days. Once
you undertake a fast, the wedding of three daughters is no excuse not to
keep it! She refuses to give herself an exemption. I fear she will faint as she
is clothed and clothed and clothed again.

The next morning, 23 January, I barge into another ritual, as related in
"Experience" at the beginning of this chapter. I don't learn its name until
many days later: it is *sandhya puja*, or threshold worship, performed quite
literally in the doorway, a ritual of in-betweenness.[11] This is one I missed
totally in Ghatiyali, I suspect because it is done early in the morning and
no one would have bothered to call me; they didn't call me here either, I
just arrived.

After this worship, the female relatives of the bride indulge in dirty
dancing. I had no idea this would happen. I had attended in Ghatiyali the
bawdy dancing that women of the groom's family enjoy after the departure
of the men for the bride's village. This event, called by different names
in different parts of North India, is well documented in anthropological
literature.[12] It was news to me that the bride's family would have similar
fun on the morning before a wedding. Needless to say I was delighted. I
joined the dancers. The song about my poor housewifery, with which I
opened this chapter, was hurled spontaneously at me in the course of this
event.

After the morning, the rush of activities became increasingly difficult to
track; they happened in multiple places. I spent quality time in various
venues, relaxing by surrendering any intent to be everywhere. After the
unexpected bawdy dancing, I went up on the roof, where I found all the
village Gujaris (Gujar women), the rural extended family, making themselves at home. Contentedly they were applying henna to one another, and
finally I too had my henna (which I had put off several times for worry of
being unable to use my hands). These country cousins had nothing crucial
to do for the time being; they were passing the time, enjoying the brief
warmth of the late morning sun, and it seemed comfortable to join them.
They gave me the basic, simple village henna pattern rather than the fine,
artistic town designs I had only been exposed to since Bhoju's family moved
to Jahazpur. Here I was pleased to ally myself with the village.

The first groom to arrive on his horse was Ghumar's Omji. The men
gathered in the tent where the stage was being erected to admire and to
appraise the gifts of gold and other adornments and cosmetic items his
family brought. Meanwhile the stage was readied and "DJ Gun-Gun" set

up his electronic equipment. Quite a bit later in the day the other two grooms (who had been sitting for exams, a rather unfortunate scheduling conflict) finally arrived. While the brides were having their final beauty treatments and makeup applied and getting into their outfits for the stage (heavy, costly outfits gifted by their in-laws), the grooms' parties danced. This was an all-male gathering except for me and Renu. It was here that I had my surprising conversation about love marriage recounted in the preceding section.

Joe was also there, snapping photographs of the men's outrageous dirty dancing. He observed in characteristically outspoken fashion, "Why don't they just project pictures of sperm entering eggs: after all that's what this is all about." Of course he was both right and wrong. If that were really all, we would hardly need the rest of it. It is a question of nature and culture. Ancient Hindu texts describe seven types of marriage ranging from capture and rape (motivated by pure lust) to devalued selling of women, and almost equally devalued arrangements of mutual desire. The apex of moral marriage is the gift of a virgin: *kanyadan*. This is supposed to be the most refined and culturally approved of the types of marriage, because it is the furthest from unrestrained sexuality as well as crass profiteering on the part of the bride's parents (R. Pandey 1969).

Yet in the course of these weddings (organized according to the model of kanyadan) other elements will have their brief moments: including valuable gifts from the bride-takers, and cutting loose in gender-segregated acknowledgements of sexuality. Women perform in the privacy of the brides' home; men of the grooms' party perform (in the absence of all but the foreign women) in the tent near the stage for this citified wedding.[13] This "dirty dancing" is an expression of just those biological elements otherwise repressed. (Will the young couples have privacy on their wedding night? Definitely not.)

The stage itself is all modernity and all show. It has no religious/ritual aspect to it. The garlanding performed appeared to replicate Sita's garlanding of Ram in the TV Ramayana. However, here it is actually an exchange of garlands, bride to groom and then groom to bride. My camera caught a lovely glimpse of Madhu and Amit, the first couple to do this, holding their garlands at the ready and glancing anxiously out toward the photographers for a cue as when actually to make the gesture.

The events on the stage seems to last just as long as the mayro. Not only close family members but friends and other relatives including us,

Figure 25. On the stage, bride and groom Madhu and Amit seek cue
from photographer as they prepare to exchange garlands.

the foreigners, pose while blessing the three couples. When all this finally
concludes, the brides immediately hurry home to change out of the outfits
their in-laws gave them and into a different set of clothes their parents gave
them that they must wear during the real wedding ritual, held in their
father's house—the ritual that will render them *parai*, belonging to others.
(It was interesting and touching to me not only that this has become the
custom, but how often they had told me beforehand, "When we do the
phere we will wear the clothes our parents gave us.")

By the time our group of four arrives at Bhoju's house the grooms on
their rented horses are already outside. Village rituals prevail here for the
prolonged (and of course times three) moment of entering. On horseback,
the groom must strike down with his sword a wooden emblem hung over
the doorway. After that he dismounts, and still the women keep him out;
each groom is playfully insulted, measured, challenged.[14]

Once the grooms are inside the house, decorum is abruptly restored.
The barber's wife was in charge of most of the prenuptial rituals; at the

stage it was definitely the cameramen who determined the action. Now a Brahmin priest, the same who wrote the lagan patra, presides with full authority. The couples worship Ganesh again and then seat themselves by two portable *havan* or sacred fires. The standard wedding ritual proceeds, couple by couple. The pot of Ganges water represents a fourth bride here as it has throughout the ritual action. There is the knotting of cloth, the joining of hands, the marking of foreheads, and the rounds themselves. Several hours pass in this culminating ritual work, but my notes are sparse.

There is one lovely breath of cherished comic relief (mentioned above in "Experience"). The couples perform the marriage rounds sequentially, oldest to youngest. When Ghumar, the third bride, got up and the priest commanded "*ghumo*," meaning "circle round the fire," she first did a little pirouette in place that made everyone crack up (it was around 3 a.m.). The story was told again and again in the hours and days thereafter, the punch line being, "Ghumar, ghumo."

The priest tells an instructional story about Shiva and Parvati, but I find I am unable to follow it and I never get a satisfactory retelling. Bali and others later assess this pandit critically: he was not a good performer; his storytelling and admonitions were dull and lifeless. There was much yawning—it was after all long past midnight and had been a thoroughly exhausting day. That is doubtless why Ghumar's charming spin became a memorable moment. Outside of that, ironically enough, the most significant ritual work, the wedding rounds or phere, were the least gripping of all the nuptial performances.

The next morning breakfast was an evident highlight, as the young couples, half starved, were so happy to eat. The sadness of the send-off or *vidai*—the farewell ritual to a new bride departing for her in-laws' home—followed. Chronicle has little to add to experience. I stood among the weeping women, my camera dangling uselessly from my wrist, and cried as if my heart would break. I was honestly not sure if I wept out of contagious collective sentimentality or if my heart were truly broken, which seemed possible.

25 January
Suman says simply, "*kya kare, parai ho gai*" ["what can you do? now they belong to others"].
I [regain self-control enough to] blurt out [my resistance], "But they will come back"; and everyone laughs [at me].

Suman's comment encapsulates Bhoju's own: "They won't belong to me anymore." It took Suman (Chapter 3) to state the obvious, to bring me back to my anthropology, to the kinship system, to the words of that classic wedding song I had translated long ago: "Little birds will fly away."[15] Bhoju as father of the brides had uttered his own version of this cultural truth with a poignant mixture of sorrow and satisfaction. To divest oneself of the burden of daughters is a significant achievement for a man. Yet Bhoju loved his daughters so much and had put so many of his hopes and dreams into their education, he himself wept without reserve.

One thing I learned from this wedding, which I had not learned in the village, where the weddings I observed were not of close relations, is that these events hardly end with the ceremony of wedding rounds, nor do they end with the departure of the bride. There was at least another week, and then some, of ritual and social work to do after the phere were concluded and the departure mourned.

Even the relatives who had come to stay and who clotted and crowded Bhoju's small house were, to my mind, awfully slow to leave again. This prolonging of familial closeness struck me as a powerful contrast to American culture. Yes, there is the brunch for out-of-town guests on the morning after, but that's it! I thought fondly of my dear uncle who expressed frankly how delighted he was to be rid of us all, after that brunch at his house at which he was the perfect host. Not so in Rajasthan. Guests linger. And the aura of sacredness lingers. The divine guest, Ganesh, the first to be invited, must be formally returned to the shrine or temple from which he was beckoned and yet another respectable feast must be served. This should be, moreover, on a Wednesday.[16]

Just two days after the wedding, I was thrilled to be able to visit Jamoli and eat their feast prepared to honor the departure of their Ganesh. I found Ghumar seated morosely on the satin coverlet of her bed—dowry goods not only beneath but all around her. The family seemed kind, but she commanded me vehemently to make sure that Papa sent someone for her as quickly as possible! She and her dowry were on display and it was clearly not to her liking. I did not get to Madhu and Chinu's in-laws' home until several years later. But when they came home they told me that they too found the days following the wedding onerous.

On the evening of 28 January Madhu and Chinu came rushing up our stairway, giggling and radiant, to announce their return a mere three days after the whole grueling business. Their amiable in-laws lingered at Bhoju's house to chat. They told us that most of the Gujar girls in Thavala are not educated. Madhu's father-in-law is convinced of the value of education, and hopes his new *bahu*, his daughters-in-law, will be models for others. I wrote about the two young women, "They seemed happy, wearing their silly red dresses and their amazing gold jewelry and their special sasural-purchased bangles." They also told me with evident pride that the people at their in-laws' places teased them that they were not truly Gujaris; surely they were *nakli*, imposters; they laughed about it.

The next day, I wandered into Bhoju's house and found the women all sitting in a tight circle opening presents:

27 January
Wah! wedding presents: lamps in the shape of boats; picture frames that plug in and light up; bangle boxes; lots of framed and interesting deities, one a neat Radha-Krishna backed by a mirror—so you could see yourself and also the divine couple; and another one of those that change in the light, so including Krishna with his flute, and Radha-Krishna together, both in one scene. And from Asma, Chinu's Muslim friend, a lovely metal jewelry box.

Like the stage, these gifts are infringements on tradition; they don't count in the ultimate reckoning of items of value presented, cash above all; they are tokens of an urban, global, modern set of practices that are added on to the old traditions without in any way supplanting them; they provide merely a thin veneer, a sheen of change over a reservoir of tradition. Many of these gifted items never even reach the girls' new homes but end up on their parents' walls or even on their parents' high storage shelves, for lack of room to display them.

The wedding's aftermath hardly stops with the pleasurable admiring of this fringe loot. On 30 January my journal declares: "Komal Kothari—when I first came to Rajasthan in 1979 to study sacred places—told me that to find out where the local shrines were, I should ask where brides and grooms go to do *dokh*. Today more than thirty years later is actually the first time I see this."

While Ghumar and Omji went separately to bow to his family gods, and Chinu and Madhu joined their husbands for theirs, all six of the young people must bow at Bhoju's family's special deities, of which there are more than I knew. Note again the gender parity. Yes, the husbands' gods are first, but the wives' household deities must be attended to with dispatch and reverence. And of course the visit to Banjari ka Devji which took place on the night of the wedding itself was a super-effort to honor a deity to which the brides' father's family owed particular gratitude.

On 29 January, not quite a full week after the wedding rounds, I was able to accompany all the newlyweds to Ghatiyali and its environs, where they paid their respects, as couples, to Puvali ka Devji, Ghanti ka Devji, Sundar Mata, and Lilurji.[17]

29 January
They go bound together as they did at the *vidai*; they go with the boys in front and girls on their sparkling leashes: what a metaphor for marriage, the sparkling leash! The impressions of the day are long and strong. The link between town and village and the distance too, for the *gaom* [village] feels on the one hand so lovely—the air is clear, there is little street or engine noise, it has an air of peace; and returning to Jahazpur jangles the nerves; on the other hand, the village seems stuck back in time: squatting in the *nohra* [cow-shed] to piss, and seeing the [unchanged] dusty lanes.[18]

Although the girls are dressed up again, only Omji comes in a groom's outfit; the other two are wearing jeans and don their turbans with good-natured humor. Everyone is much more relaxed than they were at the wedding. The main ordeal, after all, is past and went off rather well. My journal notes this restored normalcy; and I note retrospectively, as I reread it several years later, that it is a normalcy that returns them from their exacting and ritually complex Hindu wedding to a familiar shared world of schools, teachers, and the cares of students.

29 January
What do the brides and grooms talk about among themselves, when sitting in public, relaxed, no one near but Aunty Ann?
Well, they talk about school about teachers about exams; they tell humorous stories of teachers who are characters . . . like any students.

Interpretations as Partial as They Come

In the final portion of this chapter I consider three elements that emerged while I experienced and chronicled the wedding process—elements that strike me as especially fascinating, difficult, and revealing. The first and most contentious of these is dowry, especially the way it is connected with parental love and a sense of self-worth. Because these are not the dominant associations made with dowry, at least in academia, I take time to explore the topic through intimate ethnography and my quasi-familial observations. I shall not engage the vast literature, both social scientific and feminist, on the subject with more than passing references.[19]

Second, I call attention to some incidents and conversations that commented on aspects of gender hierarchy in subtle and interesting ways. These include allusions to transformative abundance as well as limited solidarities and ritual parity. Finally, I shall resume the main theme of *Shiptown* and a current already quite visible in the preceding sections. Everything connected with this wedding was inflected by a dynamic country/town interchange. This will neatly return us to the market (subject of the next and final chapter), via ritual materiality and a cash economy.

Dowry Delights and Doubts

Complexity and polyvalence reign around the relationship between dowry and women's well-being. As already disclosed, I was emotionally as well as ethnographically absorbed in every aspect of the nuptial proceedings. I never knew at any given moment whether I was an anthropologist or just part of the family. I wanted to be both seamlessly. Yet inevitably there were inner voices critiquing some assumptions and practices. Dowry was one of them. Arguably dowry's historical origins had to do with giving daughters, otherwise denied inheritance of land, a share of their paternal property. However, dowry has come increasingly in contemporary times to be one of the reasons to lament the birth of a girl or to neglect her well-being after she is born.[20] Thus the potentially ruinous economic burden of daughters is commonly considered one cause for the enduring skewed sex ratios that haunt India well into the twenty-first century.

The government has launched positive campaigns to value the girl child; it has legally banned medical tests to determine the sex of a fetus, but to little avail in many states including Rajasthan. Because of this, social activists justifiably view dowry as nothing but damaging to women. As colleagues have told me, with troubled looks, I too became complicit by passively observing rather than actively objecting. In Bhoju's family the girls were precious, beloved, and aware of being treasured, knowing that not just their mother but their father would weep at their departure. (This they confide in me: "Papa has a soft heart, he will weep," and true to their prediction, so he did.)

The decision to have a triple wedding was cost-cutting. Bhoju clearly stated his reasons: "Let me spend the money on their education!" If a triple wedding requires less expenditure than would three separate events, it was accomplished with unblemished, extravagant openhandedness, according to the social status of the participants. Nor did Bhoju stint on dowry for the three brides. Every purchase was a token of love. The girls glowed when showing these things to me. And their mother "battled" (her word) for the best choices, which in her view were those items that would solidify her daughters' status in their marital homes. Papa (that is, Bhoju) might be practical, thinking for example that such big beds were not ideal for the small rooms available to the young couples; or that well-made ceiling fans might be more convenient than cumbersome coolers. But Bali was "victorious" (her word) in each argument, on the side of ostentation versus practicality. She knew what mattered.

25 December 2010

Bali told me there was just one *larai* (battle) between her and Bhoju having to do with the beds; that she was pleased with the fridges, the TVs, and everything else. But Bhoju told me with great grumbling that Bali was also not happy with his idea of ceiling fans and she thinks he should get coolers; also he defended his choice of smaller beds because the rooms weren't big enough for the big beds.

Bali of course wants it to be that there is nothing of which the grooms' families can complain. Hence, even if it isn't practical, her daughters should bring coolers and big beds, just so that no one can say, "She only brought a fan not a cooler."

Later I said to Bali, "you said there was only one battle, but Bhoju told me about the coolers." She acknowledged this correction with a thoroughly self-satisfied smile.

In spite of her husband being a salaried headmaster and Bali being an illiterate housewife, she had serious power and wielded it unsparingly on behalf of her daughters.

As the date drew nearer, each day when I arrived at their house the girls would show me the latest additions to the ever-accumulating heap of materiality. Large items—notably three fridges, three color TVs, three wardrobes, three double beds—were stored elsewhere (in a wealthy, trustworthy neighbor's new, capacious, and still uninhabited house). But lesser items were piling up in the girls' shared bedroom—on every shelf and surface, and in protected containers beneath the bed: all kinds of outfits, accessories, blankets, bedspreads, cosmetics, and more. Normally I would ooh and aah along with them. One day in early January, as recorded in my journal, I walked into the house in a different mood and queried with a breath of Western cynicism infusing my Hindi locution: *aj kya mal a gaya*? "So what goods have come today?" I intended this jokingly, but it didn't come out that way. Or it wasn't a good joke. I had let slip a barbed phrase, semideliberately.

In my journal I wrote, "Today the brides have new purses, little cute ones. Every day more stuff. Weddings *are* stuff; *mal*. But the girls seemed embarrassed when I said it." In truth it was plain wrong of me to refer to the dowry as *mal* (goods). For a moment I disrupted the magical spell of wedding pleasure. Each item was much more than an object of desire or trade, purchased for cash. These were pure gifts. A few days later, my slip was forgotten and the revelry continued:

10 January 2011
the ecstasy of the sheets; everyone was so happy, the shiny reversible golden sheets; no jokes about sex either. Bali seemed overwhelmed with joy. Madhu seemed so excited to display the two sides of each one. Chinu and Ghumar [engrossed that day in study] were less into it.

Kanyadan (the Sanskritic term for dowry), means literally "gift of a virgin." It appears in Rajasthani women's songs, but more common in speech is Hindi *dahej*. All the dowry goods are prescriptively seen as embellishments to the bride herself. She is not the recipient of them, nor is the groom per se. Rather dowry goods adorn the girl, and she is passed along with them as a selfless, reverential gift from bride-givers to bride-takers.[21]

If in ritual theory the dowry is not "for" the girl, in the context of domestic economy, clearly it is. As Raheja tells us: "a woman's position and influence in her sasural [in-laws' home] are in some measure dependent on her in-laws' perception of the degree to which she is held in esteem by her natal kin. If they give generously to her and treat her with respect, then her husband's kin know that they will also come to her defense if she is mistreated. . . . If gifts are signs of love and regard, then refusals to give are signs that one's loyalty and affection lie elsewhere" (1995:40). In Bhoju's household, while there was no scarcity, a level-headed frugality normally prevailed. You bought what you needed when you needed it (or when the price was right). You shopped with care. Each extravagant dowry purchase was thus unprecedented and evidence of parental affection and concern.

In fact, these brides, their mother, and all their female relations (not to mention friends and neighbors) reveled in the strong testimony to their high worth that the lavish dowry and elaborate wedding unequivocally made in the local culture's language. Of course, I cannot forget that the so-called dowry system does genuine damage to females, or that to an outsider's gaze the wedding itself appears temporarily at least to render bright, ambitious, studious girls into dolled-up objects on display, led away by their grooms, literally, on sparkling leashes. If we agree that structurally and systemically, dowry has an objectionable impact on women, still in this intimate context of domestic economy and emotional attachments, I hold that it may unfold quite otherwise.

In a conversation I had with Bali and Raji after the wedding, my journal notes, "Raji says her soul is content now that the girls are married and she has no more *chinta*! [worries]." Bali agreed that in spite of the cost and in spite of the exhausting work, "No matter I am satisfied." Marriage of course changes relations with grown children of either sex. The satisfaction in having successfully placed their daughters in good marital homes remains important to their parents—even when those daughters do indeed belong to others.

My first chance to visit Thavala (Madhu's and Chinu's in-laws' village) was in 2013, two years after the wedding. Bali was with me and she took care to show me a good view of the extensive farmland possessed by her two daughters' marital family. This land was to her the prime evidence that she and Bhoju had placed their daughters successfully in good homes; her pride was tangible.

Abundance, Parity, Solidarity

In the course of our interview with Munni-bai, the barber's wife, going through all the rituals she helps to perform, we discussed the worship of the compost pile (*rori ka puja*). I asked her simply what it meant. She answered without hesitation, "You shouldn't say anything to anybody, you shouldn't fight. So, when the girl goes to her in-laws' place—well, she will be able to put up with anything—even if people quarrel with her or criticize her she must accept it [just as a compost pile accepts any spoiled or rotten food you put into it]."

Bali affirmed, in her strong voice, her louder, slower, explain-things-in-simple-words-to-Ainn-bua voice: "Be like a *rori!*" So that is one meaning—that a bride must accept anything dished out to her in her in-laws' home. The feminist gut reaction would be something akin to horror.

However, as Victor Turner insisted long ago, symbols are polyvalent and there are indeed other meanings of compost worship, which Munnibai then added to her interpretive account. An iron nail is buried in the rori at the time of the puja. Later it may be taken out again and brought to the site where the wedding feast is cooked, where it provides a charm against running short of food.[22] Compost is not just acceptance but abundance, almost magical organic transformation, fertility, nourishment. The ritual links the bride-to-be with these positive attributes.

Moreover, the groom too worships the compost pile. Is he too enjoined to "be like a rori?" I did not ask but I doubt it. The groom after all is not going to live in a new place that will put unfamiliar demands for patient agreeability on him. That granted, the groom does the compost ritual in his village on the same day that the bride does it in hers. Gender parity remains at work throughout the prenuptial ritual action.

This was one thing I had found most compelling (and initially surprising) in 1980: rituals for the bride and the groom were meticulously equivalent. Another example: women from the natal family and their neighbors sing *bana* (songs of the bridegroom-prince) for grooms-to-be and *bani* (songs of the bride-princess) for female counterparts. Equally, both future brides and grooms are feasted by friends and neighbors between the invitation to Ganesh and the wedding day. Even the rubbing of a young body with turmeric paste "to beautify" it, to make skin more fair and thus more attractive, was done to both bride and groom in their respective parents' homes.

All this remained true in 2011. When not long after the wedding we got to sit around Bhoju Ram's living room watching a DVD produced by the groom's side (in this case Ghumar's husband, Om Prakash), we saw him, stripped to his underwear, scrawnier than I ever would have imagined, in a kind of crouching position with his eyes demurely, or miserably, lowered while gleeful female relatives rubbed him vigorously with the special turmeric paste compound to enhance his youthful glow. I describe this moment in a journal entry: "Ghumar watches the video, from her in-laws' video-man, of Om sitting in his boxers, like a child, his bare arms and chest less arrogant than his clothed body, the women of his family rub turmeric on his body, and feed him sweets. . . . Ghumar laughs full-throated."

The days immediately following the wedding, when life had by no means returned to normal yet and guests were still lingering, gave me an opportunity to show my pictures to family members and to ask questions about rituals while memories were fresh.

27 January
At Bali's house, still there: Mohani, Kamalesh, Dev Raj's wife whose name is either Parvati or Lakshmi (Mohani's sons, the two brothers married two sisters and those are their names.)
We look at pictures [on my laptop]; those pictures showing smiles, teeth, dancing; and especially Sajjan dancing [dressed up like a man and making moves and gestures that are hilariously sexual] provoke delight and glee, a whole group gathers around the computer screen. Bali takes it seriously explaining to me the rituals, the rituals that are women's work totally, about which Bhoju does not just pretend ignorance but truly possesses ignorance.
Two different worlds, the pandit's and the women's. I ask about something in the Ganesh worship and Bali quickly dismisses that question, "Ask the pandit." But she knows *everything* about women's work.

In the midst of our jolly and ethnographically fruitful picture fest, the father of Dev Raj's wife appears and demands that she return with him, posthaste, to Motipura. He needs her help to irrigate his wheat crop.

Although young women are usually eager to visit their parents, this is evidently an unwelcome intrusion. She was having fun. Bali goes into the other room of the house and quickly begins cooperatively helping to gather up the young woman's belongings. No male members of the household were around, and the young woman's father (although I'm certain he was served the requisite tea) assumed an impatient pose in the sitting room, his mien grim and uncomfortable as I've noticed is often the case with solo men dealing with largish groups of high-spirited women. Suddenly, Mohani (Bhoju's elder sister, this girl's mother-in-law and an imposing figure) emerges into the sitting room, speaks to the man quickly, and ushers him out the door. She announces to the rest of us that she has dispatched him with a promise to send the girl on the following day. Everyone relaxes. We return to enjoying photographs.

This is merely an anecdote but not without significance. I offer it as a slight instance in which frivolous pleasure for women triumphs over the stern work ethic entailed by rural life, and incidentally over gender hierarchy. Moreover, Mohani's intervention also undermines the supposed antagonism between the mother-in-law and her son's bride. The mother-in-law's authority trumps the father's here, and women's prerogative for relaxed enjoyment temporarily defers the demand for productive labor. This is far from always the case; I merely make the point that, from time to time, it happens. Whether the compost stands for total submission or transformative power; whether gender parity in ritual carries over in any fashion into the everyday; whether a mother-in-law's protection of small pleasures for a young wife means women's solidarity: if certainty is out of reach, these perplexities require contemplation.

A Wedding of Village and Town

Once the date was set, as noted earlier, there was considerable debate about where to hold the wedding. The brides-to-be unequivocally desired Jahazpur. Raji, the grandma, wanted it in the village. Other family members saw both sides. Bhoju eventually determined on Jahazpur. He had his own reasons, I suspect (tense relations with some of his village relatives as well as a desire to put on a ceremony that affirmed his own status as no longer a village man). But he was frankly glad to please his daughters.

Patterns of social and demographic change are perceptible in these individual and even unique wedding arrangements. These brides had moved only a few years ago from village birthplace to town home, and moved gradually at that, so each had lived a different period of time in town. Bhoju's daughters spent their early childhoods in Ghatiyali, completed their higher secondary schooling in either Sawar (Madhu) or Jahazpur (Chinu and Ghumar), and went on to college and master's programs in nearby Devli or, in Chinu's case, Kekari. Girls like them, whose grandparents, mothers, aunts, uncles, and cousins were all by and large uneducated, were not rare among the youth from farming communities who attended Jahazpur schools.

I vividly remember an early interview with a Brahmin girl who was just Madhu's age and lived right next door in Santosh Nagar. This young woman was from a family with many generations rooted in the qasba. Her mother and several aunts were all teachers. She had female role models in the women who surrounded her, among whom she grew up. This contrasts strikingly with the Gujar girls and their Mina and Jat contemporaries, whose mothers were largely nonliterate. Those uneducated mothers' considerable skills in agricultural, horticultural, and pastoral work were not the ones their daughters now cultivated. The interview provided me with a kind of fieldwork epiphany: What a leap Bhoju's family was taking with these educated daughters! And how different for Gujars than it is for Brahmins. I suspect both these realizations would yield a justly deserved "duh" from any member of Bhoju's family (not to mention many of my readers): "You mean you just figured that out?" But knowing something is different from *getting* it, viscerally.

It was also clear that having reached the same stage of education, the young women had much in common in spite of their different backgrounds. They shared ambitions to work at salaried jobs, to be not only good housewives but financially independent of their in-laws. This kind of cross-caste and cross-class commonality among girls is a town phenomenon. In their home villages educated Gujar women remain a distinctive minority within their own community. This is why the three brides desired a town wedding so badly. Their peers from school would be sure to attend. If the wedding were in Ghatiyali, Jahazpur girlfriends who were classmates and neighbors were unlikely to be allowed to travel there.

Bali, Raji, and Sandip the youngest brother were still living in their village home at the time of the wedding. Bali came early enough to supervise arrangements, but Raji and Sandip arrived from Ghatiyali more or less along with other relatives. The grooms' families, moreover, still resided in villages. All the young men had spent some time in cities and towns for their education and also for their families' business ventures. With significant resources still rooted in the land, the grooms' families were expanding their economic horizons.

Santosh Nagar, where the brides lived and where the wedding took place is, as Chapter 3 described, a relatively new suburb to the centuries-old walled market town of Jahazpur. For many women who live there without independent transportation, it can feel village-like. But in truth it is quite different from any village I know. To hold one wedding for multiple couples is perfectly common among Gujars and other agricultural communities in this region of India. I could tell that some of the more urbanized neighbors in Santosh Nagar considered it slightly rustic, but this attitude appeared more in tone of voice or facial expression than any explicit declaration, whether of surprise or disapproval.

At the broadest level of description, my fieldwork aims for 2010–11 were to produce an ethnography of small-town life in which I would track both continuities and contrasts with village life as I knew it from earlier research. This wedding offered a priceless opportunity to do precisely that. It was in many ways a performative marriage of village and town customs, or even (we might venture to say in the anthro-speak of the early seventies) a marriage of tradition and modernity. To use marriage as metaphor to think about a wedding's sociological aspects may seem convoluted. But I suggest that it serves well to evoke more than simple union: not fusion, but alternating currents and—employing an English word well incorporated into discourse about marriage in provincial Rajasthan—adjustment.

In this triple wedding, we perceive the influence of divergent social milieux producing adaptations, oscillations, improvisations united to display a seamless, possibly unprecedented event. In the case of the hubcap, an impromptu bricolage on the part of village-born women making do with town conditions. Similarly, the first days of singing for the brides gathered neighbor women from disparate backgrounds unused to singing together, but learning to harmonize with practice.

The "stage" as already described was a new and urban element that Bhoju and his family chose to incorporate into their wedding although it served no ritual purpose.

31 January 2011
I asked the group gathered round my computer when the "stage" was introduced into weddings in Rajasthan, was it ten, fifteen years ago? Monu [younger brother to the three brides] said, "Oh among the Gujars, more like *one* year ago!"

Monu's own wedding, held along with his younger brother's almost three years later in a village not far off the highway between Jaipur and Jahazpur, did not have a stage. These brides belonged to a wealthy, landed family, active in the business world but also quite conservative about their ritual traditions. They too, however, were firmly committed to the education of girls. In the same conversation with the siblings after the wedding, I asked how many unmarried Gujar girls there might be who were as old as our brides. Madhu answered that she was the second to last of her age group from Ghatiyali to be married. Unlike Jahazpur, Ghatiyali has a large Gujar population.

The last urban element I wish to highlight for the triple wedding is its use of manufactured paraphernalia purchased from the market. There were many such small items including charm bracelets for the brides and their girlfriends; gifts for the women who came to sing twice a day; other ritual items such as the lagan (astrological chart with the blanks to be filled in by the pandit); the *toran* (emblem to be symbolically knocked down by the groom from his horse) and more.

When we interviewed the owner of Lovely, the store specializing in sea-sonal goods, he gave wedding season as determining his display and busi-ness at certain times of the year (December–January and March–April). When I walked past his store in 2015 he had renamed it "Bride House," and told us that he had shifted over from a specialization in seasonal festivals to a more thorough and dominant focus on wedding goods. In the past most of these items would be hand-made from local materials, and many of them were acquired not through cash purchases but rather through the old patron-client system that once structured relationships between farmers and artisans. For example, the toran, that wooden emblem critically mark-ing the groom's entry into his bride's home, would have been made by the carpenter who had a hereditary connection with the bride's family and a share of the grain at their harvest. Nowadays such ritual necessities are mass manufactured and part of the cash economy.

We can see an evident village-to-town economic transition exemplified in the change from hand-made items in a noncash economy to store-bought items. The prevailing use of these purchased ritual supplies is one significant part of this Jahazpur wedding's citified nature. Thus we embark on *Shiptown*'s final passage, into the heart of the qasba and its raison d'être: the market.

Chapter 8

Talking Business
Commerce and Cosmology

In composing Chapter 7's wedding stories I held one central image in my mind's eye: the pastel-colored neon valentine heart that, raised and glowing over the three brides' home, illuminated very little about the realities of marriage, but plenty about the brave new urban wedding. Chapter 8 radiates out from a different, denser, less ephemeral heart. For surely Jahazpur's market—enterprising, profit-oriented—must be the blood-pumping heart, metaphoric and literal, of the qasba and the municipality that has grown up around it. The market is where pleasures and sorrows, strivings and struggles, kindnesses and cruelties, satisfactions and disappointments, rapaciousness and generosities, friendships and enmities, collective effervescence and disturbing tensions of town life are at their most public.

Origin legends charter Jahazpur as a land devoid of compassion, as Chapter 1 elaborates. What happens when Shravan Kumar puts his foot on Jahazpur's soil? He demands the "fare" from his parents. This appeared to me to be the mentality of the market crystalized into folklore: pay your way or fail to reach your destination. But does it all really boil down to account books, recording tidy columns of profit and loss? Of course not; no more than the wedding boils down to the biology of human reproduction, as Joe had jokingly proposed. The market is methodical but equally chaotic; it may manifest as ruthless but is equally shot through with charity; it may be all about everyday necessity but provokes and nourishes many other kinds of aspiration. This is likely why only a few interviewees were ready to affirm that Jahazpur was truly a pitiless land.

Anastasia Piliavsky writes, of another Rajasthan qasba, "the marketplace threatens with its potential for complete openness" (2014:177). Piliavsky is one of the very few anthropologists who have conducted ethnographic fieldwork in a Rajasthan town comparable to Jahazpur. Her portrayal of qasba life focuses on politics, not business, and still less pleasure. I avowedly avoid political realms, ignoring or at best skirting them. I acknowledge her insights as welcome correctives to my own perspectives. I may have been tone-deaf to threats, but it seems to me that Piliavsky neglects a whole level of genuine sociability where openness is a good rather than a danger. The market is a place of leisure, of relaxed talk about things of local concern, of shared TV watching, usually of sports events. Different communities mix in the business world. Women, mostly shoppers but also shopkeepers, maintain a vocal, visible presence in Jahazpur market. The market is a place to acquire or even just admire the goods one fancies and to engage in the serious sport of combative bargaining. Tea circulates like a connective fluid among friends, acquaintances, and strangers. It is served in the tiniest cups imaginable, thus allowing large numbers of rounds of chai to be consumed in a day, each graciously proffered by one person to a small group with minimal outlay.

Beginning in late February 2011, largely with Bhoju's help, although sometimes in the company of Madhu and/or Chinu, I conducted more than forty interviews with a wide range of Jahazpur businesspeople. Most of what we called our "market interviews" began with simple questions eliciting family histories of business owners and probing the nuts and bolts of commercial practices. We were feeling our way, as this was new territory for all of us. Had I not already spent half a year looking at and listening to more poetic, affective elements of town life, these interviews would have seemed dull and shallow to me. But now I felt they held the key to everything else.

This does not mean I had been transformed into an economic determinist. The mechanics of business that filled many hours of recording and painstakingly transcribed interview notes captivated me ultimately as little as did the contents of my 1993 interviews with farmers about soil types or fertilizer application strategies. These were things I doubtless needed to learn about, because they were things that interviewees needed to know in order to feed, clothe, and educate their families; to survive, prosper, and flourish. But that did not make them inherently captivating. I was always waiting for stories, moral commentaries, even gossip to liven up the shop talk. This chapter distills a very small proportion of the many interviews supplying plain information. Some of our market interviews, the best ones in my view, moved from the details of trade into free-flowing conversations on a broad range of topics concerning not just town life but life itself. Those rarer reflections receive disproportionate space in this chapter. I argue this is not all that perverse a strategy.

If you were to interview me about my own work, you would doubtless find most interesting and significant the wandering life that brought me to anthropology and the ways my identity and my livelihood have fused, the friendships I've made, the impact an anthropological life has had on my family and my world view. Far less compelling would be my professorial routines around the construction of my stock-in-trade, so to speak: a PowerPoint lecture on the Bhagavad Gita, for example, or an essay topic handout on the anthropology of gender, or the crafting of letters of recommendation for students. Even though I expend inordinate time and mental energy producing such items and I could, if pressed, go on and on about how I do it, I would not expect outsiders to care about these labors.

The first section below offers a broad description of how my companions and I approached our market work and condenses some of the basic things we learned. I give a panoramic sketch of our efforts, mentioning many interviews whose content will not be reported but which nonetheless inform what follows. Next I ask without irony, and without foregone conclusions, "Is the qasba pitiless?" Jahazpur legends are town wide. Rather than revealing or infusing a singular group identity, they belong to all groups residing within a certain territory. If these stories serve any functions in Jahazpur lives and minds, it would have to do with establishing and/or acknowledging something as broad as the way human nature is infused with the character of a place.[1] Thus I attempt to build bridges, however flimsy (or speculative), between Jahazpur's legends and its everyday realities in the world of trade. A final segment cites three organic philosophers among our interviewees, all in varying degrees successful businessmen, although not one is from the merchant communities and not one is currently based inside the walls.

The second and third sections both reveal the ways different individuals frame their lives, struggles, and successes within and beyond the world of business; how they put together Jahazpur's life of trade with what is happening globally, even cosmically. The voices I include in the final segment are in some ways the voices of persons who possess the most unusual perspectives on life, or perhaps just of those most willing to disclose idiosyncratic perspectives. All were exceptional characters and knew it. I find their viewpoints suggestive of the contemporary ferment that seems to be steaming up from the cauldron of trade, religion, and globalization that bubbles merrily in Jahazpur as in many other twenty-first century urban settings.

Looking at the Market

We commenced our serious effort to talk with shopkeepers about shop keeping and with businesspeople about business in the main market, as seemed only proper. (I had already interviewed many such persons about other matters.) We visited shops not far from Royal Gate and a few others located at the Nau Chauk end of the main market. We spoke with persons who sold groceries, cloth, ready-made clothing, electronic goods, school supplies, shoes, cookware, plastic utensils, and more. We also tapped a few who were in service professions—including traditional ones such as barber and tailor, as well as those that have developed on the tail of new technologies such as digital photography or repairs for electronics including mobile phones. We visited a video game parlor in the qasba, with machines that appeared to have teleported directly out of the 1980s. We failed, I fear, to interview the long-suffering Shankar, to whom my husband and I were frequently lodging complaints when our Internet card failed to work and with whose shop we were therefore all too familiar.

Jahazpur has a plethora of small grocery stores, called *kirane ki dukan*. They are all of the traditional type in which there is no room for the customer to enter, browse, or choose. Grocery stores sell all kinds of nonperishable food items from the basics of tea, sugar, and many varieties of lentils to the luxuries of dried fruits and nuts. They may also diversify in various ways. To shop at these stores, you stand outside in the street and make your requests. The merchant finds the goods you request and either hands them to you or piles them up. Similar stores are run by Baniyas, Brahmins, Muslims, Taks, and others. Inside the walls such shops are often inherited, but new ones keep opening at various localities outside. These days, we learned in interviews, to open such a store can be a second- or third-choice career for those who have either not been successful in other ventures or tired of them, or in some cases retired from them.

A Brahmin grocer in Santosh Nagar told us he had kept his store for six or seven years. Before that he was a bus conductor on the route between Bhilwara and Devli. Asked why he quit the job to open his shop, he said

Figure 26. Babli Pathak, whose business acumen brought additional success to her father's shop by catering to neighborhood women's needs.

being a conductor was not like a government job. There was no security and no respect. "So I thought I should take up a line of work (*dhandha*) that has a reputation, and one in which I am my own boss." Hence a grocery store.

After her divorce, Babli Pathak commenced working in a shop with her father and brother. This was a small store also on the Santosh Nagar road. She claimed, "The business didn't go very well until I joined it but after that it started to do better." Her contribution was to begin to stock petticoats and sari falls. She told us that theirs is the first store in Santosh Nagar where you can get petticoats along with general goods. "Women from the suburb are happy because they don't have time to go all the way to the market." Moreover, she asserted that she keeps only good-quality items and "all the neighborhood women" buy from her.

Our interviewees belonged to a variety of caste communities. Diversity has certainly come to Jahazpur market, which by all accounts was originally the domain of merchant castes. True Jain and Vaishnavite merchants do remain a numerical majority, but our interviews with qasba shopkeepers inside the walls included also Brahmins, Sindhis, Taks (former wine sellers), Muslims (both Deshvali and Pathan), one Nath, and one Gujar. Inside the walls, but off the main market streets, were craftspeople such as lathe-working carpenters and smaller businesses such as the Gaji Pir Trimmings store. These interviewees were all male. However, I was able to negotiate another ten or so market interviews focused on women who actively conducted business: bangle makers in the main market (traditional, hereditary, both Hindu and Muslim) and beauticians in their homes (innovative, modern, and predictably not confined to any caste identity).

Jahazpur market originally nestled fully enclosed within the protective qasba walls. Now town businesses are rapidly spreading along the main transportation arteries, notably Shahpura Road and Devli Road, where growth is possible. Outside the walls we contacted businesspeople based just on the opposite side of Royal Gate, at the present-day bus stand. At the higher end of this group (socially and economically) were those who owned or rented permanent shops on the periphery, trading in all kinds of dry goods from soap to socks, from batteries to vitamins. The permanent shops around the bus stand also included our friend Bunty, to whom I always came for my mobile recharge, along with a few other similar places catering to all types of communication needs.[2]

Also on the bus stand periphery was Raju the Brahmin paan seller, who fondly reminisced about the days of old when lengthy lines of customers waited patiently to savor his special hand-wrapped betel-leaf delicacies on pleasant evenings. The oldest tea stall in town, a sweet store, and the tent house that rented out large items required for big feasts were also in this area. Near the shrines dedicated to Tejaji and Ramdevji were other small enterprises including a crippled tailor with a limited repertoire whose shop was more or less his sewing machine table. There was one stand that, seasonally, did a lively business in frothy green sugarcane juice; this was run by a Kir. Kirs (former boatmen) were among the communities that, we gathered from often-expressed opinions, had lagged in finding a profitable footing in the contemporary economy. However, this family was an exception. Next to the sugarcane press, they also kept a small cigarette and tobacco stall that operated year-round with other items in packets such as snuff and shampoo. At the opposite end of the market outside Delhi Gate, as Chapter 2 noted, Nau Chauk is also rimmed with shops.

Many persons do business within the bus stand out of portable stalls as well as carts on wheels. We tapped their knowledge and experience too. These were fruit and vegetable vendors (mostly Khatiks, and a few Muslims) and sellers of fried snacks. Jahazpur's vegetable and fruit market is not what most Americans deem a "farmers' market." That is, the vendors are not the growers. If you get up early and get to the bus stand sometime between 6:30 and 7:30 a.m. you can see the *boli*, an auction of fruits and vegetables in bulk lots—passing from growers (or brokers) to vendors. The morning auction takes place 365 days a year. It is the only business I recollect encountering in Rajasthan that observed neither religious, nor government, nor personal holidays. Doubtless the personnel might shift but the business itself—secular to the core—never paused. Members of the Khatik community had launched this enterprise in the mid-1980s, around the same time they built their Satya Narayan temple, which overlooks the auction and the vegetable market. Khatiks have a well-deserved reputation for persistent hard work and for keeping long hours. The fruit and vegetable auctions are certainly emblematic of that. There are now several smaller, independent auctions every morning, and every one of them is run by a Khatik.

The lowest end of bus stand business belonged by and large to SC persons. Some of them sold goods from carts such as used clothing. There were also handcart pullers who ferried goods off-loaded from transport trucks to be delivered inside the qasba where, due to the narrow streets, the passage of any kind of delivery truck remains unthinkable.

Bhoju and I also cast our nets into Jahazpur's new spaces of enterprise. We interviewed a few individuals situated at the highest end of local commerce, such as the manager of the Hero Honda showroom and the agent for Mahindra Tractors, whose establishments were out on the highway (although both came from families rooted in the old market). Rajendra Tak, manager of the local Hero Honda franchise, was the first to make clear to me that Jahazpur, besides being proverbially a pitiless land, was blacklisted by financial institutions as a bad bet for loans. He explained that his agency had to do all the financing themselves for their customers. According to Rajendra, Jahazpur was among the "*top panch chor*" (top five thieves). I misunderstood, thinking that actual motorcycles were stolen. He corrected me: the problem was that people make a down payment and then fail to make any subsequent payments. He described the need to send out a "seizer" (using an English word, although the equivalent America slang would be, I believe, "repo man"). This had gone on for long enough that at least two major banks had simply banned all vehicle loans to residents of greater Jahazpur because of the difficulties involved in repossession, as well as in taking legal action on bad loans. "They don't want to hear Jahazpur's name," was his summary of the situation.

Rajendra told us that he personally finances about 70 percent of the bikes he sells. People give a series of checks to be cashed at intervals. Sometimes of course the checks bounce, and he has to track down vehicles, but clearly there is a good profit to be had from loans as well as sales, because he was certainly not complaining. I refrained from asking him about his interest rates but can guess that they were significantly higher than the banks'. Thus the denial of credit from statewide or nationwide institutions very likely works to the advantage of local capital.

In Ambedkar Colony, a newer residential and business neighborhood inhabited mostly by former leather workers, many of whom are today employed in construction, we met the founder and manager of a large, booming recycled junk enterprise, himself a Khatik. Lower realms of the business hierarchy, out on the highway, included tire repair shops and other auto mechanics; these were almost universally owned and operated by Muslims.

In the years since my fieldwork concluded in June 2011 and my most recent visit in February 2015, additional motorcycle showrooms, the town's first automobile agency, and a new hotel-restaurant along with several new religious sites sprang up along the highways. If the government still fails miserably at provisions for waste management and basic sanitation and receives a barely passing grade for health care and primary education, it has systematically managed enormous progress with transportation infrastructure. The trip from Jaipur to Jahazpur has quickened from an inevitable five hours down to not much more than three and a half.

Sampling Qasba Commerce: Clothes, Cloth, and Bangles

Interviews with merchants of cloth and clothing were for us a good entry into the general workings of the market. They are a core element of its traditional base. I intend my detailed descriptions of a few conversations with merchants in these lines of trade to serve to exemplify much else that there is not room to include here. In addition, I discuss the bangle and cosmetics trade because they are the only stores in which women regularly and visibly sit, and because theirs is a very old business practiced by both Hindus and Muslims.

Although I will not discuss these here, I note other areas where women do business. Quite a few run beauty salons. These have proliferated in private homes over the past decade. Although they may display small signs, their proprietors are not visible to passersby. Distinctly visible and quite accustomed to public interactions with men are those women who hold their own among the produce sellers at the bus stand and Nau Chauk—many from gardening and Khatik communities. Finally, it is not unusual in Jahazpur qasba for various enterprises to find a female relative "minding the shop" when adult males have reason to be elsewhere.

One of the first qasba merchants with whom we spoke was Jittu Kumar Jain, thirty-two years old. His store, Arihant, was the place Bhoju always went first when he was looking for ready-made clothing. Directed there by Bhoju, Daniel and I had purchased some relatively costly items, notably winter sweaters. Arihant was also a place we now and then took refuge from the chaos of an interminable procession. We were confident of a welcome. Jittu had spent most of his life in Jahazpur, although his family had moved here from nearby Sarsia when he was a child. Much of what we learned from Jittu we heard from other cloth and clothing merchants as well. He told us: "Our customers include a lot of Minas; maybe I sell only 20 percent to people from Jahazpur qasba." Jittu explained that his business is linked to the harvest, and thus to the weather. People shop after harvest, and when the crops are good then business is good.

Making a valid generalization, one we would hear confirmed by many others, Jittu told us that these days his business was great in terms of volume, "but little by little the *margin goes down because there is a lot of *competition."[3] In ready-made, for example, he said, "There used to be four but now there are twenty stores." This trend is naturally connected to population growth; it also derives from an exponentially increased demand from villagers who in the past did not purchase stitched clothing.

Jittu attributed this increase in demand to two causes. First among these, he told us, is that "in villages today live people who work for the government, and they buy ready-made for their own children. Other people's children see them and want to wear the same kind of clothes. So the government servant's son is wearing an outfit worth five hundred rupees and the other children, maybe they get one worth half that much. Still they

Figure 27. Rural family shops for children's clothes; blue jeans as objects of desire.

are happy. They are happy because they too have *ready-made. It is not as if they understand quality. They just know they have *blue jeans."

Besides the desire aroused by the sight of salaried government workers' well-dressed children, Jittu also held that television had an impact on consumer desire. He said, "Everyone wants to follow Western style, after watching movies on TV—not just clothing but toothpaste, soap, cosmetics, and more." He added that these changes are quite recent, having really taken hold over the past twelve to fifteen years. "People's way of thinking (*soch*) has changed," he continued. "Even if they are not able to buy, they want to buy." The significance placed on desire is telling.

Jittu commented, as did many of his fellow middle-class townspeople, that living standards have changed in the rural areas: "They bathe more often; they get more haircuts." Returning to his own business, these desires emanating from the surrounding villages have influenced his decisions on what to stock. Contradicting his earlier assertion about his customers' lack of concern for quality, he told us, "I used not to keep any outfit that cost over four or five hundred rupees; now I have even a thousand-rupee outfit![4] People are looking for higher quality!"

Returning to the subject of sales volume, Jittu offered the example of another business: motorcycles. Jittu told us that Hero Honda was the first motorbike showroom in town and that initially it only sold three or four motorbikes in a month. Now, Hero Honda alone sells fifteen or twenty. As with clothes, a successful business stimulates competition. As previously noted, other motorcycle companies have recently opened showrooms in Jahazpur.

While we were in Arihant, our interview proceeded in fragments. Jittu was in the process of selling some clothing to a woman from the Rebari community (camel herders, once nomadic; they would be considered still more "backward" than Minas). She was driving a hard bargain. We happened to record some of the phrases he used in his repartee with her. These included, "O, Auntie, these clothes don't grow in my field!" and "I opened a store to earn money, not in order to provide selfless service (*seva*)." I suspect these are pat lines, but they are uttered with vehemence. Note that, speaking to peasant women, he draws his imagery from agriculture and religion.

Hari Prasad Tak sold cloth, not ready-made. At age thirty-five, he was of the same generation as Jittu. He too talked about increased consumer spending and lamented the shrinking of his margin even as his sales volume increased. Hari claimed that his village customers did indeed care about quality. Bhoju asked, "How have people's way of thinking about quality changed?" Hari replied dramatically, "It has changed so much, the difference is that between earth and sky! People used to think that a hundred rupees for a long skirt and a wrap is a whole lot. Now they say even a thousand for the same is OK, but they want good quality. They are thinking less about the cost. They believe that there should be a new design every fifteen months or so. Even in villages *fashion has gained importance!"

Hari did not mention government servants and their nicely dressed children but attributed the desire for new fashions that now affects village women directly to the TV. Hari brought up the purchasing of cloth for a *mayro* (gifts from a woman's brothers presented at her children's major life cycle rituals, observed in Chapter 7) to be particularly representative of huge change. "It used to be that you could manage a mayro with two or two and a half thousand [rupees], and if you wanted to make it really fancy it might be five or six thousand. But nowadays, an ordinary mayro costs twenty to twenty-five thousand and a good customer today would spend fifty to sixty thousand."

I can easily speculate that this difference of opinion between Jittu and Hari regarding discernment among village shoppers would be due to the difference between a ready-made store and a cloth store. Peasants have been purchasing cloth for centuries, while ready-made is relatively new and its quality may be more difficult for them to assess. However, several other cloth merchants explicitly told us that a person purchasing a mayro consciously seeks a bargain and will willingly purchase older, out-of-style fabrics if the price is right.

In the past, members of the Tak community manufactured and traded in spirits. They have diversified enormously in Jahazpur market. I mentioned to Hari that it seemed to me that there were a lot of stores in the market run by Taks. He immediately listed a wide variety of enterprises belonging to members of his own extended family. These included five cloth stores, one electronics store, one cement store, a motorcycle showroom, an auto mechanic shop, a sari and petticoat store, two or three small grocery stores, and (at the very end of his list) two wine stores.

Hari praised his Mina customers, comparing them favorably to other less couth communities who bargain too much. But he also talked about how he has to keep the price low on certain items or lose business. For example, he told us, at one time he purchased large towels for sixteen rupees and sold them for twenty; then the wholesale price went up to eighteen but he still sold for twenty. Now, he averred, it costs him twenty-one but he has to continue to sell large towels, at a loss, for twenty or risk his customers taking their business elsewhere. Hari said, "They get stubborn about these things, they *know* what the towel should cost. Hence I am compelled to sell it at a loss." (Of course they will buy other things from him on which there still is a good margin of profit, a calculation he surely makes when giving them the towels for twenty; as spelled out by Kisan Sindhi in the next section).

Durga Lal Regar (SC) sells used clothing at the bus stand. He explained his business to us, describing his weekly excursions to Jaipur, the care with which he selected goods, and the kind of trade he did. Sundays are his busiest because schools are closed, and people bring their children. Sweaters in winter are particularly attractive to buy secondhand. He said you might pay three hundred rupees for a new sweater but spend only thirty or forty for a comparable used one; so winter is his best season. He did not speak of his margin and I suspect it is slim. But his business embodies one of many links between Rajasthan's growing capital city and the old market town of Jahazpur. Durga Lal has found, or created, a small and lucrative enough space in which to buy and sell. He also provides a service to customers who are not able to purchase clothing necessities at current market prices. No one would buy wedding or mayro items secondhand, but for ordinary needs for a family with straitened finances, the option is evidently an attractive one. For Durga Lal, the used clothing trade offers an alternative livelihood to a person from a community that works largely in construction, except for those who have risen in the social hierarchy by qualifying for government service.

We heard estimates of between twenty and thirty Jahazpur shops dealing in bangles and other costume jewelry along with cosmetics, women's underwear, hair ornaments, and all kinds of items that come under Hindi *sringar* or the English loanword "fancy." Some of these stores have also expanded their wares to include adornment for homes: posters of the gods and other cultural icons (film stars, cricket players, cute animals, romantic scenery). The only shops where women sat both visibly and regularly within the market were bangle stores.

For the Hindu caste called Lakharas (their name deriving from the original bangle material, tree sap called *lakh*) as well as for Muslim manihars, who traditionally made and sold glass, not lakh, bangles, this was a hereditary trade. These shops specialize in items mostly desired and purchased by, or for, women. In the old days, communities associated with the bangle trade both made and sold them, and they pretty much cornered the market. Now they purchase stock in bulk from factories or distributors, and so anyone who wishes to may go into this business. Because hereditary bangle makers no longer control production, there is increasingly stiff competition from many other communities in such lucrative trade.

In one of the larger bangle shops well situated in the main market street, I always saw a woman tending the store. I persuaded Bhoju to go in with me one day. The seller was a Lakhara by caste and initially quite reluctant to be interviewed. Throughout the recorded conversation she interjected wishes to bring me to her home and serve me tea and snacks; that, to her, she declared, would be a satisfying form of interaction; our interview evidently was not. Still we learned some basics from her. She told us that her best season was the hot season, when farmers hold their weddings. As she put it, simply, "Because they are not busy in the fields, and they have

Figure 28. Bangle seller with customer, main market.

brought in the harvest, and they have money. . . . So, you need bangles for weddings!" As had the cloth and clothing merchants, she told us that Minas from the twelve hamlets composed the bulk of her customers.

I asked about the provenance of her stock and learned that she and her husband make buying trips to Ajmer together, where they purchase bangles from a wholesale dealer. These bangles are manufactured in Firozabad (notorious in the literature on child labor in the bangle industry). I queried her about changing styles, which I have noticed over the years, as I always wear bangles in Rajasthan. She agreed that fashion keeps changing, but unlike the clothing merchants she said she has no "dead stock" in her business. She is always able to sell everything she buys. I also asked whether, besides ritual necessity, people bought bangles from her just out of interest (*shauk*), and her enthusiasm warmed. Farming people, she said, *always* want new bangles and always wear them (they never take them off). Baniyas, she added, might be able to endure not having bangles, but not Minas!

We discussed the other stores in town that dealt in similar goods. She listed about five shops that belonged to members of her family, but told us there were thirty, all told: seven or eight from the Lakhara community, to which she belonged, and the rest to an assortment of others. Was such competition bad for her business? Her immediate answer: "We all get what our *kismat* [fate] gives us."[5]

Bhoju explained that she had fixed customers who always come to her shop. I followed up on this comment with a question about credit, as I knew that in other shops like grocery stores fixed customers returned to the same place because the shopkeeper kept an account for them. "Do you give credit?" I naively inquired.

"Who me? I don't keep accounts!"

"Are you educated?"

"Yes, to eight grade!"

"So, you could keep accounts if you wished to do so."

She agreed that she could indeed, and told us that she did keep the store accounts for banking purposes. But she only makes cash sales and never gives loans. Emphatically she said, "Loans do not get repaid! If I give a loan then the customer will not come back! They will go to another store!" Note that this is the opposite of the reason many shopkeepers do give loans. That is, customers return loyally to the shop that gives them credit. Bhoju joked, saying a person could go to a different shop every time they need bangles, and that there are enough bangle stores to last a lifetime.

I turned to questions about her family, asking if the Lakhara jati had lived in Jahazpur since the old times. She said they had; her husband's grandfather was born here. And, unlike many others who were psychologically invested in a future for their offspring beyond their own businesses and often the immediate locality, her own hopes for her son and future daughter-in-law were for them to carry on the same work she and her husband do. Her son is not yet engaged, but she said she is decidedly not looking for a daughter-in-law who will work at a salaried job. She wants someone to do the housework and to sit in the store in her place.

Bhoju asked this Lakhara bangle seller about the term "manihara" which is used in women's songs to refer to bangle sellers. She said that manihar is a term for "*chachi*"—aunties, that is, Muslim women bangle sellers (literally father's younger brother's wife, kinship terms conventionally used by Hindus for Muslims). Manihara would not apply to her community.[6]

Some weeks later, Chinu and her best friend from college, a Muslim girl from an esteemed qasba family, took me to a Muslim bangle shop, where I found even more resistance to an interview and general suspicion of my motives. Finally, after we had assuaged her fears, Fatima the shopkeeper seemed willing to talk a little. She was scornful of my ignorance when I attributed agency to her having become a businesswoman. I had simply asked, "How did you decide to open a store?" Emphatically, she retorted: "This is my *khandani dhandha* [ancestral trade]. My grandfather, his father, they are the ones who started it, and so it continues. The men bring the goods, and the women sell them. This business was my ancestors' and doing this business, they lived and died; and still it goes on!"

She continued to reflect on this in the context of changing times: "These days, a *naukari* [salaried position] is great, if you can get it—but if not: then do this *dhandha* until you die!" She noted that some of her family had diversified; there was a sandal store, a motorcycle repair store, and then there were others who, like her, acquiesced to family tradition and sold bangles.

Is the Market Pitiless?

To begin to answer this question, I provide long extracts from what was the most revealing of our market interviews, again with a dealer in cloth.

Kisan Sindhi is a successful, hard-working cloth merchant. His views on trade and candid explications of his own practices provide a dynamic portrait of the stereotypical nature of merchants. He seemed to express with disarming candor a perfect and perfectly justified pitiless land rapacity. Our interview with Kisan stood out in my memory because he was so articulate and frank, even boastful, about his own business tricks. Kisan's grandfather came from Sindh when that region went to Pakistan at partition. He told us that his family had first been resettled in Jaipur, but "wandering, wandering they came from Jaipur in this direction, to Mewar." They reached Bhilwara District and found it peaceful and a good place to relaunch their cloth business. "We used to go on bicycle door to door, selling cloth, door to door, village to village" he told us. Eventually, his father was able to rent a shop in Jahazpur market. Kisan said, "My father started to buy cloth from elsewhere, without any money, on credit. We purchased it and as we sold it, we paid, and then we purchased, and paid, we did that, a rotation of money."

Kisan was not hesitant to describe his family's business acumen (perhaps brought with them from Sindh rather than a result of having put their feet on Jahazpur soil; it seems likely that he would be familiar with the proverbial caricatures of cutthroat Sindhis in Rajasthani folklore).[7] No other storekeeper was quite as frank as he was. "We made our prices low; we had a low margin; the older cloth merchants in Jahazpur market were taking 10 percent profit, but my family sold with only a 6 percent markup. We did this to attract customers away from the other cloth shops."

Kisan was a practitioner of hatha yoga and a devotee of the goddess, and he claimed to embrace a relatively ascetic lifestyle. Unlike many merchants who tend to grow paunchy pretty early in life, he was a lean man without an ounce of spare flesh. He proceeded to explain to us, with little prompting and without the slightest embarrassment, about some of his less-than-noble strategies for selling to (unlearned) villagers who form the majority of cloth buyers in Jahazpur market.

> So, take a *saphi* [a small piece of cloth for a mini-turban, used as a gift item]. If a customer has cash, I will sell it for thirty rupees. But if he wants credit, I will sell it for forty-five—and he'll take it because he needs the credit. Who knows when he will pay—whether in six months or a year—there is no guarantee for six months. I don't tell them but I'm telling you, because it is the truth.
>
> If he says, "It is too much, forty-five!" I answer, "OK, don't take it." Then if he says, "I can get it elsewhere for thirty," I say [persuasively], "No, it is good quality, and you are just like a member of my own family!"

Kisan grinned, "We have so many ways to make them happy, this is the art of selling!" Warming to his theme, he told us, "The shopkeeper has other *tricks."

It took only a little encouragement from our side for him to go on revealing these "tricks" to us, continuing to use the saphi as his example.

> So say, this little saphi, its price is 30. And the customer says, "I won't pay more than 20!"
>
> So, I say to him, "OK, you will give me 20." OK, I give it to him for 20. "Now, what else do you need."

"I also need a *langa* [cloth for a lady's skirt]." Well, the correct
price of this langa is 100 rupees, but I tell him, "140."

He thinks, "I got the other item for 20" [and therefore has faith
that 140 is also a good price].

He is illiterate, and he doesn't know the real value of things! If I
know he has come *only* to buy a saphi, I won't sell it for 20, of
course! But if he is getting other things, then I don't let him go.
Until he takes the langa, I won't put the saphi in the bag for him,
so how can he take it?

These are the kinds of *tricks I mean. We are cunning [*chalaki*].
We give one thing cheap and another expensive. It doesn't matter
as long as we get it back on some other item.

Kisan then summed up his world-view: "This is the shopkeeper's motto:
'Never let the customer go!' He can't leave empty-handed. . . . Never let
him go! Whatever money he has, that money has to come in my direction
(toward me). He has to be completely drained of it!" A bit of lip service to
some sense of compunction or self-justification followed: "What can we
do? We don't want to cheat! It pains our hearts! But the market is bad, so
should we stay hungry? If we don't do business this way, what will we eat?"

Of course, there is nothing in Kisan's strategies that is uncommon to
merchants the world over, including those who set prices at the largest
chain supermarkets in my hometown. In the case of Jahazpur market, however, deceptive marketing strategies must be practiced on a more intimate
scale, person to person, and for this reason deceit could seem more, well,
pitiless. Kisan himself saw nothing in his practices to detract from his self-
image as a worthy person, honoring obligations to family, community, and
divinity.

Kisan is not alone in his attitudes toward his customers. A metal merchant who was Brahmin by caste explained his similar business strategies
as something he had learned from Baniyas. Speaking of his customers, he
said, "Yes if he sits on my carpet once I won't let him go without buying!
Because my guru, he is a Baniya!"

He continued in this mode, elaborating somewhat repetitively the same
types of practices Kisan and others had described: "Sometimes I will even sell
at my own cost. Then that customer will come back and the second time, I'll
make money. I am a disciple, and my guru is a Baniya. This is the nature of
the Baniya: he will never let a customer go!" A little further probing found

that this man had in fact worked for a bona fide Baniya before opening his own business. I could hardly deny the validity of his observations or the adeptness of his techniques, for I left the interview the proud owner of a tarnished old bronze pitcher for which I had no need whatsoever and which doubtless no one but a foolish foreigner would have purchased.

While the majority brushed it off, a significant minority, approximately 20 percent, of our interlocutors wanted to claim a clear connection between the Shravan Kumar story and the reality of Jahazpur society. My focus now is deliberately on those who did assert that Jahazpur's moral character was flawed.

I offer two examples from more extended interviews with persons rooted in the qasba who decidedly wished to attribute pitilessness to their home town. Listening to them may help us see how a place myth can be incorporated into a worldview when it is useful for various reasons to an individual. One elderly man with whom we spoke, Prabhu Lal Kairathi, narrated both "pitiless land" legends—the heartless mother and the abruptly mercenary son—sequentially, as many others had. When we asked him whether this meant that persons who live in Jahazpur were ruthless, he surprised us by emphatically agreeing. "Yes, people who live on this land are not compassionate; it doesn't matter whether he is Hindu or Muslim, he has no compassion."

Prabhu Lal's own community of lathe-working carpenters had once been the proudly skilled producers of wooden toys exported all over the region. While not located in the main bazaar, these wooden utensil and toy shops had been important to town trade in the past—so important that they were noted in colonial gazetteers as one of the chief products of Jahazpur. Japanese plastics had put Kairathis out of the toy business; members of their community had found other lines of work and many had moved away permanently (selling their qasba land to successful immigrant merchants, the Sindhis). There were only two Kairathi extended families left in Jahazpur who still made rolling pins and boards (basic kitchen equipment) and a very few other wooden items that continued to sell locally.

It seemed these remaining families were locked in a bitter feud with one another, which might well be what gave Prabhu Lal his dim view of the town's humanity. It is not hard to intuit a bridge between the decline of their craft's capacity to produce goods desired by consumers, and the bad relations among caste fellows likely rooted in competition for an increasingly limited trade.

My field notes for the day we met Prabhu Lal in 2010 record a brief but memorably upsetting experience that Bhoju and I, for once equally in the dark, had when we went to search out Prabhu Lal in his neighborhood. I had interviewed this man about his woodworking business in the summer of 2008 and wanted to give him a print of a lovely photograph I had taken then. I also of course wanted to schedule another interview. We didn't know exactly where Prabhu Lal's house was and had gone to his shop, which was closed.

> 10 October 2010, journal
>
> the strangest experience: we showed the picture to some people on the street, who we assumed would be his caste fellows as they were sitting inside a workshop/store for wooden goods. In all my thirty years of fieldwork, I've never received a reaction of utter rudeness such as I did from these people: one of them took the photograph from Bhoju's hand, studied it briefly and then threw it to the floor with violent contempt. An old lady who had also glanced at the picture shook her fan angrily at me, in a gesture that clearly meant "get away and stay away!" In rancorous silence we were momentarily paralyzed; then Bhoju, although in shock, had the presence of mind to pick up the photo from where it lay on the sawdusty floor and we retreated hastily. At last we found someone in the neighborhood who knew where to locate Prabhu Lal: at the shop where his son, not a lathe worker, repairs motorcycles around the corner, near the Mahadevji temple. He was great; we did a long interview with him in the temple that was very fruitful. He did not explain exactly what the cause of the enmity with his neighbors was . . . enmity, so deep so bitter. It shook us up, the experience. Usually people are so willing and happy to give directions!

Our interview with Prabhu Lal included very poignant reminiscing about the products the Kairathis once sold. Bhoju simply asked whether there had been change in his work; he answered volubly and at length, with just occasional interjected prompts from one of us:

> There is a huge amount of change! My work is finished! (*khtam ho gaya*). I realized that this work was going to be over. The big problem: the wood is not available. Also: there are no buyers! So I

arranged for my sons to do other work: motorcycle repairing. I put them in the mechanic line for five years (of apprenticeship). This one [the son in whose store we had found Prabhu Lal] was apprenticed in Devli, and after working in Devli he opened his own store here.

We asked, "What kinds of things did you make in your father's time?"

The same items we now make, but the quality used to be finer. In the time of the great kings [that is, pre-Independence], we made a lot of things using "*danadar*" [a special coloring technique] and we made many more of everything. Now nobody knows that technique! We used to make color with *chapari* [a gum that comes out of the pipal tree; after filtering, it would be heated and used to coat the finished wooden item]. Now you can't get chapari and you can't get wood either. So now we use paint. You can't make it shine the way it once did. . . . It used to be when we put color, you could count each and every grain but now people don't even know what it is. We made airplanes, incense holders, fans, sticks, and rolling pin rolling board sets; we made sticks to support scales; parcheesi game pieces; handles for sickles. We made every kind of thing, whatever thing you make on the lathe, even cot legs.

Note that Prabhu Lal's initial statement regarding producing the same items today as in the past turns out to be inaccurate as he recollects how many different things they once made. Queried about the wood Kairathis once used for their products, he named several species of trees, adding sadly, "My father and grandfather took them from the jungle but now the jungle is finished off and there are no trees in it."[8]

Prabhu Lal concluded that the lathe workers' business is down to about 20–25 percent of what it once was. Reflecting on the lack of demand for wooden toys, he spoke with resignation: "Even if we still made wooden toys, people can get plastic and electronic toys so they have no interest in the wooden. Electronic toys break, and they are expensive, but still that is what people want to buy. They like the ones that work with *remote. That is what pleases them! even though they are expensive and break. And for this reason our business is down." It is easy to conjecture retrospectively that a painful feud between neighbors and caste fellows, and the decline of what were once valued skills, together explain Prabhu Lal's unusually dark assessment of Jahazpur's character. Or, put another way, he may choose to explain his troubles to himself by thinking that, after all, it could not be any other way, for we live in a pitiless land.

Bunty Patriya is only in his thirties, but his eyes and mouth already show stress lines. He owns and tends a small store well located on one side of the bus stand. This was where I regularly came to get my AirTel mobile minutes recharged. Bunty was a masterful multitasker, always taking care of several customers and doing several transactions simultaneously; he never slowed down to shoot the breeze with anyone, as far as I could see. He was all business. Bunty's shop attracted a steady stream of customers who came to purchase mobile minutes. He also had a couple of photocopy machines, a fax service, and some used mobile phones and assorted accessories.

It took us many tries to set up an interview with Bunty, and this was not (as sometimes was the case with others) because he didn't want to talk with us. Rather, he was just so overworked he rarely had a moment free from business and family obligations. Eventually we arranged to meet him at his home, where he revealed himself to be a very different kind of person than what I had imagined from his store persona. At home he was not at all brusque. He was reflective, and sweetly affectionate to his little girl. He seemed to welcome our visit as a rare interlude rather than another pressure on a pressured life.

Bunty told us of his difficult childhood, in spite of being born to the privileges of a Brahmin. His mother died of heart disease after what was (in provincial India at the time) a staggering amount of medical expense all in vain. In another family tragedy around the same time, Bunty's uncle had an agricultural accident and perished painfully from tetanus. During his mother's incapacitating illness his father, a salaried government servant, had to take on household chores, and after she died he took early retirement in order to care for his children, some of whom were still young. Readers should try to understand that a man doing the cooking and child care alone is a condition of extreme pathos in provincial Rajasthan. Bunty emphasized this to us. His own immediate family was still strapped for cash.

In my market interview phase I was no longer seeking out "pitiless land" tales, as they had begun months ago to feel repetitive. Bunty however spontaneously connected his own compulsion to assist others with the legendary nature of the town; that is, he stressed his distinctively different nature as a compassionate man well aware of residing in a pitiless place. He was capable of catching himself in acts of unkindness, and redressing them. "Sometimes I say something bad to someone, and then I have remorse, and I ask forgiveness, and that person then will come back to me. From the beginning I have been a soft-hearted person, because I experienced so much sorrow in my own life. I can't bear to see someone in trouble, so I always go and help. If I see someone with a problem, I ask them if I can help." He then mused out loud, "Jahazpur is the pitiless land," and told us the story about Shravan Kumar, including the bit about the handful of soil.

It was only this day that I learned who Bunty's grandfather was. This man, Ram Prasad, was an important figure in another piece of Jahazpur history that I had investigated on one of my previous summer visits, and the subject of my first finished essay about the town (Gold 2016). The incident had to do with the former butchers, the Khatiks, and their struggle to build a Vishnu temple just opposite the bus stand. Today this temple is one of the town sights and on most persons' lists—lists I had elicited from all communities in my early, groping interviews—of the "best" places, most worth seeing.

But in the 1980s the Khatik community's plan for the temple had met virulent opposition from most members of the higher castes. When I first recorded this history, a Khatik leader told me about one local Brahmin who had supported the Khatiks in their temple-building struggle—a dedicated progressive man who had as a consequence suffered ejection from his own community. All I knew was that his name was Ram Prasad. I had done business with Bunty for over half a year but learned only now that Ram Prasad was his father's father. Bunty's thoughtfulness, his softheartedness, may have come not only from his immediate family sorrows but from his lineage's predilection to assist their fellow human beings. This family tradition of thinking otherwise from mainstream society predated Bunty's mother's illness. As Bunty reflected on it, he seemed to suggest that his nature, forged by hardship, forced him to act against the grain of the pitiless land.

Business, Morality, and Changing Times in the Pitiless Land

Interviews with merchants and businesspeople—some just scraping by at the bottom of the heap and others expanding, diversifying, and already moving beyond the local—revealed a range of worldviews and diverse assessments of the present. There were many who articulated very clearly the way both their business and their daily lives were driven by a relentless set of economic pressures. Some persons described vividly and justified practices (ruthless or pitiless?) stereotypical of business the world over. Many shopkeepers described the need to work harder even while they were earning less. Some, as we have heard, expected their children to follow in their footsteps, while others deliberately direct offspring to alternative futures.

A few younger men were eager to offer critical and novel analyses of commerce and of life. The three interview vignettes with which I close my last chapter sketch fragments of personal philosophies offered to us in recorded interviews by Jahazpur businessmen. Bhag Chand Soni temporarily left behind his hereditary profession as goldsmith to become a traveling salesman and an earnest, silver-tongued proselytizer for life insurance. Satya Narayan Khatik reveled in his success as an entrepreneurial junk dealer. Deepak Tak was a prize-winning tractor agent whose philosophy of life was unique. All three had a strong sense of self and did not hesitate to announce and even brag of worldviews discrepant from their peers'.

Two of these men explicitly distinguished themselves and their ideas from the masses. Deepak Tak, possibly the most successful of the businessmen we interviewed, described the vast majority of his contemporaries in Jahazpur as pure followers, a phenomenon he labeled *bher chal*—people who move like sheep, following the herd. He characterized himself as distinctively not sheep-like. Bhag Chand Soni estimated with a highly authoritative manner that in Jahazpur, and in fact throughout India, 80 percent of the people were content with what they had, while 20 percent were unhappy. It was his firm conviction that only the malcontents (among whom he numbered himself) invented, created, and progressed.

Bhag Chand Soni had a strong personality and an engaging manner. At the age of forty, his life experience was highly varied. He was born in a village to a family of goldsmiths by hereditary identity. As a young man he lived in Mumbai for twelve years, learning modern modes of metalwork from relatives who did business there. Following that sojourn in India's most cosmopolitan city, Bhag Chand had settled in Jahazpur because he had family and caste connections in place and wanted to be somewhere larger than a village but near to his father, whose health was poor. In Jahazpur, Bhag Chand successfully produced and sold ornaments to all levels of society. However, for a few years before our interview in 2011, he had largely abandoned that work to be a traveling salesman for the (now defunct) insurance company called Tulip.

Bhag Chand held forth on new times and religion in a fashion evidently inspired by his work for Tulip, which seemed close to a conversion experience. He wore a beautiful gold ring with a tulip on it that he himself had designed and crafted, thus bringing his old trade into conversation with his new vocation. Some of what he said sounded partly like a humanistic approach to existence such as I have rarely encountered in provincial India, and partly like a sales pitch. Here is a sample: "When you are in trouble god doesn't come to help you, only human beings come to help you. If you need money god isn't the one who gives you money, some human being comes and gives it. There are plenty of people in this world, who don't just work for money, but who like to share their happiness with others. The greatest virtue (*dharma*) in this illusory world (*duniya*) is *network [*is duniya me sab se bara dharm hai network*]."

I was never able fully to fathom the workings of this divine network; it was some kind of pyramid scheme that ultimately collapsed under a cloud. As far as I grasped it, a person who purchased an insurance policy from Tulip "joined" the company—perhaps after hearing Bhag Chand's (or any other salesperson's) hypnotic, seductive rhetoric. If that individual were then able to sell to ten others and to recruit them as additional salespersons, then they would have a share in company earnings. If they did nothing, then they had simply bought an insurance policy. In other words, it should have been a no-lose proposition. (Bhag Chand had sold one to Bhoju a few years back, and Bhoju ruefully admitted that he had never attempted to take advantage of the opportunity to join the network).

When we interviewed him in 2011, Bhag Chand made it clear to us that being a part of Tulip had transformed both his livelihood and his worldview. Although he still now and then crafted or procured gold jewelry for friends, one had to catch him on one of his brief stops in Jahazpur between long tours of his sales territories. However, Tulip's network eventually imploded, and by the time I was looking to buy a gold nose stud for my niece in 2013, Bhag Chand had reopened a jewelry store although not in Jahazpur. We could never find him at home.[9]

Khatiks, as already noted, were formerly butchers and traders in animal flesh, a community once held in contempt by clean castes and indeed classified among oppressed groups (SC) by the government of India. These days in Jahazpur the Khatik community consistently garners grudging admiration from middle-class Jahazpurites who note both their energy and progress. If we asked, as we often did, which groups were doing well and which groups were not, Khatiks appeared at the top of everyone's list for the first category. Individuals from various communities and classes would readily single out Khatiks among the so-called "lower communities" (English phrase used by middle-class speakers of Hindi) as having gone forward with the times.[10]

For example, as already mentioned in this chapter, members of Khatik society have transformed Jahazpur's entire produce-marketing process, regularizing daily morning auctions and acting themselves as the auctioneers and middlemen between growers and vendors; significant numbers are also vendors. Their fruit and vegetable enterprise has expanded over the past thirty years from just one to four small markets, each with its own auction. All of these, located at or near the bus stand, are literally backed by the same community's success in constructing in the mid-1980s and maintaining into the present the beautiful Satya Narayan temple.

The Satya Narayan temple and the vegetable markets form a creatively constructed package of progress. The Khatiks collectively take care of their image, but in several ways they have diverged significantly from a standard course of so-called Brahminization or Sanskritization. For example, few non-Khatiks, when discussing Khatik progress, failed to mention (some with thinly veiled disapproval and some with sincere appreciation) how hard Khatik women work, whether at farming, labor, or vegetable selling. Thus the Khatiks have not in any way subscribed to the often noted pattern of upward mobility which involves the increased seclusion of women. And, although the majority of Jahazpur Khatiks have totally eschewed their old trade in livestock and meat with the religiously devalued violence inherent in it, they are not afraid to soil their hands if it makes good business sense. We see this with the young entrepreneur named, not wholly incidentally, Satya Narayan. (Satya Narayan is not an uncommon name among Vaishnavites and is used by many different communities, including Brahmin.)

Satya Narayan Khatik is an enterprising man. His fleet of over twenty buyers on motorbikes fans out from Jahazpur every morning to visit villages in the vicinity, collecting junk for recycling (and peddling shiny new junk in exchange for it, thus reducing the cash outlay). They purchase every kind of unwanted material from beer bottles to women's hair to candy boxes. Satya Narayan's employees sort each day's haul. Then different categories of materials are resold to factories in diverse metropolitan areas throughout North India, and at a tidy profit. Satya Narayan is thus a highly successful dealer in recycled junk. Satya Narayan studied to college level and spoke Hindi well. He told us he quit working on his BA when he realized that he could do a lot better in the junk business than on a government salary: "I can earn in one hour what a teacher earns in one day," he boasted—a rather pointed remark given that Bhoju is a teacher on a government salary, a status most people in Jahazpur normally consider to be an enviable professional achievement.

I asked Satya Narayan what the reason was for the progress he had made, the success of his business. He gave a succinct answer in two words: awareness (*jagarukta*) and hard work (*mehant*). He did not at first elaborate on "awareness." For hard work, he gave an example from his own schedule: "Last night," he told us, "I personally loaded a truck of scrap, and didn't go home to eat until 11:30 p.m." He added, "I came back to work at 6:30 this morning."

Others, both Khatik and non-Khatik, frequently posed a connection between the visible progress of the Khatik community over the past thirty some years and their establishment of the highly visible Satya Narayan temple in 1984. Bhoju therefore asked Satya Narayan the businessman about this causal link: "How much change happened after this installation?" The immediate answer this young entrepreneur gave did not ascribe success to divine favor. Rather, he continued the twin themes of awareness and effort—which he located largely in behavioral changes among his caste fellows—linked to the temple of course but by effort, self-control, and collective action, not grace.

> There has been a great deal of change! Because our temple is at the bus stand and people from the high castes come there, from the important communities, so we [Khatiks] have to pay attention to our behavior. We have to be careful. We have begun to get some respect (*ijjat*). We have cut down on eating meat and drinking liquor, little by little; 70 percent have giving up drinking altogether and maybe only 20 percent of our caste even let others who do eat meat and drink liquor into their houses.

Bhoju pressed him again as to whether this was a miracle (*chamatkar*) from the temple. Satya Narayan answered tactfully, not wishing to deny credit to divine intervention but nonetheless insisting on the human factor: "It is due to both. But mostly, people are working hard and starting to understand their own worth," that is, to acquire self-respect, which is an attribute of "awareness" or "awakening." Thus, while stressing motivations that may in part derive from the temple, mainly he insisted on the power of human effort. He clearly views his own success in the same pattern.

As we have already seen, another community that has done well diversifying in the Jahazpur business world after giving up their traditional trade is that of the former wine sellers. Kalal, the old caste name for wine sellers, has been replaced in current Jahazpur usage by Tak, a lineage name.[11] Earlier in this chapter I recounted a conversation with Hari Lal Tak, a cloth merchant. We also met Rajendra Tak, local agent for Hero Honda. In Chapter 6 I noted that it was Bhairu Lal Tak whose hunger strike on behalf of the Nagdi River first turned our attention to local environmental activism.

In pre-Independence India the Kalals had distilled wine and sold it. This hereditary specialization had been disrupted less by religious scruples combined with status aspiration (as with the Khatiks) than by government regulatory impositions on liquor production as well as its marketing. The government totally took over production and began to auction off licenses required to sell liquor legally. Thus propelled into other lines of business, Jahazpur Taks seemed quick to find opportunities to prosper.

One of the most distinctive voices among our interviewees was Deepak Tak, who worked under his father at the Jahazpur franchise for Mahindra Tractors. Deepak was a voluble man, not yet thirty, who possessed an unusual philosophy of life about which he was pleased to hold forth. Our original plan had been to interview Deepak's father, but as our interactions unfolded, Tak senior had little interest in talking with us and seemed grateful to slip away as his son increasingly dominated the conversation. Deepak was eager to show us Mahindra's online accounting system, through which he was able to access the records for each tractor customer. Deepak explained a system of promotions for tractor sales and service that worked via mobile phones (widespread now in the rural areas), sending out voice mails (knowing that farmers who own tractors may not necessarily be able to read).

I admit to being overly dazzled by the technology in the Mahindra office. What would have been unexceptional in Jaipur or Ajmer was possibly unique in Jahazpur. Not even the town's several Internet institutes possessed such up-to-date computers and evidently high-speed connections.

Figure 29. Deepak Tak at his desk, Mahindra Tractor.

Most of Jahazpur market, including Deepak's relative at Hero Honda, still did its bookkeeping in clothbound ledgers in 2011 (although doubtless this would be changing rapidly). Mahindra's networked accounting and advertising was certainly an anomaly. Obviously this has to do both with Mahindra being a huge company with global reach and with the price of a tractor (comparable I would guess to nothing else sold in Jahazpur, unless it would be gold jewelry sets).

Deepak analyzed many aspects of town life and human society in the course of our long conversation, but I muse upon his provocative theology as I near the close of this chapter and of our conversations with the residents of Shiptown. He explained to us that god himself had changed because god had become "*samajhdar*"—that is, "discerning"—someone who understands the way the world works.

> God didn't used to be samajhdar. He is not today that Ram from
> before, that Ram in the dharmic books, that is not today's God.

In the old days, people thought, as many are born, let them come. But now God thinks there are too many people living on the earth. He thinks, "Let's kill a lot of them!" So he sends an earthquake, or a tsunami [this was about seven years after the devastating tsunami].

The old God left them alone.

. . . .

Just as many worlds below are changing, so the worlds above are changing. There are many worlds below and above and in all places it is changing.

For example, America was so proud, of its power. Then God thought, "The bastard, how does it imagine itself ahead of me?" [*sala mere se zyada tak age kaise soch rahe ho*] So he sent the terrorists to destroy the twin towers. God did that. Americans thought that they were the bravest in the world and they feared no one, but now they have again started to fear God, *and* they are afraid of terrorists too.

I could not help wondering, and wish I had asked Deepak, if this new god were not himself *nirday*—pitiless.

While acknowledging these three voices as somewhat unusual, expressing their own creative understandings of contemporary life, I would generalize that a sense of moral ferment emerged in quite a few other interviews. With the term "moral ferment" I intend to distinguish ideas I heard in 2010–11 in Jahazpur from ideas about moral *decline* that I gathered over the course of almost twenty years in nearby villages. The latter was a consistent rhetoric about the decline of love and the ascent of egotism in modern times. One thing everyone in Ghatiyali and other villages had nonetheless insisted was that God had not changed; only people had changed (Gold 2006). In Jahazpur, by contrast, as I have tried to show, there are those thoughtful persons who perceive that the cosmos itself is in some kind of flux. How are we to read this divergence? Are Jahazpur's varied views logical outcomes of a more truly cosmopolitan experience, or of a gulf between town and country based on environment and sources of livelihood? Or does this ferment represent diverse responses to the influence of global media combined with the economic pressures of life in the twenty-first century? I would hazard that all these factors are relevant.

It could seem fitting to give the last word in *Shiptown* to the tractor dealer with his modern showroom out on the highway and his outlandish theology. An epilogue follows, however, in order to report on just two significant developments that followed my brief Jahazpur sojourn. These developments, grounded in the qasba past but reaching far beyond local geographies, gesture toward other, related dimensions of present and future conditions and transformations.

Epilogue
Wondrous Jahazpur

All the world is a bloom space now. A promissory note. An allure and a threat that shows up in ordinary sensibilities of not knowing what compels, not being able to sit still, being exhausted, being left behind or being ahead of the curve, being in history, being in a predicament, being ready for something—anything—to happen, or inventing yourself to the sole goal of making sure that nothing (more) will happen. (Stewart 2010:340)

Kathleen Stewart's enigmatic words capture something restless and relentless about the common present of humankind, and they evoke not just uncertainty but potentiality, however fraught or precarious. In Jahazpur, among residents young and old, I encountered similar sensations, articulated as the necessity to strive for oneself or one's children to realize an unprecedented becoming, bypassing foreclosed futures toward glimmering if foggy horizons.[1]

Since Dan and I packed up and left our Santosh Nagar residence in June 2011, Shiptown the place kept on changing while *Shiptown* the book gradually became frozen on the page. Such has always and inevitably been the case with ethnographic texts. What has altered anthropological circumstances radically are the conditions of hyperconnectivity under which we now live. Closure comes hard when all the world's a bloom space.

Most of what is chronicled as contemporary Jahazpur in the preceding chapters drew on a fixed period of time when I lived there with a research visa, a formal affiliation, and an Internal Review Board protocol for the protection of human subjects. Since then I have been able to make three short winter trips back as a tourist—to visit, to sightsee, and above all to sustain friendships formed during fieldwork but overflowing its bounds. I revisited Jahazpur for brief periods of time (staying one to two weeks in Bhoju's Santosh Nagar house) in December 2012, December 2013–January 2014, and February 2015. Beginning in spring of 2013, some developments in the qasba became visible to me on the Internet, specifically on Facebook. Initially I followed these compulsively, downloading and filing each post. Over time my compulsion decreased; there is just too blooming much.

In 2010 when I began my long spell of fieldwork, Jahazpur's culture evidently existed in perpetual engagement with national and transnational flows of goods, images, jobs, news, money, and much more. The qasba was networked both literally and figuratively, and individuals from Jahazpur used social media well before the events of 2013. But the town's presence on the Web as a place was negligible.

In contemporary religious studies it has become commonplace to document a merged sensibility of profound reverence with high-tech aptitudes. There are evidently multifarious modes whereby the Internet intertwines with religious phenomena across traditions, as it does with pretty much every aspect of human behavior. Therefore the juxtaposition of an old-fashioned miraculous image and two new Facebook pages could seem too facile, too ready-made as a strategy to evoke ongoing change in Jahazpur, or that time-honored trope, the "modernity of tradition" (Rudolph and Rudolph 1967). Still, examined in its specificity, this is an attractive conjunction: sequestered images linked to ancient history, Facebook pages linked to contemporary projects. Therefore I risk taking this juxtaposition as a small epitomizing coda to my exploration of a place, the Jahazpur qasba and its environs. This book has argued that the town possesses a distinctive and profoundly plural culture and is a site of frequent passages and easy crossings, repeated and reversed, back and forth, between rural and urban, between older habits and newer trends. Such crossings and cross-fertilizations, however ordinary, are real and consequential.

This brief epilogue centers on two conjoined events in 2013 and their aftermaths, which continue both on the ground and in the ether. Both events could be described as emergences. First there was the miraculous and material emergence on a Muslim landowner's qasba property of yet another buried cache of centuries-old Jain images. Second, and subsequently, there was the technological and virtual emergence of Jahazpur onto the Internet as two Facebook pages about the town were launched.

In accord with a habit of this book, a caveat: although it is true that the visibility of the town of Jahazpur on Facebook originated with the Jain images' discovery in 2013, much has passed before my cruising vision since then that has nothing to do with religion. My ever-increasing numbers of Jahazpur Facebook friends offer commentary on local and national politics, farmers' movements, the launching of educational institutions, and more, not to mention posting jokes, poetry, scenery, weddings, and—that cross-cultural universal—cute babies! But these are all on personal pages, not on the two town pages that are my focus here.

As discussed in Chapter 5, Jain discoveries are old news in Jahazpur. However, the most recent incident occurred on a major Jain festival day: Mahavir Jayanti—a date on the lunar calendar (bright thirteenth of Chaitra) said to be the birthday of the twenty-fourth Jain Tirthankara, Mahavir (599–527 BCE according to tradition).[2] Not long after the images had been fully unearthed, cleaned, and temporarily housed in the Digambar Jain temple—crowded though it was with other evidence of the region's Jain heritage—miracles were reported in connection with the largest image, identified as a representation of Munisuvrata, the twentieth of the twenty-four Jinas (victors) revered by Jains. The statue, it was said, breathed; it bathed itself; a sign appeared on its forehead.[3]

It was in the immediate wake of these spectacular occurrences that two Facebook pages were launched giving visibility to the place, Jahazpur. Mahesh Parisar, a Brahmin well established as among the town's foremost Internet entrepreneurs, initiated "Wondrous Jahazpur" (Adbhud Jahazpur), www.facebook.com/jahazpur.[4] Members of the Digambar Jain community launched a page they named Swasti Dham Atishay Kshetra Jahazpur, Rajasthan (hereafter Swasti Dham), www.facebook.com/swastidhamjahazpur. As Chapter 5 noted, some interviewees, years before the 2013 emergence, referred to their town as *atishaya kshetra*. The phrase that seemed to work best to translate those terms was "hallowed ground." But the words might also be rendered accurately as "miraculous site." The entire page name would be awkwardly rendered as "Blessed Site on Hallowed Ground Jahazpur." The page describes the Mahavir Jayanti discovery as "the most beautiful moment in the history of Jahazpur" and speaks of the images coming out "from the womb of the earth."[5]

Thus the initial motivation for both pages was a single splash: the 2013 emergence of Munisuvrata and accompanying statuary. However, the pages diverge in audience, content, and intent. "Wondrous Jahazpur" has a broad scope. Certainly it publicized the Jain miracles, but it also regularly features Hindu festivals and temples and sporadically highlights civic events, extreme weather, and places of historical significance. The "Swasti Dham" page fosters interchange among Digambar Jains about Jain-specific materials. It aims evidently to let Jains from outside Jahazpur know about the wonders and building efforts in the town, as well as to alert local Jains to matters of interest within their community all over the region, and beyond it.

On my winter break in 2013–14, I stopped by Mahesh's Internet place to do some email and had a chance to chat with him about "Wondrous Jahazpur." Mahesh explained his motivations, which I paraphrased in my travel journal and summarize here. First he acknowledged that it was definitely the miraculous emergence of the Jain *murtis* that inspired him to start the page. He had thought to himself, he told me with straightforward earnestness, that outsiders initially attracted by the Jain images would naturally want to know more about the town. His page would supply information about all Jahazpur's "wonders." However, he also acknowledged that the most popular post ever on "Wondrous Jahazpur" had been a short video of the Jain image when it was said to be taking breaths; this video (still available in the sidebar) had initially attracted over sixteen hundred views in one week.[6]

In the same conversation, Mahesh expressed a sincere affection for his hometown (which incidentally supplies a helpful counterpoint to the numerous negative judgments that my 2010 interviews, described in Chapter 1, had elicited about Jahazpur's lack of progress and "backward" character). Mahesh's comments went something like this: Even though there are so many things going on throughout the whole wide world, people love the place where they are born. Out of his own love for his birthplace, he had felt moved to do something. The Facebook page "Wondrous Jahazpur" would, he believed, not only give the town some presence or heft in the minds of unknowing outsiders but would please others like himself who were fond Jahazpurites.

I probed a bit about what was to me a painfully glaring absence on "Wondrous Jahazpur": that is, evidence of the town's rich Islamic heritage.[7] Mahesh gave a somewhat troubling response, which I take as only partially disingenuous. He said that while Hindus would surely not object to posts about Muslim sites, members of the diverse Muslim community might. Thus, on grounds of not risking offense to Muslims, he disseminates a false impression on Facebook of this very plural qasba to whose history, economy, and culture Islam has made vital contributions, and whose skyline is recognizably dominated by a minaret. While I have many Muslim Facebook friends in Jahazpur, as far as I have been able to discover, the Jahazpur Muslim community does not have its own public page.

Nonetheless, Jahazpur Muslims played a role in the Jain miracle. I had known that the images were found by a Muslim on his own property. I saw nothing more than the man's name in accounts of the find by journalists and nothing at all on social media.[8] On my winter visit at the end of 2013 I happened to learn a bit more. Daniel had a particular Muslim friend in the market, Rafiq, a grocer. His shop was inside the walls a very short distance from Royal Gate. Rafiq always greeted me warmly, even when Daniel was not with me. When I ran into Rafiq in 2013, I learned that he himself had assisted in digging out the statues. He said he had been on the way from his shop to his house to eat—thus passing through a large stretch of the Muslim neighborhood. He noticed a group of people collected around a site where preliminary construction was under way to dig the foundation for a new house. These people informed him that the diggers had encountered a huge stone. He was able to reach into the excavation and put his hand on it. He said he could tell that it was an upside-down image, that it had a face, and that it might be made of *neelam*.[9] So, Rafiq thought to himself, "it must be a *murti*." Eventually seventeen images would be carefully removed from this single site.

Our grocer friend went on to tell me and Bhoju that he was one of five Muslims belonging to the neighborhood who all donated their labor to extract the images safely from the ground. Some other Jahazpur Muslims, he added, were angry about their coreligionists' participation. The implication was that dealing with images in any fashion was disapproved in the view of the town's more strict (*kattar*) Muslims, from whom our friend wished to distinguish himself. Bhoju warmly assured Rafiq that he had "done something for God" and should feel at peace. He responded simply, as my diary records, "It is my *karam* [fated action] and I have done it, so I am satisfied."

Rafiq also mentioned that the Jains had offered him a large sum of money as a reward (*inam*) but that he had immediately returned it in the form of a donation (*dan*) to the temple fund. A Hindu friend later commented that the emerged Jain images brought peace to the town. He prognosticated that this peace was a blessing that would endure, that Jahazpur would now forever remain a peaceful area. Thus he looked hopefully toward the peaceful aura of Jainism to help his town shed its unwanted reputation as a place of interreligious tension (Chapter 4).

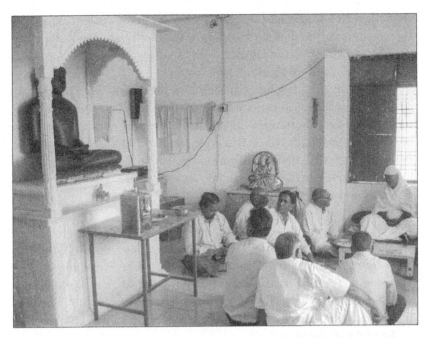

Figure 30. Downstairs at Digambar Jain temple, temporarily housing recently
emerged miraculous image; nun discourses, one listener gazes
at image, 2014 (photo by Bhoju Ram Gujar).

On this same winter visit of mine, Bhoju and I stopped in at the
Digambar temple and joined a small group seated beneath the big black
image of Munisuvrata, and gathered around a Jain nun, addressed as
Mataji. She had arrived in Jahazpur not long after the murtis emerged (and
was still there in 2015). I liked her immediately; she seemed unpretentious
and sincere. In a straightforward fashion, she interpreted the main image's
genuine power persuasively without recourse to a theology of miracles
(which are not admitted in Jain precepts, if widely acknowledged in popular
religiosity).

Mataji explained to us, in a pure but not overly flowery Hindi, that
there were profuse numbers of images in the world, but "when you go in
front of *that* murti you stay transfixed without blinking your eyes." She
told us this quality did not derive from divine power residing in and vitaliz-
ing stone. Rather, in speculative fashion, she suggested the image's power
had been endowed by the hands of the carver. "Maybe it was a particularly

religious person who made this murti." Thus she acknowledged the image's special powers of an uplifting attraction without attributing to it any other-worldly capacities. She added that when someone looks at it, the image makes contact with that person's soul (*atma*).

In spite of this religious teacher's restrained view, on Facebook, as already noted, Jains had previously reported and documented with blurry photographs and short video clips a small flurry of miracles: the image breathed, bathed itself, and on its initially unmarked forehead a sign of the moon had appeared. Bhoju had gone to the temple at my behest during the breathing miracle period in the rainy season of 2013. His email account expressed some skepticism:

> Dear, I hope you are doing well. Yesterday I went to the Jain temple and spent half an hour to see the Idol. For a long while I did not blink my eyes, but could not see anything. There were some Jains around me and also many other pilgrims from far away, up to MP. [Madhya Pradesh]. The Jains from Jahazpur were saying "look! look! it's breathing, there is some movement near around his navel!" But I do not think . . .

He went on to remark that the local Jains were in the process of collecting money for their temple-building project, and these miracles certainly provided good publicity. The email concluded: "Anyway it is good something is going on in Jahazpur for good."

Bhoju was genuinely impressed that, as he had expressed it once in another email, "God came out on his birthday." In other words, the appearance of the image on Mahavir's birthday was to him indisputably persuasive of the statue's miraculous agency. However, he considered the additional reports associated with the emerged image to be trumped up, if forgivably, for the explicit purposes of fund-raising in the interests of temple construction, a purpose Bhoju personally approved.

If Deepak, the Mahindra Tractor agent, seated by his computer screen and holding forth on a brutal new God is one portent of a global, networked Jahazpur (Chapter 8), the miracles attributed to the emerged images and the energetic temple-building efforts that followed, magnified via the Internet, are another. As the Jains complete their work on the new temple, other construction and enterprise proceed in the vicinity, along the same road. Among these additional projects I noted a new meeting hall built by followers of Jaigurudev, a group that previously gathered in a member's home (D. Gold 2013), and the Hotel Relax, another brave attempt to bring family dining to the town.

Throughout this work I have stressed that Jahazpur presents a unique qasba culture, neither rural nor urban. It is a site of multiple and bidirectional passages and crossings between an economy and society based on agropastoral production and one based on commerce via ever-expanding networks of trade, transportation, and communication. While my epilogue gestures to extraordinary events, it goes without saying that the everyday has its variegated, ongoing life full of unpredictable change. For instance, in 2015 Bhoju Ram sold his house in Santosh Nagar and moved back to Ghatiyali, his village birthplace. There in 2016 family and community celebrated lavishly Bhoju's retirement from a successful career in education. For the sake of her postgraduate studies, Chinu lived for several years in Kekari, another growing town in the region with good educational facilities; she has achieved high marks and I trust has a good chance for employment. Madhu taught for some time at a private school in her in-laws' village but more recently relocated with her husband and son to Bhilwara, the district capital, where she has resumed efforts to pursue opportunities for government service. Shiptown, as it turns out, was not a final destination for any member of my Rajasthani family, but it did provide transport. Along with the subjects of this book, its coproducers continue their not atypical, nonlinear passages toward livelihoods and personal fulfillment in shaky, yet not wholly unpromising times.

Notes

Preface

1. This observation only echoes and affirms many others; see for example Das 2013; Mayaram 2005; Olsen 2003; Ring 2006; Singh 2011.

2. While anthropologists have by and large neglected provincial towns, Indian writers have eloquently portrayed them; see R. K. Narayan's many works for loving accounts of fictional Malgudi (e.g., Narayan 2006); Aravind Adiga's *Between the Assassinations* (2008) for a much darker view; and Pankaj Mishra's *Butter Chicken in Ludhiana* (2006) for a young journalist's sometimes critical, sometimes affectionate rendering of provincial India. For reasons I cannot fathom there are scholars deeply upset by what they imagine to be an unreflective acceptance of Narayan's fiction as a source of cultural insights. I remain a staunch and unrepentant fan (which doesn't mean that I am unaware of the differences between fiction and life).

3. Gyanendra Pandey called my attention to Reza's novel by recommending it as offering a "very rich 'anthropological' account" of everyday concerns in North Indian qasba life (1988:123 n. 68).

4. See Nelson 2015:98 for potent statements about gendered apologies.

Introduction

1. See Sethia 2003 for the role of qasbas in eighteenth-century Kota, a former kingdom not far from Jahazpur; see also National Foundation of India 2011.

2. Census data obtained from Jahazpur Population Census 2011, http://www.census2011 .co.in/data/town/800593-jahazpur-rajasthan.html; according to its size, Jahazpur is a Class IV town.

3. A responsive and kind audience at the Delhi School of Economics Sociological Research Colloquium affirmed my preliminary hunch that the semantics of qasba were more nuanced than the dictionary could reveal.

4. See also Vashishta 2011 for a study of the development of Beawar market located only a few hours' driving distance from Jahazpur.

5. See for example Bayly 1980; Freitag 1989; Hasan 2004; G. Pandey 1988; Rawat 2011; Sato and Bhadani 1997; Yang 1998.

6. An Urdu term derived from Arabic, *mofussil* in its adjectival usage translates neatly as "provincial"; it carries slightly disparaging implications—insular, backwater—in British colonial usage. I rarely heard it uttered in Jahazpur.

7. English *progress* was the word used most often in my recorded interviews; but I also heard both Hindi *vikas* (development) and Urdu *taraqqi* (improvement, advance, progress); all three appear almost interchangeable in their implications.

8. Except for the large number of Khatiks who live clustered near the qasba end of Santosh Nagar, our tailors were one of two SC households in the colony; the other was a drummer family.

9. Jahazpur hospital is notoriously poorly staffed. Many recollected a better time when a competent doctor had been posted there and the beds would be full. Now they are often empty, as ill people seek better care in or beyond Devli or from alternative medical practitioners (see Das 2015a).

10. I typed a journal every day, religiously, but often it was no more than disconnected jottings, intended to keep me from losing crucial bits. Later, I went back and selectively crafted more detailed expositions, more coherent accounts out of some, but not all, of these jottings. The virtue of the field journal, as subsequent extracts will reveal, is exactly the same as its drawbacks: it is raw.

11. All my earlier fieldwork had been village based; see Prakash 2002 for an anticipatory and highly lucid synopsis of "the urban turn."

12. See for example Borneman and Hammoudi 2009; Davies and Spencer 2010; Pratt and Rosner 2012.

13. In the "had better not ignore" department I acknowledge that time constraints and my strong predilection for the personal over the institutional united to exclude other crucial areas of qasba life, including the many departments of local government and the booming business of education.

Chapter 1

1. In a new and provocative study of an Islamic saint, Ghazi Miyan, Shahid Amin addresses and critiques the same literary source. Amin writes, "By underlining a mere linguistic switch—Gadipur/Ghazipur—Rahi Raza was being faithful, no doubt, to a composite view of India's medieval past, where even if Ghazis and Rajas cross swords, no real trace of that conflict—not even toponymic—survives on the ground." Amin disagrees, speaking of a "momentous rupture amidst the quotidian" (2015:192–93).

2. In a short story by Ghulam Abbas, a triple name change occurs—first from Husnabad, "the home of the beautiful," to Hasanabad, after an important Muslim figure—in a bid for respectability (as the town originated with a brothel). As Abbas describes it in his fictional account, "After going through scores of rotting volumes and old manuscripts, it was found that hundreds of years ago, there used to stand here a city by the name of Anandi, which is what it is called now" (1996:55). To shift from Husnabad to Hasanabad to Anandi is to transition from Perso-Arabic vocabularies to Sanskrit, the opposite direction from both the Jahazpur example and Reza's. See also Green 2012.

3. In February 2015 I visited the site, where ground had been broken and construction had commenced.

4. For a full translation see van Buitenen 1973:44–123. Sanskrit scholars have commented extensively on the peculiarity of the epic snake sacrifice; see for example Minkowski 2001:169–86; O'Flaherty 1986:16–44; Reich 2001:142–69.

5. In this method of irrigation, known as *panat ka kam*, women's traditional part is considered the most strenuous and backbreaking agricultural labor. They use their hands and a small tool to construct mud barricades in order to direct the precious irrigation water into channels surrounding different portions (*kyari*) of the field so that the entire crop will be uniformly watered.

6. Of the thirty-some recorded interviewees who spoke of Yagyapur, approximately half only gave the tale of Janamejaya; another 15 percent gave us only the Shravan Kumar story when asked about Jahazpur as a place. Over a third, then, told the two sequentially, often with barely a pause in the narration. The sole link between the two stories is that crucial trait assigned to Jahazpur territory: a land without compassion.

7. This is recounted in the Ayodhya Kanda, the second book of the Sanskrit Ramayana said to be authored by the sage Valmiki. Apparently the popular image of Shravan Kumar with shoulder baskets, one parent in each basket, is nowhere in Valmiki, or even in retellings that follow Valmiki closely; see Chandrasekhar 2001:21–28; Prime 1999:50–51. Thanks to Philip Lutgendorf for insights into this narrative's place in the Ramayana epic.

8. At a workshop where I first presented this tale, an audience of mostly senior South Asianists was flabbergasted; they racked their brains for any similar myth, but the only one who came up with something was Phyllis Granoff. She kindly provided me with her own translation of a Jain text that shows that the Marwar desert leads to pitilessness in the form of abandoning one's old parents (under desperate circumstances). Thus it poses a kind of ecological determinism, linked as A. R. Vasavi (personal communication) points out with the very name Marwar, a land of death.

9. The Banas is a major river approximately twelve kilometers from the town of Jahazpur; the Nagdi, which flows through Jahazpur, is a tributary of the Banas.

10. We learned a lot from him; as it transpired, sadly, he passed away not many months afterward. I had taken a candid photograph of him, in his everyday clothes, and Bhoju and I were able to give it to his family when we visited them to pay our respects during the mourning period.

11. See Ortner 2016 for an illuminating discussion of "dark anthropology."

Chapter 2

1. Bhoju doubtless thought the same of my life when he spent a semester living in my house in Ithaca in 1998.

2. See Gold, Gujar, Gujar, and Gujar 2014 for Bhoju's description of the difference between his work in Ghatiyali and in Jahazpur.

3. Henceforth I will use the English "municipality" when referring to the institution and the Hindi "Nagar Palika" when referring to the building as a place people go, where various things happen.

4. The installation of Maharana Pratap discussed later in this chapter was energized by Rajputs from other places in the region, not Jahazpur. Rajputs are still powerful in the state of Rajasthan; their diminished status in Jahazpur is idiosyncratic and localized although not unique.

5. Actually the big gates have small windows (*khirki*) in them for human passage; but the small gate *is* a window. Its name, Bari Gate, means "window gate"; English *gate* is very often used in place of Hindi/Urdu *darvaza*, but Bari Gate would never have been called a darvaza (entranceway).

6. Vijay Kumar Vashishtha, for example, writes of Beawar that the city wall, which was raised in 1841 for extending protection "from the plunderers," had four gates opening into the town (2011:142). See Narayanan 2015 for an extended and eye-opening discussion of "old walled cities" and urban planning in India.

7. Here I must credit a conversation with Anand Pandian when I was driving him from Ithaca to Syracuse in October 2011 shortly after returning from my year in Jahazpur. I told him I was thinking about my book as "windows on Jahazpur" and he suggested that I also think of it as "windows from Jahazpur," thus causing me to catch myself whenever tempted to imagine a gaze that is not two-way.

8. The name refers to the special seat for an esteemed saint, a cushion, although one Jahazpur Muslim elder told us simply, "When Muslims sit to pray they call it *takiya*."

9. I say men because women in Jahazpur do not appear as drivers of cars, motorbikes, or even bicycles. This is characteristic of Jahazpur's provinciality, for women regularly drive in larger cities.

10. In 2010 it was said to be a sign of Jahazpur's lack of progress that its one garden restaurant had gone under financially. In 2014 the Hotel Relax had opened to give the idea another try. Neither was at the bus stand or in the qasba; both were out on the highway.

11. For a recent and fascinating discussion of Tejaji in Rajasthan see Singh 2015:164–96.

12. A great deal has been written on the Ram Lila, as performed and televised throughout India; see for example Hess 1993; Lutgendorf 1995.

13. For Ramdevji see Khan 2003.

14. Processions also halt and performances also take place at Nau Chauk, another of Jahazpur's pivotal sites, as the next section will discuss.

15. Three others are the Circle Inspector of the Police Department; the Abkari (liquor excise) office; and the Ayurvedic Hospital.

16. Rima Hooja notes that Kumbha "asserted his control over certain areas that showed signs of independence. Among these were Yagnapur (Jahazpur), Joginipur (Jawar), Vardhavan (Badnor), and Hammirpur (Hamirgarh). Kumbha's vigorous policy resulted in an unprecedented expansion of the boundaries of Mewar, besides the acquisition of immense wealth, including ransoms, indemnities and loot!" (2006:340).

17. So much of the history of Rajasthan has been written around kings and battles and forts, but see Sethia 2003 for refreshing attention to markets. See also C. A. Bayly, who makes this claim about a qasba called Kara in today's Uttar Pradesh: "We see here the emergence of the town as a definite corporate entity with traditions and history of its own which long survives the vicissitudes of violent political change at the center"(1980:43). This is quite germane to Jahazpur.

18. The wine-seller woman or *kalali* is an alluring and ambiguous figure, seductress and trickster, in Rajasthani oral traditions, both in song and in oral epics such as that of the Bhagaravat Brothers (Miller 1994).

19. I don't know enough to tell it myself, but I hope someone will write the story of the empty pedestals where Ambedkar ought to be. It is not just Jahazpur where Ambedkar Circle has no permanent statue of Ambedkar. I discovered the same situation in Devli.

20. "Bindi is small village located in Jahazpur Tehsil of Bhilwara district, Rajasthan with total 17 families residing. The Bindi village has population of 94 of which 52 are males while 42 are females as per Population Census 2011." Census 2011, http://www.census2011.co.in/data/village/95908-bindi-rajasthan.html (accessed 17 June 2016).

21. Neither, I would argue, are Hindu-Muslim tensions; gender discrimination; laments about corruption; or religious devotion, pouring energies and rupees into temple building or mosque building, as the case may be, the dominant subjects. All these play a part, but it

seemed to me that earning a living and taking care of the family were the true centers of concern for most Jahazpur people, around which the others ranged themselves with greater or lesser significance given to them.

22. Stefano Bianca on Arab cities helped me to understand the importance of such gateways in Islamic cultures. He captions the image of a mosque gateway: "Within the traditional Muslim city: the transition from the market street to the ritual space of the mosque courtyard" (2000:22).

23. For Rajasthan as a whole, see "Rajasthan's Population," http://www.indiaonline pages.com/population/rajasthan-population.html (accessed 23 March 2015); for Jahazpur see "Jahazpur Population Census 2011," http://www.census2011.co.in/data/town/800593 -jahazpur-rajasthan.html (accessed 20 June 2016).

24. The *Rajasthani–Hindi–English Dictionary* (Suthar and Gahlot 1995) defines *Deshvali* as "those Muslims who had to pay the *jajiya* tax," which was a tax levied on non-Muslims living under Muslim government; the *Rajasthani Sabad Kos* (Lalas 1967) glosses *Deshvali* as "a caste of Rajputs who became Muslim." Neither dictionary definition fully covers Jahazpur Deshvali usage, but taken together they at least point the way toward an understanding of Deshvali Muslims as converts with known Hindu antecedents and residual genetic identity. Clearest on this point and of course geographically closest to our fieldwork region is the *Bhilwara District Gazetteer*: "In practice, however, there are two distinct groups among the Muslims namely foreign and native. Sayyad, Shaikh, Mughal and Pathan come in the former category and the latter comprises the Indian converts" (Sehgal 1975:103).

25. For more on this saint and his shrine, by all accounts the most important such place in South Asia, see Currie 1989; Suvorova 2004; Troll 1992.

26. See Gottschalk 2000 and Das 2013 for similar observations. Veena Das observes, "Thus my argument is not that Hindus and Muslims live in complete peace and harmony but rather that they inhabit the same social world in a mode of agonistic belonging" (2013:76). In Jahazpur, I'm not even sure if "agonistic" would be appropriate most of the time.

27. See Tambiah 1990 on the potency of ethnicity, which in this case seems to trump religion.

28. See Laurent Gayer and Christophe Jaffrelot's very important discussion of Muslim roles as crucial in the development of a qasba culture around small towns. They write, "In North India, for instance, the Mughal gentry started acquiring land-rights at the end of Akbar's reign . . . and from then on started investing in the small market towns known as qasbas. They were integrated with surrounding villages through the collection of land revenue and the consumption of agricultural and non-agricultural surplus—as well as with larger towns, offering a broader canvas of services" (2012:15).

29. Bhoju Ram's willingness to eat whole meals with relish at Muslims' homes (even though he said he ought not to do so) versus his absolute unwillingness even to drink tea at a Hindu leather worker's house is worth noting in this regard: that is, for Bhoju, a residual gulf between clean and unclean Hindu castes trumps the seemingly vaster gulf between Hindu and Muslim (see Gold, Gujar, Gujar, and Gujar 2014).

30. The question "do you do *bethi buhar*" means "do you intermarry?" and "do you do *bhojan buhar*?" means "do you attend one another's feasts?" These queries may be further condensed into "Do you do *beti-bhojan buhar*?" *Buhar* is a variant of *vyavahar*, which means transactions.

31. Jasani 2008 and Simpson 2008, both based in Gujarat, offer insightfully nuanced ethnographic approaches to Islamic reform movements including the ways such movements are received in specific circumstances. For a lucid historical treatment see Metcalf 2002.

32. Nonetheless, my picture was in the local Hindi newspaper no fewer than three times in the course of the year: at the idgah, at the Ram Lila, and when Bhoju's enthusiasm for exploring oddities took us on an ultimately irrelevant but nonetheless fascinating excursion to a village, Piplund, where a rash of uninvited spirit possession attributed to a malign ghost had been shaking up a particular government school.

33. For Bhoju's very frank account, see Gold, Gujar, Gujar, and Gujar 2014.

34. For the role and importance of all human senses in ethnographic research, see for example Seremetakis 1996; Stoller 1989.

Chapter 3

1. Limits on driving for women are very place specific; in cities such as Ajmer and Jaipur you see many women driving motorcycles and cars. It is completely normal. But this is not the case in a provincial town such as Jahazpur.

2. See Lohokare 2016 for a nuanced and illuminating ethnography of place and gender in a Pune neighborhood, with a focus on masculinity; Jeffrey 2010 also explores ways men inhabit public space in urban, but not cosmopolitan, settings.

3. These first two sections incorporate, with alternations and reframing, material that has appeared in two earlier publications: Gold 2014b and Gold, Gujar, Gujar, and Gujar 2014.

4. *Chavundia* is the local pronunciation of the name of a well-known goddess, Chaumunda.

5. When I long ago attempted to ask Rajasthanis, "What is the Hindi word for 'colony'?" the answer given without skipping a beat was always "*kaloni.*"

6. As Gayatri Jai Singh Rathore explains in reference to Rajasthan's capital, Jaipur, historically a mohalla, was inhabited by and associated with a specific caste: "Each *mohalla* therefore represented an extended ethnic group, homogenous in terms of caste and religion" (2012: 84). In Jahazpur qasba, many neighborhoods are named after one caste but are no longer homogeneous. Others are named after lineages, temples, trees, and so forth.

7. For Bhils see Unnithan-Kumar 1997; Weisgrau 1997.

8. There are references to Ghanta Rani in the District Gazetteer (Sehgal 1975) because of notable commerce at the large annual fair held there: "About 150 shops of sweets, brass utensils, ironware etc., come from Mandalgarh, Jahazpur, Kotri and Devoli. Total sale is about Rs. 20,000. Income from the fair held in 1969 was Rs. 50.25" (Sehgal 1975:217). Tod notes in his personal narrative of 1820 that the "outlaws" of the region "sacrifice a tithe of their plunder to 'our Lady of the Pass' (Ghatta Rani)" ([1832] 1978:542). See Gold 2008b for the temple origin story. Since my fieldwork concluded in 2011, a new temple has been inaugurated with a great deal of fanfare.

9. After thirty years or so, the Sindhi family vacated their large home and shifted to Kota. In 2015 that house still stood empty; Bhoju rented a room to store the overflow of dowry items he received at his two sons' marriages.

10. Writings on middle-class identity in India are burgeoning, and consumption is a major focus. Ethnographic fieldwork contributing to many of these studies is based among urban populations significantly larger than Jahazpur's; see Fernandes 2006 (Mumbai); and

Saavala 2010 (Hyderabad). Derné 2008 (Dehra Dun), and some chapters in Donner 2011 treat smaller cities, but none under one hundred thousand.

11. While her book does not treat Rajasthan, Sunila Kale (2014) offers important insights into uneven development and distribution of electric power in India. Jahazpur power cuts were erratic in a fashion that made it difficult to plan and sometimes very frustrating; inverters provide a welcome buffer between middle-class consumers of power and the realities of its distribution.

12. I refer to Karuna Morarji (2010), who offers an excellent discussion of provincial education and its relationship to aspiration. For a much darker view of aspiration and its discontents, based on research in Kerala, see Chua 2014.

13. See Gujar and Gold 1992 as well as Gold, Gujar, Gujar, and Gujar 2014.

14. Definitions from the Web dictionary *Hindkhoj* (2012), which offers colloquial English usage include "knowledge, dope, know-how, information."

15. Not only is it strange to find an ancestor included as a "fifth wheel" in Shiva's inner circle, but I had never before seen an ancestor enshrined as a likeness of a person rather than the generic "hero-stone." Unlike heroes in days of old, Makhanji's unexpected death took place while he was home eating dinner; see Harlan 2003 for divine heroic ancestors in Rajasthan.

16. For my own work on women's ritual storytelling associated with vows, see Gold 2002; Raheja and Gold 1994. Numerous other wonderful studies and stories are available; see for example Narayan and Sood 1997; Pintchman 2005; Wadley 1983.

17. According to one dictionary (Suthar and Gahlot 1995), *panoti* is an astrological term referring to a period of good and bad fruits caused by the planet Saturn's influence, or more generally an inauspicious time period. Presumably the fast would work to ward off the bad influences and channel the good.

18. See Gold 1988:7–9.

19. What she says to the king in Rajasthani is "Mere vrat me bhanda patka"; a more literal translation, I believe, would be: "You have thrown ill fame into [the practice of] my vow." I am condensing into "abuse" the notions of disregard and obstruction that the phrase seems to imply.

20. For a classic take on bhakti's "anti-structural" messages regarding both ritual hierarchy and gender hierarchy see Ramanujan 1973. Saavala 2010:149–76 offers an interesting discussion of rituals offering a "non-hierarchical interpretation of Hinduism" among middle-class persons in Hyderabad.

21. See Raheja 1988 for the ethnographic classic on gifts to Brahmins taking away sin.

22. For a helpful elucidation of issues swirling around and between gender and place in anthropology see Pellow 2003; Casey 1998:322–32 muses philosophically and insightfully on gender, body, and place.

23. An incomplete list of women's rituals I noted during my Santosh Nagar year, confined to those with some collective community element, includes Dasa Mata, Gangaur, Govardhan, Chauth (four times a year, the most important being Karva Chauth), Sitala Mata, and Tij. It would be impossible to enumerate individual vows.

24. Jhumpa Lahiri's widely read novel *The Namesake*, written in English, explains a Bengali version of this practice.

25. Journal text is indented. Brief explanatory insertions I signal with square brackets; anything in parentheses was in the journal originally.

Chapter 4

1. For more on Krishna pageantry, including *jhanki*, see Hawley 1985; Hein 1972.

2. While I know that the majority of spectators must enjoy the band music that is an omnipresent feature of parades in Jahazpur, several people closer to my own age revealed to me that they plugged their ears with cotton on such occasions. Anand Taneja (personal communication) read this chapter in draft and called my attention to a recurrent emphasis on noise that remains uninterpreted. That is, I repeatedly mention sound, mostly as a field-work peril, but do not reflect on why it is so pervasive in public religious events. His comments made me more conscious after the fact of the deliberate use of sound in filling and claiming space. See N. Khan 2011 for compelling discussion of Islamic concerns regarding religious uses of loudspeakers in Pakistan.

3. These draw on Book Ten of the Bhagavata Purana; see Bryant 2004.

4. On processions in and beyond South Asia, see Husken and Michaels 2013; Ingold and Vergunst 2008; Jacobsen 2008; see Narayanan 2015:125–58 for a fine-grained discussion of space and religion including processions and Hindu-Muslim relations in Rajasthan's capital, Jaipur.

5. See also Ashutosh Varshney's straightforward statement, "Pluralism would indicate the coexistence of distinctive identities (A respects and lives peacefully with B)" (2002:62). For an excellent historical and cultural overview of pluralism in India, see Madan 2003. I am also taken by some meaningful abstractions proposed by Gary Bridge, who seeks "an understanding of the city that is full of communicative difference but in which there can be an evaluation of claims across dissensus and difference, the resources for which come from the range of transactions rather than any appeals to transcendence" (2005:2).

6. For one such group in Jahazpur qasba see D. Gold 2013.

7. For anti-ritual teachings in South Asian religious thought, see for example the trenchant critiques by fifteenth-century poet-saint Kabir (Hess and Singh 1983; Hess 2015).

8. RSS is a right-wing Hindu organization. Daniel was surprised to learn that some of our acquaintances were members; for a time he envisioned a project titled, "friends and neighbors in the RSS," but ultimately he did not pursue it. See however Menon 2010 for insights into the appeal of RSS to otherwise sympathetic people.

9. For Gaji Pir's legend see Chapter 6; see also A. Gold 2013:317–18.

10. There is considerable literature on festivals and communal disturbances in South Asia; see for example Freitag 1989. In some cases near "professional" provocateurs may aid and abet the deterioration of amiability between different groups.

11. Each study varies and authors at times contentiously debate or refute one another's conclusions. Nonetheless there are some convergences; see Brass 2003; Hardgrave 2001; Varshney 2002; Wilkinson 2004.

12. I encountered, for example, a Muslim gambler who sought help from a Hindu Tantric specialist, and a Muslim farmer who spoke of ritually respecting the snakes in his field, as did Hindus, inspired by Jahazpur's origin legend.

13. Those middle-class and middle-aged Muslims with whom we spoke talked freely and neutrally about the 1980 riots; it would have felt awkward to query them specifically about 1947, and it was not volunteered; this makes it likely that the tale we gathered was a Hindu interpretation (with Muslims not only offending the sacred tree but also acting cowardly, in their precipitate flight from the aggressor Minas).

14. A hakim was an agent or deputy of the king, and at this time Jahazpur would still have been governed by the princely state of Mewar; Rajasthan had not yet transformed into a democratic state. See Gold and Gujar 2002 for many accounts from individual memories of the hakim and their respected and resented but unyielding authority.

15. Other accounts simply said, "They beat the drum on Malaji's hill."

16. Other accounts said they went to the fort.

17. Galgatti is in ward number six; a possible translation of the neighborhood's name is "small alleys"; but I am uncertain about this.

18. Although I make light of the loss of one branch, in my own ethnographic history is the story of a priest who agreed to cutting the branch of a sacred neem tree and who died mysteriously not long after, a death attributed by many to his sin against the tree (Gold 2010).

19. Much of the literature on Muharram in India has focused on the practices of Shi'a Muslims, which involve extreme forms of bodily mourning (e.g., Hyder 2006; Pinault 2000). For a firsthand ethnographic portrait of Sunni and Shi'a practices and differences at Muharram in the city of Ajmer, quite near Jahazpur, see Olsen 2003. For Sunni/Shi'a divergence and conflict at Muharram in colonial Lucknow see Ilahi 2007. Frank Korom reminds us that the mela atmosphere at Muharram in Lahore, which surprised the early ethnographic observer Omam, should not surprise South Asianists, writing that "melas virtually always accompany public religious processions in South Asia . . . any public event is going to draw in vendors" (2003:85). For women's roles in Muharram, with several chapters focused on South Asia, see Aghaie 2005.

20. The original Karbala is in Iraq, but it is common for Muharram processions to culminate in symbolic Karbalas. Here there was a well whose water was required to "cool" the taziya, a Jahazpur practice of whose extent I am unsure. Because of lowered water tables and poor rainfall, a tanker had to be called to fill the well in 2010 so that there would be enough water for the ritual.

21. Unaccustomed as I was to following Islamic festivals, I was naively shocked and even dubious to learn that there would be a "second Muharram" forty days after the first, which I confess had felt so grueling that I could not imagine there would be another like it so soon. The Muslim period of mourning the dead is forty days long; the first Muharram marks the burial of the martyrs and the second ends the mourning period. I was not able to follow the second Muharram in January 2011 as it came on the same day as Bhoju's daughters' weddings (see Chapter 7). Daniel, less involved in the wedding, did go out to see it and reported that he did not observe any great differences from November.

22. A pipal tree–taziya encounter is so typical as to be suspect (Freitag 1989:135). See also Mushirul Hasan, whose counterexample indicates again that a taziya–pipal tree encounter is somehow paradigmatic of inter-community relations. Hasan translates from the memoir of Hosh Bilgrami, who looks back from darker times: "During Muharram, Hindus and Muslims walked shoulder to shoulder reciting elegies and dirges. Music did not provoke violence *nor did the Pipal tree cause conflict*" (Bilgrami cited in Hasan 2004:127; my italics).

23. The difficulty of telling members of one religion from another comes up in many stories of partition's horrors; forcing men to pull down their pants and reveal whether they were or were not circumcised was the ultimate (and degrading) test but only worked for males. For women, of course, clothes could provide a complete disguise; see Shauna Singh Baldwin's moving novel *What the Body Remembers*, about a young Sikh girl whose childhood

whim to have her name tattooed on her hand in Urdu saves her by causing Muslim attackers to assume she is Muslim (2001).

24. This movement had to do with Hindu right-wing agitations against the Babri Masjid, a mosque built, according to the political claims of the Hindu right, atop the deity Rama's ascribed birthplace (Ramjanambhumi) in the town of Ayodhya. In the 1980s when Jahazpur's troubles took place, bricks intended to construct a new Ram temple were ceremonially processed from all over India. In 1993 a Hindu mob destroyed the mosque. The scholarly literature on all of this is vast; see for example Nandy et al. 1995.

25. When I presented some of this material to a South Asia seminar at Brown University in 2014, several members of the audience picked up on this point; it is rare. In the troubles in Gujarat in the early 2000s the police were definitely not neutral; nor were they in Mumbai in the 1990s.

26. When we were typing out this interview, Bhoju observed that Muslim shops which were burned were all outside the market; he assured me that there had never been arson inside the market, or near the bus stand.

27. A "history-sheeter" is a police term in India for a criminal with a long record of serious crime. See Brass 2003 on professional riot workers.

28. See Peabody 2009 for nearby Kota, where a danga in the same fraught year, 1989, led to deaths and serious, enduring disruption of relationships between Hindus and Muslims; or is it that the disruption of relationships preceded violence? Peabody's account, especially regarding the use of blades and drawing of blood in Kota, made me newly alert to the wording of Jahazpur testimonies, "not a drop of blood was spilled."

29. The most belligerent Hindu we met was a priest not a businessman, and therefore could afford to encourage trouble; but he also seemed quite unbalanced. We found him an unreliable source on all topics.

30. Both Tejaji Tenth and Water-Swing Eleventh were celebrated on a smaller scale in Ghatiyali, the Rajasthan village where I lived through almost two festival cycles in 1979–81.

31. For a recent and very stimulating discussion of Tejaji's worship in Rajasthan, see Singh 2011.

32. Anthropologists have devoted considerable effort to analyzing such distinctions in Hindu contexts. For one classic work, see Babb 1975. The same distinction appears in published works, many in Hindi, by scholars of folklore and popular religion. For recent and helpful reflections on related concerns see Singh 2015:275; Peterson and Soneji 2008.

33. Harijan were sweepers by caste; the municipality employed them to perform their community's hereditary work. They had the dignity and economic advantage of salaried positions combined with the ongoing stigma of sweeping.

34. This was the Padmanabhaswamy temple in Thiruvananthapuram, Kerala; the revelation about the wealth stored there broke not long before these festivals in Jahazpur.

35. Bhoju confided to me later as we made our notes on this interview that people in Ghatiyali "used to say 'Ramdevji is a Regar.'" According to his legend, Ramdevji was actually a royal personage who formed indelible bonds with an untouchable "sister."

36. Stanley Tambiah's observations on crowds and rhythmic conduct are germane (1996:304).

37. I am not counting a few hours spent at a regional urs in the summer of 2006; see Gold 2013.

38. See Qureshi 2006:97 for *milad* as expressing "devotion and exultation"; see also D. Gold 2015:86.

39. The term *sadbhavana* (good feeling) is wielded by both of India's primary national political parties, the BJP and the Congress, as part of a broader public discourse on sustaining intercommunity relations.

40. The sources of my epigraphs, Bigelow 2010 and Heitmeyer 2009, both offer invaluable insights into the worth and workings of an institutionalized peacekeeping system, based on fieldwork in Punjab and Gujarat, respectively.

41. CLG is an official category; one hundred members' names are recorded on the Internet for Jahazpur Circle: http://police.rajasthan.gov.in/ActualPoliceStationWiseCLG.aspx ?Circle = JAHAJPUR&CircleIdCLG = 21722 (accessed 7 July 2016).

42. Holi, with its charter for reversals and transgressions, is quite muted in Jahazpur doubtless due to the potential for disturbances. I will not discuss Holi here, but based on my experience, it seems that as a festival Holi has for many of Jahazpur's residents passed largely from the domain of public religion into private pastime; the bonfires are still public but the color play hardly is. Bhoju's wife felt that Holi in Ghatiyali was far more satisfying.

Chapter 5

1. Recorded interviews included twelve with Jains: three in Santosh Nagar, nine in the qasba; and ten with Minas: one in Santosh Nagar, and nine in one or another of the twelve hamlets. In spite of the very recent history of antagonism in Rajasthan between Minas and Gujars (Mayaram 2014), Bhoju himself was a Gujar who possessed long-established, deep bonds with Mina friends. Through his friendship networks, as part of his extended family, I spent uncounted hours just relaxing, chatting, or participating in life cycle events together with Minas, but few such hours in the company of Jains. The only exception to this was one good-hearted neighbor in Santosh Nagar, a shopkeeper whose business was slow enough that she welcomed any diversion including a foreign presence; she allowed me to observe the trickle of small transactions that make up a small-scale grocer's everyday life.

2. Fussman et al. 2003 shows what a research team effort including art historians and archaeologists together with ethnographers might do to produce a fuller portrait of a qasba.

3. Excellent studies exist on the role of merchants in Rajasthani towns, both historically and in contemporary times; see Carstairs 1970; Cadène 1997; Ellis 1991; Jones 1991; Sethia 2003; Vashishta 2011.

4. For my approach to the use of memory see Gold and Gujar 2002.

5. Hardiman is particularly useful on this nomenclature and commonalities across Jain and Hindu religious identities: "No sense of antagonism was posed between the belief systems and practices of the Jain and Vaishnavite Baniyas. Many rituals, prayers and ceremonies were common to both" (1996:80).

6. If a Muslim or Gujar or former wine seller takes up shopkeeping, as quite a few have, people do not refer to them as mahajan or baniya—terms apparently reserved for persons regarded as members of the third *varna* or social class, according to Vedic categories.

7. See Harlan (1992), who well supports a similar argument for female influence among Rajputs, who could be thought of as the ultimate patriarchal group.

8. Sehgal (1975), for example, tells us that there is evidence of strong Jain presence in the region in the twelfth century CE. K. G. Sharma (1993:88) also documents Jain inscriptions at nearby Dhaur to around the middle of the twelfth century CE); Sethia (2003:25) refers to

an inscription from Dhaur dated 726 CE. Chattopadhaya 1994 also makes reference to Dhaur, citing inscriptions from the seventh century (but not specifically Jain); see also Jain 1963, 1972; Somani 1982.

9. Some conventional lore holds that Jains turned to trade because of the violence to living beings inherent in agriculture.

10. While I am not aware of others who have focused extensively on interactions of Jains and Minas, there exist a considerable number of important studies (covering a variety of time periods between the seventeenth and twenty-first centuries) treating crucial roles played by merchants in economic life and princely polity; in city, town, and village; and in various regions. Particularly detailed and relevant to Jahazpur are Bayly 1988; Cadène and Vidal 1997; Hardiman 1996; Haynes 2012; Sethia 2003; Yang 1998.

11. For fragmentary regional oral histories of this area positing Minas as the original settlers and rulers who predated the Rajputs, see Gold and Gujar 2002:59–64. For one colonial depiction of Minas, see M. Singh (1894) 1990:51–56.

12. Prior to 1970 Trilok Patriya was Sarpanch or leader of the town council; he became the first chairman when the nagar palika came into being. According to gossip gathered by Bhoju Ram Gujar, this Brahmin chairman was involved in some scandal, decamped from town and, to quote Bhoju's email, "till today no one know where is he?" The following list of subsequent mayors (chairmen) of Jahazpur municipality is in chronological order. Names and dates are as listed on the wall of the town hall; annotations appear in brackets.

Mathura Prasad Vaidhya [nominated not elected]; served from 29 September 1970 to 20 October 1972 [2 years]; Chirangi Lal Bangar; served from 20 October 1972 to 5 August 1977 [almost 5 years] [During the national "emergency" declared by Indira Gandhi from 1977 to 1982 there were no elections and no chairman]; Dayanand Arya; served from 19 September 1982 to 31 March 1985 [2.5 years]; [Between 1985 and 1990, during the period of time between Jahazpur's first "riot" and including the second and worst disturbance (see Chapter 4), there were no elections and no chairman.] Gaiga Ram Mina [Borani]; served from 1 September 1990 through 29 August 1995; [he was therefore the first to be in office for a complete five-year term]. Mohan Lal Mina [Bindhyabata]; served from 29 August 1995 to 16 February 1997 [1.5 years]; Gaiga Ram Mina [Borani]; served a second term, from 16 February 1997 to 18 December 1998 [almost 2 years, in addition to previous 5-year term]; Sarif Mohammad Chita; served from 18 December 1998 to 18 August 2000 [about 1.5 years]; Kali Devi Mina [Borani, wife of Gaiga Ram]; served from 1 September 2000 to 18 August 2005; Kanta Devi Mina [Bindhyabhata]; served from 19 August 2005 to 21 August 2010; Kali Devi Mina [Borani, wife of Gaiga Ram]; served from 21 August 2010 through 2015 [5 years, in addition to previous 5-year term].

13. The above characterizations are synthesized from Rizvi 1987; Sethia 2003; Tod (1832) 1978.

14. According to Bhoju the Khairar is a large area between the Banas River and the Aravali hills, an area predominantly populated by Gujars and Minas. See Gupta 2007 for Mindesh or "the country of the Mina," which in his map does not quite extend to include the area where Jahazpur is.

15. See also Mayaram 1991 on Meos (another liminal community in Rajasthan) and Minas and the designation "criminal."

16. Hooja 2006 similarly mentions Mina roles in Rajasthan's history in passing but never attempts to treat Mina history. For a Mina perspective, see Mina 1991.

17. The twelve hamlets (barah pal), are incorporated into Jahazpur in the 2011 census. For some of the hamlets Bhoju Ram Gujar provided an approximate number of households, figures he obtained orally. These numbers serve simply to give an idea of the size range in the hamlets' populations. I list the hamlets alphabetically by name, including diacritics: Bhakton kā Bāṛā; Bhart Kherā (not included in Jahazpur municipality today; rather it is part of Sarsiya panchayat); Bindhyābhāṭā (c. 208 households); Borāṇī (c. 198 households); Chavundiya (now part of Jahazpur proper, but formerly numbered among the twelve); Ghāṭī kā Bāṛā (c. 71 households); Lālāṃ kā Bāṛā (c. 109 households); Mātolāī (c. 30 households); Muṇḍībhaṭṭā (c. 28 households); Pāṃchā kā Bāṛā (c. 104 households); Radghi kā Bāṛā; Sailādāṃtā (c. 88 households).

18. In one journal entry I exclaim: "How I loved the old Minas who in spite of having been in the global world of the army, of banking, love their stories and their place so much, are so animated, so happy to show us and tell us everything they can."

19. See Connerton 1989 on how collective memory is embodied and sustained through repeated rituals.

20. *Chant* means sprinklings, or drops of water; *bharna* means many different things, but here you could merge two of the dictionary definitions: "to fill" and to "satisfy someone in exchange for something." Thus the practice means quite literally "to sprinkle water for the ancestors in exchange for their blessings."

21. Due to my sister's stepping off the plane in Delhi with a festering infection, I was unable to be in Jahazpur in time to see Diwali. My plan had been for her and her family to be with me there for the festival, but alas I spent Diwali 2010 in a hospital in Jaipur, striving to keep her moderately comfortable and learning to hate forever the sound of fireworks. Bhoju made a detailed photographic record of the Minas' use of Jahazpur spaces during their annual ancestor worship.

22. That Minas so readily shifted their profession from soldier to farmer always struck me as a little odd, but I have to place it in the context of the universal desire for agricultural land as the basis of all wealth and respect.

23. See Somani n.d., a reference to Jahazpur's Digambara heritage for which I am indebted to John Cort, who photographed the relevant pages for me while engaged in his own archival research.

24. For more about Rajasthan's Jains, past and present, see for example Babb 1996, 1998; Cort 1998; Babb, Cort, and Meister 2008; Saxena 2014.

25. The conventional attribution of iconoclastic zeal to the Mughal emperor Aurangzeb (ruled 1658–1707) is common in Jahazpur as it is throughout north India; for correctives see Eaton 2001.

26. Several Indian scholars to whom I first showed photographs of these archaeological finds reacted with some astonishment at the piety with which such ancient treasures have been treated. They would have expected someone discovering a clearly valuable artwork to put it up for sale, not to install it in a temple. But as far as I know, all the emerged Jain images have been reverentially housed. This is perhaps another sign of provincialism.

27. The Maurya emperor Ashok is of course famous for spreading Buddhism throughout the South Asian subcontinent. His grandson Samprati in turn embraced Jainism and is sometimes called the "Jain Ashok." Samprati's reign is dated from the third century BCE.

28. Besides Chavundia Mata, the same temple complex houses Bijasen Mata. Bijasen Mata is a powerful although far less ancient goddess; her worship priest belongs to the potter community. She also receives goat sacrifice.

29. For the iconography of Padmavati see Hegewald 2009:98 ff.

30. I am grateful to friends and colleagues who specialize in art history, especially Pika Ghosh and Anisha Saxena, for pointing me to other examples of reuse of divine images; see Brilliant and Kinney 2011; Meister 2008; Saxena 2014.

31. See Davis 1999.

32. *Chaudhary* is a generic term for a headman or leader, especially from an era before the days of elections or elected chairmen, well before the municipality was established. Chaudhary is also used as a last name in families from diverse communities if a particular lineage once held such leadership positions, but I have not seen it used among the Jains in that way. That Jahazpur's chaudhary was Jain, of course, is another indication that Jains were preeminent in the market town's recollected past.

33. Bans on animal sacrifice continue to be enacted by different states in India. Thanks to the Religion in South Asia listserv, I have encountered a rich and fascinating body of recent writings focused on contemporary animal sacrifice and the legal, ethical, moral, and devotional complexities surrounding it; see for example Arumugam 2015; Elmore 2011; Govindrajan 2015; Halperin 2012; Moodie 2014; Pandian 2005. These studies cover the map from Himachal to Tamilnad to Bengal.

34. For Agarwal identities see Babb 2004:201 ff.

35. *Lag* was a part of the old taxation system and usually referred to a gift required on top of a basic rent; this is a somewhat odd usage of the term.

36. See Kelting 2009 for Jain sati narratives, which are significantly not about women widowed through war.

37. *Ghorla* is a generic term for a person who becomes possessed, so that name would refer to a medium for the sati spirits, avoiding naming their lineage.

Chapter 6

1. For fuller accounts of these cases see these earlier publications coauthored with Bhoju Ram Gujar treating one of the two hills (Gujar and Gold 2007) and the river (Gold and Gujar 2011; Gujar and Gold 2011; Gold and Gujar 2013); Gold 2017 incorporates some of this chapter's observations, framing them in broader arguments about ecologies of urbanism.

2. As Orlove and Caton observe, water "circulates through practically all domains of social life, rural as well as urban" (2010:403); see also Bear 2015. For water, religion, and sewerage in Jaipur see Narayanan 2015:186–92.

3. One day, Dev Narayan's mother, Sadu Mata, and Malaji's mother, Jagmal De, happened to bathe at the same time in Pushkar Lake, Rajasthan's foremost pilgrimage site. While dressing after bathing, the two women accidentally put on one another's blouses. Because of this incident they became "blouse sisters." Accordingly, their sons, Dev Narayan and Malaji, are considered cousin-brothers. Moreover, since that time, Gujars and Minas collectively are understood to be related as maternal cousins, at least by those among them (not the majority, I would caution) who know Malaji's tale.

4. For the trope of the headless horseman in Rajasthan lore see Gold 1988:46–48; Harlan 2003:95–100; B. Singh 2015: 33–58.

5. See Cheifer 2015 for an ethnographic study of the All World Gayatri Parivar at its main center in Hardwar.

6. *Mar-sa* is a colloquial condensation of "Master-Sahib," commonly used to address a teacher respectfully.

7. The case of Jahazpur's Nagdi River thus displays attributes of "cityness" as Simone defines it: "a sense that behind the present moment there is another time operating, other things taking place, unfolding, waiting, getting ready or slipping away, and that we know only a fragment of what is taking place (2010:9).

8. For scholarly fascination with the paradox of India's scripturally and ritually revered sacred rivers and their pollution with a toxic combination of industrial and human waste see Alley 2002; Haberman 2006. Colopy 2012 offers a vivid journalistic portrait in *Dirty, Sacred Rivers*.

9. See Taneja, forthcoming, whose insight from the areas adjoining the capital of Delhi is germane here: "The coming of piped water supplies to the villages drastically changed their relationship to local water bodies" (ms., 241).

10. We have not been consistent enough to claim to practice what has come to be called public anthropology, but it was certainly a leaning in that direction (McGranahan 2006).

11. I translate *Bhamashahs* as "esteemed donors"; this refers to a fifteenth-century historical figure who generously supported the Rajasthan hero Maharana Pratap when he was broke.

12. Of course this could be labeled a perfect "neoliberal" resolution. However, keep in mind that the success of these nongovernmental efforts would never have been achieved without the government's prior construction of new gutters, as David Gilmartin pointed out (personal communication, April 2015).

Chapter 7

1. Hindi speakers find Shaitan (Devil) to be an unusual name. Although it is a nickname, and this young man does have a formal name, he uses only Shaitan. It appeared on the wedding invitations, for example.

2. In graduate school in the late 1970s I avidly absorbed Inden and Nicholas (1977) concerning the transformation of a Bengali Hindu bride through wedding rituals into her husband's "half-body." During my first fieldwork in Rajasthan I discovered that such transformations were less complete than the anthropology of kinship had led me to expect. Many women, even those long married, when asked for a lineage name would give their fathers' gotra first and only recollect their husbands' on second thought.

3. Here is a joke about child marriage I heard in 2011; I cannot date its origins: As is not uncommon, given the length of wedding ceremonies and the lateness of the hour at which they are normally conducted, a five- or six-year-old groom falls asleep during the long ritual proceedings. When the time arrives for the crucial transformative rite of the wedding rounds, his father gently shakes him awake and tells him, cajolingly, "Wake up, son, it is time to take wedding rounds." Like other incorporative actions in Hindi such as receiving a beating or getting lost, the verbal phrase is neither "to do" nor "to take," but literally "to eat": to eat rounds: *phere khana*. When his father thus instructs the little boy "Wake up, it is time to 'eat rounds,' " the sleepy child answers plaintively "But I'm not hungry."

4. It certainly would take an entire monograph to begin to do them justice; see Archer 1985; Fruzzetti 1982; van der Veen 1972.

5. These include the verses reproduced at the opening of this chapter, and another quite a bit raunchier that described my tossing a lice-infested skirt onto a treetop while copulating.

6. Banjari ka Devji is a shrine near Bhoju's father's birth village, where the family's special deity (the god responsible for Bhoju's birth and survival) resides; it is not easy to reach as it

is off all the main roads. They all drove there to bow after the wedding ritual and before the breakfast and the brides' departure.

7. Iqlaq is the Muslim studio man, a close friend of the brides' father. He produced both the treasured four-DVD set of wedding memories and the lavish and costly album of stills. See Abraham 2010 for the role of the photographer and how it has transformed weddings in Kerala. Rajasthan, and I suspect everywhere on the subcontinent, is remarkably similar; for albums in Tamilnad see Wilson 2015.

8. This date, 14 January 2011 was Makar Samkrant, the holiday marking the winter solstice in India. In the morning I fed cows for merit and later with my husband walked all around the qasba, taking pictures of kites in the air and of kids on rooftops holding their kite strings and sometimes jousting with them.

9. Raji lived long enough to play with Madhu's son, Nandu, her first grandchild; she passed away in November 2014.

10. For further discussion of women's songs as chorused conversations see Raheja and Gold 1994:42–43.

11. Two dictionaries yield meanings such as these for the feminine noun *sandhya*: juncture, twilight, intermission, between day and night; boundary; a goddess.

12. My favorite account of such gatherings is K. Narayan 2002, a delightful fictionalized ethnographic story.

13. At rural weddings, the groom's party would be camped somewhere, likely on the edge of the village, and without benefit of a DJ would be able to perform uninhibited dances of their own devising.

14. See Schomer 1994 for a description of the challenges and riddles faced by Rajasthani bridegrooms.

15. See Raheja 1988 on *parai*; as well as Raheja 1995 explicitly on the pain of losing (and having) daughters: "Crying when she's born and crying when she goes away."

16. Cyclicity prevails in many regards and probably bears more thought: for example, Ganesh must return; the lagan comes back from the grooms; a "return mayro" is brought to the brothers' home, and so forth.

17. The first two are, like Banjari ka Devji, shrines to Lord Dev Narayan, a deity worshipped by Gujars above all, although generally popular in this region (Gold 1988; Malik 2004). For Sundar Mata, a Ghatiyali goddess shrine, see Gold 2008b.

18. Although tempted to edit out with ellipses my cliché about the village being "stuck back in time," I have let it stand to reveal my apprehension, as a newly minted town person, of what Ghatiyali has and doesn't have to offer as a place of residence. Echoing in my brain are the words articulated by an old acquaintance, Shiv Karan Gujar, who remembered me from 1980, when we met again by chance in 2010: "O, Ainn-bai, jo vikas hona chahiye tha nahi hua." (O, Ann, the development that ought to have happened did not happen.) We were standing in front of my former home in the Rajput neighborhood looking at the rutted unpaved lane into which drains ran from houses without benefit of gutters.

19. A few important works on dowry in India include Bradley, Tomalin, and Subramaniam 2009; Oldenburg 2002; Raheja 1995.

20. Veena Oldenburg, author of the best historically grounded study of dowry I know, has persuasively described her own journey toward understanding the complexity of the practice and resisting oversimplified conclusions about what it does for, or to, women. She writes,

"I had to discard the notion of a simple universal hierarchy of gender . . . and begin to grasp the far more complex and reticulate distribution of power. This involved the realization that adult male or female identity is not that of a single, unitary self . . . but a more fluid notion of self that describes itself variously in different contexts. . . . The Hindu woman is legion unto herself and unto others; her multivalence is often mistaken for a single-dimensional powerlessness" (2002:221).

21. As Oldenburg writes: "Dowry *demands*, a cultural oxymoron, are unscrupulous ploys that bear no resemblance to the historical and traditional meanings of dowry" but are "simple blackmail, extortion, or insurance fraud—crimes common to all societies" (2002:219, emphasis in original).

22. To run out of food is a major blemish on someone's reputation and on their event's success. Sometimes antagonistic guests may even try to make this happen by taking far more than they can eat.

Chapter 8

1. For this sense of biomoral connection between person and place as a South Asian concept, see Daniel 1984.

2. I made an attempt to elicit names for the various built structures housing different businesses. *Dukan* is a permanent shop. The English loanwords "cabin" and "stall" are both used to refer to small sheds that have permanent places but are architecturally less substantial. Cigarettes and small cosmetic packets are sold from cabins, tea and snacks from stalls. Then there are wheeled and thoroughly movable carts called *thela* from which fruits, vegetables, used clothing, plastic utensils, and so forth may be vended.

3. In our market interviews English terms are common, although sometimes the usage differs from that of English speakers as occasionally noted. "Margin" is used regularly as shorthand for "profit margin."

4. The word I translate regularly as "outfit" is actually the English word "dress," which in Hindi usage has come to mean a complete set of clothing for either gender. What Americans would call a dress, worn only by females, is in Hindi referred to with another English loanword "frock." Frocks in this region of North India are only worn by little girls, not by adults.

5. While editing this interview text, I checked on caste names for bangle sellers in Singh's 1894 survey and was shocked to find this written about Lakharas. "The Lakheras are very rarely rich, and are generally found *superstitiously contented with their present condition*," attributed to a curse from the goddess Parvati (M. Singh [1894] 1990:165; my italics). Thus, oddly to me, in contemporary Jahazpur an interviewee spontaneously confirms a stereotype from colonial times.

6. In Singh's 1894 survey of Marwar castes, Manihar is noted as a subcaste of Muslim bangle sellers that works in glass ([1894] 1990:165). In the Hindi-English dictionary *manihar* is "a maker and trader of bracelets, beads etc." Crooke ([1879] 1989:39) describes the tools of a glass-bangle maker or *manihar*. It would appear that the Hindu/Muslim distinction between Lakhara and Manihar lines up with the difference between lakh and glass, which in the old days would have been far more salient because the crafting of these ornaments required different raw materials, tools, and skills. Professions blur today because the sellers are no longer the makers.

7. Paradigmatic was this one: "If you meet a snake and a Sindhi on the road, kill the Sindhi first." I learned this in Rajasthan several decades ago but find it now widely discussed on the Internet. Other caste names, of groups deemed untrustworthy or cutthroat, may of course be substituted.

8. See Gold and Gujar 2002 for causes and consequences of pervasive deforestation in this region.

9. Concerning the demise of Tulip Global Private Ltd., it was reported in an Internet newsletter, *City Matters*, dated January 2012, that the company had duped over 300,000 investors on the promise of providing high returns (http://www.cuts-international.org/CART/TCS/pdf/City_Matters1–12.pdf, accessed 3 October 2014).

10. Gill 2010 is an excellent book on Khatik entrepreneurs in the recycled plastic business in Delhi; Gill, too, stresses Khatik willingness to deal with garbage if it becomes a viable, profitable enterprise. See D. Gold 2013 on Khatik participation in the Jaygurudev sect in Jahazpur.

11. According to Singh, the Taks are a division of Kalals that "claim descent from a Tak Rajput" and hold a social ranking superior to other Kalal lineages ([1894] 1990:190).

Epilogue

1. See Kantor 2016 for similar observations based on ethnographic research in provincial Bihar.

2. In her massive study of Jain architecture, Julia Hegewald (2009:41–45) discusses the frequent emergence of buried images often deemed miraculous and how Jain communities in various parts of India have responded.

3. On wonder, see Srinivas 2015; for miracles in South Asia see Dempsey and Raj 2008.

4. The dictionary spells as *adbhut* the word I translate as "wondrous"; however, the Facebook page in Devanagari, not English, employs an idiosyncratic spelling that would transliterate as *adbhud*.

5. By coincidence (through an old Syracuse connection) I knew the woman who was a divisional commissioner at the time with a special interest in the arts: Kiran Soni Gupta. She told me in a conversation we had in 2014 that on receiving word of the archaeological find, she had gone to Jahazpur, initially intending to arrange to transport the images to a Jaipur museum. Spokespeople for Jahazpur's Jain community were able to persuade her that it would be better to house the images locally so that local people, who rarely if ever travel to Jaipur, would have access to them (personal communication).

6. One of the comments on the page, from a Gujar professor of chemistry based in Ahmedabad, warns that it is a "fake page"; his comment received just one "like" and numerous rebuttals.

7. Cruising through three years of the timeline on "Wondrous Jahazpur," all I could find on the Muslim community was a single post of a congratulatory newspaper article about a local Muslim religious teacher having achieved his doctorate.

8. Bhoju told me that the Jains wanted to purchase this property after the discovery, although I don't know if negotiations were successful.

9. All dictionaries define *nilam* as a blue jewel, or blue sapphire. I have heard other temple images in the region described as made out of nilam. In consultation with John Cort and several art historians, the most we can conclude is that the image is carved from a hard, greenish-black stone quarried in western India and used primarily for main temple icons.

Glossary

āratī—prayerfully circling a tray usually with a lamp and sometimes other offerings in front of a revered image or person; common action for Hindu rituals in temples and homes

atishaya kshetra—hallowed ground; miraculous site (in Jainism)

bali, balidān—sacrifice, sacrificial animal, sacrificial offering

baniyā—merchant, shopkeeper

bevān—chariot or seat in which a deity's image is carried in procession

bhajan—devotional hymn; may also refer to devotional practice more broadly including meditation

bhāv—person possessed by a deity; the phenomenon of a deity possessing and speaking through a person

chaudharī—the leader of a community or occupational group; a headman; a hereditary title of honor

chillā—a term for a forty-day period of seclusion or retreat; commonly refers to an Islamic shrine associated with a saint's spiritual practices

dangā—a brawl, a riot

Deshvālī—literally "of the land"; used in Jahazpur to designate a community of Muslims understood to be descended from local converts

dhandhā—business, occupation, trade, profession

Gūjar—jati traditionally associated with herding and dairy production

hākim—an official of status; someone delegated by a ruler to give orders and exert authority

hathāī—a place to sit; often designates public meeting place for a specific community

idgah—a designated site, often on the edge of town, where Muslims gather to pray on certain festival days

jāti—group to which a human or other living organism belongs by birth; caste

Jina (in Jainism) victor or conqueror (over all desire); one among the twenty-four liberated teachers; also *Tīrthankara*

kaṭṭar—unyielding or strict; used to describe religious practice

Khaṭīk—SC jati historically associated with trade in animals destined to be butchered or sometimes with meat trade; Jahazpur Khatiks today run the fruit and vegetable market as well as other successful business enterprises

Kīr—jati (also known as Kevaṭ) traditionally associated with ferrying others across rivers in small boats

lagan; lagan-patra—an astrological document prepared by a priest as one significant ritual preliminary to a marriage

mahajan—literally "great person"; used to describe members of the merchant class

māhaul—atmosphere, mood, ambiance

māyro—gifts of clothing and cloth from a woman's natal family, ritually bestowed on the occasion of a life cycle ritual for her children; gifts from a mother's brother; refers both to the goods given and to the ritual of giving

mazār—tomb; enshrined tomb of Muslim saint

melā—Hindu religious fair, uniting a festival day such as a deity's birthday with regional commerce

Mīnā—ST jati understood to be among the first residents of the Banas basin region

mohallā—neighborhood

mūrti—image or icon

nagar pālikā—city corporation; municipality

nirday—pitiless, cruel, without compassion

pāḍā—male buffalo calf

Pardeshi—literally "foreign"; used in Jahazpur to refer to those Muslims whose ancestors are understood to have come from elsewhere

pherā (plural *phere*)—circling of a sacrificial fire by bride and groom; the central and culminating wedding rite

pīr—Muslim elder or spiritual guide; a revered teacher; sometimes a pir's tomb becomes a shrine

prasād—grace; commonly used for food offered to a deity and returned to worshipper as a blessing

Regar—SC jati associated in the past with leather work; many today work in construction

sadbhāvanā—good feeling; term used in government initiatives to sustain amiable relationships between communities

sasurāl—a spouse's natal place; used most frequently to refer to a woman's conjugal village or home

satī—literally "virtuous woman"; a woman who casts herself on the flames of her husband's funeral pyre

SC—Scheduled Caste, government category used to refer to those jatis formerly disadvantaged as "untouchable"

ST—Scheduled Tribe, government category used to refer to jatis considered to be indigenous peoples

suvidhā—amenity, comfort

Ṭāk—one lineage within a jati formerly known as wine sellers (Kalāl); in Jahazpur today members of this group have diversified greatly in the business world

tāziyā—ornamented representation of the tombs of martyrs Hasan and Husain, carried in procession during Muharram

tehsīl—subdistrict; an administrative unit within a district

Tīrthankara (in Jainism) one who establishes a crossing place; one among the twenty-four liberated teachers; also *Jina*

'urs—ceremony and associated events (processions, qawwali performances and other entertainments) marking the death anniversary of a Muslim saint; literally a wedding, as a saint's death is understood to be the union of their soul with God

vrat—vow; individual devotional practice normally involving a fast, a ritual, and often including ritual storytelling

References

Abbas, Ghulam. 1996. *Hotel Moenjodaro and Other Stories*. Translated by Khalid Hasan. New Delhi: Penguin.

Abraham, Janaki. 2010. "Wedding Videos in North Kerala: Technologies, Rituals, and Ideas About Love and Conjugality." *Visual Anthropology Review* 26 (2): 116–27.

Adiga, Aravind. 2008. *Between the Assassinations*. New York: Free Press.

Aghaie, Kamran Scot, ed. 2005. *The Women of Karbala: Ritual Performance and Symbolic Discourses in Modern Shi'i Islam*. Austin: University of Texas Press.

Alley, Kelly. 2002. *On the Banks of the Ganga: When Wastewater Meets a Sacred River*. Ann Arbor: University of Michigan Press.

Ambos, Eva, and William S. Sax. 2013. "Discipline and Ecstasy: The Kandy and Kataragama Festivals in Sri Lanka." In *South Asian Festivals on the Move*, ed. Ute Husken and Axel Michaels, 27–57. Wiesbaden: Harrassowitz.

Amin, Shahid. 2015. *Conquest and Community: The Afterlife of Warrior Saint Ghazi Miyan*. New Delhi: Orient Blackswan.

Archer, William G. 1985. *Songs for the Bride: Wedding Rites of Rural India*. New York: Columbia University Press.

Arumugam, Indira. 2015. "'The Old Gods Are Losing Power!': Theologies of Power and Rituals of Productivity in a Tamil Nadu Village." *Modern Asian Studies* 49:753–86.

Babb, Lawrence A. 1975. *The Divine Hierarchy*. New York: Columbia University Press.

———. 1996. *Absent Lord: Ascetics and Kings in a Jain Ritual Culture*. Berkeley: University of California Press.

———. 1998. "Ritual Culture and the Distinctiveness of Jainism." In *Open Boundaries: Jain Communities and Cultures in Indian History*, ed. John E. Cort, 139–62. Albany: State University of New York Press.

———. 2004. *Alchemies of Violence: Myths of Identity and the Life of Trade in Western India*. New Delhi: Sage Publications.

Babb, Lawrence A., John E. Cort, and Michael W. Meister. 2008. *Desert Temples: Sacred Centers of Rajasthan in Historical, Art-Historical, and Social Contexts*. Jaipur: Rawat Publications.

Baldwin, Shauna Singh. 2001. *What the Body Remembers*. New York: Anchor.

Bayart, Jean-François. 2007. "The Paradigm of the City." In *Cities of the South: Citizenship and Exclusion in the 21st Century*, ed. Barbara Drieskens, Franck Mermier, and Heiko Wimmen, 23–44. Berlin: Heinrich Böll Foundation.

Bayly, C. A. 1980. "The Small Town and Islamic Gentry in North India: The Case of Kara." In *The City in South Asia: Pre-Modern and Modern*, ed. K. Ballhatchet and J. Harrison, 20–48. London: Curzon Press.

———. 1988. *Rulers, Townsmen and Bazaars: North Indian Society in the Age of British Expansion, 1770–1870*. Cambridge: Cambridge University Press.

Bear, Laura. 2015. *Navigating Austerity: Currents of Debt Along a South Asian River*. Stanford: Stanford University Press.

Bhuyan, Ragini. 2013. "Living Together in the Shadow Lines of Plural, Global Cities." *Sunday Guardian*, 20 April 2013.

Bianca, Stefano. 2000. *Urban Form in the Arab World: Past and Present*. New York: Thames and Hudson.

Bigelow, Anna. 2010. *Sharing the Sacred: Practicing Pluralism in Muslim North India*. New York: Oxford University Press.

Borneman, John, and Abedellah Hammoudi, eds. 2010. *Being There: The Fieldwork Encounter and the Making of Truth*. Berkeley: University of California Press.

Bradley, T., E. Tomalin, and M. Subramaniam, eds. 2009. *Dowry: Bridging the Gap Between Theory and Practice*. New Delhi: Women Unlimited.

Brass, Paul. 2003. *The Production of Hindu-Muslim Violence in Contemporary India*. Seattle: University of Washington Press.

Bridge, Gary. 2005. *Reason in the City of Difference: Pragmatism, Communicative Action and Contemporary Urbanism*. New York: Routledge.

Brilliant, Richard, and Dale Kinney, eds. 2011. *Reuse Value: Spolia and Appropriation in Art and Architecture from Constantine to Sherrie Levine*. Aldershot, UK: Ashgate.

Bryant, Edwin F., ed. and trans. 2004. *Krishna: The Beautiful Legend of God* (*Srimad Bhagavata Purana, Book X*). New York: Penguin.

Cadène, Philippe. 1997. "The Part Played by Merchant Castes in the Contemporary Indian Economy: The Case of the Jains in a Small Town in Rajasthan." In *Webs of Trade: Dynamics of Business Communities in Western India*, ed. Philippe Cadène and Denis Vidal, 136–58. New Delhi: Manohar.

Cadène, Philippe, and Denis Vidal, eds. 1997. *Webs of Trade: Dynamics of Business Communities in Western India*. New Delhi: Manohar.

Carstairs, G. Morris. 1970. *The Twice-Born: A Study of a Community of High-Caste Hindus*. Bloomington: Indiana University Press.

Casey, Edward. 1998. *The Fate of Place: A Philosophical History*. Berkeley: University of California Press.

Census 2011. http://www.census2011.co.in/data/village/95908-bindi-rajasthan.html, accessed 13 May 2016.

Census of India. 1994. *District Census Handbook, Bhilwara*. Jaipur: Census Operations.

Centre for Science and Environment. 2003. "Sacred Groves: Last Refuge." *Down to Earth*. Electronic document, http://www.cseindia.org/dte-supplement/forest20031231/sacred_disconnect.htm, accessed 15 March 2014.

Chandrasekhar, Holalkere. 2001. *Tales from Indian Epics*. Bangalore: Ila Printers.

Chattopadhyaya, Brajadulal. 1994. *The Making of Early Medieval India*. New York: Oxford University Press.

Cheifer, Daniel. 2015. "The All World Gayatri Pariwar: Religion, Science, and the Body in Modern India." PhD dissertation, Syracuse University.

Chua, Jocelyn Lim. 2014. *In Pursuit of the Good Life: Aspiration and Suicide in Globalizing South India*. Berkeley: University of California Press.

Colopy, Cheryl. 2012. *Dirty, Sacred Rivers: Confronting South Asia's Water Crisis*. New York: Oxford University Press.

Connerton, Paul. 1989. *How Societies Remember*. Cambridge: Cambridge University Press.

Cort, John E., ed. 1998. *Open Boundaries: Jain Communities and Cultures in Indian History*. Albany: State University of New York Press.

Crooke, William. (1879) 1989. *A Glossary of North Indian Peasant Life*. Ed. Shahid Amin. Delhi: Oxford University Press.

Currie, P. M. 1989. *The Shrine and Cult of Mu'in al-din Chishti of Ajmer*. Delhi: Oxford University Press.

Dāngī, Shāh Manohar Singh-jī. 2002. *Shāpura rājya kā itihās* [History of Shahpura kingdom]. Shahpura: Shāh Madansingh Manoharsingh Dāngi Smriti Samsthan.

Daniel, E. Valentine. 1984. *Fluid Signs: Being a Person the Tamil Way*. Berkeley: University of California Press.

Das, Gurcharan. 2010. *The Difficulty of Being Good: On the Subtle Art of Dharma*. New Delhi: Penguin Books India.

Das, Veena. 2010. "Engaging the Life of the Other: Love and Everyday Life." In *Ordinary Ethics: Anthropology, Language, and Action*, ed. M. Lambek, 376–99. New York: Fordham University Press.

———. 2013. "Cohabiting an Interreligious Milieu: Reflections on Religious Diversity." In *A Companion to the Anthropology of Religion*, ed. J. Boddy and M. Lambek, 69–84. Malden, Mass.: Wiley Blackwell.

———. 2015a. *Affliction: Health, Disease, Poverty*. New York: Fordham University Press.

———. 2015b. "Between Words and Lives. A Thought on the Coming Together of Margins, Violence, and Suffering: An Interview with Veena Das." In *Wording the World: Veena Das and Scenes of Inheritance*, ed. R. Chatterji, 400–412. New York: Fordham University Press.

Davies, James, and Dimitrina Spencer, eds. 2010. *Emotions in the Field: The Psychology and Anthropology of Fieldwork Experience*. Stanford: Stanford University Press.

Davis, Richard H. 1999. *Lives of Indian Images*. Princeton: Princeton University Press.

Dempsey, Corinne, and Selva Raj, eds. 2008. *Miracle as Conundrum in South Asian Religious Traditions*. Albany: State University of New York Press.

Derné, S. 2008. *Globalization on the Ground: Media and the Transformation of Culture, Class, and Gender in India*. New Delhi: Sage Publications.

Donner, Henrike, ed. 2011. *Being Middle-Class in India: A Way of Life*. London: Routledge.

Eaton, Richard M. 2001. *Essays on Islam and Indian History*. New York: Oxford University Press.

Ellis, Christine M. Cottam. 1991. "The Jain Merchant Castes of Rajasthan: Some Aspects of the Management of Social Identity in a Market Town." In *The Assembly of Listeners: Jains in Society*, ed. Michael Carrithers and Caroline Humphrey, 75–107. Cambridge: Cambridge University Press.

Elmore, Mark. 2011. "Bloody Boundaries: Animal Sacrifice and the Labor of Religion." In *Secularism and Religion-Making*, ed. Markus Dressler and Arvind-Pal Singh Mandair, 209–25. New York: Oxford University Press.

Fernandes, Leela. 2006. *India's New Middle Class: Democratic Politics in an Era of Economic Reform*. Minneapolis: University of Minnesota Press.

Freitag, Sandria. 1989. *Collective Action and Community: Public Arenas and the Emergence of Communalism in North India*. Berkeley: University of California Press.

Fruzzetti, Lina. 1982. *Gift of a Virgin: Women, Marriage, and Ritual in a Bengali Society*. New Brunswick, N.J.: Rutgers University Press.

Fussman, Gérard, Denis Matringe, Eric Ollivier, and Françoise Pirot. 2003. *Chanderi: Naissance et déclin d'une qasba*. Volumes 1 and 2. Paris: Diffusion de Boccard.

Gayer, Laurent, and Christophe Jaffrelot. 2012. "Introduction: Muslims of the Indian City: From Centrality to Marginality." In *Muslims in Indian Cities: Trajectories of Marginalisation*, ed. Laurent Gayer and Christophe Jaffrelot, 1–22. New Delhi: HarperCollins Publishers India.

Gill, Kaveri. 2010. *Of Poverty and Plastic: Scavenging and Scrap Trading Entrepreneurs in India's Urban Informal Economy*. Delhi: Oxford University Press.

Gold, Ann Grodzins. 1988. *Fruitful Journeys*. Berkeley: University of California Press.

———. 2001. "Shared Blessings as Ethnographic Practice." *Method and Theory in the Study of Religion* 13:34–50.

———. 2002. "Children and Trees in North India." *Worldviews: Environment, Culture, Religion* 6 (3): 276–99.

———. 2006. "Love's Cup, Love's Thorn, Love's End: The Language of *Prem* in Ghatiyali." In *Love in South Asia: A Cultural History*, ed. Francesca Orsini, 303–30. Cambridge: Cambridge University Press.

———. 2008a. "Blindness and Sight: Moral Vision in Rajasthani Narratives." In "*Speaking Truth to Power*": *Religion, Caste, and the Subaltern Question in India*, ed. Manu Bhagavan and Anne Feldhaus, 62–77. Delhi: Oxford University Press.

———. 2008b. "Deep Beauty: Rajasthani Goddesses Above and Below the Surface." *International Journal of Hindu Studies* 12 (2): 153–79.

———. 2010. "Why Sacred Groves Matter: Post-romantic Claims." In *Village Matters: Relocating Villages in the Contemporary Anthropology of India*, ed. D. P. Mines and N. Yazgi, 107–29. Delhi: Oxford University Press.

———. 2013. "Ainn-Bai's *sarvadharm yatra*: A Mix of Experiences." In *Lines in Water: Religious Boundaries in South Asia*, ed. Eliza Kent and Tazim Kassam, 300–329. Syracuse: Syracuse University Press.

———. 2014a. "Sweetness and Light: The Bright Side of Pluralism in a North Indian Town." In *Religious Pluralism, State and Society in Asia*, ed. Chiara Formichi, 113–37. Religion in Contemporary Asia series. London: Routledge.

———. 2014b. "Women's Place-Making in Santosh Nagar: Gendered Constellations." In *Routledge Handbook of Gender in South Asia*, ed. Leela Fernandes, 173–88. London: Routledge.

———. 2015. "Waiting for Moonrise: Fasting, Storytelling, and Marriage in Provincial Rajasthan." *Oral Traditions* 29 (2): 203–24.

———. 2016. "Carving Place: Foundational Narratives from a North Indian Market Town." In *Place/No-Place in Urban Asian Religiosity*, ed. Joanne Punzo Waghorne, 205–26. New York: Springer.

———. 2017 (in press). "Discrepant Ecologies in a North Indian Qasba: Protected Trees, Degraded River." In *Places of Nature in Ecologies of Urbanism*, ed. Anne Rademacher and K. Sivaramakrishnan. Hong Kong: Hong Kong University Press.

Gold, Ann Grodzins, and Bhoju Ram Gujar. 2002. *In the Time of Trees and Sorrows*. Durham: Duke University Press.

———. 2011. "The Plight of the Nagdi and the Future of Us All." *Seva Mandir Newsletter*, 4–10.

———. 2013. "A Thousand Nagdis." *Anthropology Today* 29 (5): 22–27.

Gold, Ann Grodzins, Bhoju Ram Gujar, Madhu Gujar, and Chinu Gujar. 2014. "Shared Knowledges: Family, Fusion, Friction, Fabric." *Ethnography* 15 (3): 331–54.

Gold, Daniel. 2013. "Bābā Jai Gurudev in the Qasbā: The Ruralization of a Modern Religion." *International Journal of Hindu Studies* 17 (2): 127–52.

———. 2015. *Provincial Hinduism: Religion and Community in Gwalior City*. New York: Oxford University Press.

Gottschalk, Peter. 2000. *Beyond Hindu and Muslim: Multiple Identity in Narratives from Village India*. New York: Oxford University Press.

Government of India. 2008. *District Groundwater Brochure*. Jaipur: Central Ground Water Board, Ministry of Water Resources.

Govindrajan, Radhika. 2015. " 'The Goat That Died for Family': Animal Sacrifice and Inter-species Kinship in India's Central Himalayas." *American Ethnologist* 42 (3): 504–19.

Green, Nile. 2012. *Making Space: Sufis and Settlers in Early Modern India*. New Delhi: Oxford University Press.

Grindal, Bruce T., and Frank A. Salamone. 2006. "Introduction." In *Bridges to Humanity: Narratives on Fieldwork and Friendship*, ed. Bruce T. Grindal and Frank A. Salamone. Long Grove, Ill.: Waveland.

Guha, Sumit. 2013. *Beyond Caste: Identity and Power in South Asia, Past and Present*. Leiden: Brill.

Gujar, Bhoju Ram, and Ann Grodzins Gold. 1992. "From the Research Assistant's Point of View." *Anthropology and Humanism Quarterly* 17 (3): 72–84.

———. 2007. "Malaji's Hill: Divine Sanction, Community Action." *Indian Folklife*, no. 26, 9–14.

———. 2011. "Nāgdī kī durdaśā aur hamārā bhaviṣya" [The bad condition of the Nagdi and our future]. *Mīmāṃsā: Sanskriti Kendrit Bulletin* 3 (1): 3–5.

Gupta, Basant. 2007. *Environmental Perception and Tribal Modernization (a Study of Meena Landscape)*. Jaipur: Ritu Publications.

Haberman, David. 2006. *River of Love in an Age of Pollution: The Yamuna River of Northern India*. Berkeley: University of California Press.

Halperin, Ehud. 2012. "Haḍimbā Becoming Herself: A Himalayan Goddess in Change." PhD dissertation, Columbia University.

Hardgrave, Robert L., Jr. 2001 "Introduction to Ethnic Conflict and Civic Life: Hindus and Muslims in India: A Review Symposium." *Commonwealth and Comparative Politics* 39 (1): 96–97.

Hardiman, David. 1996. *Feeding the Baniya: Peasants and Usurers in Western India*. Delhi: Oxford University Press.

Harlan, Lindsey. 1992. *Religion and Rajput Women*. Berkeley: University of California Press.

———. 2003. *The Goddesses' Henchmen: Gender in Indian Hero Worship*. New York: Oxford University Press.

Hasan, Mushirul. 2004. *From Pluralism to Separatism: Qasbas in Colonial Awadh*. New Delhi: Oxford University Press.

Hasan, Mushirul, and A. Roy, eds. 2005. *Living Together Separately: Cultural India in History and Politics.* New Delhi: Oxford University Press.

Hawley, J. S. 1985. *At Play with Krishna: Pilgrimage Dramas from Brindavan.* Princeton: Princeton University Press.

Haynes, Douglas E. 2012. *Small Town Capitalism in Western India: Artisans, Merchants and the Making of the Informal Economy, 1870–1960.* Cambridge: Cambridge University Press.

Hegewald, Julia A. B. 2009. *Jaina Temple Architecture in India: The Development of a Distinct Language in Space and Ritual.* Berlin: G & H Verlag.

Hein, Norvin. 1972. *The Miracle Plays of Mathura.* New Haven: Yale University Press.

Heitmeyer, Carrie. 2009. " 'There Is Peace Here': Managing Communal Relations in a Town in Central Gujarat." *Journal of South Asian Development* 4 (1): 103–20.

Heitzman, James. 2008. *The City in South Asia.* London: Routledge.

Hess, Linda. 1993. "Staring at Frames till They Turn into Loops: An Excursion Through Some Worlds of Tulsidas." In *Living Banaras: Hindu Religion in Cultural Context*, ed. C. A. Humes and B. Hertel. Albany: State University of New York Press.

———. 2015. *Kabir Oral Traditions and Performative Worlds in North India.* New York: Oxford University Press.

Hess, Linda, and Shukdev Singh. 1983. *The Bijak of Kabir.* San Francisco: North Point Press.

Hooja, Rima. 2006. *A History of Rajasthan.* New Delhi: Rupa and Company.

Husken, Ute, and Axel Michaels, eds. 2013. *South Asian Festivals on the Move.* Wiesbaden: Harrassowitz.

Hyder, Syed Akbar. 2006. *Reliving Karbala: Martyrdom in South Asian Memory.* New York: Oxford University Press.

Ilahi, Shereen. 2007. "Sectarian Violence and the British Raj: The Muharram Riots of Lucknow." *India Review* 6 (3): 184–208.

Imperial Gazetteer of India Rājputāna. (1908) 1989. New Delhi: Usha Publications.

Inden, Ronald B., and Ralph W. Nicholas. 1977. *Kinship in Bengali Culture.* Chicago: University of Chicago Press.

Ingold, Tim, and Jo Lee Vergunst. 2008. "Introduction." In *Ways of Walking: Ethnography and Practice on Foot*, ed. T. Ingold and J. L. Vergunst, 1–19. Aldershot: Ashgate.

Jacobsen, K. A., ed. 2008. *South Asian Religions on Display: Religious Processions in South Asia and in the Diaspora.* New York: Routledge.

Jain, Kailash Chand. 1963. *Jainism in Rajasthan.* Solapur: Jaina Samskriti Samrakshaka Sangha.

———. 1972. *Ancient Cities and Towns of Rajasthan: A Study of Culture and Civilization.* Delhi: Motilal Banarsidass.

Jasani, Rubina. 2008. "Violence, Reconstruction and Islamic Reform: Stories from the Muslim 'Ghetto.'" *Modern Asian Studies* 42 (2/3): 431–56.

Jeffrey, Craig. 2010. *Timepass: Youth, Class, and the Politics of Waiting in India.* Stanford: Stanford University Press.

Jones, J. Howard M. 1991. "Jain Shopkeepers and Moneylenders: Rural Informal Credit Networks in South Rajasthan." In *The Assembly of Listeners: Jains in Society*, ed. Michael Carrithers and Caroline Humphrey, 109–38. Cambridge: Cambridge University Press.

Kale, Sunila S. 2014. *Electrifying India: Regional Political Economies of Development.* Stanford: Stanford University Press.

Kantor, Hayden. 2016. "'We Earn Less Than We Eat': Food, Farming, and the Caring Family in Bihar, India." PhD dissertation, Cornell University.

Kelting, M. Whitney. 2009. *Heroic Wives: Rituals, Stories and the Virtues of Jain Wifehood.* New York: Oxford University Press.

Kent, Eliza. 2013. *Sacred Groves and Local Gods: Religion and Environmentalism in South India.* New York: Oxford University Press.

Khan, Dominique-Sila. 2003. *Conversions and Shifting Identities: Ramdev Pir and the Ismailis in Rajasthan.* New Delhi: Manohar.

Khan, Naveeda. 2011. "The Acoustics of Muslim Striving: Loudspeaker Use in Ritual Practice in Pakistan." *Comparative Studies in Society and History* 53 (3): 571–94.

———. 2015. "River and the Corruption of Memory." *Contributions to Indian Sociology* 49 (3): 389–409.

Korom, Frank. 2003. *Hosay Trinidad: Muharram Performances in an Indo-Caribbean Diaspora.* Philadelphia: University of Pennsylvania Press.

Kumar, Nita. 2007. *The Politics of Gender, Community, and Modernity.* New Delhi: Oxford University Press.

Laiten, David. 2001. "Civic Life: Hindus and Muslims in India." *Commonwealth and Comparative Politics* 39(1):98–110.

Lalas, Sitaram. 1962–78. *Rajasthani Sabad Kos.* 9 vols. Jodhpur: Rajasthani Shodh Sansthan.

Lohokare, Madhura. 2016. "Making Men in the City: Articulating Masculinity and Space in Urban India." PhD dissertation, Syracuse University.

Lutgendorf, Philip. 1995. "All in the (Raghu) Family." In *Media and the Transformation of Religions in South Asia,* ed. L. A. Babb and S. S. Wadley, 217–53. Philadelphia: University of Pennsylvania Press.

———. 2007. *Hanuman's Tale: The Messages of a Divine Monkey.* New York: Oxford University Press.

Madan, T. N. 2003 "Religions of India: Plurality and Pluralism." In *The Oxford India Companion to Sociology and Social Anthropology,* 775–801. Delhi: Oxford University Press.

Malik, Aditya. 2004. *Nectar Gaze and Poison Breath: An Analysis and Translation of the Rajasthani Oral Narrative of Devnarayan.* New York: Oxford University Press.

Massey, Doreen. 1994. *Space, Place, and Gender.* Minneapolis: University of Minnesota Press.

———. 2005. *For Space.* London: Sage.

Mayaram, Shail. 1991. "Criminality or Community? Alternative Constructions of the Mev Narrative of Darya Khan." *Contributions to Indian Sociology* 25:57–84.

———. 2005. "Living Together: Ajmer as a Paradigm for the (South) Asian City." In *Living Together Separately: Cultural India in History and Politics,* ed. M. Hasan and A. Roy, 145–71. New Delhi: Oxford University Press.

———. 2009. "Introduction: Rereading Global Cities: Topographies of an Alternative Cosmopolitanism in Asia." In *The Other Global City,* ed. Shail Mayaram, 1–32. New York: Routledge.

———. 2014. "Pastoral Predicaments: The Gujars in History." *Contributions to Indian Sociology* 48 (2): 191–222.

McGranahan, Carol. 2006. "Introduction: Public Anthropology." *India Review* 5 (3–4): 255–67.

Meister, Michael W. 2008. "Sweetmeats or Corpses? Community, Conversion, and Sacred Places." In *Desert Temples: Sacred Centers of Rajasthan in Historical, Art-Historical, and Social Contexts,* 23–41. Jaipur: Rawat.

Menon, Kalyani Devaki. 2010. *Everyday Nationalism: Women of the Hindu Right in India.* Philadelphia: University of Pennsylvania Press.

Metcalf, Barbara Daly. 2002. *Islamic Revival in British India: Deoband, 1860–1900.* New Delhi: Oxford University Press.

Miller, Joseph C., Jr. 1994. "The Twenty-Four Brothers and Lord Devnarayan: The Story and Performance of a Folk Epic of Rajasthan, India." PhD dissertation, University of Pennsylvania.

Mina, Lakshmi Narayan. 1991. *Mīnā Janjāti: ek Parichay.* Bhopal: Madhya Pradesh Hindi Granth Academy.

Mina, Ram Svarup Motis, et al. 2009. *Shrī Mālājī mahārāj līlā amrit.* [Nectar of Lord Malaji's divine play]. Jahazpur: Jain Printers.

Minkowski. C. Z. 2001. "The Interrupted Sacrifice and the Sanskrit Epics." *Journal of Indian Philosophy* 29:169–86.

Mishra, Pankaj. 2006. *Butter Chicken in Ludhiana: Travels in Small Town India.* London: Picador.

Moodie, Deonnie G. 2014. "Kalighat Temple: Discursive Productions of an Ambivalent Antiquity." PhD dissertation, Harvard University.

Morarji, Karuna. 2010. "Where Does the Rural Educated Person Fit? Development and Social Reproduction in Contemporary India." In *Contesting Development: Critical Struggles for Social Change*, ed. Philip McMichael, 50–63. New York: Routledge.

Nanda, Meera. 2009. *The God Market: How Globalization Is Making India More Hindu.* Noida: Random House India.

Nandy, Ashis, et al. 1995. *Creating a Nationality: The Ramjanamabhumi Movement and Fear of the Self.* Delhi: Oxford University Press.

Narayan, Kirin. 2002. "The God of Doorways." In *Mementos, Artifacts, and Hallucinations from the Ethnographer's Tent*, ed. Ron Emoff and David Henderson, 61–79. New York: Routledge.

Narayan, Kirin, in collaboration with Urmila Devi Sood. 1997. *Mondays on the Dark Night of the Moon.* New York: Oxford University Press.

Narayan, R. K. 2006. *Malgudi Days.* New York: Penguin Classics.

Narayanan, Yamini. 2015. *Religion, Heritage and the Sustainable City: Hinduism and Urbanisation in Jaipur.* London: Routledge.

National Foundation of India. 2011. *Svashāsan kī dishā mem racanātmak kārya: Chhoṭe shahro? aur kasbāī bastiom ke jan-jīvan me sudhār lānā.* New Delhi: National Foundation of India.

Nelson, Maggie. 2015. *The Argonauts.* Minneapolis: Graywolf Press.

O'Flaherty, Wendy Doniger. 1986. "Horses and Snakes in the Adi Parvan of the Mahabharata." In *Aspects of India: Essays in Honor of Edward Cameron Dimock, Jr.*, ed. Margaret Case and N. Gerald Barrier, 16–44. New Delhi: Manohar.

Oldenburg, Veena Talwar. 2002. *Dowry Murder: The Imperial Origins of a Cultural Crime.* New York: Oxford University Press.

Olsen, Keri. 2003. " 'We All Eat Pickles, Don't We?': Negotiating Identity in the City of Ajmer." PhD dissertation, Syracuse University.

Orlove, B., and S. C. Caton. 2010. "Water Sustainability: Anthropological Approaches and Prospects." *Annual Review of Anthropology* 39:401–15.

Ortner, Sherry B. 2016. "Dark Anthropology and Its Others." *HAU: Journal of Ethnographic Theory* 6(1):47–73.

Pandey, Gyanendra. 1988. "'Encounters and Calamities': The History of a North Indian *Qasba* in the Nineteenth Century." In *Selected Subaltern Studies*, ed. R. Guha and G. C. Spivak, 89–128. New York: Oxford University Press.

———. 2013. *A History of Prejudice: Race, Caste, and Difference in India and the United States.* Cambridge: Cambridge University Press.

Pandey, Rajbali. 1969. *Hindu Samskaras: Socio-religious Study of the Hindu Sacraments.* Delhi: Motilal Banarsidass.

Pandian, M. S. S. 2005. "Dilemmas of Public Reason: Secularism and Religious Violence in Contemporary India." *Economic and Political Weekly.* May 28–June 4: 2313–20.

Peabody, Norbert. 2009. "Disciplining the Body, Disciplining the Body-Politic: Physical Culture and Social Violence Among North Indian Wrestlers." *Comparative Studies in Society and History* 51 (2): 372–400.

Peletz, Michael. 2009. *Gender Pluralism: Southeast Asia Since Early Modern Times.* New York: Routledge.

Pellow, Deborah. 2003. "The Architecture of Female Seclusion in West Africa." In *The Anthropology of Space and Place*, ed. S. M. Low and D. Lawrence-Zuniga, 160–83. Malden, Mass.: Blackwell.

Peterson, Indira V., and Davesh Soneji. 2008. "Introduction." In *Performing Pasts: Reinventing the Arts in Modern South India*, ed. Indira V. Peterson and Davesh Soneji, 1–40. New Delhi: Oxford University Press.

Piliavsky, Anastasia. 2014. "Against the Public Sphere: The Morals of Disclosure and the 'Vernacular Public Sphere' in Rural Rajasthan." In *Democratic Transformation and the Vernacular Public Arena in India*, ed. T. A. Neyazi, A. Tanabe, and S. Ishizaka, 172–89. London: Routledge.

Pinault, David. 2000. *Horse of Karbala: Muslim Devotional Life in India.* New York: Palgrave Macmillan.

Pintchman, Tracy. 2005. *Guests at God's Wedding: Celebrating Kartik Among the Women of Benares.* Albany: State University of New York Press.

Prakash, Gyan. 2002. "The Urban Turn." *Sarai Reader* 2 (The Cities of Everyday Life): 2–7.

Pratt, Geraldine, and Victoria Rosner, eds. 2012. *The Global and the Intimate: Feminism in Our Time.* New York: Columbia University Press.

Prime, Ranchor. 1999. *Ramayana: A Journey.* New York: Welcome Rain.

Purohit, Dev Nath. 1938. *Mewar History: Guide to Udaipur.* Bombay: Times of India Press.

Qureshi, Regula. 2006. "Islam and Music." In *Sacred Sound: Experiencing Music in World Religions*, ed. Guy Beck, 89–111. Waterloo, Ontario: Wilfrid Laurier University Press.

Rademacher, Anne M. 2011. *Reigning the River: Urban Ecologies and Political Transformation in Kathmandu.* Durham: Duke University Press.

Raheja, Gloria G. 1988. *The Poison in the Gift.* Chicago: University of Chicago Press.

———. 1995. "'Crying When She's Born, and Crying When She Goes Away': Marriage and the Idiom of the Gift in Pahansu Song Performance." In *From the Margins of Hindu Marriage: Essays on Gender, Religion, and Culture*, ed. Lindsey Harlan and Paul Courtright, 19–59. New York: Oxford University Press.

Raheja, Gloria G. and Ann Grodzins Gold. 1994. *Listen to the Heron's Words: Reimagining Gender and Kinship in North India.* Berkeley: University of California Press.

Ramanujan, A. K. 1973. *Speaking of Śiva.* Baltimore: Penguin Books.

Rathore, Gayatri Jai Singh. 2012. "From Occupation-Based to 'Communal' Neighbourhood?" In *Muslims in Indian Cities: Trajectories of Marginalisation,* ed. Laurent Gayer and Christophe Jaffrelot, 81–103. New Delhi: HarperCollins Publishers India.

Rawat, Ramnarayan S. 2011. *Reconsidering Untouchability: Chamars and Dalit History in North India.* Bloomington: Indiana University Press.

Reich, Tamar C. 2001. "Sacrificial Violence and Textual Battles: Inner Textual Interpretation in the Sanskrit Mahabharata." *History of Religions* 41:142–69.

Reza, Rahi Masoom. 2003. *A Village Divided.* Translated by Gillian Wright from the Hindi *Adha Gaon* (1966). New Delhi: Penguin.

Ring, Laura A. 2006. *Zenana: Everyday Peace in a Karachi Apartment Building.* Bloomington: Indiana University Press.

Rizvi, S. H. M. 1987. *Mina: The Ruling Tribe of Rajasthan (Socio-Biological Appraisal).* Delhi: B. R. Publishing.

Rudolph, Lloyd, and Susanne H. Rudolph. 1967. *The Modernity of Tradition: Political Development in India.* Chicago: University of Chicago Press.

Saavala, M. 2010. *Middle-Class Moralities: Everyday Struggle over Belonging and Prestige in India.* New Delhi: Orient BlackSwan.

Sato, Masanori, and B. L. Bhadani. 1997. *Economy and Polity of Rajasthan: Study of Kota and Marwar.* Jaipur: Publication Scheme.

Saxena, Anisha. 2014. "Landscape, Memory and History: Claims and Conflicts in the Constitution of Sacred Geographies in Western India." PhD dissertation, Jawaharlal Nehru University.

Schomer, Karine. 1994. "Testing the Groom: Riddling at Rajasthani Weddings as Cultural Performance." In *The Idea of Rajasthan,* ed. K. Schomer et al., 110–42. New Delhi: South Asia Publications.

Schwarz, Henry. 2010. *Constructing the Criminal Tribe in Colonial India: Acting Like a Thief.* Chichester, UK: Wiley-Blackwell.

Scott, James. 1999. *Seeing Like a State: How Certain Schemes to Improve the Human Condition Have Failed.* New Haven: Yale University Press.

Sehgal, K. K. 1975. *Rajasthan District Gazetteers,* vol. 17. *Bhilwara.* Jaipur: Directorate of District Gazetteers, Government of Rajasthan, Jaipur.

Seremetakis, C. Nadia. 1996. *The Senses Still.* Chicago: University of Chicago Press.

Sethia, Madhu Tandon. 2003. *Rajput Polity: Warriors, Peasants and Merchants (1700–1800).* Jaipur: Rawat Publications.

Sharma, K. L. 1999. *Chanderi 1990–1995.* Vol. 2. Paris: Collège de France Publications de L'Institut de Civilisation Indienne.

———. 2003. "The Social Organisation of Urban Space: A Case Study of Chanderi, a Small Town in Central India." *Contributions to Indian Sociology* 37 (3): 405–27.

Sharma, Krishna Gopal. 1993. *Early Jaina Inscriptions of Rajasthan.* New Delhi: Navrang.

Sharma, Mukul. 2012. *Green and Saffron: Hindu Nationalism and Indian Environmental Politics.* Ranikhet: Permanent Black.

Simone, A. 2010. *City Life from Jakarta to Dakar: Movements at the Crossroads.* New York: Routledge.

Simpson, Edward. 2008. "The Changing Perspectives of Three Muslim Men on the Question of Saint Worship over a 10-Year Period in Gujarat, Western India." *Modern Asian Studies* 42 (2/3): 377–403.

Singh, Bhrigupati. 2011. "Agonistic Intimacy and Moral Aspiration in Popular Hinduism: A Study in the Political Theology of the Neighbor." *American Ethnologist* 38 (3): 430–50.

———. 2015. *Poverty and the Quest for Life: Spiritual and Material Striving in Rural India.* Chicago: University of Chicago Press.

Singh, Munshi Hardyal. (1894) 1990. *The Castes of Marwar Being (Census Report of 1891).* Jodhpur: Books Treasure.

Smith, E. Baldwin. 1978. *Architectural Symbolism of Imperial Rome and the Middle Ages.* New York: Hacker Art Books.

Somani, R. V. 1982. *Jain Inscriptions of Rajasthan.* Jaipur: Prakrit Bharati Sansthan.

Somani, Ramballabh. n.d. *Jahāzpur ke Chauhānkālīn Digambar Jain mandiroṃ ke khaṇḍahar.* *Vīr bāṇī.*

Srinivas, Tulasi. 2015. "Doubtful Illusions: Magic, Wonder and the Politics of Virtue in the Sathya Sai Movement." *Journal of Asian and African Studies,* Fall 2015: 1–31.

Stewart, Kathleen. 2010. "Worlding Refrains." In *The Affect Theory Reader,* ed. M. Gregg and G. J. Seigworth, 339–53. Durham: Duke University Press.

Stoller, Paul. 1989. *The Taste of Ethnographic Things: The Senses in Anthropology.* Philadelphia: University of Pennsylvania Press.

Suthar, Bhanwar Lal, and Sukhveer Singh Gahlot. 1995. *Rajasthani-Hindi-English Dictionary.* Jodhpur: Rajasthani Sahitya Samsthan.

Suvorova, Anna. 2004. *Muslim Saints of South Asia: The Eleventh to Fifteenth Centuries.* New York: RoutledgeCurzon.

Tambiah, Stanley J. 1990. "Presidential Address: Reflections on Communal Violence in South Asia." *Journal of Asian Studies* 49 (4): 741–60.

———. 1996. *Leveling Crowds: Ethnonationalist Conflicts and Collective Violence in South Asia.* Berkeley: University of California Press.

Taneja, Anand Vivek. forthcoming. *Jinnealogy: Time, Islam, and Ecological Thought in the Medieval Ruins of Delhi.* Stanford: Stanford University Press.

Tod, James. (1832) 1978. *Annals and Antiquities of Rajasthan.* Vol. 2. New Delhi: M. N. Publishers.

Troll, C. W., ed. 1992. *Muslim Shrines in India.* Delhi: Oxford University Press.

Unnithan-Kumar, Maya. 1997. *Identity, Gender and Poverty: New Perspectives on Caste and Tribe in Rajasthan.* New York: Berghahn Books.

van Buitenen, J. A. B., trans. 1973. *The Mahabharata.* Vol. 1. Chicago: University of Chicago Press.

van der Veen, Klaas. 1972. *I Give Thee My Daughter: A Study of Marriage and Hierarchy Among the Anavil Brahmans of South Gujarat.* Amsterdam: Van Gorcum.

Varshney, Ashutosh. 2002. *Ethnic Conflict and Civic Life: Hindus and Muslims in India.* New Haven: Yale University Press.

Vashishtha, Vijay Kumar. 2011. "Growth of Beawar as an Urban Centre During the Nineteenth Century." In *Urbanization and Trade Routes of Rajasthan,* ed. S. P. Vyas, 140–49. Jodhpur: Books Treasure.

Wadley, Susan S. 1983. "Vrats: Transformers of Destiny." In *Karma: An Anthropological Inquiry,* ed. E. V. Daniel and C. Keyes, 147–62. Berkeley: University of California Press.

Weisgrau, Maxine. 1997. *Interpreting Development: Local Histories, Local Strategies.* Lanham: University Press of America.

Wheatley, Paul. 1971. *The Pivot of the Four Quarters: A Preliminary Enquiry into the Origins and Character of the Ancient Chinese City*. Chicago: Aldine.

Wikan, Unni. 2012. *Resonance Beyond the Words*. Chicago: University of Chicago Press.

Wilkinson, Steven I. 2004. *Votes and Violence: Electoral Competition and Ethnic Riots in India*. Cambridge: Cambridge University Press.

Wilson, Nicole. 2015. "Middle-Class Identity and Hindu Women's Ritual Practice in South India." PhD dissertation, Syracuse University.

Yang, Anand A. 1998. *Bazaar India: Markets, Society, and the Colonial State in Gangetic Bihar*. Berkeley: University of California Press.

Index

Page numbers appearing in italics refer to illustrations

Acknowledgments

I am grateful for the generous support of a Fulbright-Hays Faculty Research Abroad Fellowship for my 2010–11 fieldwork. I was affiliated with the Institute for Development Studies in Jaipur, where Varsha Joshi served as my advisor; she and the late Surjit Singh, who was then IDS director, were supremely generous with their time and guidance. In academic year 2014–15 a fellowship from the John Simon Guggenheim Foundation supported the writing of *Shiptown*, and a residential fellowship from the National Humanities Center gave me the perfect space in which to work—not to mention unparalleled library services, congenial interdisciplinary company, and luscious cookies. I am extraordinarily grateful to the College of Arts and Sciences at Syracuse University, which has generously supported both my research and the production of this book. I thank my former department chair Jim Watts for his administrative gifts, and our office manager Debbie Pratt for inimitable and tireless path-smoothing and spirit-soothing services. Discretionary funds from the Thomas J. Watson Chair (to which I was appointed while in India in 2011) allowed me to make three return visits to Rajasthan, sustaining connections with people and place. At University of Pennsylvania Press, Peter Agree has offered stalwart support for this project from its inception, while Amanda Rose Ruffner and Noreen O'Connor-Abel have seen its preparation through several laborious stages. For all such bounty my gratitude is boundless and ongoing. I can only feel abashed that so much good fortune has been mine in these straitened and challenging times in academia.

Colleagues, students, friends, and family members have helped me in numberless ways since I began to imagine a project in Jahazpur, to the final stages of producing a readable text. Every interaction makes a difference for the better, and I am grateful to editors, reviewers, readers, and listeners. My attempt to acknowledge every person who contributed will certainly fail, and I beg forgiveness in advance for omissions. Without this community, *Shiptown* (the book) could not have come into being. I take sole responsibility for inevitable residual flaws.

For close, critical, and enormously helpful readings of entire chunks of draft manuscript I am particularly indebted to Alan Babb, Joyce Flueckiger, Daniel Gold, Eli Kabir Gold, Jonah Gold, Mariam Grodzins, Nita Kumar, Anand Taneja, A. R. Vasavi, core members of the informal "Place" seminar at the National Humanities Center (including David Ambaras, Beth Berry, Anat Biletzki, Sandra Greene, Noah Heringman, Elizabeth Hornbeck, Jo McDonagh, Chris Melchert, Bonna Wescoat, Chris Whitmore), the terrific, engaged students in the fall 2015 edition of ANT/REL 699 (Writing Religions and Cultures), and one of the press's reviewers who remains anonymous.

Other colleagues, students, and former students happily metamorphosed into colleagues have responded to queries, contributed invaluable knowledge, edited, critiqued, corrected, otherwise improved, supported with recommendations, or generally cheered along multiple presentations and writings that eventually coalesced into *Shiptown*. They include Anthony Acciavatti, Rick Asher, Jason Cons, John Cort, Veena Das, Corinne Dempsey, Wendy Doniger, Julie Edelman, Leela Fernandes, Chiara Formichi, Pika Ghosh, David Gilmartin, Sondra Hausner, Dan Heifetz, Susan Henderson, Edward Hower, Craig Jeffrey, Sarah Lamb, Madhura Lohokare, Alison Lurie, Aditi Mehta, Ajay Mehta, Kalyani Menon, Townsend Middleton, Diane Mines, Haripriya Narasimhan, Anand Pandian, Leela Prasad, Anne Rademacher, Priti Ramamurthy, Mahesh Rangarajan, Anisha Saxena, Angela Rudert Shulman, Ed Simpson, Bhrigupati Singh, K. Sivaramakrishnan, Tulasi Srinivas, Ashutosh Varshney, Joanne Waghorne, and Ian Wilson. It was a pleasure to work with Syracuse University cartographer Joseph W. Stoll, who produced the two maps.

From my heart, I express special gratitude to a smaller set of persons, fellow travelers in all senses of the phrase: Joyce Flueckiger, Lindsey Harlan, Ron Herring, Nita Kumar, Philip Lutgendorf, Kirin Narayan, Gloria Goodwin Raheja, Peggy Trawick, and Susan Wadley. These sustaining friendships have endured for around a quarter-century and constitute for me the worth and meaning still at the heart of an academic life increasingly plagued by trivia and stress. I thank each one for conversing, challenging, encouraging, nourishing, and several for agreeing repeatedly and with sublime good nature to write in support of multiple grant applications.

Bhoju Ram, Madhu, and Chinu Gujar coproduced this book, and their whole wonderful family including Bali, Ghumar, Monu, and Sandip fostered me and my family in hundreds of ways: I fondly recollect surprise spinach pakoras delivered warm one rainy evening, and the very best chai in all of Bharatdesh consumed year round. I am honored to be the "Great Nani" of Nandu, whose first and repeated communication to me, accompanied by a two-year-old's surprisingly powerful blows, was "Hup!" Now he has become *samajhdar* and is as courteous and sweet as all the rest of the family.

Jahazpur's citizens of all ages were unfailingly gracious, patient, and hospitable. How might I ever thank them all? I hope this book will not disappoint them, and that they will recognize their hometown. Among my Santosh Nagar neighbors whose kindnesses were legion I must single out the Pathaks young and old, Madhu Tripathi, Da-ji's whole family (four commodious houses full), Bhag Chand Jain's family, and especially Suman Vaishnav and the members of her household. In and around Jahazpur qasba, many friends of Bhoju Ram's became friends of mine and helped in all kinds of ways. These include, together with their hospitable families, Ehsan Ali, Iqlaq, Satyabala, and Shiv Lalji, who makes his home (where I've consumed many a fine feast) in the village Gadoli but who was nonetheless a Jahazpur regular.

Daniel Gold as colleague reads my work both generously and critically, pointing out shortcomings and excesses; as husband he has been as ever a steadfast companion through fieldwork ups and downs, and I thank him with all my heart. My sons Eli and Jonah Gold—nonacademic readers with excellent sensitivities to language—provided invaluable feedback when they read and commented on different pieces at different times. I thank Eli in addition for his hard work on both aesthetic and technical aspects of image selection and production.

I dedicate *Shiptown* to my sister Mariam Grodzins, my niece Colorado Maria Kagan, and my great-niece, Cheyenne Maria Costanza. Mariam, when she must have known (but would not say) that she was seriously ill, embarked on a grueling journey to India with a wish to visit Jahazpur—to see my place. She got only as far as Jaipur, where she lay suffering for too many days—suffering not only from a painful infection but from the acute disappointment of not being physically able to complete the Rajasthan tour she had so fondly planned. My beloved brother-in-law Simon Wurtzburg stayed by her side in Jaipur so that Colorado and Cheyenne were able to spend one night with me in Santosh Nagar. There, in spite of a bleak winter drizzle, they did get to see some sights, spend time with Bhoju's family, get elegantly hennaed by Chinu, and learn more about Aunt Annie's work.

"The singer may die but the song will remain." (Steeleye Span)

CPSIA information can be obtained
at www.ICGtesting.com
Printed in the USA
BVOW08*2251180517

483809BV00002B/3/P